D1088683

THE INTERNATIONAL WINE AND FOOD SOCIETY'S GUIDE TO

THE WINES OF
Bordeaux

To my wife Meg, who has shared more bottles
of Bordeaux with me than anyone else

Also in the series

THE WINES OF BURGUNDY
H.W.Yoxall

THE INTERNATIONAL WINE AND FOOD SOCIETY'S GUIDE TO

THE WINES OF

Bordeaux

Edmund
Penning-Rowsell

The International
Wine and Food Publishing Company

STEIN AND DAY / *Publishers* / New York

First published in the United States of America
by Stein and Day/*Publishers* 1970

Published under the auspices of
The International Wine and Food Society Limited
Marble Arch House, 44 Edgware Road, London, W2

President: Andre L. Simon

© Edmund Penning-Rowsell, 1969

All Rights Reserved. No part of this publication may be
reproduced, stored in a retrieval system, or transmitted,
in any form or by any means, electronic, mechanical,
photocopying, recording or otherwise, without the prior
permission of the International Wine and Food Publishing Company.

This book was designed and produced by
George Rainbird Limited
Marble Arch House, 44 Edgware Road, London, W2

Printed and bound in England by A. Wheaton & Co., Exeter

Editor: Robin Howe
Line drawings by Stewart Black
Cartography by F. R. Coombs
Index: M. Penning-Rowsell

Library of Congress Catalog Number 77-106797

Stein and Day/*Publishers*
7 East 48 Street, New York, N.Y. 10017

SBN 8128-1272-7

Contents

	Foreword	7
1	The Setting and the Wine	11
2	Bordeaux and Wine	28
3	The English in Bordeaux	37
4	After the English	52
5	The Rise of the Estates	59
6	The Bordeaux Wine Trade from the Eighteenth Century	71
7	The Wine Merchants of Bordeaux	89
8	The Médoc I–Pauillac and St-Estèphe	104
9	The Médoc II–St-Julien, St-Laurent and Margaux	136
10	The Médoc III–Cantenac and the Lesser Communes	156
11	The Graves	172
12	St-Emilion	187
13	Pomerol	203
14	Fronsac, Bourg & Blaye	214
15	Sweet White Wines	223
16	The Entre-Deux-Mers, Côtes	242
17	The Classification of the Médoc	247
18	The Bordeaux Vintages	264
	Appendix A Opening Prices	305
	Appendix B Rainfall in the Gironde 1952–67	309
	Appendix C Wine Organizations	310
	Appendix D Table of Minimum Strengths	311
	Bibliography	313
	General Index	315
	Index of Wine Châteaux	318

Maps

	page
The Médoc	139
Graves	177
St-Emilion	189
Pomerol	205
Fronsac with Coutras and Guîtres (1)	217
Bourg and Blaye with Cubzadais (2)	219
Sauternes and Barsac	225
Entre-Deux-Mers	245

Foreword

Oddly enough this appears to be the first book written in English to be devoted to a reasonably comprehensive account of the wines of Bordeaux. Odd because by and large there has been a closer wine connection between Bordeaux and Britain over the past six hundred years than between the Gascon city and any other of its foreign customers. Claret, from *clairet*, a clear and light rather than a dark wine, is the English term by which red Bordeaux is known throughout much of the world. Of course there have been books on claret, and no lack of English writing on Bordeaux wines; and on these I have gratefully drawn when necessary to provide a rounded account of the wines of a region which in my view produces the finest red wines in the world and at least some of the best whites. This is not to deny the appeal of the rival in Burgundy, particularly the incomparable white wines, or the charm of the Moselles and Rhine wines. But among beverage wines no other region can touch Bordeaux for range of quality, style and price. To paraphrase—and correct—Dr Samuel Johnson, he who aspires to be a serious wine drinker must drink claret.

However, this book does not set out to be a professional bible of Bordeaux. Even were it possible to write a 'complete' book on the subject, I would not be the one to attempt such a task; and the result would be very dull. The pages of the invaluable Cocks et Féret's *Bordeaux et Ses Vins* are not exactly easy reading. Like most other books on wine this one has been written by an interested amateur for others who care to look beyond the bottle and the label. Inevitably, therefore, errors as well as gaps will be found, and I hope that they may be dealt with charitably. In defence of amateurs it can be said that they may feel more free to state their opinions in print than those professionally engaged in wine.

Moreover exact information is not always easy to secure in Bordeaux. The detailed statistics of vineyard area and output vary, as they may do in any agricultural community made up of a great many comparatively small units. I cannot always vouch for their accuracy any more than I can for the figures of the composition of the vineyards in terms of grape varieties. For the latter I have had to rely upon information given me by proprietors, *régisseurs* and *maîtres de chai*; I sought these facts

7

only when the opportunity presented itself and have included them only where they seem of interest. At least all such statistics should be sound enough to afford bases of comparison.

I have not attempted completeness for another reason. Although my publisher accepted uncomplainingly a manuscript more than twice as long as the length stipulated, basically I have written the book with wine drinkers in Britain and America in mind. While trying to provide a general account of Bordeaux wines, I have given much more attention to the wines of those districts and growths that they are likely to meet than to the lesser communes and minor growths whose wines are not much seen outside France. A list of the châteaux producing *appellation contrôlée* wines in the commune of Sainte-Foy might be impressive, but it would be of little practical value to those who may read this book.

For similar reasons I have paid much more attention to the red wines than to the white. Although Bordeaux usually produces more white wine than red, it is generally of far less interest, with the exception of the fine Sauternes and a handful of Graves.

For wine drinking is a highly personal and subjective matter, and to a great extent this book is founded on personal experience and judgements. I hope that the long chapter on vintages will prove useful and give readers an opportunity to compare their own views, but it cannot be definitive in so elusive and changing a wine as claret; and that variation is one of the great charms and attractions of Bordeaux.

I have made a point of visiting every one of the Médoc châteaux that were classified in 1855 and which exist today, as well as all the Sauternais estates similarly honoured. I have covered so far as I have been able the leading red wine growths of the Graves, St-Emilion and Pomerol. As others who have spent a day or two chai-visiting may agree, this is a formidable task, especially for a non-resident of the region. It is one thing to pass through the almost always open doors of the great châteaux with world-wide reputations and quite another to enter the small back-country farms, where the proprietor is out, and his child-girt wife does not venture to unlock the *chai* and allow one to taste. It took three persistent visits even to penetrate the cellars of one of the smaller *crus classés*.

Also where possible I have tried some critical assessment of the châteaux and their various vintages. It has always seemed to me a failing of many books on wine that the authors, through kindness, diffidence or unwillingness to risk giving offence, have been insufficiently critical of various estates' wines. Their comments have been diluted (or sweetened) by unjustified addition of sugariness; and criticism has not gone much beyond such remarks as 'one of the first growths (un-named) has not in recent years been producing wines up to its glorious reputation'. My comments have been based purely on personal experience and are entirely without malice; for all of us surely want every grower to produce wine superlative in its class. So if my comments, commendatory or otherwise, have obviously been influenced and limited by the extent of my experience, in neither direction have they owed their origin to anything else than my own taste; which may well be different from others as well as deficient.

I have tried to give some historical perspective to the wines of an area, whose vinous history is probably richer than that of any other wine region in the world; as well as having a particular association with the English-speaking world. Indeed there is a wealth of material to be drawn on, except in the case of the individual châteaux where it is often unexpectedly sparse; and I have had to resist the temptation to fill the bottle with too much historical sediment.

Although this is a book written by an amateur, it would be churlish as well as dishonest to deny or depreciate the amount of professional help that I have enjoyed, not merely in the compilation of this book but over long years of wine drinking. There can be no calling more generous with its products, articles of commerce, information and time than the professional wine world. In England my knowledge of Bordeaux and in particular of claret owes much to Mr Ronald Avery of the distinguished Bristol firm and to Mr Harry Waugh, formerly of Harveys of Bristol in its independent days. Among wine drinkers of my generation both have done a great deal to encourage an appreciation of fine claret. Harry Waugh has also done me the additional service of reading my manuscript.

I owe equal and even more widespread thanks to proprietors and merchants in Bordeaux. First I must acknowledge the help I have had from Christian Cruse, doyen today of those Chartrons merchants who historically have put Bordeaux wines on the world map. M. Cruse's experience, extending over sixty years, and his exceptional memory have been immensely valuable; directly and through his wide contacts he has supplied many items of information and checked various facts. He has also read the manuscript and made many suggestions. With him I must bracket his son Edouard, who for many years has been a constant guide on my visits to Bordeaux and the surrounding châteaux, not least in Pomerol and St-Emilion. He also has read much of the manuscript. The special love of him and his father for old claret have opened many rare and interesting bottles for me.

It is also a pleasure to acknowledge in print the help given me by that wine prince among the nobility, Baron Philippe de Rothschild and his wife Pauline, who have made me as welcome in their unequalled wine cellar at Mouton as in their comfortably equipped library, which several times has provided a base for some of my researches and expeditions. To one long associated professionally with books, to be able as I have at Mouton-Rothschild, to dine and drink exceptional wines amid the unusually designed, book-filled presses of this charming room, has been a special experience.

Another very hospitable host and source of information who has also read part of my manuscript, has been Mr Ronald Barton of Langoa. Not only have I had the benefit of his wine and wine knowledge, but with my family I have more than once camped in his garden, occasions enriched by a steady flow of bottles from the joint private cellar of Langoa and Léoville-Barton.

So many other people in Bordeaux have helped me with information that it is impossible to mention all, but I must single out M. Henri Binaud of Cantemerle; M. Pierre Ginestet of Château Margaux; M. Philippe Cottin of La Bergerie; M. Jacques Théo of Alexis Lichine & Co.; Mr Peter Sichel of Sichel & Co.; M. Henri Woltner of La Mission-Haut-Brion; M. Delmas of Haut-Brion; M. Guy Schÿler of

Lafite; M. Fourcaud-Laussac of Cheval-Blanc; M. Roger Danglade of Libourne; M. Gaston Marchou of Bordeaux, M. Yves Foureaud of Eschenauer who arranged accommodation at Rausan-Ségla; International Distillers and Vintners, who have afforded me hospitality at Loudenne and access to the Gilbey diaries there; and all those wine merchants in Bordeaux who enabled me to write the chapter on The Wine Merchants of Bordeaux. I must also acknowledge the help of the *Conseil Interprofessional du Vin de Bordeaux* in Bordeaux and the *Institut National des Appellations d'Origine des Vins et Eaux-de-Vie* in Paris.

In Britain I have had assistance on points of detail from a number of people, including one or two already mentioned. I must also express my thanks to Mr Cyril Ray for allowing me to read the manuscript of his *Lafite* in advance of publication, and to Mrs Pamela Vandyke Price, whose reading of the completed manuscript for the publishers was also of considerable help to me; also to Mr Norman Alexander who read the proofs with concentration suitable to the subject and to the staff of Rainbird Reference Books Ltd for their punctilious attention to detail. I am also grateful to Christies and to Mr Michael Broadbent of their wine department in particular, for access to their catalogue archives. Finally I must thank my wife for compiling the extensive index.

1. The Setting and the Wine

Bordeaux, set upon the last great curve of the Garonne before that broad river joins the Dordogne at Bec d'Ambès and both become the Gironde, is one of the most agreeable cities of France. Although its cathedral and churches are medieval, the chief imprint from the past is from the eighteenth century: Victor Louis' splendid colonnaded Grand Théâtre (1773 – 80); the Allées de Tourny, named after the intendant who helped to plan the heart of the city but failed to restrict the growing Bordeaux *vignoble*; the Jardin Public; and the merchants' tall houses on the Chartrons and the Cours Xavier Arnozan, formerly known as the Pavé des Chartrons. Thrust among them is the Place des Quinconces with its columns to the reforming, rejected Girondins. Even after seventy years the huge square still seems not quite at ease among its elders; a little *arriviste*. Wine, at least in the historic areas, seems to exert a conservative influence, and although Bordeaux has had its moments of revolt and counter-revolt, this is a conservative, bourgeois city.

The wine on which it still principally lives is largely produced some way away, and much comes from flat and, except to *amateurs* of level country, rather dull surroundings. Broadly speaking the better the wine, the duller the Bordeaux countryside. The most attractive country is certainly that known under its modest wine classification as the Premières Côtes. This lies upstream from the city, opposite the white wine areas of Graves, Cérons and Sauternes, and edging the Entre-Deux-Mers. It is charming, hilly country, with hedges, small fields and curving roads, together giving an impression of England, perhaps of Devon. From its crests overlooking the Garonne, there are delightful views of the river, of the vineyards opposite and the dark shadow of the Landes on the horizon. Yet the wine is not very distinguished.

Just inland from the Premières Côtes, on the south-east of the department of the Gironde, which includes all the Bordeaux vineyards, is the white wine country of the Entre-Deux-Mers where the vine shares the fields with other crops. The country looks rich and contains some splendid châteaux and manoirs. On the northern edge it adjoins and almost surrounds the small Graves de Vayres district, through which runs the main road from Bordeaux to Libourne. This is not, as many people believe, a source of Graves wine, but takes its name from the gravelly soil.

North and east of the sprawling Entre-Deux-Mers – it runs far enough north to be traversed by the main Bordeaux-Paris road (*RN.10*) – there is across the Dordogne some agreeable country, particularly in and around St-Emilion, which describes itself as 'the pearl of the Gironde'. With few rivals in the region, it may fairly claim this title. Along by the Dordogne the land is flat and marshy – the *palus* – but rises with the valley sides to the town of St-Emilion and to the plateau which lies beyond, merging into Pomerol to the west and north-west, Montagne to the north, and on the other sides with the other outlying St-Emilion communes, mostly sanctified in name if not specially blessed in the quality of their wines. Montagne is a relative term of description but it is lofty for Bordeaux. Whereas the average height above sea level in the Médoc is a mere 55 feet, in St-Emilion it is around 230 feet, and about the same in the Entre-Deux-Mers.

Fronsac, downstream from Libourne, the port of St-Emilion and Pomerol and the centre of that part of the Bordeaux wine trade, is in part hillier still. The steep La Tertre de Fronsac is the high point of the Côtes de Fronsac, with a splendid view from the summit. Towards the sea and beside the Dordogne and the ensuing Gironde there runs the gently rolling country of Fronsac, with plenty of trees in the valleys and a general air of modest agricultural prosperity. Both Bourg and Blaye afford excellent views of river and estuary, and both towns have the air as if history, of which they had their fair share in the past, has now passed them by. The rolling country behind them is an agreeable contrast to the flat, persistent Médoc opposite, and many Médocain château families in summer cross by the ferry from Lamarque to Blaye to picnic in the arcadian valleys of the twin districts. The soil is clearly much richer and heavier on this side of the river than on the left bank, and this alone accounts for the fuller, less elegant wines, which can rise to near-Burgundian richness in Pomerol and St-Emilion.

As the mean altitude demonstrates, the Haut-Médoc is by no means high. It is, of course, flattest near the river, and it rises slightly to the 'back' villages like St-Laurent, Listrac and Moulis. It undulates slightly by St-Estèphe, descends appropriately into the Bas-Médoc, as it used officially to be called, and the country then becomes Lincolnshire-like in its near-flatness, dykes and the feeling of being far away from the busy world. Indeed Lesparre, the main centre, is forty miles from Bordeaux, while St-Vivien on the edge of the vineyard area and not far from the Pointe de Grave and the Atlantic, is over fifty miles away from the Girondin capital; almost as far as Oxford is from London. The Bas-Médoc has the slightly sad, forgotten air of a district that has seen better days; and so it has.

The Graves area, which strictly speaking includes the city of Bordeaux, is either

12

flat and suburban or flat and forested. The soil, as the name implies, is gravelly and the sandy Landes encroaches on it. The vineyards of the more remote parts look as if they have been carved out of the tree-belts. The sweeter white wine areas further up the Garonne have similar soil, but in the vineyard area here the country is generally less tree-enclosed.

So much, very briefly, for the lie of the Bordeaux vineyard land.

Grape Varieties

Now must be mentioned the kinds of grapes which grow on it, producing wines of great but often subtle variety in the biggest fine wine area in France, and indeed in the world. Two to three thousand vines in full production are needed to produce one *tonneau* of wine, more in the leading vineyards.

No grape names are on record in Bordeaux until the sixteenth century when *La Bidure* was named as the common plant. Today the leading red wine grape variety of Bordeaux is the Cabernet-Sauvignon; the grape on which claret's reputation is founded. In the Graves it is sometimes called the *Vidure*, which in patois can easily be rendered as *Bidure*, and this is claimed to be the same as the Latin *Biturica*, named by Pliny; but this is speculation only. It is the Cabernet-Sauvignon which produces much of the deep colour, the 'bloom' of the aroma, the finesse and the 'cut' in the flavour of a fine Médoc; the 'backbone' of an elegant claret. Its influence can be best noted in the fairly young wine of growths like Latour and Mouton-Rothschild. In the vineyards of both these leading Pauillacs at least 80 per cent of the grapes are Cabernet-Sauvignon. Like the leading grape of Germany, the Riesling, it flourishes in not too easy conditions, and is more resistant to rot than Bordeaux's second grape, the Merlot. It normally ripens later than the latter, and in the vineyard is picked afterwards.

The Cabernet-Franc variety is usually to be found in most Médoc vineyards, and is sometimes counted in as part of the Cabernet proportion of the *cépage*. It is however an inferior variety and produces a less coloured wine with rather less body. Some say it is half way towards the Merlot but that is an exaggeration. Across the river in St-Emilion there is the Bouchet, a variety of Cabernet somewhat similar to the Cabernet-Franc.

The Merlot, the second most important red wine grape of Bordeaux, is particularly associated with St-Emilion and Pomerol. In the Médoc it was only known towards the end of the eighteenth century. It produces much softer wines than the Cabernet-Sauvignon, as can be seen *par excellence* in Cheval-Blanc, where Merlot is prolific in the vineyard; although of course the relatively rich soil of St-Emilion is another factor in the flavour. The Merlot is also fairly prominent at Lafite and Palmer and contributes to the delicacy of these wines. It has the advantage of being productive, but with a tendency to bud early it is subject to spring frosts, which the Cabernets may escape. In a poor season it is liable to rot. A vineyard with a heavy proportion of Merlot may suffer particularly badly from wet weather at vintage-time. The wine from the Merlot matures more rapidly and in these commercial times this is a temptation to the growers. Unkind proprietors in the Médoc may whisper, with a pleasurable shake of the head, that their neighbours have unfortunately planted too high a proportion of Merlot; almost as bad as if the neighbours' daughters had taken to the streets! In St-Emilion Merlot is more acceptable, but then no Médocain will admit their wines to equality with a Médoc.

The other well-known red wine grape is the Malbec. It produces a big quantity of fairly large grapes, matures early, and the wine is inclined to be soft like the Merlot. It is, however, subject to the disease of *coulure*, when the flowers fall off without forming grapes. The least used of the four main varieties, it probably does not represent more than 10 per cent of a vineyard, and less in the fine growths. In St-Emilion it is called the Pressac. Generally it is in decline in the Gironde.

There are two other red wine grapes worth mentioning. One is the Verdot, of which there are two sub-varieties, the Gros and the Petit. The former makes rather ordinary red wine and is grown in the riverside *palus*. The Petit-Verdot, a late ripener, may be found in more distinguished surroundings, for it can give body to a wine. A few years ago Ronald Barton opened for me at Langoa two bottles of his Léoville-Barton of that light and not very renowned year, 1938. One was made from the normal blend of grapes; it was drinkable but rather faded. The second had been made exclusively from Petit-Verdot; this had much more fruit and flavour than the first. However, it is only grown marginally, being subject to *coulure* and to rot in a late harvest.

The other black grape is the Carmenère, to be found only in the Médoc and even there on a tiny scale for although producing good wine, it is difficult to grow, and flourishes only in a successful season.

A typical fine Médoc vineyard may be planted with 55 per cent Cabernet-Sauvignon, 20 per cent Cabernet-Franc, 20 per cent Merlot and 5 per cent Malbec; whereas a common 'blend' in St-Emilion might be 60 per cent Merlot, 30 per cent Bouchet and 10 per cent Pressac (Malbec). More exact proportions will be found in the chapters devoted to the various districts.

It will be appreciated that the secret of success in planting a vineyard is to secure a balance of the most appropriate and successful varieties for the situation and soil. In the leading vineyards of the Médoc too high a proportion of Cabernet-Sauvignon may mean a small crop and a big, slow-maturing wine. One of the reasons given for the traditional backwardness of Latour is said to be the high proportion of Cabernet-Sauvignon. Another reason is that until recent years the Cabernet was picked fairly early there, resulting in rather a hard wine. Yet Mouton-Rothschild claims at least the same proportion of Cabernet-Sauvignon and the wines are usually more forward. Here the soil is playing its decisive role. Too much Merlot or Malbec will mean a large production of rather soft-centred wines. At Haut-Brion their proportion is 55 per cent Cabernet-Sauvignon, 22 per cent Cabernet-Franc and 23 per cent Merlot. The lower proportion of Cabernet-Sauvignon compared with the two Pauillac leaders may be one reason for the rather soft texture of many Haut-Brions; but there is the Graves soil to be considered.

Certain soils and situations may demand a different amalgam of varieties. In the statistical survey of the Gironde published in 1874 by Féret and quoted by Germain Lafforgue in *Le Vignoble Girondin* (1947), the commune of Pauillac was shown as being planted with 75 per cent Cabernet and 25 per cent Merlot and Malbec, whereas in Pessac in the Graves it was 50 per cent Cabernet and 50 per cent Merlot and Malbec; and in St-Emilion, Pomerol and Fronsac, it was one-third of each of these three grapes. As today, the further away from the Médoc, the more the productive Merlot and Malbec was grown.

To alter the balance of a vineyard is a long-term matter. To root up productive vines at the height of their quality – perhaps from 10 to 25 years old – is uneconomic, as they have to be replaced by vines that will not be productive for three years and not fully extended for several more. Unless a vineyard can be territorially increased, it takes time to plant enough vines of another type to make a difference to the final blend of the wine. Too great a proportion of young vines of any variety will result in a green, stalky wine. This was the case, it seemed to me, with La Lagune, whose vineyard had been allowed to run down. In 1957 and the following years almost the whole of it had to be re-planted. Not only must a balance of suitable varieties be maintained, but also a fair proportion of old and new vines.

In the white wine areas there are only two important grapes: the Sauvignon and the Sémillon. The former, also known as the Petit-Sauvignon, produces a big quantity of fruit, but not so much as the Sémillon, less subject to disease. The Sauvignon produces the finer quality wine but its flavour is too pronounced unless blended with a good proportion of Sémillon. On the other hand the former is particularly prone to the *pourriture noble*, essential for fine Sauternes.

Another white wine grape is the Muscadelle. This is never used on its own, for – like all Muscat-style grapes – it has too penetrating an aroma and flavour, but makes a valuable contribution as a small proportion of the blend in the sweeter wine areas; but not in such outstanding estates as Yquem.

There are other white wine grapes grown for wine in the Gironde, and as one goes further from the leading areas, so their use, although controlled, is less discriminate. They include varieties such as the Merlot-Blanc, the Folle-Blanche (best known in the Charente) and the Colombar. They are to be found in Blaye and in the lesser areas whose *appellation contrôlée* is only Bordeaux. In the sweet white wine district the Ugniblanc is grown, and the Riesling can occasionally be met in the Graves. Occasionally too minor vines appear.

Diseases of the Vine

While discussing the grape varieties it is appropriate to mention the diseases to which now or in the past they are or have been subject. The most famous, the oidium and the phylloxera, are frequently mentioned later, so it is as well to deal with them right away.

The three most serious attacks of disease and parasites suffered in the Gironde area followed in historical sequence; so it is easiest to describe them thus.

The first was the oidium. This is a small mushroom growth which attacks young wood, young leaves and young grapes. Small, whitish spots are formed and soon cover the whole branch, leaf or berry. The leaves curl up and drop off; the grapes darken in colour, split and dry up. It was first discovered in England in 1845 on some plants imported from the tropics in a greenhouse in Margate, by a gardener named Tucker and a naturalist called Berkeley. As a result it was named *Oidium tuckeri*. It had been noticed in the Gironde early in the 1850s, but really struck the Bordeaux vineyards in 1852–3. When it first appeared widely in the department in 1852 the oidium started in the white wine areas of the left bank of the Garonne, and spread rapidly through the Graves, attacking particularly the best grape varieties which apparently were less resistant. The leading white Sauternes were especially badly hit. The drop in production at Yquem shows this. In the fine vintage of 1847 it had made 140 *tonneaux*; in 1853 only 18 was produced. By the following year production was only a quarter of the previous year. The four red Bordeaux *premiers crus* produced between them only 22 *tonneaux* in 1854, compared with 254 two years earlier; but it was very quickly and successfully treated by the application of sulphur. By 1858 the position was restored and there was a very large crop, with the *premiers crus* producing 333 *tonneaux* between them. One lasting effect, however, was a steep rise in prices. The end of the oidium period marked for growers and merchants the beginning of the era of great prosperity which closed with the onslaught of Bordeaux's second and most serious enemy – the phylloxera louse.

The phylloxera is an aphid, about one millimetre in size and stout in shape. It feeds on the sap of plants, from the leaves down to the roots. No fewer than twelve generations can be produced in one year. Native to the eastern part of the U.S.A., where apparently it lives chiefly on the leaves, forming galls, in Europe the creature is more addicted to the roots, producing nodules on the young roots which eventually die. The insects then come to the surface in search of nourishment and proceed to spread the disease further.

An English greenhouse was again the setting for the first discovery in Europe of this largely subterranean invader. It was found in a Hammersmith greenhouse in 1863 and studied at Oxford by Professor I. O. Westwood, who did not name it as he could find no males; at one stage it is parthogenetic. Later it was suitably named *Phylloxera vastatrix*. About the same time it was discovered on the Rhône in three communes near Avignon, including Villeneuve-les-Avignon. It spread very rapidly in the Midi, particularly after 1869. It is said the disturbance caused by the Franco-Prussian War in 1870–1 was partly responsible for neglect in dealing with this invader, which in the end cost France more than the Prussian one. A contemporary estimate was £400 million.

In the Gironde it was first observed in 1866 and 1867 in the *palus* at Floirac a few miles across the river from Bordeaux. Initially the advance was slow but it began to spread into the Entre-Deux-Mers, and then along the right bank of the Dordogne, attacking Blaye, Libourne and St-Emilion. The Médoc was not seriously affected until after 1878, and there were those who claimed that this mysterious disease was an effect rather than a cause. Some thought it was a malady of the vine owing to impoverishment of the soil and lack of fertilizer in the outlying areas. Others, led by

M. Laliman, a grower, as early as 1869 believed that re-planting with resistant vines was the only cure.

By the end of the 1870s between a half and a third of the vineyards of St-Emilion and Fronsac had been devastated. A visitor at this time to Ch. des Tours, a large property in Montagne-St-Emilion, referred to the debilitated branches almost bare of leaves, and even those were yellow and impoverished. The grapes were scanty and dried up. The proprietor pulled at a 40-year-old vine and it came out of the ground without any resistance; the roots were mutilated and reduced to a spongy state. The Gironde area was one of the worst hit in France and 138,000 hectares out of 141,420 were affected by 1882.

It will be understood that Laliman's radical solution first to plant resistant vines and then, in 1871, to graft French vines on resistant American stock, was far from popular. It was well known that the American vines produced a foxy-tasting wine (*un goût de renard*), and who was to know whether the splendid, unique flavour of the Bordeaux wines would be lost for ever? In 1874 M. Théophile Malvezin, a distinguished historian of Bordeaux, published a 56-page pamphlet in the form of a letter to the Bordeaux Chamber of Commerce, in which he suggested alternatives to re-planting.

One suggestion made was that *la chasse* should be prohibited in all the viticultural departments of France (nearly all then), except for shooting, as it was thought that the snaring of small birds, who ate the insects, was a cause. Secondly flooding the vineyards, as had been practised successfully in Vaucluse, was advocated, but this was scarcely practicable in most other vineyard areas. All sorts of insecticides were advised and tried, from coal tar and phenic acid to ammonia, sulphuric acid, carbon-bisulphide and potassium sulpho-carbonate. The last two were probably most extensively used, but they were very expensive to apply over wide areas. In 1883 at Loudenne, which had been bought only eight years previously by the Gilbeys, no less than £600 was spent on treating the vines.

The diaries of the visits of the Gilbeys still preserved at Loudenne give a picture of the long and uncertain struggle against the phylloxera, which in the Gironde alone did not cease abruptly, as is sometimes imagined, in the same way as the oidium was conquered. It was 1879 when the Gilbeys first noted the presence of the phylloxera in the Médoc, although it was already established in the adjoining Charente. By 1882 potassium sulpho-carbonate was being used in the vineyard, and there was a reference to American vines being planted. 'This method will probably be adopted.' But in 1886 over £300 was spent on the chemical treatment which was thought to fumigate the soil, and up to £700 in later years. The problem was, of course, to avoid killing the vines as well as the attacker. This treatment was certainly temporarily successful, so was carbon-bisulphide as used at the Ch. des Tours.

The Bas-Médoc was thought to be more vulnerable than the Haut-Médoc, as the standard of cultivation was lower in the former. In the 1892 diary there is a reference to the planting of American stock, but even in 1894 some French ungrafted Cabernet-Sauvignon vines were being planted, although a further note that year states that they were satisfied that American stocks were essential, as the phylloxera was still

17

present in the Loudenne vineyard. Gilbeys were probably not backward in coming to this decision, but in the Loudenne diary for 1889 there is a reference to the fact that chemical treatment was still being used at Pontet-Canet.

Even as late as 1890 nearly half the Gironde *vignoble* was still planted or re-planted with old French vines, mostly in the Médoc, Graves and Sauternes, where the sandy soil was less favourable to the phylloxera louse. In the 1893 edition of Cocks et Féret's *St-Emilion*, it is stated nearly all the vines in that district were French vines. Moreover mass re-planting was extremely expensive. In 1895 the Gilbeys reckoned that to re-plant 12 acres would cost £720, a figure which probably has to be multiplied five times to correspond with present-day values. As late as 1898, treatment was necessary in that part of the vineyard not yet re-planted.

The disaster was increased by the appearance of Bordeaux's third plague – the mildew. This was first reported widely in 1883 in the south-west of France. Mildew affects the leaves only, leaving white spots on the under side and yellowy-brown patches on the top. This occurs at the flowering. The result is an imbalance in the plant reflected in the wine itself. The means of combating this was discovered as quickly as the cure for the oidium; it was the spraying with copper sulphate – *bouillie bordelaise*, or Bordeaux mixture – which also destroys other vine diseases and parasites. As a result recovery began in 1887 and was complete by 1888.

There was some controversy as to whom the credit for the treatment was due. Apparently it was customary for the Médoc proprietors to have the lines of their vines nearest the roads or paths to be sprayed with copper sulphate to discourage amateur grape pickers. It seems certain that M. David, the *régisseur* (manager) of the two properties of Nathaniel Johnston, Ducru-Beaucaillou and Dauzac, had a hand in this, but the scientific basis for the counter-measures in the mid-1880s was certainly laid by M. Millardet, Professor of Botany at Bordeaux University.

In a way mildew had a more immediately disastrous effect than the phylloxera, for the latter affected quantity rather than quality whereas the former spoiled the wines. Otherwise, for example, it seems almost certain that 1884 would have been a fine vintage. Consequently Ch. Margaux '84 sold for 5,000 frs. a *tonneau*, of four *barriques* of 225 litres each, as it had not been touched by the disease, whereas Lafite which suffered badly was only able to secure the derisory price of 1,500 frs. a *tonneau*, or £15 a *barrique*. The wine was so poor that it was rejected by the Bordeaux trade. By 1887 Lafite was recovering and produced 120 *tonneaux*, and in the following year 300 *tonneaux*, including its subsidiary vineyard on the Carruades plateau.

One result of the combined phylloxera-mildew period was that a few vineyards at the lower end of the Bordeaux social scale went out of production; but an equally contributory factor to this was the slump in France during the 1880s. The Gilbeys in their 1884 diary wrote: 'The complete stagnation on the Bordeaux market had compelled proprietors to submit to prices that had not been known for *very* many years'.

Contrary to common belief, however, while output fell in the Gironde as a result of phylloxera and mildew, the acreage under vines did not substantially decline. In 1875 the total was a record 145,000 hectares, and 144,000 in 1889. In the succeeding period up to the First World War it varied between 129,000 and 142,000, and in 1911 was 136,000. This was owing to poor economic conditions rather than to the effects of disease. Nevertheless during the 1880s property values dropped sharply and the Gilbeys mention in 1886 one property in the Bas-Médoc valued at 200,000 frs. in 1878 and now worth below 150,000 frs.

For later generations of wine drinkers the big question about the phylloxera and the consequent re-planting of French vines of the variety *Vitis vinifera* on to American stocks of *Vitis riparia* and *Vitis rupestris*, is whether the wines are so fine as they were. Wine drinking is to some extent a looking-over-one's-shoulder occupation and nostalgia deepens as the second and third bottles are reached. It was therefore natural for a certain generation of wine drinkers to believe that wines 'would never be so good again'; not altogether discomforting either, as these gentlemen often had enough of the pre-phylloxera wines below stairs to see them out!

But I believe that the great pair of 1899 and 1900 killed this pessimism, and I see no reason to believe the wines less good since the 1880s. On the other hand the extraordinary longevity of the great pre-phylloxera clarets does suggest that perhaps the wines do not last as long now as they did; and this without taking into consideration contemporary methods of vinification developed since the last war to make the wines ready to drink earlier. There has not been yet sufficient time to judge the results of this, but it might be that they have had a more decisive effect on the life-span of claret than the adoption of American stock.

It is also possible that the vines do not last so long; yet earlier uprooting may be owing to the need for higher yields; as the vines age, so their crop falls. It is said too that the grafted vines yield more grapes and have to be pruned more severely to maintain quality.

Here it should be pointed out that these three major diseases have been contained but not cured. To re-plant non-resistant French vines would be an invitation to the lurking phylloxera, and only the repeated applications of sulphur and copper sulphate keep at bay oidium, or powdery mildew, and the downy mildew or peronospora.

There are, of course, other diseases with which the Gironde growers have to contend. There is *millerandage*, which results in a proliferation of small grapes which fall off and never swell. There is black rot, which attacked the French vineyards towards the end of the last century and had a disastrous effect on the 1897 vintage, but has not otherwise been a great problem in the Gironde. Allied to *millerandage* is *coulure*, which is the dropping of the flowers or of the newly produced berries, owing to bad weather at the time of the flowering. This occurs to some extent nearly every year. The rot which affects the grapes in wet years is *pourriture grise*.

There are a number of somewhat specialized diseases which modern methods of treatment have rendered no great risk. These include anthracnose, which forms stains on leaves, grapes and young shoots; cochylis, which produces grubs feeding on grapes, and which was a danger soon after the phylloxera; altise, a beetle feeding on leaves; and red spider. However these and other disorders are normally under control, and while they may occupy the *vigneron* by day they do not keep him awake at night as the three plagues of the last century certainly did.

Wine Making

This book is in no sense a technical work, but after describing the grapes and their diseases, some account is needed of the vineyard year and the making and ageing of wine in the Gironde. In practice there are variations not only from district to district but from château to château. At Lascombes in Margaux they plough the vineyard four times a year, at Palmer in adjacent Cantenac three times; others plough twice and then remove the weeds by harrowing. When it comes to the making of the wine the differences are widespread. However the general principles are much the same, with the aim being to make as much good wine as is either consonant with the vineyard's reputation and prospects of sale or within the limit allowed under the regulations of *appellation contrôlée*. The two alternatives do not, of course, always produce the same results.

The vineyard year begins after the grapes have been picked. Except in Sauternes this will be over by the end of October at the latest, but in the sweet wine areas the final picking may go on into November. Then the vineyard is cleared of any debris and a preliminary ploughing may take place to earth up the vines as a protection against winter frosts.

In December pruning begins and continues through the winter; it should be completed before the sap begins to rise in the spring, although there are advocates of late pruning to protect the vines against spring frosts. Vine pruning is a technical affair and very important. Basically in the Médoc each vine is allowed two widely spaced branches, which are tied to the three rows of wire that run along the lines of vines. These vines are usually planted one metre apart, and there will be at least one metre between each row. It is usually more in the Sauternes, in St-Emilion and the lesser districts; and the needs of mechanization are tending to increase this distance. The two permitted branches – it is three in the *palus* – will have sprung out in the previous spring and summer; for the grapes are borne on last year's wood. In the old days these branches were supported on stakes, as they still are in some vineyards, but in Bordeaux wire is almost universal. Each of these branches is allowed to keep two or three buds apiece. In St-Emilion and Sauternes one fruit-bearing branch only is permitted, with 7 – 10 buds per branch. Great care is taken in the pruning to remove all unnecessary wood.

In January the vineyard may be manured. This is not done too frequently as it would encourage too much foliage; usually once every five years. Any defective staves are replaced, and some growers have a winter spraying against various diseases, notably red spider.

The important ploughing begins after the winter frosts, normally about 20 February. This 'opens up' the vine, by uncovering the ridge in which the foot of the vine lies, and transferring the earth to the ground between the vine lines; the earth which cannot be removed by the plough is hoed away from the vines. Ploughing is finished by the end of March, and in the following month a new ploughing takes place, with a different type of plough, the object now being to replace the earth round the foot of the vine. At the beginning of May a further opening up of the vine may be done by the plough, followed immediately by a final operation to cover the base of the vine trunk, as a protection against hot weather.

Planting and grafting continues until April. Any suckers that have emerged from the American root-stock below the graft are removed, the young leaves being sprayed against mildew and oidium and surplus buds removed. There is a danger of late frosts in May, which are more damaging than those earlier in the year, for with the sap risen, once the vine is in leaf a very slight frost can devastate the vineyard. The most disastrous frosts in recent history were those in February 1956, when some vineyards were practically wiped out at temperatures as low as −24 degrees C., but this was also partly caused by a very mild January which had encouraged the sap to rise prematurely. Indeed after the diseases, particularly rot, frost has always been the chief hazard of Bordeaux. It was recorded in 1354 that the vineyards were frozen in Saint-Genès near Bordeaux, and in 1406 nearly all the vineyards of Guyenne were ruined by frost. The terrible winter of 1766 devastated the Bordeaux vineyards; and when Lafite was sold in 1797 after the Revolutionary confiscation, the sale notice prominently mentioned that the vineyard was free from the danger of frost. Today perhaps the low-lying Graves area is most subject to it.

At the beginning of June comes the flowering or *floraison*, when fine warm weather is needed to set the flowers without delay. The flowering should be over within three weeks, and the rule-of-thumb estimate is that the vintage will take place 100 days after the completion of flowering. Bad weather at this time will produce *coulure*, when the flowers or tiny berries fall off; and *millerandage* when the grape clusters may be composed of a mass of tiny grapes that will not develop. There is spraying in June and trimming of excessive vegetation.

Spraying continues in July and August, particularly after rain; the vine lines are kept trimmed and the ground below freed of weeds by ploughing or harrowing. Viticulturally there is no finer sight than a well-kept Bordeaux vineyard. Otherwise, August and the beginning of September is a quiet time in the vineyard, and the workers in the vineyards and cellars (*chais*) as well as the working proprietors usually take their holidays at this time.

Ideally the vintage begins about 15 September, although it normally begins later. The earliest vintage on record since 1795 was 1893, when it started on 15 August, with excellent results. The only other such summer vintage known was in 1822 when it began on 27 August; the vintage was not exceptional. Of the great years in Bordeaux's modern history, the starting dates were as follows:

1798 – 13 September	1899 – 24 September
1802 – 23 September	1900 – 24 September
1811 – 14 September	1920 – 22 September
1815 – 25 September	1921 – 15 September
1828 – 15 September	1928 – 25 September
1858 – 20 September	1929 – 26 September
1864 – 17 September	1945 – 13 September
1870 – 10 September	1961 – 22 September

It will be noted that few of the outstanding years had vintages beginning before 15 September. Few leading years, however, started as late as October, although 1926 (4 October) and 1953 (1 October) succeeded. The latest modern vintages on record were 1816 (27 October), described in Tastet et Lawton's records, to which I am indebted for these details, as 'detestable', 1932 (15 October), 'execrable', and the notorious 1956 (14 October).

It is a fact nowadays that the vintage takes place later than it did in the last century. Prior to the development of modern instruments to test the sugar and acid content of the grapes before picking begins, there was a natural tendency not to risk bad autumnal weather, and therefore to pick early rather than late. This meant that the grapes were often not completely ripe and the wine tended to be harder and slow-developing. Nowadays owing to modern methods the grapes in a good year should be *à point* when picked, and the resulting softer wines will develop more quickly.

Not all the vineyards will start picking simultaneously; and St-Emilion and Pomerol normally begin a few days before the Médoc. Much depends on the weather and the forecasts put out by the meteorological office in Bordeaux, as well as on the maturity of the grapes in the vineyards. These are usually tested for sugar and acid content. Some proprietors hope to squeeze the last drop of '*surmaturité*' out of their grapes before picking, but this can be risky, as was shown in 1964 when rain spoiled the latter half of a vintage that began only on 28 September. At Mouton-Rothschild during the vintage something like a council of war, armed with weather and vineyard reports, is held regularly, to decide when to pick and when to stop. Before picking in the fine wine areas, the sugar content of the grapes should be a minimum of 11 per cent degrees of alcohol and a maximum of 7 grammes of tartaric acid. To pick or not to pick is the most momentous decision in the wine-making year in Bordeaux.

Harvesting is done in the big estates by teams of imported labour, often Spanish, who are accommodated and fed for the two or three weeks necessary to complete the picking; more in the Sauternes where the vintage will last for 4 – 6 weeks. Some growers will employ local labour, particularly in the Sauternes, for obvious reasons, to ensure that the grapes are ripe to the point of noble rottenness, discussed in the chapter on sweet white wines. At the end of the picking, which is arduous, particularly in bad weather, there is usually a party, and on some estates it is still the custom to present the wife of the proprietor with a large bouquet of flowers – the *gerbaude*. I remember a few years ago at Mouton-Rothschild a bouquet, splendid enough to have gladdened any first-night *prima donna*, presented to the Baroness by the *vendangeurs*.

After the picking, the paths of red and white wine-making diverge. Black grapes go through the process of *égrappage*, in which the stalks are removed; the white rarely except at a few Sauternes châteaux including Yquem, after the first pressing. This is usually done by a revolving cylindrical machine, which also breaks the skins lightly, and is known as a *fouloir-égrappoir*. The operation can also be carried out by hand on a kind of table with a grill top (*table d'égrappage*), as practised at Palmer and Cantemerle, but is not now common. If the stalks were not removed there would be an excess of acidity and tannin in the wine. At Yquem, one is assured, the grapes are never in contact with metal.

For red wine the grapes, skins and juice are at once pumped into large vats which have been scoured and put in sound, clean condition in the weeks prior to the vintage. Most fermentation vats (*cuves*) in Bordeaux are of oak, but some are of concrete and even of steel. Some châteaux such as Pontet-Canet and Mouton-Rothschild have an upper floor in their press-houses (*cuviers*), and the grapes are taken up from outside and poured into the tops of the vats; elsewhere they are tipped in from ladders placed against the sides of the vats. The fermentation usually begins within 24 hours, but in cold weather it can be delayed up to three days, and the *cuviers* may have to be heated. The period of fermentation varies from three or four days to a fortnight. In good conditions this may be over within four to six days, and the wine stays thereafter in the vats for varying lengths of time.

The object of the fermentation is, of course, to transform the sugar into alcohol by means of the natural yeasts on the grape skins; it is seldom necessary to add yeast during the fermentation, although it is said to be more common with modern sterile vats. The great risk is of the must becoming overheated to such an extent that the yeasts are killed and fermentation ceases; to re-start the process is very difficult, and the wine with unconverted free sugar may turn to vinegar. This happened at Lafite in 1921, and occurred very widely in the excessively hot vintage of 1895.

Accordingly it is desirable to keep the temperature below 30 degrees C., although it often goes up to 33 degrees; the top limit is 35 degrees, and at 37 degrees the fermentation begins to slow down. To keep the temperature low two methods are used. Ice is lowered in canvas sacks into the *cuves* – and at Mouton-Rothschild they bring in a ton a day during the fermentation period. The wine is pumped out of the bottom of the vat, through a piece of equipment consisting of a serpentine series of pipes cooled by ice or water, and then back into the top of the vat. This has another purpose. The skins float to the top of the fermenting must and form a hard crust known as the *chapeau*. This can be a foot or more thick and prevents essential air reaching the must as well as reducing the contact of juice with the skins. This is broken up by men with poles, and the wine released from the bottom of the vat is poured into the top. This process is known as *remontage*. Another way the *chapeau* is prevented from forming is by the laying of planks across the vat, a few inches below the top, as is done at Branaire, following the practice in Algeria.

At La Mission-Haut-Brion Henri Woltner installed vitrified steel vats, which keep the must relatively cool, and not over 30 degrees C. This is what he calls '*fermentation froide*'.

During the fermentation period, attached to every vat in the press house is a chart, showing the arc-like rise and fall of temperature and the drop in sugar content expressed on the Baumé scale.

This raises the question of *chaptalisation* or the addition of sugar to the must in order to raise the alcoholic strength. The term comes from Jean André Chaptal (1756 – 1832), a chemist who became Minister of the Interior and Comte de Chanteloup under Napoleon. He wrote a book on wine-making *L'Art de faire, de gouverner et de perfectionner le Vin* (1801) and was a pioneer in France of beet sugar production. As the sugar should all be converted into alcohol the wine's degree of sweetness ought not to be altered, but if one tastes an off-vintage claret, which has had to be *chaptalisé* a sweetish flavour can often be detected; alcohol from cane sugar is likely to taste different from that produced from grape sugar. Moderate sugaring is unlikely to be noticed. There is a legal limit to the amount of sugar which may be added: 3 kilograms per hectolitre of must. Also no more than 200 kilos of sugar may be added per hectare of vineyard under production. As 1·8 kilograms of sugar will raise the alcoholic content by one degree, this means it may only be increased by just over 1½ degrees. *Chaptalisation* is only allowed when the wine already has the minimum alcoholic strength permitted for its *appellation*. The various minima of strengths are given later, under the districts, but the minimum for a wine to qualify for the lowest red wine *appellation contrôlée* of Bordeaux is 10 degrees, although a fine château wine will not be less than 11·5 degrees and should be nearly 12. So *chaptalisation* may be resorted to not only in a bad year but also when the wine is a little below the desirable strength. This occurred in 1966 when many proprietors wanted to bring the wine up by half a degree.

Common in Burgundy and elsewhere for many years, *chaptalisation* was only legalized in Bordeaux in 1938, for that year only, and then not again until 1951, although on occasion it was certainly practised there long before this. Since 1951 it has only been allowed on an annual basis by the Minister of Agriculture at the request of the *Institut National des Appellations d'Origine* (*I.N.A.O.*), through the Prefect of the Gironde on the representations of the growers and the advice of experts. As permission usually is given only a day or two before the vintage – or even after it has begun – one wonders how the growers manage to secure the necessary sugar so promptly. Sugar used for *chaptalisation* is taxed at ·80 frs. a kilo. Some people consider that Bordeaux sold out its birth-right of natural wine when this sugaring was permitted, but certainly it has saved a great deal of wine otherwise unsaleable or unpalatable. Permission is given with great frequency these days, even in successful years like '64 and '66. The addition of sugar to a wine after the fermentation is strictly illegal. *Chaptalisation* applies only to red wine.

There has been much talk in recent years of wine being made differently, with a view to producing quick-maturing wines. In so far as this is true, it arises from the length of time the newly fermented wine is left with the skins in the vats before being drawn off into cask. The purpose is to give further colour and tannin to the wine, thus increasing its body and power of development; the skins, pips, etc., which contain the tannin, macerate in the wine. In the old days the wine lay on the skins for three or four weeks, before the latter were taken out and pressed. Nowadays the normal period among the *crus classés* is more like ten to fourteen days, while elsewhere as at La Mission-Haut-Brion the wine is taken off the skins once the fermentation is completed. At some châteaux, including Haut-Brion, the wine is left in the vats for a couple of months after the skins have been removed. Others leave it in vats until the first racking at the turn of the year or even longer. This keeps the wine fresh, but it develops more slowly than in wood, and takes longer to fall bright. In some small growths the wine is kept permanently in vats until bottled; this is of course a cheaper method of storage, and there will not be the same loss from evaporation, but the development will not be as good. Certainly longer contact with the skins will increase tannin content.

Whether the shorter period of maceration will adversely affect the quality and above all the longevity of the wine is still in question. There is little doubt it has done so in Burgundy, but the wines there naturally have less tannin. Until such vintages as 1959, 1961 and 1964 demonstrate whether they can or cannot last the twenty to thirty years of their pre-last world war predecessors we shall not know the answer; and only a few then may care.

Another reason for leaving the wines in vats for a certain period is to try to have part at least of the second or malo-lactic fermentation over by the time the wine goes into cask. This fermentation transforms malic acid into lactic acid, and is an essential stage in a red wine's development. Only in fairly recent times has this been understood. It cannot be speeded up, and it may not take place until the spring after the vintage, or even later. A wine that ferments in bottle may well have not completed the malo-lactic fermentation before bottling. So if the growth is lucky this fermentation will follow hard on, or even occur almost simultaneously with the alcoholic fermentation. A wine that ferments in bottle seldom, if ever, completely recovers.

It should be mentioned also that a second wine, the *vin de presse*, is made by pressing the skins after the vats are emptied. This can be good wine, and a proportion is normally added to the first wine even in the leading growths. After that the grapes are distilled for *marc*, but by specialists in that process rather than by the growers. It is compulsory for the growers to produce some distillate, and this is how they do it. Before the development of the *fouloir-égrappoir* a *vin de queue* was made by pressing the stalks, but was generally added to the workers' *piquette*.

Ideally the young red wine should go into new Limousin oak casks; they make a splendid sight in those châteaux that can afford a complete new range every year. They are hardly worth it in off-years like 1963 and 1965. The new oak certainly adds something to the wine's flavour, and the wine is said to clear and fall bright more quickly in new oak. Most proprietors even of the classed growths buy only a proportion of new casks each year, for they now cost about £14 apiece, compared with less than £1 at the beginning of this century. When the wine is bottled at the château the hogsheads may be sold to second-hand dealers.

The continence of the *barrique bordelaise* is strictly controlled. In earlier times it varied from 215 to 230 litres, but it was officially designated in 1866 at 225 litres (49·5 imperial gallons, 59·4 U.S. gallons), with four *barriques* making a *tonneau* of 900 litres. A tolerance of 2 per cent is allowed on either side. The shape, circumference and number of iron bands, etc. are also specified. This should provide 300 bottles of ·75 litre apiece, but in practice only 288 bottles or 24 dozen are allowed for, and when a customer has his wine château-bottled this is the quantity he will expect from each *barrique*.

For the first ten months or so of its life the claret is in a cask with the bung on the top. Since there is loss by evaporation, it is necessary to top up the cask once or twice a week to replace the ullage (*ouillage*). At the end of December or early in January the wine is racked off (*soutirage*) the accumulated lees into a clean cask, and this is repeated quarterly for the first year, and probably three times in the second. The wine from the lees is collected, and also racked off, fined and later bottled as *vin de lie*, which can be excellent but is never marketed, and consumed in the château. It is always laid down that racking should take place in dry, still weather, as then the lees will more readily lie at the bottom of the cask, but this is not always followed today.

Early in the New Year will take place the *égalisage* or *assemblage* of the wines made from the different grapes in the vineyard, and hitherto kept separate. This is the moment of truth for the proprietor, the *régisseur* or the *maître de chai* (cellar master). The wine from each vat is carefully tasted to decide which is good enough to be included in the *ensemble* and sold under the château label, in bottle or cask as may be; and which will be rejected. The rejection may be owing to the grapes from a particular vat being too young, or they may have been picked under unfavourable conditions; fine sunny weather throughout the vintage cannot be expected.

The temptation to include too much in the *ensemble* must be considerable, since the difference in price between the château wine and the commune wine, or even a wine sold at lower *appellations*, is great indeed. Each vat rejected involves the owner in substantial financial loss, and the wine therein may have to be sold at less than the cost of production. On the other hand there is the château's reputation to be protected; too high a proportion of wine from young vines of indifferent wine may affect adversely the good name and perhaps the sale prospects of the estate. At Palmer in the very poor year of 1963 all the vats were rejected, in 1964 about one-third were not accepted; with over half rejected in 1965, but none at all in 1966. Along with the decision when to pick, this is the greatest problem each year for the proprietor or his deputy; and whereas the former decision is to some extent a collective one, for others are making up their minds publicly by sending the pickers out to collect the grapes, the *assemblage* is made in the isolation and privacy of the *chai*.

In the second year the casks will lie with their bungs half way over on the side of the cask, so there will be no more ullage. Accordingly samples will be drawn not by removing the bung, but via little spigots inserted in the cask ends. Usually the wine will undergo one fining (*collage*), to clear away the impurities, which are carried to the bottom by white of egg, blood, isinglass or patent chemicals. If a wine is very tough a second fining may be given it, to reduce the tannin. Fining is normally carried out shortly before the cask is despatched or bottled off. Incidentally what are known as keeping charges and fining for all wine sold are paid for by the customer. The former work out at ¾ per cent per month of the purchase price, and 2 per cent per fining. When Bordeaux wines were generally inexpensive this was no great addition, but it is no small matter these days when the customer has to pay up to 20 per cent on the purchase price of £150 or more per *barrique*. Some merchants quote prices including these charges. The prices of the four *premiers crus* and Mouton-Rothschild always include keeping charges but not the compulsory château-bottling.

The time of bottling or shipping in cask varies considerably. It depends to some extent on the vintage and the state of the wine, but despatch of wine in cask is not undertaken either in the cold winter months or in mid-summer. The lesser wines probably will be shipped in cask in the late spring or early summer of the second year after the vintage. Bottling at source is likely to take place in the summer of the second year or before the second vintage, but should not be carried out in hot weather; although it often is. The finest red Bordeaux is bottled when the wine is over two years old, either in the third autumn or in the third spring; clear, dry weather is advised. After bottling or shipping in bottle all wine may be out of condition or 'bottle-sick' for a matter of months.

Red Bordeaux should be bottled in green bottles, and white Bordeaux in white bottles.

The principal difference in the fermentation of white Bordeaux is that the grapes are pressed up to three times and for the finest wine the fermentation then takes place in the casks into which the expressed juice is immediately run. For lesser wines and for many well-known Sauternes the fermentation is carried out in vats. The third pressing should not be used in the best quality wine. In the Sauternes district before picking, a sugar content that will produce 20 per cent of alcohol is desirable. The fermentation will stop at about 15 per cent, thus leaving 5 per cent of free sugar to give the wine its special lusciousness. The high alcoholic content will prevent the wine turning to vinegar. At Yquem the *égrappage* is done only after the first pressing, and each pressing takes about an hour. The fermentation in cask may last anything from fifteen days to three months, but the most satisfactory period is one month. In the Sauternais where the picking may take place over an extended time there are likely to be bigger variations from cask to cask than with the red wines; so an *égalisage* has to take place to ensure a consistent wine. This is usually done when the wine is a year old. Bottling of these sweet wines may be carried out anything from two to three and a half years after the vintage, but the dry wines are put in bottle after fifteen to eighteen months, though these days some are bottled after only six months.

Rosé wine or 'Bordeaux clairet' is made in Bordeaux by taking the must off the skins in the vats almost at once; then the grapes are pressed and the juice is fermented out on its own in hogsheads, as with white wine. The bottling is usually done as with dry white Bordeaux. As mentioned later this *rosé* used to be known as *vin de goutte*.

There are many variations in wine-making in Bordeaux, and some of these are described in succeeding chapters. I have come upon small growths in Bourg and Blaye where a red wine is still in vat after two years. This may be because the grower thinks it will develop best that way, or he may be short of money to buy casks. Certainly the wine will keep fresher in vat. Most growers have their own methods and even secrets of viticulture and wine-making. It is a hazardous and highly individual occupation, and so long as we have good Bordeaux, long may the individuality of Bordeaux – its chief glory – remain.

2. Bordeaux and Wine

It seems likely that Bordeaux was a wine trading centre before it was a wine growing region. The argument against it first being a wine growing area is that it is not mentioned as such by the geographer Strabo, who wrote about 63 B.C. Burdigala is indeed included but as an *emporium,* and it is thought that if there had been vine growing in any scale he would have said so. Broadly speaking the vine in France spread north and west from Provence and the Rhône Valley. One of the oldest wine areas of France was Gaillac, which continued to be important until the nineteenth century. From this town the wine could be shipped down the Tarn and Garonne and thence to Bordeaux. There is an inscription of the 1st or 2nd centuries A.D. which mentions the presence at Bordeaux of a *negotiator britannicus.* What else was this English merchant doing in Bordeaux if not buying wine? Surely he was one of the pioneers of the Anglo-Bordeaux wine trade, whose successors in good times and bad, in peace and often in war, have visited Bordeaux in order to buy wine for the British market. Our British negotiator was not concerned with wine grown in and around Bordeaux, but with the young wine brought down from what later was known as the Haut-Pays. He would have been in character if he remarked to the Bordeaux merchant, 'A little lacking in body this year's Gaillac, don't you think?'

Moreover although the Edict of Domitian in A.D. 92, by which vineyards outside Italy had to be pulled up, was never fully implemented, it would have discouraged the planting of vines in an area which was not at that time regarded so suitable for wine making as the country further east and south. For the soil was poor and the climate uncertain in a district subject to Atlantic weather. Much of the area was little above water level, and Dion (*Histoire de la Vigne et du Vin en France des origines au*

28

XIXième Siècle, 1959) suggests that it took very hard work to establish the Bordeaux *vignoble*, by cutting down the forests and draining the land, and this was only possible out of the profits of the export trade.

When Probus became Emperor in A.D. 276 he took a much more enlightened view of vineyard planting throughout his empire, and Domitian's restrictions were officially relaxed in 280. Ausonius the poet owned vineyards in the Bordeaux area in the fourth century, and his is one of the earliest testimonials to their presence. His quite considerable vineyard probably overlooked the Garonne and it would seem likely that it was in what is now the Premières Côtes area of the Entre-Deux-Mers, or in the Graves or possibly opposite Bordeaux near Cenon, where the Paris road climbs the hill towards Carbon-Blanc.

The Bordeaux trade was certainly adversely affected as a result of the decrees of the Roman Emperors forbidding trade with the barbarians, and in the fifth century the Saxon pirates harassed their maritime commerce.

In 412 the Visigoths invaded the region and brought their usual devastation. They were succeeded by the Franks under Clovis but, as elsewhere when the Romans withdrew, history is very sparse. In the Merovingian period (sixth to eighth centuries) Plassac on the Gironde south of Blaye was a vineyard centre. Charlemagne passed through the area on his way to Spain; later the Norman long boats reached up the Garonne and Dordogne, pillaging the surrounding country. It is thought that the vineyard area slowly increased, but there are no documents giving facts about the trade in wine until the arrival of the English in 1152, following the marriage of Henry Plantagenet and Eleanor of Aquitaine. The period of the English association is dealt with in the next chapter. Here we are concerned with the general methods of viticulture and wine commerce in the Middle Ages, when Bordeaux became an important wine centre.

In the Middle Ages the grapes were either planted in closely spaced lines, as today, or widely, so that other crops could be cultivated between the vine rows. The vineyards were small, for they were worked by hand, an exception in the fourteenth century being the one in Pessac, belonging to the archbishop, which was worked by ox-drawn ploughs.

Diseases of the vine were regarded as being sent from the Devil and they were accordingly exorcized. There was no limitation on production per hectare as there is now, and output was probably fairly large. It should be borne in mind that in normal times, grape cultivation has always been among the most profitable of cash crops. Hence the tendency of the vineyards to spread at the expense of other and more necessary agricultural products, such as wheat.

In the Middle Ages and indeed until the end of the *Ancien Régime*, the crop could not be picked until the authorization was given by the landlord to his tenant. This *Ban de Vendange* was suppressed at the Revolution, as it inflicted severe loss on the peasants. Today the *Ban* is still proclaimed in the Médoc, but in fact it is no more than an occasion for jollification: the election of members to the order of the *Bontemps de Médoc et des Graves*, followed by an excellent luncheon or dinner. This is held in one or other of the leading châteaux. In the Middle Ages anyone who picked early was liable to prosecution, although sometimes special permission was given. In St-Emilion the start of the vintage was signalled by the ringing of the town bells. The date varied from the end of August to early in October.

It is to be remembered that until our reform of the calendar in the eighteenth century the dates do not correspond with our own. In the archbishop's vineyards the vintage in the fourteenth century started from the third week of August to the fourth week of September, according to conditions; at that time the calendar was about eight days behind. Therefore 12 – 15 September was the equivalent of the 20 – 23 September. In the late vintage of 1410 they started picking the grapes in Pessac on 23 – 24 September (old style). By 1500 the old Julian calendar was about nine days in arrears.

Unlike Burgundy, where old presses may be seen in the *Musée du Vin* in Beaune and at Clos de Vougeot, there are no ancient presses extant in Bordeaux, but they must have been similar contraptions of huge beams and counterweights. The pressing (*foulage*) was done by feet, although afterwards there was a second pressing by a hand-operated press. This was not considered to produce as good wine, any more than the *vin de presse* is regarded today. The 'cake' of grapes, or the *marc*, was then liquefied with water and pressed again; the result was a thin wine, the *vin lymphaté* mentioned below, short-lived even by the standards of the time.

The fermentation usually took about ten days, and it should be noted that white wine was made in exactly the same way as red, with the fermentation taking place in large fermenting vats and not in casks. This did not begin for white wines until the seventeenth and eighteenth centuries. Even in bad years there was no sweetening of the must. Sugar was as rare as spices in the Middle Ages and the earliest known example of sugaring was at Ste-Foy-la-Grande in the eighteenth century; clearly it was a novelty.

Four types of wine were commonly produced: red, white, *clairet* and *vin lymphaté*. *Clairet*, from which our own word claret is derived, was made from a mixture of red and white grapes put together into the fermenting vat, thus producing a *vin gris* or *rosé*. Much more red than white wine was produced in Bordeaux until about three hundred years ago; in the Middle Ages the proportion of white wine was very small. The *vin lymphaté* was watered wine. The new wine was racked off its lees a few months after the vintage, but there is no evidence that fining (*collage*) was used to clear the wine, although this process had been used by the Romans with white wine.

After fermentation the wine was put into casks of oak from the upper Garonne, Périgord, the Saintonge or the Angoulême region. The *barrique bordelais* was a kind of trade mark for the wines of the area. Not only were its dimensions carefully specified and supervised, but neighbouring wine areas were not permitted to use a cask of the same size. As is well known, the Bordelais reckon their output in *tonneaux*, although these 900-litre casks no longer exist, any more than do Bordeaux pipes, which contained 450 litres. They did exist, however, in the Middle Ages, and not only for wine: corn and honey were kept in these large casks. They were in use until the sixteenth century, when their unwieldy size for transporting by road caused their gradual disappearance. By 1789 the *barrique* was normal. The coopers (*tonneliers*) formed an important skilled trade in Bordeaux, and in medieval times they tended to congregate in the St-Michel quarter of the city.

Certainly normally the new wine was blended, sometimes to give more colour to a light one. In the days when the wine was drunk immediately – the archbishop was recorded as having drunk his 1361 new wine in September – it was light in colour and alcohol, and doubtless was appreciated like that. Blending the wine of one year with another was, however, strictly forbidden, not only in Bordeaux but in London also. The wine was often shipped on its lees, i.e. un-racked.

It is difficult for us, accustomed to the fine gradations of vintage wines, to appreciate the conditions under which the trade operated and their customers drank wine. Both lived from cask-to-mouth until the arrival of the bottle in the seventeenth century. There was no means of keeping wine to mature, so it had to be consumed as speedily as possible. For last year's wine was likely to be a dead loss. In 1342 the *vin nouveau* sold at an average price of 21 *livres** per *tonneau*. The *vin ancien* for only 12 *livres*. In 1226 Henry III ordered that his stock of wines of the previous year held in Bristol be sold, and new wine bought with the proceeds. The Bordelais to protect themselves from loss did their best to ensure that their wine was sold promptly and that they secured every advantage to this end.

The burghers' wine was free of all taxes, both the *Petite Coutume* which applied to all wines sold retail in Bordeaux, and the *Grand Coutume* on exports; and could circulate freely anywhere. Their wines, along with those of the archbishop, two Chapters and of the nobles resident in the city, alone could be sold retail from the end of September until early June. Even neighbouring but 'foreign' wines from the Haut-Pays (of which more below), whose arrival in Bordeaux was delayed until the feast of St Martin (11 November) or even until Christmas, had to be sold by a citizen of Bordeaux; and of course the imported wines were taxed. Bordeaux certainly looked after its own and had a reputation for commercial shrewdness which it has by no means lost today.

As elsewhere, the Bordeaux innkeepers were always suspect and were subject to strict supervision. They were particularly firmly forbidden to indulge in blending. In 1342 London innkeepers were not allowed to keep a Gascon wine in the same cellar as one from the Rhine; and the purchaser must be able to see the wine drawn from the cask.

The expansion of the Bordeaux vineyard area probably began in the eleventh century, as the forests surrounding the town were cut down. The Church was a powerful influence in the extension of the vineyards, first because wine was necessary for the holy offices, secondly for hospitality, and thirdly for the excellent revenue return from their estates that wine usually provided. Later on wine growing became very profitable. In the fourteenth and fifteenth centuries the revenue in a good year of a Bordeaux vineyard in full production might be as much as four times the out-goings; for the largely serf labour was very poorly remunerated. Vines were also

---

* The livre tournois was the approximate equivalent of the franc. In 1795 the modern franc was instituted, and 80 francs = 81 livres. At 25 frs. to the £, the franc remained the equivalent of 10d. in English money and 19 cents in American money until 1914.

planted on the right bank of the Garonne, increasingly as the marshes were re-claimed in the *palus* near the river. These riverside vineyards spread considerably in the twelfth and thirteenth centuries, upstream as far as Cadaujac, near Léognan. Until 1200 the Bordeaux *vignoble* was largely composed of the vineyards of the Côtes – Blaye, Bourg, the lower Dordogne and Garonne valleys – and the Graves area around Bordeaux. Until the fourteenth century vineyards were numerous inside the city's boundaries. Where the Allées de Tourny now stands there were once vines. Across the unbridged river, Cenon and Lormont were centres of wine growing.

By the fifteenth century all the cultivable land within easy access from Bordeaux was under vines. Indeed the history of the Bordeaux *vignoble* is one of advance as the forest retreated in face of the vines, and then of decline in the nearer suburbs, as the town itself spread; but this came later, in the nineteenth and twentieth centuries.

The principal and most prolific medieval wine-growing district was the Graves. It was predominantly a red wine area, as indeed was the whole region now entitled to the *appellation* Bordeaux. The chief wine villages were Pessac, Talence, Merignac, Gradignan and, further out, Cérons. In Pessac by the fourteenth century was prob-ably the now oldest named vineyard of the region: Ch. Pape-Clément, as it is now known, although it was no château in those days, but rather part of the estate of the archbishops of Bordeaux. It had been presented to the See in 1305 by the Arch-bishop Bertrand de Goth, who had succeeded to the papacy as Pope Clement V. From here probably came the finest wine of the archiepiscopal estates, for although these included a good deal of vineyard property, the other main vineyards were on the right bank at Lormont and Queyries, now part of the Premières Côtes. These vineyards across the river remained archiepiscopal property until the Revolution. Lormont lies slightly down-stream from Bordeaux, and Queyries is on the flat land. It was opposite what was then the village of Bacalan, beyond the suburb of the Chartrons, named after the Carthusian monks who, in 1383, built their chartreux in the marshy land by the river. Now Queyries is occupied by factories and somewhat decrepit suburbs, through which runs *Route Nationale 10*, prior to climbing the hill in the direction of St-André-de-Cubzac. On this slope were produced the *vins de côtes* of Lormont and Cenon, which were superior to those of the Queyries *palus* which never-theless had a special reputation up to the eighteenth century. In the fourteenth century this *palus* area was owned by the de Grailly family, one of the first identifiable secular vineyard-proprietor families of Bordeaux. Another medieval family with large vineyards in Queyries was that of Puy-Paulin. In the late eighteenth century the deep coloured wines of Queyries (*'vin fort noir'*) were much appreciated in America where they apparently matured well.

Further inland on the right bank there was always a good deal of wine made in the Entre-Deux-Mers, and the English kings held vineyards there. Even before this, vines were recorded as existing in the eleventh century in Vayres and St-Sulpice-d'Izon. There were also vineyards at Carbon-Blanc, Beychac, Langoiran, Cadillac, as well as further south at Loupiac and St-Macaire on the edge of the province of Bordeaux. In the twelfth century the Entre-Deux-Mers was the most widespread and developed vineyard area.

Upstream also, but on the left bank, were vineyards in Sauternes, Barsac, Pujols, Podensac and Cérons. Wine was certainly grown in the Sauternes and Cérons districts in the thirteenth century, and in the church of the latter village is a carving on a capital of a Bordeaux *barrique* placed under a human head. In this southern section the wines were white, but although probably fairly sweet, they did not at all resemble the luscious wines we associate with Sauternes and Cérons today; for this was long before the discovery of the properties and possibilities of *pourriture noble*.

In the Médoc, named after a Celtic tribe, the vineyards were few and scattered, except in the vicinity of Bordeaux. This was owing to their inaccessibility and to the marshy, waterlogged nature of the ground. So there were few vineyards in the Bas-Médoc to the north of St-Estèphe although there were church properties up in Soulac near the Atlantic in the thirteenth century. Where they existed they were sparse and insignificant. The vineyards of the Haut-Médoc (the name is modern) were naturally concentrated in the villages nearest to the city or near the main road to Lesparre. The Chapter of the cathedral of St-André, which by the fourteenth century was nearly as substantial a vineyard owner as the archbishop, had properties in Blanquefort, Solesse and Le Taillan north of the Jalle de Blanquefort and further afield at Listrac, Moulis and Avensan. Among the place names associated today with Médocain wine growing where there are records of medieval vineyards are Castelnau, Avensan, Bégorce near Soussans, Cantenac and Issan. The wines from the remoter villages, such as Moulis and Castelnau, probably came to Bordeaux by boat. Macau, then bounded by streams and considered an island, was full of vines by the thirteenth century. Its watery past is recalled today by the lake in the grounds of Cantemerle, which takes its name from the noble family who held the estate in the century following the English expulsion. Corn was also grown in quantity in the Médoc, and in the Middle Ages it cannot be regarded as essentially wine country; this did not come about until the seventeenth century.

However a part of the Graves area was sometimes partly known as the Médoc, particularly Pessac (Pessac-de-Médoc). The cathedral authorities owned property here, and also in Léognan and Villenave-d'Ornon. The Pessac vineyard was considered unusual in the fourteenth century for being ploughed with an ox-plough, whereas it was commonly drawn by hand with a *marre*, a special vine tool, between a hoe and a spade, which was certainly in use as late as the beginning of this century.

If the Médoc was largely undeveloped in vineyards, St-Emilion was a well-established wine area in the days of the English kings. The town of St-Emilion was accorded the rights of a commune in 1199, and Libourne in 1270. Edward III extended the commercial privileges of Bordeaux to the latter after some disturbances near the end of the thirteenth century; the burghers of St-Emilion only regained in 1312 the right to elect their mayor and to maintain other privileges by promising to deliver to the English king 50 *tonneaux* of '*vin clair pur et bon*' before Easter. No doubt the provision as to the latest date each year was because thereafter it would be less good. There was also a fair-sized vineyard area in Fronsac by the thirteenth century, but if one existed in Pomerol it had no separate identity.

In the Middle Ages both Bourg and Blaye were important wine areas, with the convenience of having ports some way down the Gironde towards the sea. They were often viewed somewhat uneasily by the Bordelais. Bourg wines in particular had a high reputation, greater than they have enjoyed since.

Broadly speaking, and excluding the Médoc, the whole Bordeaux *vignoble* at its peak of expansion in the fourteenth and fifteenth centuries was not very different in extent from its appearance on the eve of the phylloxera in the nineteenth century. By the time the English were expelled Bordeaux relied on wine for its prosperity, while corn had to be imported from outside the region to feed the population; it was paid for by the sale and export of wine.

The export trade was much more important than the sale within Bordeaux. Each year there were two shippings of the young wine: the autumn shipping, known as the vintage shipping; and the spring or rack shipping, after the wine had been racked off its lees into fresh casks. The latter was the better. As already mentioned, the Bordelais took good care that their own wine had priority over that of the Haut-Pays, which was more consistent and less affected by Atlantic climatic conditions than Bordeaux. The Haut-Pays wines had to be kept outside the city walls, and this is why the Chartrons suburb grew up to the north of the town. This area in the fifteenth century was divided from the city by the Château Trompette, built by Charles VII (1403 – 61) after the expulsion of the English in 1453 as the new 'seat of government', in place of the English-built Château de l'Ombrière, which was turned into the law courts. The Haut-Pays wines, contained in casks distinct from the Bordelais type, and subject to tax which made them 10 to 20 per cent dearer than the burghers' wines, had to be removed from the area by the 8 September each year if unsold, i.e. before the next vintage wine became available.

The Haut-Pays wine producers carried on a fight for over 300 years against the discrimination suffered by their wines. In 1500 they managed to secure some improvement by permission for Languedoc wines (which chiefly meant Gaillac) to reach Bordeaux by St Martin's Day (11 November), provided they were not put on sale before the Feast of St André (30 November), nor – showing the importance of the English trade to the Bordelais – sold to the English before Christmas.

The Haut-Pays growers, no less fly than their successors today in the south, and adept at blending and 'assisting' the wines of other areas, adopted several stratagems to send their wines down the river Garonne. Wine was shipped to the Bordeaux 'frontier' town of St-Macaire and taken overland to Bergerac, which maintained its ancient liberty of trade, first granted by the English kings. Thence it was shipped down the Dordogne to the Gironde and the open sea. How often must the Bordelais have bewailed the geographical fact that their city was placed above rather than below the confluence of the two rivers at the Bec-d'Ambès!

Nevertheless the Bordelais merchants wished to control rather than exclude the Haut-Pays wines, to secure priority for their own wines but also to trade in the wines of their neighbours. For the Haut-Pays wines were not inferior. They included Gaillac, Quercy, Nérac and Bergerac, and they were normally drunk both at the English and French courts. Later on, in the middle of the seventeenth century, the wines of Quercy were considered superior to those of Bordeaux. Moreover the

Haut-Pays wines provided important business for the merchants and shipping interests, as well as for blending. The Bordelais wished to sell their merchandise to the adjacent territories as well as to buy corn therefrom. Further, the Bordeaux wine and shipping trades could not subsist on the burghers' wines. The Haut-Pays was also a valuable source of trade for the Bordeaux shipping interests. They were great producers of woad (*pastel*) which, until superseded by indigo, was the source of blue dye throughout Europe, and particularly used in the Iberian peninsula.

From the sixteenth century onwards, the alternative to returning the unsold wine to source after 8 September was to sell it for *eau-de-vie*. In the Middle Ages there is no evidence of wine or *marc* being distilled, but in 1559 the *jurats* of the city forbade the distillation of wine within the walls for fear of fire. In the following century distillation became more common, and in the eighteenth century the *eaux-de-vie* of Bordeaux were classed along with those of La Rochelle, i.e., from the Cognac area. But the superiority of the more northerly brandy, along with the greater commercial acumen of the Charente traders in marketing their product put cognac firmly ahead; and today the chief distillation for normal sale in Bordeaux is of liqueurs. The well-known firm of Marie Brizard et Roger was formed in 1755, and by 1791 employed 29 '*distillateurs liquoristes*.' But the Vieille Cure and Cordial Médoc liqueurs are made at Cenon. There are also other distilleries.

Some of the Haut-Pays wine areas gave up the protracted, unequal struggle with the Bordelais, who controlled the normal exit way of their wines. Agen, for example, took to prunes instead of wine, and fruit-growing displaced vineyards here and elsewhere on the Garonne. Yet the Bordelais never relaxed their vigilance and right into the eighteenth century inspectors were stationed at the Dordogne 'frontier post' of Castillon to make sure that no 'mislabelled' wine entered the Bordeaux region. It is fair to add that they were concerned with the quality of the wines of Bordeaux as well as with their own narrower commercial interests.

Even after the Revolution finally swept away the ancient privileges of Bordeaux in 1790, efforts were made to retrieve them. When Bordeaux made a last attempt in 1803, the town council of Cahors denounced the Bordelais, saying that they could not face fair competition from the Haut-Pays wines, which were more consistent. They alleged that the costs of viticulture in the Gironde were exorbitant, while their own were very low. However, although Bordeaux never recovered its legal privileges, what centuries of policing and discouragement had failed to do was largely achieved by the phylloxera and economic slump of the late nineteenth century. Thereafter the Haut-Pays vineyards, like those elsewhere in France including parts of the Gironde department, were never again so extensive.

The second potential rival to Bordeaux reads oddly in modern times: the Médoc. It was not so much the rather scattered wine producers of whom the burghers were afraid; they feared to lose the trade in those parts of the Médoc remote from Bordeaux, and particularly the carrying trade. Far too much wine went through the ports of Libourne, Bourg and Blaye for the liking of the Bordelais merchants, although it was only a fraction of what was handled in the Gascon capital; and they feared the development of ports on the Médoc bank of the Garonne and Gironde. The virtues of commercial competition are usually more readily appreciated in theory than in practice by those in the business. Accordingly the Bordeaux burghers contrived to secure from Edward III and later from Henry V (1413–22) a ban on wine being loaded anywhere from Crébat, on the city outskirts, to Castillon-de-Médoc in the commune of St-Christoly far up towards the Atlantic. No doubt this contributed substantially towards retarding the development of the Médocain *vignoble*, but the problems of clearing the forests, establishing vineyards, securing the necessary labour and above all the provision of transport by road along the fairly narrow strip of cultivable land were even more important obstacles. Etienne de la Boétie, friend of Montaigne, in the middle of the sixteenth century wrote a work entitled *Historique description du sauvage et solitaire pays du Médoc.*

Although until the sixteenth century, trade with England was much the most important for Bordeaux, and is discussed in the chapter on The English in Bordeaux, there was always a brisk trade with Brittany, northern France and with Flanders. At the beginning of the thirteenth century, only fifty years after the marriage of Henry Plantagenet and Eleanor of Aquitaine, the Gascon merchants were given by Marguerite, Countess of Flanders, the same protection granted to those of La Rochelle and other Atlantic ports. This was a reciprocal gesture, for the Flemings were prominent in the carrying trade, taking wine to England, Scotland and to northern European ports. They were particularly useful to the Scots, for in times of Anglo-Scottish warfare, the English merchants could not deliver the Gascon wines themselves. So it was shipped through 'neutral' Flanders. All attempts by the English authorities to prevent wines destined for England from being carried in other than English ships failed; there were not enough of the latter, and the Netherlanders were the chief beneficiaries.

However they did not only carry Gascon wine, and when once the special relationship between Bordeaux and England ceased in the mid-fifteenth century, the Bordelais had to compete not only with German and Spanish wines, but with those from further north in France. These included wines made right up to Normandy, which produced wine in quantity until the nineteenth century. No doubt this was far less good wine than from Bordeaux, but it was conveniently placed for transport across the narrow sleeve of the English Channel.

The account of Bordeaux wines and their sale is continued in later chapters. Meanwhile it is timely here to consider the role of the English in Bordeaux.

3. The English
in Bordeaux

Having surveyed briefly the story of Bordeaux in its early days and in the Middle Ages, it is necessary to go back slightly to outline a very special and significant enclave in the history of Gascony.

Although the first part of this chapter is not immediately connected with wine, I believe it to be an essential part of any but a superficial account of Bordeaux and its wines. Most of us are broadly aware that for three centuries Bordeaux came under the English Crown; few of us remember many details of this connection. That one of our English kings was born in Bordeaux, and two others who ruled over it are buried in France is not all that widely known, nor that one positive feature of the luckless King John's reign (1199 – 1216) was the encouragement of Bordeaux wine growing and trading. No one can doubt that inevitably a great wine district would have developed in what is now the Gironde department, but if Henry Plantagenet had married a Burgundian princess, or if a successor had found himself possessor of a great strip of northern and eastern France instead of the bulk of the south-west of the country, might we not have become a nation of (still) Champagne and Burgundy drinkers instead of the leading consumers of Bordeaux? True the wine from the Gascon capital came easily by sea, subject to the hazards of piracy, but under favourable political conditions, the Marne, the Seine and the short sea crossing might have provided comfortable routes for the rivals of Bordeaux wine.

However, it was from the English tenure of territories in Gascony that stemmed a commercial connection between Bordeaux and Britain which has never been broken except in time of war, and often not even then. It was Gascon wine that was called for in the medieval taverns of England; and although some of it may have come from what is now the Charente area and been shipped from La Rochelle, most certainly derived from Bordeaux; particularly in the latter part of the period.

It is worth noting here that the terms Gascon and Gascony have often been used loosely, and with good reason: the region called Gascony varied considerably. At its greatest extent in the early Middle Ages it ran from the Pyrenees to the Gironde, and from the Bay of Biscay to the Garonne. But the more southerly part was hived off and Gascony became roughly the country around Bordeaux south of the Gironde. Guyenne, which usually included Gascony, roughly covered the present Gironde department, as well as areas to the east associated with the Dordogne, Tarn and Lot rivers. The Gers region, where armagnac is now distilled, was once part of Gascony.

The association with Bordeaux began when Henry Plantagenet, aged nineteen, married in May 1152 Eleanor of Aquitaine, then about thirty years old. She may fairly be described as being the most eligible young woman of her time, with a dowry that included most of the western part of France up to Brittany. Poitou, Gascony, the Auvergne, the Limousin, Périgord, as well as parts of Touraine and the Berry were all hers; while Henry filled in with the rest of Touraine, Anjou, Maine and Normandy. Eleanor had already been married in 1137, reputedly at the age of seventeen, to the French King, Louis VII (1137 – 1180) at Bordeaux, but an annulment was arranged on the convenient grounds of consanguinity. Henry and Eleanor were married in Poitiers. Two years later on the death of King Stephen (1135–1154), they became King and Queen of England, with enormous territories in France. In 1156 Henry II visited Bordeaux for the first time.

From the beginning, the English possessions in France were a source of trouble, as the French kings naturally regarded the English presence as an affront, as well as a sore loss of revenue, trade and military manpower. It has to be remembered that the French Crown did not then control the source of that other great centre of French wines, Burgundy. This was ruled by its own Dukes and, although they usually collaborated with the French monarchs, Burgundy only finally came to the French kings in 1477, twenty-four years after the final expulsion of the English from Bordeaux.

An intermittent series of wars was conducted against the English-ruled provinces, and in these the French were helped by having interior lines of communication, while English aid had to come by sea. Various English attempts were made by means of skilful marriages to divide and rule the French opposition; the other weapon was the appointment of English rulers of Guyenne, Poitou or Gascony, as the situation warranted and the breadth of territories permitted. The first of these was the future Richard Coeur-de-Lion, who at the age of 12 was installed in Poitiers with his mother Eleanor. By this time Henry's relationship with Eleanor was highly unsatisfactory and she abetted struggles against her husband's rule for much of his life. Their tombs lying side by side today in the great church of Fontevrault near Saumur give a false picture of uxoriousness.

However Queen Eleanor was very popular in her own country, and she and her son Richard, who was made Duke of Aquitaine and Count of Poitou, ruled their territories from 1169 to 1173. Then a revolt of the French nobles instigated by Eleanor broke out, but was easily crushed by Henry; in 1174 he sent his wife back to

England to semi-imprisonment, but forgave his young son. Richard continued to spend much of his time in France, and held courts in Bordeaux in 1174 and again in 1176. Shortly before his father's death in 1189, Richard liberated his mother and they both returned to Bordeaux where they were warmly welcomed. He left the Gascon capital in 1190 to go on his Crusade, and only re-visited it once more in 1199, just before his death. He too is buried in Fontevrault, although his heart is in Rouen Cathedral.

During their reigns neither Richard nor his brother John were very much interested in Bordeaux politically, as it presented no military problems. John, however, was by no means unconcerned with its commercial significance. Not long after his accession he arrived to visit his mother who lived at the Château de l'Ombrière, which over-looked the Garonne and was sited not far from the present city end of the fine Pont de Pierre. The present-day Rue du Palais de l'Ombrière marks its position. During the entire English occupation Ombrière was the headquarters of the English ad-ministration – a kind of Dublin Castle. Edward I (1272 – 1307) later re-built most of it, including a *Tour du Roi* which was reserved for the English kings on their somewhat rare visits to Bordeaux. It was at the château that John, having managed to divest himself of his marriage to Isabella (Avice) of Gloucester, who had been his wife for 11 years, married in 1206 another wife with the same Christian name, Isabella of Angoulême. She being only twelve had little choice in the matter, although already betrothed to a French noble named Adhémar.

However, whatever John's shortcomings in other fields, he did a great deal to establish firmly Anglo-Bordelais commercial relations. Although the origins of the Bordeaux wine trade with England are obscure, this certainly began as early as 1203 in John's reign. It was he who, in order to secure the support of Bordeaux, Bayonne (which supplied most of the ships for carrying the wine to England) and Dax against the French king, gave their burgesses considerable commercial privileges and tax exemptions. In particular John exempted the Bordeaux burghers from paying the unpopular export tax known as the Great Custom (*Grande Coutume*), levied on all outgoing ships. This was the Crown's direct revenue, and no other town's citizen-merchants obtained Bordeaux's privilege. The Haut-Pays merchants who exported their wine were subject to this levy. He also made free grants of land mostly covered with wood or marsh near Bordeaux on condition that the land was redeemed and planted with vineyards. Henry III (1216 – 1272) and Edward I (1272 – 1307) made similar grants, so the original planting of a part of the inner Bordeaux *vignoble* owes something to the English connection. In 1214 John exempted the nobles and burghers of Bordeaux from all taxes on the wines emanating from their vineyards, and these privileges were confirmed by the succeeding English kings.

Yet when John died two years later he owed the large sum of £720 to Bordeaux merchants, who after five years' negotiation never recovered more than £400. How-ever he had been a good customer for Gascon wines. In 1212 out of 348 casks bought for the royal household, 267 came from Gascony. Most of the rest came from the Orléanais and the Ile de France. That they were Gascon wines did not mean that they were all grown in the Bordeaux region. A considerable proportion came from

Gaillac and Moissac, whose wines at that time were more esteemed and highly-priced than the red Bordeaux. They were probably more powerful and full-bodied.

However to keep Gascon goodwill the monarchs extended to their merchants privileges in London similar to the citizens, often to the disgust of the latter. Unlike most other foreign traders they were allowed to stay long in the capital, were not obliged to live in a specified quarter, and often settled in England. Later on English merchants began to settle in and around Bordeaux, a practice which has survived to this day.

A side-effect of the development of the Anglo-Gascon wine trade was the gradual decline of domestic viticulture in England.

In 1225 Henry III sent his younger brother Richard, Earl of Cornwall and Count of Poitou, to Bordeaux. He at first repelled the French, capturing St-Macaire and Bazas on the 'frontier', but in the following year he nearly lost Bordeaux, for the French troops arrived before its walls and only the timely death of Louis VIII (1223 – 6) and the accession of Louis IX (1226 – 1270) caused the French to make a truce, saving the city. Richard stayed until 1227 but the king himself did not pay his first short visit to Gascony until 1230, when he had been on the throne fourteen years. Twelve years later he came again to meet the threat of French advances. Landing at Royan in May 1242, he was heavily defeated at Saintes and retreated with difficulty to Blaye, a town of considerable strategic importance on the Gironde, which long held out for the English connection.

King Henry spent the winter of 1242 – 3 in Bordeaux and did his best to win the support of the nobles. He also bought largely of the fine 1242 vintage, making substantial purchases from the archbishop, whose spiritual duties did not preclude him from dabbling in the wine trade. In September 1243 he left France, but Gascony remained unsettled and in 1248 Simon de Montfort, Earl of Leicester and son of the savage leader of the Albigensian 'crusade', was sent over to establish order in Gascony with a seven-year appointment of office as Seneschal in his pocket. Bordeaux was divided between two rival factions: the Coloms, the head of the wine traders, and the Delsolers, representing the nobles and feudal power rather than the trading class. Simon de Montfort supported the Coloms and imprisoned some of the Delsoler faction, thus directly or indirectly supporting the trading faction. Unfortunately in the process he made himself extremely unpopular, and by 1252 his rule was over; in the following year Henry III paid his last visit to Gascony, lasting 15 months. He did his best to appease the Delsolers, but the Coloms still remained dominant in Bordeaux. A royal viceroy seemed to be expedient and in 1254 Prince Edward, later King Edward I, married Eleanor of Castille and spent more than a year in Gascony, much of it in Bordeaux.

Of the ten English kings who numbered Bordeaux among their possessions, Edward I was probably the most successful in dealing with his Gascon subjects, who were more inclined to regard their rulers as Dukes of Gascony than Kings of England. When Edward first arrived he conciliated the Bordelais, still angry after Simon de Montfort's severe rule. For example the burghers of Bourg and St-Emilion were exempted from taxes on their vines for five years. The quarrels between the Coloms and the Delsolers were probably not entirely unwelcome to Edward, who was able to take the nomination of the important post of mayor into his own hands, and so diminish the independent political power of Bordeaux.

Edward spent a further year in and around Bordeaux in 1260 – 1, and after he became king in 1272 he made two more visits: from August 1273 to May 1274; and it was his chief residence from August 1286 to August 1289. Considering his preoccupations at home, not least in Scotland and Wales, Edward paid much attention to his French possessions. As Eleanor C. Lodge remarks in her valuable *Gascony Under English Rule* (1926), 'The connection of Gascony with England was closer than ever before, and perhaps for the first time it could be considered an English possession rather than merely an outlying bit of royal property.'

Edward had his reward, for he received not only monetary taxes but Gascon soldiers to help him in his campaigns at home. Yet he had to tread warily. Even in 1261 when he had secured the right to nominate the mayor, he and the Seneschal had to swear to observe the customs of Bordeaux before the leading citizens swore fealty to him. He conciliated the nobles but relied on the townspeople. Later he also had the nomination of the mayoralty of St-Emilion in his hands, and in 1268 he ordered Jean de Grailly, the Seneschal of Gascony, to build a bastide on the Dordogne at an important spot which was to become a centre of the wine trade, and remains today the headquarters of merchants who specialize in the wines of St-Emilion, Pomerol and Fronsac. This was Libourne, said to be named after the English Seneschal of Guyenne, Roger de Leyburn, who is alleged to have been responsible for the erection of the town and its fortifications.

These fortified towns or bastides are a feature of south-west France, and were strong points created by the English or the French in their long struggle in this frontier country. The best-preserved of them today, such as Domme and Monpazier, still retain their fortifications and their gridiron pattern of streets which is the admiration and source of pilgrimage of modern town planners. Their other readily recognizable feature are squares surrounded by arcades, an example of which may be seen today in the Place Abel Surchamp in Libourne. Another relic is the fine Tour du Grand Port on the river-front. The English kings used to stay nearby at the castle of Condat. The Captain of Fronsac was usually an Englishman. One of these, Sir William Faringdon, later became Constable of Bordeaux.

Relations with the French Crown were always uneasy, and it must be remembered that Edward I held Gascony as a fief of the French Crown. He and the other kings who accepted this situation did not try to claim the French throne; indeed they swore loyalty to the kings of France, who took care to assert their dominance even when they were not actually engaged in fighting a war or planning the renewal of hostilities against their reluctant English subordinates.

In 1294 Philip the Fair (1268 – 1314) actually sent troops to occupy Bordeaux and the surrounding places. Although an English expedition later that year succeeded in recapturing Castillon and Macau in the Médoc as well as Bourg and Blaye, the French held the Gascon capital until peace was signed in Paris in 1303. The French occupation did not endear itself to the Bordelais, and the last years of Edward's reign were spent in repairing the damage, including the payment of large sums in compensation.

The close connection between England and Bordeaux in Edward's time may be shown by the fact that Henry de Galeys who was Mayor of London in 1274 was Mayor of Bordeaux in the following year. In the following reign of Edward II the Bordeaux merchants in the English trade formed a trade association: The Merchant Wine Tonners of Gascony. The origin of the Vintners Company of London in the fourteenth century was very much bound up with the Gascon trade, and its privileges initially were limited to Gascon wines.

Edward II, born in 1284 and reigning from 1307 to 1327, who married Isabella of France and paid homage in person to Philip the Fair in 1308, did not leave much impression on Bordeaux, but near the close of his reign there was a war unsuccessful from the English standpoint. When Edward III (1327 – 1377) ascended the throne he possessed only a strip of land from Saintes to Bayonne. Aggrieved by the failure of the French kings to observe the terms of the treaties or to treat them fairly as vassals, Edward laid open claim to the French throne. This in 1337, precipitated the Hundred Years' War which eventually led to the loss of Bordeaux in 1453. The maintenance of English rule in Gascony was a focal point of the war throughout its intermittent course.

This is not the place for a detailed history of this struggle, which began with the French seizure of Blaye by the stratagem of blocking the gateway with a provision waggon. Libourne and other places fell, but were recaptured in 1345 by Henry of Lancaster, Earl of Derby, who led a very successful two-year campaign right up into Poitou. After a truce in 1347 the war was renewed in 1355 and this time the Black Prince was in command. He played a considerable part in the history of Bordeaux during the period, and on his first arrival he presented his letters of patent to the notables of the city in the cathedral of St-André. The following year he led the campaign which culminated in the Battle of Poitiers which, it should be remembered, was not just an English victory, but an Anglo-Gascon one, for the Black Prince's army contained Gascon troops.

King John (1350 – 1364) of France was captured and taken to Bordeaux, being civilly treated there before being sent over to England whence he was ransomed in 1360, but returned to London in 1364 and died there. Meanwhile following the Treaty of Bretigny in 1360, in which the English claim to the French throne was given up in return for full sovereignty in much of South-West France, there was another interval of peace, and the Black Prince was given the Principality of Aquitaine and Gascony. On 9 July 1363 Bordeaux witnessed a ceremony of oath of fealty made to the Black Prince by the nobles, mayor and jurats of Bordeaux, and the municipal leaders of such wine towns as Bourg, Blaye, St-Emilion and Langon. For seven years he ruled the country, often residing in Bordeaux where he organized lavish entertainments – perhaps on the principle of wine and circuses – which cost the principality a great deal in taxes. He also gave the top posts to the English. When war was resumed in 1369, the Prince was failing in health and he departed from France finally in 1371, leaving his brother John, Duke of Lancaster, in command. But John was no match for Bertrand du Guesclin, and by 1375 the English/Gascon side was in poor shape. Only Bordeaux, Bayonne and Dax remained to them.

Richard II who succeeded Edward III in 1377 was born at Bordeaux on Twelfth Night 1367, the son of the Black Prince and his wife Joan the Fair Maid of Kent. He has been popularly known as Richard of Bordeaux. Although he left Bordeaux when a small child and never re-visited it after becoming king, this unfortunate monarch managed to establish a favourable local impression. During his reign truces persisted, and in 1390 he sent his uncle John of Gaunt to Bordeaux and appointed him Prince of Aquitaine. This title was extremely unpopular with the Bordelais, who without direct access to the English crown feared isolation, to be followed by a French take-over. It was then agreed that the new Prince should be received only as a representative of the King. When Richard was dethroned in 1399 by Henry IV the Bordelais for some time refused to accept the new king and sent strong protests to England; although the nobles were quietened by an envoy of Henry, the common people were not and in 1403 started an insurrection and attacked the Ombrière, but without success. In 1406 the French under the Duke of Orleans, brother of Charles VI, (1368 – 1422) took the field again and assailed Bourg and Blaye, 'the keys to Bordeaux and Gascony on the north', as they were described. Bourg was besieged from October 1406 to January 1407. However ships from Bordeaux sailed down the Gironde and destroyed a French squadron, with the result that Blaye held out until the customary truce in 1407.

But the sands of English rule in Gascony were beginning to run out. Neither Henry IV (1399 – 1413) nor Henry V (1413 – 1422) ever entered Bordeaux during their reigns. The latter was more interested in securing the French throne than in his Gascon territories. The Bordelais had to rely increasingly on their own efforts to keep the French at bay, for they were deeply concerned to maintain the English connection, which gave them a considerable measure of independence, while the towns under the French Crown were steadily losing their powers to the centralizing control of the royal administration. To clear the 'enemy' from her neighbourhood and to secure the freedom of trade on the Garonne and Gironde, Bordeaux began her own war in 1420 and captured St-Macaire and La Réole upstream.

However, Joan of Arc came to the fore and in 1429 Charles VII (1422 – 1461) was crowned at Rheims. He was determined to clear the English from France, but it was not until 1442 that he felt able to attack and invest Bordeaux itself.

By now the chief defender of Bordeaux against the French and the leader of the pro-English party was the remarkable archbishop of Bordeaux, Pey Berland, the son of a peasant, who had been born in the Médoc. He was made archbishop in 1430, and became the chief founder of the university in 1442. When Charles attacked and captured Dax, so long an English stronghold, Pey Berland organized the defence of Bordeaux and set off for England to secure help from Henry VI (1422 – 1461). He procured some aid, and in 1444 there was a truce which lasted for five years. However in 1451 a much more serious investment took place and at last Blaye fell, followed by Bourg, Libourne and St-Emilion. Only Fronsac held out for a time but that too surrendered. Henry VI was far too occupied with the domestic Wars of the Roses to send any help to the Gascons. Archbishop Pey Berland treated with the French commander, Dunois, and secured favourable terms from him. The French were more concerned to conciliate rather than to humiliate this important city. On 30 June 1451 Dunois clad all in white and on horseback led a victory march into the city via the Chartrons, where so many Bordeaux wine merchants today have their offices and cellars. The only English stronghold left was Lesparre far up the Médoc.

Soon however the Bordelais had second thoughts. They lived by trade, principally by selling their wine to England. How and where were they going to sell their 1451s? When in 1452 they were asked to pay a tax for the defence of France, and their objections that it was contrary to the capitulation terms were waved aside by Charles VII, they began secret talks with the English. Henry, better placed now to send an expedition to Gascony, despatched John Talbot, Earl of Shrewsbury, in command of a fleet up the Gironde in October 1452. He landed in the Médoc and during the night of 22 October the gates of Bordeaux were opened to him by the welcoming citizens. There was another triumphal entry and the English commander, whose name is commemorated in the name of the St-Julien château, was hailed as 'Le Roi Talbot'. He went on to secure Libourne, Cadillac and Castillon. Again only Fronsac held out, this time for its new French rulers, but was captured during the winter.

However the next campaign was the last. Although the English king sent more reinforcements from England, Charles VII personally took over the French forces. His general was Jean Bureau, still today a well-known name in the Bordeaux district and borne by the celebrated *maître de chai* of Yquem. On 15 July Talbot sallied out of Bordeaux, paused at Libourne and then surprised the French advance guard at Castillon a short way up the Dordogne. He made the mistake of not awaiting the arrival of his main force, and on 17 July 1453 his troops were routed at the Battle of Castillon; he and his son the Earl of Lisle were both mortally wounded. It is said that as the result of a promise given to the French king upon his release from captivity on a previous occasion, not to bear arms against the French, he went unarmed into the battle of Castillon. His exact age is a matter of conjecture, but he was an old man, probably over 70, and possibly as much as 80. Talbot is a prominent, noble figure in Shakespeare's *Henry VI*, Part One, where his defeat is attributed more to the fraud of a delaying fellow-Englishman than to the French forces. According to Shakespeare, Talbot appears before the walls of Bordeaux but does not capture the city, and then there is a scene actually at Castillon, described merely as 'A Field of Battle'. Talbot's son John is killed first, and his body placed in his father's arms who dies with the words:

> Soldiers, adieu! I have what I would have,
> Now my old arms are young John Talbot's grave.

St-Emilion, Libourne and Fronsac immediately fell, and Bordeaux was encircled. The French king's soldiers invaded the Médoc in pursuit of the fleeing English, and the song ran:

Tous les jours, les Francoys courroient
En l'isle et pays de Médot,
Où Angloys et leurs biens prennoient
Sans ce que aucun leur dist mot.

In Bordeaux they held out until October, but then even Archbishop Pey Berland recognized that the end had come. The French troops entered the city on 19 October. Although the lenient terms of two years previously were cancelled, the Bordelais were not badly treated. If the French behaved comparatively moderately towards the Bordelais, with only one or two executions and some imprisonments, there was savage devastation of much of the previously English territory. Places such as Castillon, Libourne, St-Emilion, Cadillac, Bourg and Blaye were ravaged, and the countryside devastated. The Médoc was particularly severely treated, with vineyards destroyed by soldiers and animals. Macau is mentioned as a substantial sufferer; and, as throughout this sporadic but savage Hundred Years War, the common people paid dearly for their doubtless often enforced loyalties to one side or the other. The English were allowed to depart in their ships, even being permitted to take with them cargoes of wine, a gesture which must be considered to have been a clever publicity move for the wines of Bordeaux. It is said that before leaving the shrewd English merchants hastily purchased the 1453s.

It cannot be said that the Gascons were soon reconciled to French rule. In 1457 the French king wrote to the Scottish king, James II (1437 – 1460), saying 'as for the county of Guyenne, everyone knows it has been English for 300 years, and the people of the district are at heart entirely inclined to the English party'. Even 30 years later a chronicler wrote: 'the majority were so strongly for the English (and still are) that they did not know how to like the French, since for three centuries without a break they had been English.'

The basis of this support of the English connection had been commercial and economic rather than sentimental, and for reasons closely connected with the vital wine trade. Where could the Bordelais sell not only the wine from their immediate surroundings but also the wine that came down the Dordogne and the Garonne from the Haut-Pays?

Moreover the three hundred years of English rule in Bordeaux should not be thought of as English 'occupation' of French territory. Bordeaux and its surrounding region was indubitably no part of England, but no more was it French; it was Gascony. More than a century after the French take-over of Bordeaux, the *jurats* of Bordeaux declared in 1585, '*nous sommes en pays de conqueste*'. One of the attractions of the English connection was its remoteness. The distance of Bordeaux from England had been the best guarantee of its liberty, while the French kings, with their centralizing policy, were now all too near at hand. Even two hundred years later this antipathy existed. The autocratic, ambitious Louis XIV (1643–1715) was by no means popular in Gascony, and until the end of his reign the Bordelais retained a somewhat idyllic picture of the '*époque anglaise*'. In addition to economic considerations, the memories of the savage re-conquest, particularly in the Médoc and in the Graves near the capital, remained as vivid as the brutalities of Cromwell in Ireland did among the Irish.

The Wine Trade with England

The beginnings of the Bordeaux wine trade with England can be firmly dated as not being substantial until the thirteenth century. In an edict of King John of 1199, the regions from which came the wines chiefly drunk in England were enumerated, and Gascony was not even mentioned; the leading supplies came from further north in the Poitou. It was in the thirteenth century that the Bordeaux vineyards really began to be extended, and then expanded rapidly in the fourteenth century – a period of great prosperity for medieval Bordeaux – and further still in the fifteenth century. All other forms of agriculture became of minor importance. In the thirteenth century the most prolific area was the Graves, pressing in on Bordeaux itself, where several of the parishes contained vineyards. There was even one in the garden of the archbishop, who was one of the largest vineyard owners, a prominence he shared with the dean and Chapter of the cathedral of St-André. The former owned vineyards in Pessac and Merignac; the latter possessed vineyard properties in the main Graves communes, including Pessac, Léognan and Villenave d'Ornon, as well as others in Listrac, Moulis, Avensan, Blanquefort and Le Taillan in the Médoc. But neither archbishop nor Chapter seem to have spread their vine properties so far afield as those communes in the Médoc most famous today, such as Pauillac, St-Julien or Margaux.

The reason for this expansion of wine-growing must have been based on the trade with England, and later to some extent with the Low Countries. There was no great market for Bordeaux wines in Paris or in other French centres of population. For one reason, overland transport was too arduous, and for another, regions as far north as Normandy produced their own wine, while Paris relied on the wine from districts relatively easy of access, including Burgundy, whose produce came down the Seine, and Champagne whence still wine was transported down the Marne. The Bordeaux trade was sea-borne and its natural outlets were maritime, non-wine producing countries, including England, Scotland, Ireland, the Low Countries and the Baltic States. Of these England was the most accessible, with its convenient ports at Bristol and Southampton, the chief English landing places for wine imports from Bordeaux in the Middle Ages.

Wine was indeed the leading French export of this period, and Bordeaux was almost certainly the chief exporter. It remained so for many hundreds of years, for until internal transport improved in the eighteenth and nineteenth centuries, Bordeaux could not depend on a substantial domestic demand outside the region. For much the same reason the English had to rely on Bordeaux for their table wines until the struggles with France that began at the end of the seventeenth century and continued intermittently until the defeat of Napoleon. This may explain the comparative rarity of Burgundy in England right up to the end of the last century; it was difficult and expensive to transport to England and a ready market could be found nearer at hand.

Throughout the English connection, the burghers of Bordeaux, well aware on which side their bread was buttered, set out to win the support of the English kings in the thirteenth century. They had three possible competitors: La Rochelle; the wine growers of the Haut-Pays; and, as the Bordeaux vineyard began to be developed, the more distant part of the Médoc, with its ease of access to the sea.

La Rochelle was a thriving rival wine port long before Bordeaux became important for wine, and had the advantage of being right on the sea, whereas to reach the Girondin port, ships had to make the difficult sixty-mile passage up the estuary – a disadvantage with which the Bordelais have to reckon even today. Fortunately for Bordeaux its rival was much more open to attack and capture by the French king. When in 1224 the latter's troops struck south and captured several Atlantic ports, the Bordelais were quick to write to Hubert de Burgh, the King's Justiciar, the head of the royal administration, reaffirming their loyalty to the English Crown and contrasting this with the infidelity and frailty of those towns further north which had surrendered. Therefore, as the French gradually encroached over the years onto the English king's possessions, the commercial standing of Bordeaux was improved.

Although demand from the Low Countries and others beyond the English Channel could take up the greater part of Bordeaux's wine exports, these markets could only be reached with the approval of the English king and his fleet. Accordingly the Bordelais were enthusiastic for the English connection for 200 years after the rest of the English territories in France had largely been taken over by the French kings. From the fall of La Rochelle in 1224 can be dated the supremacy of Bordeaux as a wine trading centre and port.

Meanwhile it appears as if the Bordelais decided that to have the English king on their side was not only a matter of politics and business, but also for the sake of what now would be called publicity. We all know these days that for some curious reason if a well-known personality, be it king, queen, president or film star, is known to be partial to a particular wine or brand of drink, this is a valuable commendation for other consumers. As the expertise of such personalities lies in other fields, this might seem a doubtful recommendation, but in view of the successful association of cognac with Napoleon and a Scotch whisky with a British Commander-in-Chief in the First World War, there is no doubt this works even in the twentieth century. Certainly it did with Bordeaux in the thirteenth century.

There was in England then a taste for the wines of Anjou and of the Rhine, but were it known that the king drank the red wines of Bordeaux, this should assure their success. So it did. Whereas in 1199, the Gascon wines were not even mentioned among the leading wines consumed in England, from 1206 onwards they appear among those bought for the royal table or offered as presents by the king. In 1214 John was thanking the Governor of Bristol for apprising him of the arrival there of a consignment of Bordeaux wines; and in 1215 he had bought 120 *tonneaux* of Gascon wines for his personal use. It was John who first authorized the Bordelais to organize themselves into a commune and appoint a mayor; and it was he who exempted the citizens from paying the unpopular Great Customs (*Grande Coutume*) export tax.

Such was the royal interest in Bordeaux wine, that by 1219 Henry III was writing to the Mayor of Bordeaux, complaining that a check had shown a shortfall in the amount of wine gauged in the *tonneaux*, and denouncing this fraud. By 1224 three-quarters of the wine drunk in the royal palaces came from Bordeaux, and by the middle of the century it was the customary wine to celebrate any solemn or festive occasion, as champagne is today. Sixty years later so much gold was being sent out of England to pay for the royal wines that Parliament protested (Simon, *History of the Wine Trade in England, 1906 – 1909*).

The Bordelais did not confine their attentions to the king. They made suitable presents to the English notabilities and entertained the British merchants who made their annual trip to Bordeaux to buy the young wine. In the accounts of the arch-bishops of Bordeaux for 1382 and 1386, there are entries relating to the entertainment of 'the merchants of England and Britain'. The English wine fleet left the English shores late in September, arrived in the Gironde in the first half of October, when the young wine was just about made. They spent 8 – 10 weeks in Bordeaux, tasting and bargaining, and then returned to England in time for Christmas. The voyage from Bordeaux to the English Channel ports took about 10 days. The royal butler had first choice of their purchases. The wine, of course, was drunk at once – *le vin de l'année*, as this would now be called. It had to be drunk young, as before the develop-ment of the wine bottle and the cork no wine could be kept sound for any length of time.

Another problem for the Bordelais was to enlist the support of the English kings against the wines of the Haut-Pays. The wine that the English kings, and no doubt private citizens also, secured from Bordeaux did not come only from the area of the present Bordeaux *vignoble*, as confined by the modern boundaries of the department of the Gironde. King John bought wine in 1206 and 1207 from the vineyards of the Abbey of Moissac, situated some way up the Garonne and renowned now for its splendid romanesque cloister. Moissac wine is also recorded as being sold to England late in the thirteenth century. In 1225 the wines of Cahors and Gaillac were imported into England. These wines were sold and shipped by the Bordeaux merchants, except for the Dordogne wines from centres like Bergerac; these were often handled in the latter part of the Middle Ages by Libourne, the leading wine-shipping rival of Bordeaux.

However as the Bordeaux vineyards spread rapidly in the thirteenth and succeed-ing centuries, so did the Bordelais try to ensure that their wine was first on the market each year. They petitioned the English kings to this effect. As long as part at least of the Haut-Pays was English the kings were not anxious to practise discrimination against wine from such centres as Agen on the Garonne and Bergerac on the Dor-dogne, but once they had fallen to the French, they were in 'enemy territory', and might be punished to help the loyal Bordelais. Thus the latter were permitted to keep out 'foreign' wines until the feast of St Martin and even until Christmas. By this time their own new wine was on the high seas or even being consumed in the taverns of the City of London, as the *beaujolais de l'année* is today drunk in the Paris restaurants by the Christmas following the vintage. As the vineyards spread in the Bordeaux region, so did the other crops contract. Accordingly, in 1401 King Henry IV imposed the condition on the merchants in 'enemy-held territories' that they must send one *tonneau* of corn for every two *tonneaux* of wine. As the merchants had nowhere else to dispose of their wine, they had no option but to comply.

If wine was France's chief medieval export, it was also England's largest import, and although separate statistics for Gascon wine imports are rare, most French wine to be found in England then was from Gascony. At its height in the fourteenth century it represented 31 per cent of our imports, compared with 1 per cent today. Indeed on *per capita* basis the amount of Gascon wine imported into England in the early fourteenth century has never been equalled. According to the estimate of Marjory K. James (*The Fluctuations of the Anglo-Gascon Wine Trade During the Fourteenth Century – Economic History Review* 1951), over 20,000 tuns came in annually, representing between a quarter and a fifth of Bordeaux exports. Translated into hectolitres this amounted to 180,000. Yet in so recent a year as 1962 the total quantity of Bordeaux wines exported to Britain was no more than 318,000 hectolitres. Early in the fourteenth century the Bordelais were exporting from Bordeaux, Libourne and the smaller Gironde ports as much as 90,000 – 100,000 *tonneaux* a year.

It must be added that these exports included large amounts of wine – up to 50 per cent of the total – that had originally come from the Haut-Pays, beyond Castillon on the Dordogne and St-Macaire on the Garonne. Although restrictions were placed on their sale in Bordeaux, for export purposes these wines were privileged. While the citizens, nobles and clerics did not pay to the English king the Great Custom on exports, the other Bordelais did pay it in full, but the Haut-Pays wines secured a reduction. The wine from the tax-exempt vineyards of the privileged classes of Bordeaux only amounted to between one-eighth and one-fifth of the whole. Incidentally there was no exemption from the Custom of Royan, which they paid as the wine-laden ships passed into the open sea.

What good customers the English kings were to their wine merchants is shown by the fact that in the early fourteenth century the normal 'annual order' given by the royal butler for the use of the court varied from 1,000 – 2,000 *tonneaux*; and to celebrate his marriage with Isabella of France in January 1308, Edward II ordered 1,000 *tonneaux*. By modern reckoning this would have produced something like 1,152,000 bottles. Quite a wedding!

The first half of the fourteenth century was the time of greatest economic prosperity, but this began to decline as the Hundred Years' War got under way. As the fighting affected the hinterland on which the great trading centre depended for much of its supplies, and to some extent its markets, so exports declined. The Haut-Pays largely passed into French hands, and henceforth only a trickle of wine from the privileged districts that had enjoyed customs preference reached Bordeaux.

When the Earl of Derby's successful campaign of 1345 – 6 freed the nearer territories, notably St-Emilion and Libourne, trade improved. Yet the fighting had caused terrible devastation to the vineyards all the way from Blaye up to St-Emilion on the Dordogne and St-Macaire on the Garonne. Moreover the English kings had to organize convoys of ships to collect the wine, harassed by French and Spanish alike. Already before the war English shipping was taking an increasing share of this carrying trade, and by 1330 it was estimated that more Gascon wine was brought to London by English merchants than by Gascons.

Then in 1348 the Black Death reached Bordeaux, and recurred intermittently throughout the century. By mid-century half the greatly reduced quantity of Bordeaux wine exports came to England. As the war became increasingly unsuccessful for the English, so did the fortunes of Bordeaux run down. In 1348/9 Bordeaux shipped only 6,800 *tonneaux*.

Moreover prices rose sharply in mid-century. The king's wine which had cost him only £3 or less a *tonneau* at the beginning of the century reached £7 to £8 in 1348. Total Bordeaux exports dropped from about 30,000 *tonneaux* to seven or eight thousand. Only the record crop of 1376 raised the total in 1376 to nearly 29,000 *tonneaux:* the last substantial total of the century. But in 1372 the English king had to pay up to £8.10s. a *tonneau*, and although prices dropped at the end of the century, they were still twice as high as at the beginning. By this time England virtually monopolized the Bordeaux export wine trade, accounting for three-quarters or four-fifths. They were taking probably between 15,000 and 20,000 *tonneaux*, a figure which dropped in the next century after England finally lost Bordeaux. Even by 1428 – 31 when Bordeaux exports were down to an average of 13,000 *tonneaux*, the English took the great majority. However, they still remained loyal to Gascon wine, and at the beginning of the fifteenth century only about 300 – 400 tuns of Rhine wine reached England each year, while the wine from Spain, Portugal and the Mediterranean producers were only a fraction of the total imports. The last decade of the English 'ascendancy' included years with the highest imports of French wine into England in the fifteenth century; from 1444–1449 imports averaged about 13,000 tuns each year.

The value to Bordeaux of the English connection has been made clear. But what did the English and particularly the English kings receive in return? First and obviously, they received wine which was a basic essential at a time when water was usually undrinkable and ale had not taken over as the drink of the better-off classes. If it had not been for the recurrent conflicts with the French kings, no doubt more wine would have reached England from the then extensive wine areas in northern France and from Burgundy, via the prosperous port of Rouen. However, as it happened, Gascon wine became the English staple.

The English kings not only needed wine in enormous quantities for the consumption of the royal household, but they also expected a good deal of credit. At times they were very bad payers, but no doubt the Bordeaux merchants, who certainly flourished according to the standards of their period, made up for this in the prices they charged their other customers. The Bordeaux merchants even lent money to the kings, and Edward I was a borrower in 1280. Furthermore the king took a 'prise' of two casks of wine per ship-load entering an English port, although the Cinque Ports were exempted from this tax owing to their services against the adjacent French. Some of this wine will have been used in the royal household, but the monarchy was not above a little state trading on its own.

This was not the only form of wine taxation benefit received by the English kings. Wine from the Haut-Pays had to pay a tax of 15s. a cask if from the English dominions, but two or three times that amount if from French territories. Only Bordeaux and Libourne were exempt from this tax, a valuable relief afforded them by Eleanor of Aquitaine in 1188 and confirmed by Edward I in 1302. The English kings had other benefits. They secured the help of Gascon soldiers not only for their domestic campaigns against the Scots and Welsh but also against the French king.

There were also commercial rewards. The English sent to Bordeaux consignments of herrings, beans, corn, dairy produce and above all cloth. From Cornish ports dried fish was dispatched to the Gironde. Bristol was the main port for the Gascon trade, and much of the cloth needed by the Gascons passed through the port of Bristol. In fourteenth-century records one reads of the Archbishop of Bordeaux buying his dried fish from Cornwall and cheese from England. In view of the excellent partnership between the milder English cheeses and claret, it is high time this medieval trade was renewed and mature English Cheddar, Wensleydale, Double Gloucester and Scottish Dunlop be found in the circular Bordeaux market just off the Allées de Tourny; many of the French cheeses are too powerful for the delicate red Bordeaux.

The other, and in the long run perhaps the most beneficial result of the English ascendancy in Gascony, was the development of our shipping. As already indicated, over the 300 years of English rule, the proportion of English shipping used in the trade with the Gascon ports increased at the expense of the native shipping. This was helped in Edward III's reign by a ban on the export of capital, as it would now be described. One recorded exception was in 1364 when a group of English merchants were allowed to take the large sum of £2,000 to buy Gascon wines. The development of the English shipping also assisted the Bordeaux wine merchants. After the venturesome voyage from England and the anticipated dangers on the return trip from ships of the French Crown, pirates and the winter gales, the English shipmaster wanted a full load of wine aboard to repay him for his risks. Since there was only a relatively short period in which the new wine could be bought for current drinking, the Bordeaux merchants were often able to exact high prices for their newly vintaged wine. By the end of the fourteenth century a shipload might include 200 – 300 *tonneaux*.

The gradual passing of the carrying trade into English hands was to stand England in good stead, building up a tradition of seamanship which in the centuries following their expulsion from Gascony, was to pay dividends in the wars against the Spaniards, the Dutch and the French. In the formation of this tradition the Bordeaux wine carrying trade played its part.

It is not clear, however, that from a balance of trade point of view the possession of Bordeaux and a gradually shrinking portion of Gascony was an asset to the English economy. These territories were not colonies, as the term was later understood. Accordingly, when the English lost Bordeaux in the same year that Constantinople fell to the Turks, there were no great lamentations. This was owing partly to domestic preoccupation with the Wars of the Roses, but also because the loss was not obviously detrimental to the English economy.

4. After the English

For the first few years of the French occupation, the Bordelais were politically and economically punished for their welcome of 'Le Roi Talbot' in 1452 and their obstinate adherence to the English connection.

According to Robert Boutruche in *Bordeaux de 1453 à 1715* (1966), perhaps 2,000 Bordelais emigrated to England, some of them nobles but also merchants. London, Southampton and Bristol were their places of refuge, and in the City of London many established themselves in the parish of St Martin Vintry. As with other refugees, this led to some bad feeling between the newcomers and the English merchants. When the French king pardoned them in the following decade, a number returned to Bordeaux. The pro-English Archbishop Pey Berland died in 1456.

The French king took the nomination of the mayor into his own hands. However, what the French kings wanted was possession of Gascony and its capital, not the prohibition of profitable trade.

So although Charles VII built the Château Trompette to overawe the citizens, his successor Louis XI (1461 – 83) immediately gave Bordeaux the Parlement (a legal court not a proper assembly) which they had been promised ten years earlier. The famous Bordeaux privileges extorted from the English kings were confirmed. These by now included no taxes on burghers' wine on entry into the city or export, reduced taxes for wines from the *Sénéchaussée* (broadly speaking the present Gironde Department), full taxes on wines from neighbouring wine areas, and restrictions on the date of arrival and duration of such wines' stay in the city and its suburbs.

Louis XI also enforced the rule preventing the loading of any wine between Bordeaux and the Atlantic, save for wine intended for the city; and in 1462 he prolonged until Christmas the prohibition on Haut-Pays wines entering the Bordeaux region.

Anglo-Gascon trade went through a difficult time. At first it was quite possible for the English ships to maintain their trips to Bordeaux, except during the autumn of 1455, when access was barred to them. However, their ships were now controlled from the time they entered the Gironde. They were obliged to stop at Soulac to pick up their permits, and again at Blaye to deposit their arms. Residence for English merchants in Bordeaux was restricted to certain houses; they could only stay there for a maximum of a month and were subject to a 5 p.m. to 7 a.m. curfew. They were shadowed, and could only make purchases outside the city if accompanied by a Bordeaux merchant or official. During this period of economic warfare, which lasted from 1455 to 1463, trade dropped off. Whereas English wine imports from Bordeaux were as high as 10,000 *tonneaux* in 1447 – 8, and were as much as 6,000 *tonneaux* in the critical year of 1453 – 4, after a spurt to 9,500 *tonneaux* in 1454 – 5 they shrank to 3,000 *tonneaux* a year until economic peace was restored in 1463, and the kings of both countries once more issued trading licences to their subjects.

From Bordeaux's point of view this was high time, and it was the French king who initiated the truce. As quoted by Miss E. M. Carus-Wilson in an article in the 1947 *Bulletin of the Institute of Historical Research* on the effects on the wine trade of the English acquisition and loss of Gascony, Louis XI accepted the advice of a councillor 'that the whole basis of Bordeaux's wealth was the isle of England, that no other country could take England's place as purchaser of its wines and supplier of its needs, and that the English should therefore be allowed to trade once more as freely as they would'.

Allowed they were, but commercial relations were often strained, and sometimes interrupted, until the Treaty of Picquigny in 1475, after which English merchants were no longer required to have safe conducts; they also secured a reduction in the *Grande Coutume* export tax. From 1482 restrictions on their stay and movements were removed. However, the visits of English merchants were personally hazardous; so much so that in 1483 the English king asked the French king for assurances as to the safety of English merchants visiting Bordeaux. These were given. Nevertheless the French Court always regarded a re-invasion as on the cards, and in 1485 Charles VIII (1483 – 1498) assisted the repair of the fortifications of Bourg, for the town was 'in great danger of being taken by our old enemies – the English'.

After the English left Bordeaux, the wine merchants there certainly had to fight harder to maintain their trade. From now on the Bordelais had to compete in the English market with the wines of Spain, Portugal and even of Greece. It is possible that this competition led to an improvement in the quality of Bordeaux wines. They had little success in other parts of France, but they did begin to build up the important trade with Flanders, the Low Countries and the Hanseatic cities which was to be their mainstay later on.

In France economic conditions in the second half of the fifteenth century were poor, and the price of wine tended to drop. In England, however, according to André Simon in his invaluable *History of the Wine Trade in England* (1906 – 1909), wine prices rose, and for a time imports fell. In the first twenty years of the fifteenth century they had averaged 15,000 tuns (a tun was 252 old gallons, a hogshead 62 old gallons). Then in the middle of the century they dropped as low as 8,000, since wine had become too expensive for the ordinary people; about the end of the century they rose to 20,000 – 25,000 tuns, and to 50,000 in the boom years of 1509 – 18. Thereafter they fell back to 20,000 – 30,000, except for a spurt in Queen Elizabeth's reign (1558 – 1603) to an average of 58,000. Yet by the end of the sixteenth century they were only 35,000 – 40,000 tuns for a population much larger than it had been a century or so earlier.

For wine prices in England continued to rise. In 1580 wine was 2s. a gallon in Oxford, and in 1598 Gascon wine cost 2s. 8d. a gallon in London. The gallon was the old gallon, five-sixths of the present one, and equivalent to the American gallon. The rise in wine prices was part of the general increase in the cost of living in the second half of the sixteenth century, following the discovery of gold in the New World.

Much of this wine continued to be Gascon wine (it was not called claret in the modern sense until later. Simon quotes Edward Tremaine using the term as meaning a red Bordeaux in 1565). After the loss of Gascony, the English kings continued to send an agent each year to buy the young wine, and until the end of the sixteenth century, the English wine fleet made its annual autumn voyage to Bordeaux, returning in mid-December each year. Henry VII (1485 – 1509) and others tried to enforce a decree that all wine from Gascony should come in English, Scottish or Welsh ships, but this was modified. Later on Charles I (1625 – 1649) tried to do the same.

Bordeaux wines remained popular in England for much the same reason that they have been for the last hundred years: they were relatively cheap for their good quality, compared with other wines such as Sack, Rhenish and those from further afield. Good relations were maintained between the traders of both nations. Simon quotes the French authorities as complaining in 1517 about the number of English merchants and sailors – seven to eight thousand of them at times – in the Bordeaux area. The merchants were on such friendly terms with the country people around Bordeaux and in the Médoc that in the event of war the English would have no difficulty in landing troops.

The wines that these English preferred above all were the Graves, followed by those of the Médoc fairly near Bordeaux and then the *palus* growths beside the river. Until the development of the big Médoc estates in the 17th and 18th centuries, it was the red Graves that won most esteem. It is for this reason that the first of the *premiers crus* to be mentioned in print, and in England to be praised by Pepys, was Haut-Brion. White wines were a minor consideration until a demand was created for them by the Dutch. The principal source of white wine was an estate in Blanquefort, the nearest Médoc commune to Bordeaux, owned by the Pontac family. This, therefore, strictly was a Médoc not a Graves, although the boundaries then were not rigidly fixed as they are now today. As mentioned earlier, Pessac was partly at least described as being in the Médoc.

At the beginning of the sixteenth century the Chartrons was only an entrepôt and that great arc of the Garonne was known as the *Port de la Lune*. It was not even a parish, and was full of cellars rather than dwelling houses. The products of the Haut-Pays caused the rapid development of the Chartrons in the sixteenth century; not only for wine but for corn and other up-country commodities.

During this century annual Bordeaux wine exports varied from 20,000 – 30,000 *tonneaux* a year to 80,000 – 100,000 in exceptional years. But the English connection was no longer dominant.

As the trade with England began to flag towards the end of the sixteenth century that of the newly formed Netherlands took its place. The Dutch and the Hanseatic traders had first made a noteworthy appearance in Bordeaux in the middle of that century. Then the declared independence of the Dutch states in 1579 led to a great increase in the commerce in French wines. For the next hundred years the Dutch Republic was at the height of its economic power. How powerful it was in the carrying trade may be gauged from the fact that in 1669 the French Minister of Marine, Colbert, estimated the French fleet at 500 – 600 vessels, the English at 3,000 – 4,000 and the Dutch at 15,000 – 16,000. So it was they who carried the wine up the continental coast and round to the Baltic, notably to the Hanseatic towns who established a reputation as wine trade centres which they have never entirely lost. Dutch merchants took up residence in Bordeaux as the English had done before them. Indeed the oldest existing firm of merchants in Bordeaux today is Beyerman, a Dutch firm founded in 1620.

But it was a different trade from that of the English, for the economically-minded Dutch and their Flemish neighbours preferred cheap white wines, particularly sweet Sauternes, and this caused an enormous increase in the production of white wine in the Graves area and further up the Garonne; but also in most other areas outside the stubbornly red wine areas, as the Médoc and St-Emilion seem to have remained. The white wine area included Ste-Foy as well as Bergerac, outside the Bordeaux region as we know it today.

Moreover while the English always maintained a preference for what were then the 'quality wines', the Dutch were interested in buying, drinking or re-selling cheap wines to other northern countries. It was reckoned by Colbert that they drank only a third of what they bought each year, and re-exported two-thirds. For this purpose they did a great deal of blending of what we would call *vin de consommation*. This 'mass production' blending was unpopular with the producers and merchants having interests in the fine wine districts. By the early eighteenth century there was more white wine produced in Bordeaux than red. As an example Dion states that 26,800 *tonneaux* of white wine and only 2,700 *tonneaux* of red were exported in 1738 – 40 to Scandinavia, Pomerania, Danzig, Lubeck, Riga and Hamburg. On the other hand in 1725 the Bordeaux Parlement complained that the English had maintained their tradition of buying '*grand vin*' at an 'excessive price', originating from only a dozen or fifteen sources, and representing only 2 per cent of the output. Today, perhaps, this complaint might be transferred to the other side of the Atlantic.

Nevertheless the Dutch certainly helped to develop the Bordeaux vineyards at a time when English interest was reduced and later was actively hostile to French wines – initially under the influence of Dutch William. And for all their preference for inexpensive white wines, it was, ironically, the Dutch who laid the foundation of the great red wines by their assistance with draining the Médoc marshes. A Dutchman, Conrad Gaussen, led the work. As for the English trade, at the beginning of the seventeenth century James I (1603 – 1625) was partial to Bordeaux wines, partly perhaps owing to the traditional popularity of claret in Scotland, but also because he was economically careful; Bordeaux wines were fairly cheap. He sent a buying envoy to Bordeaux each vintage. At one point he issued an order forbidding the purchase of new wine in Bordeaux before 1 December each year, owing to the number of complaints about the poor quality. That the wine was not all that cheap can be demonstrated by the fact, quoted by Simon, that the price per hogshead then was £5.10s., yet three hundred years later, in the Inter-War years of the twentieth century, classed-growth clarets of good vintages could be bought for £12 and less a *barrique*. Owing to his arbitrary government, Charles I's reign (1625 – 1649) was not encouraging either for wine traders or wine drinkers. In 1637 he clapped a tax of £2 per tun on all wine. This was abolished by the Long Parliament in 1640. Moreover like other taxes the duty on wine was farmed out. The Vintners' Company, which had attempted to monopolize the wine trade, in 1640 was denounced in Parliament by John Pym. The Company had paid Charles £30,000, had taken £80,000 themselves and by retailing had recovered £232,000. Charles himself was very abstemious and Simon says he was 'probably the soberest monarch who ever ruled over England and the one who spent less for wine'. Just before his execution it is recorded that he 'drank a small glassful of claret wine'.

During this period it is interesting to have a record of Henry Thompson, perhaps the first 'modern' English wine merchant resident in Bordeaux, buying wine from the Graves, Médoc, Blaye, Ste-Foy, St-Emilion and Langon. There is no evidence that all this wine was destined for England and perhaps the cheaper qualities went to the Low Countries who were by then dominant in the Bordeaux wine trade.

The prices that Thompson paid, and the relative standing of the wines of the various districts can be estimated from the statistics given by Malvezin in his *Histoire du Commerce de Bordeaux* (1892). In 1647 they averaged as follows:

Graves and Médoc	78–100 livres (per *tonneau*)
Côtes	72–84
Bourg	66
Entre-Deux-Mers	60–75
Blaye	54
Barsac, Bommes, Sauternes	84–100

As converted by Malvezin into the franc value of his own time, Blaye wines cost 430 frs. (£17) and the top Graves, Médoc and Sauternes were 800 frs. (£31).

Under the Commonwealth the Anglo-Gascon wine trade improved, for the Roundheads though Puritans were not, as some might imagine, teetotallers. Cromwell himself drank French and Spanish wine. However like some of his predecessors he made an attempt to confine the carrying trade, but in a different form. By the 1651 Navigation Act foreign shipping could bring in only the produce of their own country; a heavy blow at the Dutch who went to war over it, not very successfully. It also hit the French wine trade, for neither they nor the English had sufficient ships, as the earlier reference to Colbert's estimate indicates.

Inside Bordeaux during this period there were some political difficulties. In 1675, following the imposition of bitterly resented taxes from which the burghers had been traditionally free, there were riots. The city was occupied by the military, some walls and gates were demolished, and a number of the ring-leaders were put to death.

Ten years later the Revocation of the Edict of Nantes, which had given tolerance to the Protestants, had a very bad effect on the Bordeaux wine trade. For its foreign markets largely lay in the Protestant countries, particularly in Holland and England, which did not care to buy from the persecutors of the Huguenots. Also in 1684 the expulsion from Bordeaux of 93 Portuguese Jewish families had been ordered, but was cancelled in 1686, as they had influential friends abroad, particularly in the Low Countries. Not many English merchants chose at this time to remain in the city; non-Catholics were not made very welcome.

As the conflict began with France, to last intermittently until Waterloo, so did the Anglo-French wine trade run into increasing difficulties; and of all areas Bordeaux, the source of most French wine, was worst hit. In 1667 the imports into England of French and Canary wine were briefly prohibited. Later, from 1679 to 1685, French wines were again forbidden entry. There were loopholes in this embargo, but trade was certainly discouraged, and if the French growers had not found other markets, including, later on, America, they would have been in a bad way.

It must be added that the English discrimination against the French was not unilateral. It was Colbert who in 1677 inflicted a steep tariff on English cloth goods, and a few years later the import of English cloth into France was forbidden; the English retaliated on wines. The Bordeaux merchants repeatedly tried to have the cloth embargo lifted and to secure special privileges and exemptions for themselves, but they failed. The English merchants on their side complained during Charles II's reign (1660–1685) of excessive French taxes on wine, and that they were not allowed to buy their wine outside Bordeaux itself. They also alleged that Haut-Pays wines were sold as Médoc, and that the Bordeaux merchants blended their wines. Familiar complaints!

No doubt blending was practised but in fact Colbert reiterated its illegality, and his ban assisted the development of 'quality' Bordeaux production, as well as a reduction in the amount of Haut-Pays wine passing through Bordeaux.

In 1693 William III (1689 – 1702) started the long drawn-out discrimination against French wines that was not finally dropped until W. E. Gladstone's Budget in 1860. William raised the duty against French wines to £22.2.10d. a tun, or 2s.1d. a gallon. The duty, high enough indeed, on Portuguese and Spanish wines was £17.13.3d. But within a few years worse was to follow. While the Iberian wines had to pay £21.12.5d., the duty on French wines shot up to £47, and in 1698 to £51.2s. or over 1s. a bottle. The cost of claret itself averaged £16.

The effect on French wine imports was of course catastrophic. Simon quotes the

English imports for 1700 as 13,649 tuns from Spain, 7,757 from Portugal, 1,430 Rhenish and only 664 from France. The situation was slightly relieved by a certain amount of smuggling and by the import of French wines in Portuguese and Spanish casks. The Bordeaux merchants carried out this little operation quite openly. Yet with Britain the French wine trade, which meant above all the Bordeaux trade, dwindled almost to nothing; in spite of protests, claret became nearly unobtainable except by the rich. The English Whigs took to port and only the Scots and some Tories, in protest against the Hanoverian monarchs, maintained precariously the French wine connection and the tradition of claret drinking.

5. The Rise of
the Estates

It is often thought that the famous château estates and the named growths that we know today are of considerable antiquity. Generally, this is not so. There is nothing in Bordeaux to match the old monastic *'clos'* of the Côte d'Or, unless we except the archiepiscopal vineyard in Pessac, partly now known as Ch. Pape-Clément. As has been pointed out in *Gods, Men and Wine* (1966) by William Younger, the role of the church in the development of viticulture has been exaggerated. Certainly it was not a prominent feature of Bordeaux, although the two chief Chapters in the city as well as the archbishop owned considerable vineyards, which were cultivated by tenants on the basis of a share of the crop. This share generally varied from one-quarter to one-tenth, irrespective of whether the landlord was ecclesiastical or lay; but the archbishop took half the crop of his Pessac vineyards (there were two). These rents were known as *agrières*. In 1558 Jacques de Bécoiran, *seigneur* of Lafite, sold to Simon de la Bégorce, the *agrières* due to the noble house of Lafite in Milon, Pauillac, St-Laurent etc.

Until the seventeenth century there were no large compact estates as we know them today, and the vineyards were worked by peasants or small tenant farmers. How small they were may be judged from the *récolte* of the Pape-Clément estate in the middle of the sixteenth century. Allowing for the fact that the archbishop received half the crop, the total output was only 24 *barriques* in 1562; 40 in 1563; 48 in 1564 and 13½ in 1575. Judging by the very small output in 1575, it looks as if the vines were stricken by frost or hail, to which they are subject even today, notably in the Graves. In this period the vintage began between 12 and 23 September. Ten days must be added to these dates for modern comparison, as this was just before the Gregorian

Calendar was adopted in France in 1582. From that year the dates in the annual calendar are the same as today, except it must be remembered that England was very slow to adopt this papal-inspired reform, and not until September 1752 did we fall into line with most of Europe.

As the Graves was the original heart of the Bordeaux *vignoble*, it is not surprising that the first secular estate that we know of was Haut-Brion in Pessac not far outside the city walls. As already mentioned, it was known to Pepys in 1663, but as 'Ho Bryen'. The name was a difficult one for the English to master, and it appears in curious forms right down to the nineteenth century. In *Bottlescrew Days* (1926) André Simon, quoting from the unpublished diary and expenses of John Hervey, first Earl of Bristol, mentions a purchase in 1705 of Obrian. Much later in the same century it appears, rather charmingly, in a Christie's auction catalogue as Oberon. We may discount the late Maurice Healy's ingenious suggestion that it was really O'Brien. The Irish arrived later on the scene in Bordeaux. Then John Evelyn in his Diary (16 July 1683) refers to Pontac and Haut-Brion 'whence the best Bordeaux wine comes'.

The development of the big estates largely coincided with the extensive plantation of the Médoc, which began in the sixteenth century, was accelerated by drainage of the marshes in the seventeenth century, and by the enrichment of the new *noblesse de robe* and of the merchant classes in the eighteenth century. With the seventeenth century came the decay of the old aristocracy, the *noblesse d'épée* and the rise of the new families, the Montesquieus, d'Alesmes and Pontacs among them. The Léoville estate was created in 1638 by M. Moytié, a Bordeaux merchant, who called it Mont Moytié. These families acquired much of their rank originally from positions in the legal hierarchy of the Bordeaux Parlement. These appointments often became hereditary and their recipients amassed wealth. Arnaud de Pontac, first President, had his revenues officially estimated in 1663 at 25,000 livres a year. The de la Tresne family, later associated with Haut-Brion, were one of the Parlement dynasties, and Jean-Baptiste de la Tresne was President in the middle of the seventeenth century. Another dignitary, who gave his name to a vineyard, was President Pichon who died in 1684.

In the following century, according to Mr Robert Forster in the *Economic History Review* (August 1961), of the 68 families of the robe in Bordeaux, 73 per cent of their income came from the sale of wine. A mature vineyard yielded 8 per cent on its purchase price.

French colonial expansion early in the eighteenth century also brought wealth to the French trading classes and a big extension of the Bordeaux vineyards. What had been lost by way of the trade with England had been compensated for by the demand for French wines in the colonies.

Boucher, intendant from 1720 – 1743, predecessor of Tourny and the first of the three great eighteenth century Bordeaux intendants, described the 'fury of planting' as starting about 1709, following the devastating frosts and disastrous vintage of that year. Writing in 1724 to his chief in Paris to demand the pulling up of all vines planted since that year except in the 'Graves de Médoc, the Graves de Bordeaux and the Côtes', he stated that since the beginning of the century, everything had been put under vines, and that for ten leagues (*c.* 25 miles) around Bordeaux one saw nothing but vineyards. Thus were revived the fears of the Emperor Domitian in the first century A.D.

The government was afraid of vineyards being planted at the expense of other crops, especially wheat. It was also believed that an extension of vineyards throughout France would lead to a drop in the price of wine and result in heavy losses to the proprietors. So from 1725 – 1766 all the efforts of the central government were in the direction of restraining wine output, of maintaining prices and preventing new plantations. From 1725 onwards strict laws were passed, forbidding the planting of new vineyards; and heavy penalties were imposed, including the ploughing up of new plantations.

The important Gironde *vignoble* was particularly affected, and the two intendants – a title carrying powers somewhat similar to the present-day *préfet*, and like him responsible to the central government – Claude Boucher (1720 – 1743) and Louis-Urbain, Marquis de Tourny (1743 – 1757), who did so much to embellish Bordeaux, were no friends to the growers wishing to expand their vineyards. Boucher earned the indignation of Montesquieu by refusing the latter permission to plant vines in land adjoining Haut-Brion, and Tourny in 1745 ordered an enquiry into the new planta-tions of vines in the Médoc since the beginning of the century. The results of this investigation came to light three years later when ten proprietors in Margaux, Cantenac, Soussans, Castelnau and elsewhere were heavily fined and their vines, some of them now very old, pulled up. Among those fined was the Président de Gascq at Cantenac, predecessor of General Palmer. He had to pull up about three hectares.

Certainly these measures had a retarding effect on the whole Gironde *vignoble*, especially at a time when Bordeaux was facing new competition from the expanding vineyards of Spain and Portugal, whose wines were cheap. However, in 1739 the total Bordeaux vineyard area was said to be double the size it had been 20 years previously, and just before Tourny retired in 1757 he admitted that in spite of all his efforts the area under vines was larger than 25 years earlier.

Nevertheless government policy changed in 1766, and new planting was en-couraged. However, the terrible winter of that year resulted in a considerable temporary decline in the vineyards. Severe frost damage led to extensive re-planting, and the restrictions lapsed; not to be renewed effectively until the 1930s when the law of *appellation contrôlée* came into being, with its consequent control over the vineyards and their output.

By the second half of the eighteenth century the pattern and extent of the Bordeaux *vignoble* was not all that different from that of the present day, although St-Emilion and Pomerol were not so heavily cultivated. This 'fury of planting' was part of Bordeaux's eighteenth century 'renaissance', with the leading estates owned and extended by the nobles of the Parlement, the prosperous *noblesse de robe*. R. Pijassou in his chapter on the Bordeaux *vignoble* in *Bordeaux au XVIIIe Siècle* (1968), on which I have drawn freely about the rise of the estates, shows how important this newly rich, mostly newly-ennobled bourgeoisie was in the development of the various districts. As the Parlementaires were all legal men, though some of the posts were hereditary, it can be said that the Médoc was first developed by the lawyers. Soon they bought out and over-shadowed their peasant neighbours, and made considerable fortunes from their new estates, often worked by tenant farmers on a 50 – 50 share-cropping basis.

The Parliamentary Councillor d'Arche of Sauternes (who gave his name to Ch. d'Arche) received from his estate there between 20 and 65 *tonneaux* of wine, produced entirely by share-croppers. The average annual revenue was 9,928 livres, of which the share-croppers received 3,367 livres, and the proprietor, after deduction of expenses, 3,801 livres (38 per cent). In some years the share-croppers received nothing at all, as they had been obliged to borrow from the owners and were heavily in debt. Many under-privileged peasant owners and tenants had to sell out, and between 1755 and 1790 the size of the noble properties greatly increased. The Président Pichard paid over 1 million livres to Ségur for Lafite. There were great profits to be made, for the expenses on a mature 60-acre vineyard were only one third to one half of the gross receipts.

No wonder that the Bordeaux proprietors and the intendants were at loggerheads. No wonder, either, that the Médoc vineyard proprietors from 1730 to 1750 fought a plan of the Bordeaux merchants to have a road built from the city to the extremity of the Médoc. The merchants stated that this would be a better way of transporting the wine than by ships, as the latter often went aground. But the noble proprietors feared that the merchants would have access to the smaller *vignerons*. Among the successful opponents were Ségur, Pontac, Fumel and Villeneuve. The bitterness that was building up among the exploited 'little men' throughout the eighteenth century can be imagined from what happened in the Bordeaux region, and it is not surprising that the Président Pichard ended his days on the guillotine.

The *noblesse de robe* was often provokingly rich; also the Church. In Villenave d'Ornon at the Revolution 69 small proprietors owned only 34 hectares of vineyard; the Church, including the monks of Carbonnieux, and the emigrated proprietors, owned 384 hectares.

For example, the Président Nicolas Alexandre, Marquis de Ségur, owned Latour, Lafite, Mouton and other properties in St-Laurent and the Graves, and was not exaggeratedly known as '*le Prince des Vignes*'. It was he certainly who established the reputations of Lafite and Latour. After his death, in 1755, it was officially estimated that the annual turnover of these two estates alone was 100,000 livres (*c.* £4,000 in the money of that day), of which 60 per cent was net profit. After a bad year in 1744 Ségur asked Tourny for a tax reduction owing to the sad state of his Lafite and Latour vineyards, but his gross income was estimated at 272,000 livres, with expenses at 34,400.

Ségur's only rival was the Marquis d'Aulède, who possessed Ch. Margaux, part of Haut-Brion, and the estate of Pez in St-Estèphe. From these his net annual revenue was about 25,000 livres (*c.* £1,000).

Lesser Parlementaires were M. Brossier, who owned Beychevelle as well as properties in Lamarque and Moulis, M. Pichon of Longueville, and others with less well-known estates. In the Sauternes seventeen properties were owned by members of the Bordeaux Parlement, including the Président de Gascq at Barsac, the Councillor de Filhot in Sauternes, and the Marquis de Saluces at Preignac, Fargues and, of course, at Yquem. It is perhaps worth mentioning that présidents proliferated in the Bordeaux Parlement. In the eighteenth century out of a staff of 117 officers there was a *premier président*, nine *présidents à mortier*, and six *présidents* of three courts. The *présidents à mortiers*, so-called because of their mortarboard head-gear, were in fact vice-presidents, and of these Ségur was one.

The Church also contributed to the development of the vineyards. In 1740 the Benedictines of the Abbey of Ste-Croix in Bordeaux bought Carbonnieux for 120,000 livres, and made a good profit out of this Graves estate. Some of the local priests too did very well out of wine. The *curé-prieur* of Cantenac in mid-century had a total revenue from wine of 25,000 livres a year.

Early in the eighteenth century all the first growths*, as they were later to become, must have had some entity, for we find them mentioned in the Earl of Bristol's records: 'Margoose' in 1703 at £27.10s. a hogshead; 6 dozen flasks of 'La Tour' for £14.8s. in 1720; 'Laffitte' at 50s. a dozen in 1721 and 'Chasteau Margoux' at £47.7s. a hogshead, including bottles, corks and carriage in 1723. Cyril Ray in his *Lafite* (1968) quotes an advertisement in the *London Gazette* of 1707, announcing the sale of 'an entire parcel of New French Claret . . . being of the Growth of Lafitt, Margouze, and La Tour'. Dr. J. H. Plumb in his *Men and Places* (1961) mentions that in 1706 Robert Walpole imported wine in bottle, as it came in chests. In 1732 – 3 he bought four hogsheads of Ch. Margaux at a time and a hogshead of Lafite regularly every three months for his lavish entertaining at Houghton Hall, Norfolk, and in London. Pontac was the only other wine mentioned by name. Bottles then were not cheap at 2s.6d. a dozen, although they were returnable at 2s. a dozen, and long French corks were 2s.6d. a gross. The importance of the English 'quality' market may be gauged from the fact that in 1737 Walpole spent £1,160 a year on wine, much of it French. The way that some wine entered England is indicated by the example of Walpole who, when a high Admiralty official, smuggled champagne in by using an Admiralty barge!

If the fame of the individual first growths had penetrated to England by the first quarter of the eighteenth century, they must have been well established by then in France. Indeed the late P. Morton Shand in his *A Book of French Wines* (revised edition 1960) claimed that there were references to Haut-Brion in chronicles prior to 1480. Certainly one of the oldest present-day estates with a firm vinous connection is La Mission-Haut-Brion, which had the un-usual record of passing from secular into religious hands. For in 1630 it was left by the widow of a president of the Parlement of Guyenne to a clergy organization; and in the settlement there is mention of vines, a *'grand chey cuvier garni d'une fouloire en pierre de taille'*. Thence it passed to the Lazarist order of preachers, who built the still-existing chapel attached to the château and gave the vineyard its name.

* It is necessary in this and following chapters to refer to the classified growths prior to the full dis-cussion on them in the chapter on the Classification of the Médoc. Readers unaware of the main facts and features of the classification codefied in 1855 may turn to the relevant chapter on page 247.

In many cases, however, there were châteaux before there were vines, or any record of them. Ch. Margaux was Ch. Lamothe in the Middle Ages; Latour has associations with the Anglo-French Wars, and there is the splendid moated château of Issan. It is said that the English retreating after the battle of Castillon in 1453 were able to embark at the harbour of Issan on the Gironde and to take their wine with them. But whether the wine was from this area is another matter. Much of the Médoc was undrained marshy land, until reclaimed by Colbert's orders in the middle of the seventeenth century. The Fort de Médoc on the estuary was built as late as 1689.

Not the least interesting references in the Earl of Bristol's records are to bottles and corks. For until the development of the bottle and the use of cork, probably about the turn of the seventeenth century, there was no serious possibility of keeping and maturing wine. Until then the young wine was drunk up quickly while still sound, as had been the custom for centuries. The new estates of the enriched and often ennobled proprietors could not develop and show the quality of their wines until towards the end of the eighteenth century when they could put them into bottles that might conveniently be laid down on their sides and the wine permitted to mature. There were bottles as such earlier than this, but designed for holding rather than maturing wine. R. Pijassou, who has examined the records of the Beychevelle cellar in 1748 in which there were only 24 glass bottles containing wine for immediate use, points out it was the *vin de l'année* that was drunk.

Latour probably accurately dates its wine-production records as a compact estate from 1670 when it was bought by a M. de Chavanas, who sold it in 1677 to the Clauzel family. Thence it passed by marriage to the Ségur family, who also owned Calon in St-Estèphe, to which estate the Vice-President of the Parlement gave his name. More details are given in the chapter on Pauillac.

Evidence of the firm establishment of the four *premiers crus* by the 1730s is given in official tax documents quoted by Franz Malvezin in his *Histoire de la Vigne et du Vin en Aquitaine* (1919). Not only were the production costs given, but also the size of the crops and the prices at which they were sold. In the decade from 1735 – 1744, the output of Lafite averaged 77 *tonneaux* of '*grand vin*' and 30 of '*second vin*'. The comparable figures for Latour were 49 and 22. At this period Margaux was producing about 65 *tonneaux* of its first wine, and Haut-Brion about 50. The opening prices varied according to quality from 1,400 to 2,000 livres (roughly equivalent to francs).

Many of the classed-growth names that we know today derive from eighteenth-century proprietors, for although the four first growths and Mouton are named topographically – La Fite means a height, and Mouton is similarly derived from *Motte de terre*, an eminence, and has no ovine associations – many of the others were named by and after their proprietors, a custom that still persists today, as may be evidenced by Mouton-Baron-Philippe and Prieuré-Lichine. It is true that a certain Jean de Lafite is said to be mentioned in a document of 1355 as living in Pauillac, but as likely as not he took his name from the locality. Among those châteaux which commemorate their former owners are Rausan, named after a seventeenth-century merchant, Léoville, previously named Mont-Moytié, but re-christened by Mme la

Présidente de Léoville, who died in 1769, and Gruaud-Larose. This had been known as Fonbedeau, but the rich, eccentric M. Gruaud bought it in 1757, and after his death in 1787 it was acquired by M. Larose, who added his name. Malescot takes its name from Simon Malescot, *procureur* in the *Cour du Parlement* in Bordeaux, who bought the property in 1697. The two Pichon estates were owned by branches of the Pichon-Longueville family, and St-Pierre took its name from the man who bought it in 1767. Grand-Puy-Lacoste was in the hands of the Lacoste family from the first half of the eighteenth century. The pattern of origin, name and period in the history of Bordeaux is clear from these examples. Mouton was known as Brane-Mouton, (or Branne-Mouton), after the family who had owned it since the reign of Louis XV.

Whatever the reputation inside France of the Bordeaux growths, other than the *premiers crus*, it seems clear that in the eighteenth century they were little known in England, where in spite of duty discrimination a trickle at least of the best Bordeaux wines continued to infiltrate.

As good an indication of the general anonymity of claret at this period can be obtained from the wines sold by Christie's, the London auctioneers, who conducted their first auction in 1766 and their first all-wine auction in 1769. Claret occupied a minor position, compared with madeira then at the height of its esteem, port or sherry, and it was usually listed merely as 'fine claret'. Very often it was sold by the colour of the seal: red, black and green, but there does not seem to have been a recognized colour code; for sometimes the black seal fetched the best price, sometimes the red. This of course may have been accounted for by the quality of the wines themselves. Later on in the early nineteenth century, it appears as if the black seal was the better, but by then a great deal of claret was sold under the name of the merchants.

Meanwhile the first Bordeaux bearing a name of any kind in the Christie sale catalogues was 'a hogshead of Canon claret' and another of 'Pontack', sold in 1778. Perhaps the first was a St-Emilion or even a Fronsac. If so it was the first to be mentioned by name for the better part of another century. Otherwise the first growths alone were singled out by name, but not always then. The first reference to them was in 1787 when 19 hogsheads of 'High Flavoured Claret of the First Growth' were offered. They fetched £34 in hogshead and 36s. a dozen in bottle. At the same sale a pipe of port (115 gallons, more than double the Bordeaux *barrique* in size) fetched £35.

In the following year 4 dozen 'Lafeete' fetched 66s. a dozen and 15 dozen of 'Ch. Margau' reached 49s. St-Julien and Médoc – unusually specific entries so early – went for 60s. and 43s. respectively. Pontac (which was probably Haut-Brion) made 45s. But this was an exceptional sale, for it was the stock of the retiring French Ambassador to the Court of St James, Count d'Adhémar, and no doubt he had rather more precise ways of identifying his Bordeaux than was usual in England. Whatever the cause this was the first time in which estate names were mentioned in Christie's catalogues, so far as I have been able to discover. Slowly, thereafter, they became more frequent. In 1794, at the height of the French Revolution, 30 dozen Lafite, 24 dozen 'Château Margeau' and 50 dozen Latour were sold. The Lafite fetched 41s. the Latour 40s. and the Margaux 39s. a dozen. No vintage was given, but in 1797 six hogsheads of 1791 'first-growth claret' were offered, still in hogshead. The catalogue note states that it was 'considered the best that France has produced for many years and similar is difficult at this time to be obtained and now in high order for Bottling'. Six years in wood!

In a trade sale in 1792, ten lots of 'the growth Latour' 1785 were sold in cases each containing '50 quart bottles'. They fetched from 41s. to 44s. a dozen.

By 1802 Ch. Margot (*sic*) and La Fitte (*sic*) were fetching 54s., but fine claret grew rare as the Napoleonic Wars dragged on and the prohibition of trade with France had its effect. In 1815, in the sale held a month after Waterloo, of Count Merveldt, the retiring Austrian Ambassador, Ch. Margot fetched 112s.6d. a case and Lafite and Latour 100s., while St-Julien reached 84s., and 'vin de Sauternes' 100s.

In the second half of the eighteenth century there seems no doubt that Lafite was the leading first growth. During the Revolution it passed to a Dutch company and its later history is referred to in the chapter on the Médoc. By the end of the century many of the Médoc estates were producing large quantities of wine. The average production of Ch. Margaux was 110 *tonneaux*, and Brane-Mouton 130 *tonneaux*, while the large estates of Léoville and Canet were averaging 160 and 175 *tonneaux*.

During the revolutionary years a number of the Médoc estates were confiscated and sold. This was not so much owing to the extermination or expropriation of the owners but to their emigration, as happened at Lafite. The Marquis de Ségur was one of these, and so his properties were confiscated, including the part of Latour which he owned. But the ownership of the rest of it, held by Ségur's daughter, the Countess of Miromesnil, was not disturbed, and she bequeathed it to her daughters. One of these married into the Beaumont family.

Haut-Brion was also partly confiscated at the Revolution, because the proprietor, Joseph Fumel, emigrated. The Brane family was not disturbed at Mouton. When the Marquis de Las-Cases-Beauvoice emigrated, the whole large Léoville estate was taken over by the state; but the three members of the family who owned three-quarters and who had not left the country demanded and secured restitution. The emigré's portion was eventually acquired by Mr Hugh Barton, partly in 1822 and the rest in 1826. Giscours was another estate confiscated, owing to the emigration of its owner, M. de Saint-Simon.

In the Graves both La Mission-Haut-Brion and Carbonnieux, which had been in Benedictine hands since 1740, were confiscated along with other ecclesiastical estates, and were bought by secular owners.

Since the purchase of Latour by the Cowdray family in 1962, a careful scrutiny of the château's archives has been made and, although not completed, a good deal of fascinating information as to the production and marketing of leading wines like Latour in the late eighteenth and early nineteenth centuries was made available to R. Pijassou for his chapter on the Bordeaux *vignoble* in *Bordeaux au XVIIIe Siècle* (1968). *Egrappage*, removal of the stalks before the fermentation, was seldom practised and the wine was only left in the vats for eight days before being drawn off into new casks of Baltic oak, where the fermentation continued for about 20 days. The wine was racked twice a year and in the second year it was 'roused', or mixed up, to aid maturity. At the end of the eighteenth century the wine was no longer sold on its lees, but by the spring following the vintage, most of the *barriques* which had been sold were shipped via the little port of St-Mambert to the cellars of the Chartrons merchants who had bought them. These cellars were more suitable for keeping the wine than out in the Médoc, and there was less ullage in the cooler temperatures. The wine was racked every six months, in April and October, and was kept in cask for a minimum of four years, and even up to six or seven years. Not only was the wine generally sold in cask by the château; the merchants did the same. Neither kept any bottle stock beyond their own needs; it was too expensive a capital outlay. Consequently when in 1801 one of the Latour proprietors, the Comte de La Pallu, asked the *régisseur* to send him an assortment of the best wines of Bordeaux, the latter replied that the only way would be to buy a cask of old wine from each estate and either send it in bottle or in cask; and this would be a very expensive matter. Was it the quality or the cost of the wine to which this *régisseur* was referring when he said 'The wines of Latour, they are like gold bars'.

The revolutionary epoch was an extremely bad period for the whole French wine trade, and particularly for Bordeaux, so dependent on export markets. From 1803 when war with England broke out, the French colonies were largely cut off, trade with England was at a standstill, and the markets in northern Europe were at the mercy of the British Navy. Moreover although the system of heavy indirect taxation on wine under the *Ancien Régime* had been abolished during the Revolution, it was replaced by other taxes scarcely less onerous. Napoleon's later campaigns also fell heavily on the French taxpayer, so that the fall of Napoleon in 1814 and his exile to Elba were by no means unpopular among the wine growing and trading sections of the Bordeaux region. For example Count Lynch, born in 1749 of Irish extraction and proprietor of Dauzac, from the end of the eighteenth century was mayor of Bordeaux in 1814 when Napoleon was exiled for the first time and the English Army entered Bordeaux on 12 March. He told the English commander, General Beresford, that if the latter was an ally of Louis XVIII he would offer the general the keys of the city. He then proceeded to tear off his Napoleonic decorations, throw away his tricolour sash of office and put on a white one, white being the Bourbon colour. He then mounted the tower of St-Michel to cry: '*Vive Le Roi! Vive les Bourbons!*' If Napoleon's return had been more protracted and successful, Count Lynch might have paid for his ostentatious loyalty to the Bourbons. As it was he fled temporarily to Plymouth aboard an English merchantman, but then returned, was made a peer by Louis XVIII (1815–24) and lived another 20 years, to die in 1835.

It is worth noting that at the beginning of the nineteenth century there were no notable estates in St-Emilion or Pomerol. That is not to say that there were no vineyards of repute. Both Ausone and Figeac were well established, but their wines had no very wide renown, and this remained true for more than another fifty years. No doubt, also, wine was made on great estates like that of the Ch. du Bouilh, whose immense, unfinished pile by Victor Louis, the famous eighteenth-century Bordeaux architect, still today dominates the Cubzadais; but the wines were not well known.

A certain number of the classed growth estates changed hands in the post-revolutionary period, but the next period of prosperity followed the Restoration in 1815 and more particularly, in the reign of Louis-Philippe (1830 – 48), when the new French capitalist class really came to the fore. Bordeaux then was prosperous. Some of these new château buyers were also wine merchants, such as Mr Hugh Barton, whose firm of Barton & Guestier had been established in Bordeaux in 1725. In 1825 Haut-Brion was sold to a Paris stock-broker and to M. Beyerman, the Bordeaux wine merchant of Dutch origin, and he ran it until it was acquired by M. Eugène Larrieu. Brane-Mouton changed hands in 1830, and M. Vivens had bought Durfort in 1824 and added his own name; and in the following year Giscours, which had been partly owned after the revolutionary confiscation by two Americans, John Gray and Jonathan Davis, passed to a Bordeaux merchant, M. Marc Promis. Mr Brown, an English merchant in Bordeaux, gave his name to Cantenac-Brown.

Some of the estates well known today were created at this period. For example Montrose was developed from woodland in St-Estèphe and acknowledged as a second growth in 1825. Château Palmer was named after the English general who bought the estate of Ch. de Gascq at the Restoration, and greatly extended it, winning recognition as a third growth. Details of these estates will be found in succeeding chapters.

The fifty years from 1830 to 1880 marked the peak of expansion among the Médoc châteaux. The 'new men' with new money moved into Bordeaux, buying up vineyards and building the often incongruous châteaux that lie heavily on the flat land, from the suburbs of Bordeaux to the extremities of the Haut-Médoc and even beyond. No comparable shift in ownership and development took place until the 1950s, when moneyed proprietors from Algeria and financial groups from elsewhere once more decided that vineyards were a profitable form of investment. But then they spent the money on the vineyards and the *chais*, not on new châteaux. In 1830 M. Thuret bought Mouton from the Baron de Brane (or Branne), and in 1836 the Franco-Spanish family of Aguado acquired Château Margaux. In 1853 Baron Nathaniel de Rothschild took over Mouton; and fifteen years later his cousin, Baron James de Rothschild secured Lafite. Palmer had passed to the banking family of Pereire in 1853, and later on Beychevelle was to go to the Foulds, the financiers. How profitable these investments proved has not been publicized, but it is a fact that Lafite paid no dividend from 1868 to 1948. Yet perhaps the Rothschild owners preferred to plough the profits back into the soil and the *chais*; or to take them in kind.

As the nineteenth century progressed the initiative and influence passed more and more from the growers and proprietors to the merchants of Bordeaux who had the capital, the accommodation and the sales organizations which the growers lacked. As will be seen later, many of these merchants bought châteaux out of their profits; but in no case of which I am aware did château owners buy merchant houses.

There were, of course, set-backs in this era of proprietorial prosperity. The 'spectre haunting Europe' in 1848 had an unsettling effect in Bordeaux, and the proprietors could not easily sell their wines, as is mentioned in the chapter on the Bordeaux wine trade. Then in 1852 the growers had a spectre of their own: the oidium. It was worse in the following year and crops were severely reduced until 1857. Probably that is the reason why M. Thuret lost money on his sale of Mouton to Baron Nathaniel de Rothschild in 1853. When he bought it in 1830 from the Baron de Brane he paid the then enormous sum of 1,200,000 frs. but twenty-three years later he recovered only 1,125,000 frs. It was a buyer's market in the stricken vineyards and Baron Nathaniel had to wait for five years until he secured much of a return on his investment.

However from 1858 to 1878 the leading growths did very well. For after the high prices of the '58s came the unequalled series of fine and plentiful vintages in the 1860s and 1870s. The attraction of the Médoc châteaux is demonstrated by the unusual number that changed ownership during the sixties. In 1860 M. Armand Lalande, a Bordeaux wine merchant, bought Cantenac-Brown and went on to buy the part of the Léoville vineyard belonging to the Baron Poyferré de Céres. This was in 1866 when the two Rausan vineyards, soon to be split, Ducru-Beaucaillou, Durfort, Vivens and Batailley also changed hands. Ducru cost Mr and Mrs Nathaniel Johnston, of the Bordeaux wine family, 1 million frs. Three years earlier they had acquired Dauzac. Another successful member of the Chartrons wine trade, M. Herman Cruse paid 700,000 frs. for Pontet-Canet in 1865, and in the same year Lynch-Bages was purchased by another wine merchant, M. Cayrou. However the most notable sale of the decade was when Baron James de Rothschild bought Lafite in 1868 for the huge price of 4,140,000 frs.

These sales continued in the seventies. In 1870 the not very prominent growth of La Tertre in Arsac was acquired by M. Koenigswater for 530,000 frs. Cruse paid 1 million frs. for Giscours in 1875, and M. Labar bought Carbonnieux for 400,000 frs. in 1878. At the very beginning of the phylloxera devastation Ch. Margaux passed to Comte Pillet-Will for 5 million frs. in 1879. Speculation ran a little mad, and unlikely-looking châteaux were erected amid unprofitable vineyards.

Among the vineyard purchasers of this period should be included the English firm of Gilbey who purchased Loudenne in the Bas-Médoc in 1875 for 700,000 frs. or £28,000. Although acquired after a good deal of careful enquiry it was not exactly a fortunate deal, for four years later the phylloxera was upon them. However, publicly the Gilbeys never regretted their purchase, and Mr Alfred Gilbey senior, the partner principally concerned with Loudenne, optimistically compared its situation on a mild slope overlooking the Gironde with that of Cliveden on its steep crest above the Thames near Maidenhead. A palpable but pardonable exaggeration. However it has remained in the hands of the Gilbeys and their successors to this day, and ships passing up and down the Gironde will notice the Union Jack flying from the terrace of the charming, turreted, pink-washed château.

With the descent of the phylloxera on the vineyards, and the mildew which followed it, there came a change in the affairs of Bordeaux and the estates. The *vignoble* had reached its fullest extent and was never again to be quite so large again. Château construction was at an end, and the building in 1880 within the precincts of the

Mouton-Rothschild *chai* courtyard of the *Deuxième Empire* style villa, now called Petit-Mouton, must have been about the last for many years.

Yet châteaux continued to change hands: Durfort was sold again in 1882 for 450,000 frs. and La Lagune in 1886 for 340,000. In 1892 M. Dubos paid 770,000 frs. for Cantemerle, as affairs were rather better then. But henceforth the châteaux on the whole had a very thin time until the post-war boom years of the 1950s.

More details of the individual estates are given later in the appropriate chapters dealing with the districts.

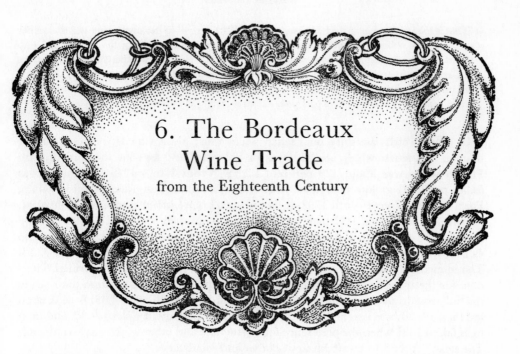

6. The Bordeaux Wine Trade
from the Eighteenth Century

This chapter is about commerce, and that inevitably means many facts and figures. Those who wish to skip them can do so without much loss of wine information, but they are important for those interested in the background of Bordeaux.

To sketch in briefly the history of the wine trade in Bordeaux from the eighteenth century onwards it is necessary to retrace our steps. In an earlier chapter I have shown that during the seventeenth century the Dutch largely came in to take the place of the English; the Chartrons became the Quartier Hollandais. At the beginning of that century English imports of Bordeaux wine averaged about 8,000 *tonneaux* a year. By 1663, after the restoration of Charles II, they had risen to 11,000 *tonneaux*, but there were periods of Anglo-French economic warfare; in 1678 and 1689 temporary total prohibitions were imposed on the import of French wines; and as soon as William III's wars with France began they fell away more or less permanently. In 1699 – 1703 Portugal and Spain already provided 90 per cent of annual English wine imports, with the other 10 per cent equally divided between Germany and France. Even a generation later when trade between England and France was rather better and England was importing 5,000 *tonneaux* from Bordeaux, the emergent French North American colonies were shipping 7,000 *tonneaux*.

For punitive duties and the Methuen Treaty with Portugal in 1703 combined to turn the English away from the French, and above all Bordeaux wines. By 1707 the English duty levied on a *tonneau* of Bordeaux wine was £55, thirteen times the price of a modest red Graves wine. The key formula had been devised in Article Two of the Methuen Treaty. In return for a Portuguese promise to admit in perpetuity British woollen goods, this Article in part says:

'That is to say, that her sacred Majesty of Great Britain shall in her own name and that of her successors, be obliged for ever hereafter to admit the wines of the growths of Portugal into Great Britain; so that at no time, whether there shall be peace or war between the kingdoms of Great Britain and France, anything more shall be demanded for these wines, by the name of customs or duty . . . than shall be demanded from like quantity or measure of French wine, *deducting or abating a third part of the custom or duty*.' (My italics.)

In other words the duty on French wines must always be 50 per cent higher than on Portuguese wines; and so it was for 128 years, and for 85 of them the duty on French wines was about 120 per cent higher. From 1707 – 1745 the impost was 5s.3d. per (old) gallon, compared with 2s.5d. for Portuguese (and Spanish) wines. For a further 37 years until 1782, it was 6s. (£63 per *tonneau*) compared with 2s.9d. for the Iberian wines, and then for four years it jumped to 9s.5d. (4s.10d.). More liberal ideas temporarily prevailed from 1786 – 1794 and the duty was dropped to 4s.10d. with a corresponding decrease in the duty on the favoured wines to 3s.1d. The immediate result was a doubling of French wine imports into the United Kingdom for the three following years. But as the Napoleonic Wars got into their stride the duty rose to over ten shillings per gallon, and higher still after 1803. A peak of no less than 19s.8d. was reached in 1813, and not until 1825 did it sink to 7s.3d. and then to 5s.6d. in 1831 when the preference for Portuguese and other wines was abandoned. The next step had to await Messrs Cobden and Gladstone.

As described earlier it was the Dutch who had saved the Bordeaux wine trade from the mid-sixteenth century onwards, and particularly since the seventeenth century. Not only in wine but also in *eau-de-vie*. In 1640 they were already importing 3,000 *barriques* from Bordeaux, whose reputation for *eau-de-vie* up to the eighteenth century was on a par with the *eau-de-vie* of La Rochelle or what is now called cognac. In 1677 a certain Jean Deschamp of Bordeaux was described as a '*brusleur d'eau-de-vie*'. In the exceptionally prosperous year of 1700 – 1 the Bordelais exported 90,000 hectolitres of spirit, of which 60 per cent went to Holland. Not all of this came from the Bordeaux area; much came from the former Gascon district of Armagnac. Also unsold Haut-Pays wine was often distilled in Bordeaux.

As to wine, in 1684 the Dutch bought 30,144 *tonneaux* of Bordeaux, 33,217 in 1699 – 1700, and no less than 43,733 in the following boom year. In these two latter years Dutch purchases were responsible for 65·5 per cent and 73·2 per cent of total Bordeaux wine exports by quantity. By 1717 the Bordeaux Chamber of Commerce, founded in 1705, was reporting an export to England of only 6,000 *tonneaux* of wine and *eau-de-vie* (perhaps 10 per cent of the total), compared with 34,000 to Holland, 6,500 to northern Europe, and 4,000 to the developing French colonies.

After the Revocation of the Edict of Nantes in 1685 many Huguenots of Bordeaux and South-West France emigrated to northern Europe and established commercial links with Bordeaux. In the same way Englishmen, Scotsmen and Irishmen of Jacobite sympathies and/or Roman Catholic religion came to Bordeaux to trade with their home countries. In return for wine Ireland used to send salt beef to Bordeaux; England was interested in the export of woollen goods.

The pattern of the export trade a little later was described in a memorandum of 1739, quoted by Malvezin in his *Histoire de la Vigne et du Vin en Aquitaine* (1919). The English consumption of Gascon wines was small, and then only the *grands vins*, selling for between 400 and 2,000 livres per *tonneau*. The second wines went to Scotland and Ireland. Holland drank very little of these types. They were mostly interested in the '*vins blancs de côtes*', from the sweet wine areas, the Entre-Deux-Mers, but above all from Bergerac (outside the region) and Ste-Foy. As for the Germans, they took the red *palus* wines and much the same whites as the Dutch. It was the Rhine wines that were fashionable in Germany, and only the common people drank Bordeaux.

Yet Bordeaux then as always had to live on exports; northern France drank other wines (the Paris region exported wines to Normandy and Picardy well into the eighteenth century), and the regional domestic market adjacent to Bordeaux was not nearly large enough to absorb the produce of a growing wine area. The surplus was one of the reasons for the distillation of *eau-de-vie*, until the Charentais took over most of the trade. Bordeaux's wine exports represented three-quarters of all French wine exports. Wine was the third most important item in the trade of Bordeaux after sugar and coffee, which were imported from the West Indies.

In fact, although the eighteenth century was an epoch of almost uninterrupted expansion for Bordeaux, the wine trade had its ups and downs. In addition to the continuing and increasing defection of the English there were the hazards of the vintage and the variations in the market. A notoriously bad vintage early in the century was the 1709. Then with the expansion of the *vignoble* there was over-production in the first quarter of the century; and from 1720 – 1730 a slump in wine prices.

Furthermore, as the Dutch increasingly lost their prominent economic position in Europe, so Bordeaux's wine trade with the Low Countries declined. As the Dutch had largely replaced the English earlier on, so northern Europe and particularly the North German Hanseatic cities stepped in during the second half of the eighteenth century. The Germans who had previously bought through Holland now imported direct, and the Netherlands substantially lost its entrepot role. By the Revolution the German colony in Bordeaux was larger than the Dutch; and henceforth until the First World War it was Germany which supplied the mass demand for the cheaper and medium-priced Bordeaux, particularly the red wines which had not directly interested the Dutch.

Also towards the end of the century other Baltic markets became important for Bordeaux: Sweden, Denmark, Prussia and even Russia, which by 1789 was taking 5 per cent of Bordeaux's exports.

The other developing market for Bordeaux wines were the French colonies, particularly the West Indies. In 1717 Bordeaux had exported 4,000 *tonneaux* to the French colonies; in 1788 the quantity had risen to 32,000 *tonneaux*, although by then French Canada had been lost.

Oddly enough the decline in trade with England helped the development of the leading estates in Bordeaux. As the duty was the same on a *premier cru* as on a *palus* wine, the rich English who could afford to drink claret naturally bought the finer wines, which relatively were better value for money. In Ireland and Scotland the duties against French wines were not so heavy, so they bought more but cheaper wines. For example, in 1740 Bordeaux sent 1,000 *tonneaux* to London, 2,500 *tonneaux* to Scotland, and 4,000 *tonneaux* to Ireland, but according to F. Crouzet's estimates their respective values came to 1 million livres, 1·5 million livres, and 1·6 million livres. In spite of everything the proprietors of Lafite, Haut-Brion and such second rank wines as Léoville and Rausan could count on selling their wines to the English aristocracy. Thus even in 1787 when the total exports to the British Isles only accounted for about 7 per cent in volume, the value was as high as 26 per cent. The cheap white wines that satisfied many of Bordeaux's customers were not worth a tenth of the fine wines.

An extract from a table of F. Crouzet in his chapter on the commerce of Bordeaux in *Bordeaux au XVIIIe Siècle* (1968) shows the changing pattern of the Gironde wine exports by percentage of volume.

Percentage Totals of Bordeaux wine exports by volume to the principal destinations

	Netherlands	Northern Europe	British Isles	French Colonies
1717	67	13	12	8
1751–1753	41	37	6	14
1775–1777	35	36	4	23
1787	14	39	7	32
1789	10	46	5	34

The 1787 figures for Britain given above are a little misleading, as they reflected a jump in exports following the relaxation of duties in 1786. It is worth noting that the rise in exports was not particularly vigorous in the eighteenth century. From 62,000 *tonneaux* in 1700 – 1, they dropped to 50,000 *t.* in 1715, reached a 128,000 *t.* peak in 1765, slumped badly in the 1770s, and achieved a pre-Revolutionary maximum of 113,000 *t.* in 1785; and this rise in exports was entirely accounted for by the colonial trade. Yet the value rose between 1728 – 1734 and 1774 – 80 from 6 m. livres to 20 m. livres – far more than the rise in the domestic French price of wine. This M. Crouzet attributes to the rise in the quality of Bordeaux wines, and in particular the birth of the *grands crus*.

The French colonies not only helped to solve the Bordeaux merchants' quests for new export markets; they also eased the difficulties of the Haut-Pays wine-growers, whose produce was largely marketed and exported by the Gironde trade. During the century the proportion of '*vins de haut*' exported rose from 10 per cent of the total to 25 per cent in the 1770s. Libourne was a great port for the wines of Monbazillac and Bergerac.

After American Independence in 1776 Bordeaux's trade with the former English colonies increased, but was not considerable in wines and spirits for which there was little demand. In 1789 only 27,000 livres-worth of wine was included in total Bordeaux exports to the U.S.A. of 373,000 livres; but Bordeaux was the chief French port for the American trade.

Altogether wine became decreasingly important in the economy of Bordeaux.

Whereas in the first third of the eighteenth century it was the major export in terms of money, as the general export trade with the French colonies increased – and it was this import-export colonial trade which was responsible for the city's great prosperity in this century and not wine – so did the share of wine drop. Between 1778 and 1786 there was another slump in wine prices, and on the eve of the Revolution wine accounted for not much more than 25 per cent of the total trade of a port, which from a comparatively modest size in 1715 had now become the largest in France. Nevertheless wine remained a vital part of the commerce. In 1760 – 1768 wine exports averaged 76,000 *tonneaux*, and certainly less than a half was drunk in the region. In the middle of the century when output had been about 130,000 *tonneaux* domestic consumption had accounted for only 55,000 *tonneaux*.

Although the Revolution in its early, anti-monarchical stages had the support of the middle class Bordelais – hence the Girondins – trade suffered. This was basically owing to the wars with the English that broke out towards the close of the century and continued intermittently until the final fall of Napoleon in 1815. Also the merchants, who had clearly done very well for themselves in the pre-revolutionary epoch, were heavily taxed on their wines. The size of the Girondin *vignoble* contracted from 135,000 hectares in 1789 to 99,000 hectares in 1808, and did not recover its pre-revolutionary extent until 1835 when it reached 133,000 hectares. Yet total production in 1808 was only slightly less than twenty years earlier. The average price of Bordeaux wines, excluding the classed growths, was almost halved in the post-revolutionary era and did not recover and surpass its 1789 level until the Elba exile of Napoleon in 1814. There was then a brief inter-war boom, including a flood of exports to Britain, which did not recur after the final defeat and exile of Napoleon a year later. Throughout the period of the Revolution, Directory and Empire wine exports fell away sharply, from a maximum of 100,000 *tonneaux* a year between 1783 and 1789 to 25,000.

Moreover although this period comprehended some very fine vintages (including 1795, the exceptional and plentiful 1798, followed by 1802, 1803, 1807 and the famous Comet Year of 1811), growers and merchants had great difficulties in selling their wines. This was partly owing to the drop in exports, partly to the problems of selling Bordeaux through France (Napoleon drank Burgundy). When the short 1814 boom arrived many proprietors still had on their hands wines from the 1802 to 1811 vintages. However demand for the leading wines improved towards the end of Napoleon's reign, and between 1811 and 1814 the price of first growths doubled; in 1814 buyers came in from Britain, Holland, Germany, Scandinavia and even from Russia.

Yet with the Bourbon Restoration, in spite of promises of reduced taxation, trade again declined. A strongly protectionist policy was followed, with consequent harm to the export trade. As shown above, the English duties on French wines were not reduced dramatically on the Bourbons' return; they remained largely political in intent and a weapon of economic warfare. Nevertheless when the English did equalize their duties on foreign wines in 1831, this was a liberalizing measure which was later followed by French trade agreements with other countries. In 1843, for example, a Franco-Belgian commercial treaty improved trade with one of Bordeaux's important customers. With the United States trade was increasing but difficult, owing to double duties: one on quantity and a second *ad valorem*. There were stories of the American customs authorities, traditionally zealous, seizing shiploads of Bordeaux wines if the paperwork did not tally as to the value. However over the years Bordeaux exports did improve, and between 1815 and 1850 the annual average for the world was 50,000 *tonneaux*.

In the 1850s the Second Empire prosperity was interrupted for the wine trade by the sudden incidence of the oidium disease, described in Chapter One. It came on very quickly in 1852 – 3, and was conquered by 1857, but in the intervening years the Bordeaux crop was heavily reduced. From over $2\frac{1}{4}$ million hectolitres in 1850 it dropped to 726,000 hectolitres in 1854 and 319,000 in 1855. Throughout France the vine crop slumped from over 55 million hectolitres down to 10 million hectolitres; it had the effect in Bordeaux of raising prices sharply and they never went back.

How sharply they rose is demonstrated by comparing the average prices of the classed growths as given in the 1853 and 1868 editions of Wilhelm Franck's manual, *Traité sur les Vins du Médoc*. In the earlier year prices, which no doubt reflected the onset of the oidium, were little changed from the first edition (1824), as mentioned in the chapter on the Classification (page 253).

	1853	1868
First growths	1800–2400 frs.	4500–5000 frs.
Second growths	2000–2100	3500
Third growths	1800	3000
Fourth growths	1500	2000–2500
Fifth growths	1200	1500–1800

In the same period the prices of Sauternes went up from 450 – 1,200 frs. in 1853 to 1,000 – 3,000 frs. The wide range is explained by the high prices reached by the few top growths. By 1868 Yquem was much dearer than the others. It will also be noted how the first growths had outdistanced their rivals in price. In the heyday of Victorian and Second Empire luxurious living, the rich were calling for the well-known 'names'.

Commercially Bordeaux's chief target at this period was Britain, which in 1840 had actually increased slightly the duty on wine to 5s.9$\frac{1}{4}$d. a gallon, although without any discrimination against the French. In 1846 Frédéric Bastiat, who lived in the Landes and was a great agitator for free trade on the British model, organized in Bordeaux an Association for Free Trade, and in August of that year the association gave a banquet in Paris for Richard Cobden, the British apostle of free trade. The tenaciously tariff-minded French industry and administration had to be converted, and the successful 1855 International Exhibition in Paris, which was visited by Queen Victoria and for which the Médoc classification was prepared, was a step on the road. However the final adherence of the French Government, whose chief negotiator with Cobden was Michel Chevalier, was only secured by the agreement of the British Government to reduce the duties on French wines.

After long negotiations an Anglo-French Commercial Treaty was signed on 23 January 1860, and the duty on table wines was at once reduced to 3s. a gallon, and then to 1s. a gallon (2d. a bottle) the following January. W. E. Gladstone, the Chancellor of the Exchequer, is generally associated with this reduction in duty, and rightly so, for it was he who secured the agreement of the British Cabinet and Parliament to the terms of the treaty. 'Gladstone's Claret' and 'Chancellor's Claret' became known for many years, and British wine drinkers of left-wing sympathies do not forget that the next chancellor who made a substantial reduction in the duty on table wines was the Labour Chancellor, Sir Stafford Cripps, in 1949.

The President of the Bordeaux Chamber of Commerce described the Treaty as 'a commercial action of the highest importance', and British wine imports from France rose from 700,000 gallons in 1859 to 2,227,000 gallons in 1861; the great majority came from Bordeaux.

To complete this happy and all too rare reduction in wine duties, some argument followed with the British wine trade, because the 1s. a gallon duty applied only to wines up to 18 degrees of proof spirit on the British scale, the equivalent of between 10 and 11 per cent of alcohol on the French (Gay-Lussac) scale. This was lower than any fine Bordeaux wines, and at the 1862 International Exhibition in London it was demonstrated that the average strength of the wines shown was over 18 degrees (Sikes). Higher duties obtained on stronger wines, with an overall rate of 2s. 5d. on all wines imported in bottle. Finally in April 1862 an amendment was made by which all table wines not exceeding 25 degrees (Sikes), or just over 14 per cent alcohol (Gay-Lussac) came in at 1s. a gallon, those not exceeding 42 degrees (24 per cent) paid 2s. 6d. and the wines in bottle incurred what became known as 'the bottle surcharge of 2s. 6d. a gallon, i.e. the additional duty on château-bottled claret was 5d. Today the British duty rates are still levied at these levels of strength, although in the 1880s the maximum for table wines was temporarily raised to 30 degrees (17 per cent). The Gladstonian duties remained unchanged until the close of the century; in 1899 the duty on table wines imported in cask was raised to 1s. 3d. a gallon, but the bottle surcharge being correspondingly reduced by 3d. to 2s. 3d. Nowadays when we in Britain consider ourselves fortunate if the duty is not increased every year, such stability for nearly 40 years seems inconceivable.

These figures are given in some detail, because they had a profound and immediate influence on the Bordeaux trade. Not only did sales to Britain soar; the position of the growers and merchants alike was strengthened. Moreover the charges led to a succession of commercial treaties reducing duties with other countries: another Franco-Belgian Treaty in 1861, a Franco-Prussian Treaty in 1862 and a Franco-Zollverein Treaty in 1865. For a few years in Europe there was a spirit of economic optimism and expansion. Yet during a short economic crisis in France in 1867 already there were manufacturing interests calling for the cancellation of the tariff concessions on British manufactured goods made by the French Government in the Anglo-French Treaty of 1860.

The purchase of classed-growth châteaux in the Médoc by the merchants, mentioned in the last chapter, demonstrated the prosperity of the Bordeaux trade in the

1860s, the second half of the Second Empire, and a period of economic expansion for France and of great wealth for the bankers, railway builders and other entrepreneurs; though not for their employees as the Paris Commune was to show in 1871. The cream of the wine trade was in the hands of a comparatively small number of firms – the commercial aristocracy of the Chartrons. Until 1860 about forty merchants dominated the export trade, each specializing in its own class of wine suited to the various markets. An example of the expansion of markets in the 1860s was Argentina. Her imports of Bordeaux wines rose from 35,000 hectolitres in 1859 to 233,000 in 1869. U.S. imports were about 200,000 hectolitres in the late 1860s.

Between 1846 and 1870 exports tripled, from an average of 445,000 hectolitres in the decade ending in 1846 to 1,187,000 in the five years culminating in 1870. By 1875 they had risen even higher to 1,500,000 hectolitres.

Several firms well known today opened their doors between 1860 and 1870, as described in the chapter on the wine merchants. Moreover the growers were able to assert themselves. Previously, apart from the first growths and a few well-known 'names', a great deal of wine exported from Bordeaux was sold under the importing merchants' names rather than of the châteaux or communes. Now these, particularly the better-known châteaux, began to publicize their names.

As indicated, the prosperity began before 1860. It was really the after-effects of the oidium in the mid-1850s which touched it off. The result was a tremendous increase in price for the diminished supplies available. Whereas in 1852 the average price of Bordeaux wine in cask was 30 frs. per hectolitre, by 1854 – in the middle of the oidium period – it was 145 frs. and even 120 frs. in the celebrated and plentiful vintage of 1858. The peak was reached in 1862, a moderate year for quality, with an average price of 221 frs. per hectolitre. For wine was still short overall; there had not been a harvest exceeding 2 million hectolitres since 1850.

However a series of exceptionally plentiful years lay ahead, beginning with the indifferent vintage of 1863, when 2·2 million hectolitres were produced. From then on until the last good pre-phylloxera vintage in 1878, only in two years were less than 2 million hectolitres produced, with 4·5 million hectolitres in 1869 and over 5 million apiece in 1874 and 1875. In these latter years this was partly owing to extensive planting in the later sixties, which bore fruit by 1873. The Gironde *vignoble* which hitherto had never exceeded 135,000 hectares suddenly expanded to 145,000 hectares. This growth was common throughout France, and in 1875 the fantastic national total of 83·8 million hectolitres was produced, compared with an average of 60 million hectolitres today. Naturally in this period of plenty the average price of Bordeaux wine dropped sharply, and by 1870 it was down to 80 frs. per hectolitre.

The Anglo-French Treaty of 1860 also had a big effect on wine drinking in Britain. If 'Gladstone's Claret' and 'grocer's Claret' became terms of disdain in some circles, since it was now possible for licensed grocers to sell this inexpensive wine carrying only a duty of 2d. a bottle, the demand for claret greatly increased in Britain.

Nevertheless it must not be imagined that in Britain claret flowed like water. True, imports in 1860 – 2 were three times higher than in the three pre-treaty years, but they started at a very low ebb, at around 20,000 hectolitres a year. André Simon pointed out in *Vintagewise* (1945) that in 1859 the little island of Mauritius was importing 40,000 hectolitres, while in the U.S.A. the total of Gironde wine imported was just on 150,000 hectolitres. Owing to the Civil War American imports suffered later in the 1860s, but recovered afterwards. The British market was still above all a 'quality' one, for only the well-off could afford to drink wine. Nevertheless of the wine drunk in England the percentage of French wine rose from 9·5 per cent in 1859 to 41·9 per cent in 1880. Thereafter it fell back slightly.

The popularity of claret was also linked with the improvement in the vintages of the Sixties compared with the Fifties. Christie's wine sales show the shortage of mature clarets until the later years. In 1862 the miserable '54s with their flavour of oidium rot, were fetching over 60s. a dozen. The Lafite '54 made 73s. The pre-oidium Lafite '51, no great vintage, made 139s. per case of 6 magnums. Two years later Lafite '48, 'magnificent and almost matchless wine', sold for 130s. Thereafter prices appeared to decline for all but particular wines of outstanding vintages of the 1840s or of 1858. In 1867 magnums of Latour '41 from Lord Bath's cellar fetched the very high price of £16 a case, though bottles of Lafite '41 from Christophers made only 88s. At this sale Lafite 1848 'château seal, bought of M. Goudal' (manager of Lafite) went for 126s., and Lafite '58, 'bottled at the château bought of M. Goudal 1864' attained 105s. In the same year the celebrated Lafite '64 reached Christie's and sold at 68s. At this sale Yquem '47 went for 120s. and the '51 at 92s. The value of money was at least five times higher than it is today.

So far as Bordeaux was concerned the years up to 1878 were the sunshine before the storm; with the onslaught of the phylloxera, the area under vines diminished slightly and the output of wine sharply declined. Although Bordeaux suffered less than other French wine districts, there was not another 3 million hectolitre vintage until 1893. The Gironde *vignoble* did not decline substantially, unlike the rest of France, whose overall vineyard area by 1899 was only two-thirds of its peak in the mid-1870s. In 1889 total French wine output was only 23 million hectolitres compared with 70 million ten years earlier. By the end of the century the total French vineyard area was less than 1·7 million hectares; three-quarters of a million hectares fewer than before the phylloxera.

This decline was not, as often attributed, solely owing to the phylloxera and the succeeding mildew. A general crisis in France in 1873 set off a slow decline in prices that continued for over 20 years. There was another crisis in 1882, which affected Britain, Germany and the U.S.A. as well as France. By 1896 when the drop in prices was arrested, they were down by 40 per cent compared with 1873. Thereafter they slowly rose, being 20 per cent up on the 1896 level by 1906 and 40 per cent by 1912. Yet in that latter year, according to A. Viallate in *L'Activité Economique en France de la fin du XVIIIe Siècle à Nos Jours* (1937), the price index was 118 compared with 144 in 1873.

The result of the recurrent economic difficulties in France led to the growth of a tariff lobby antagonistic to the free trade principles which had inspired the 1860 Anglo-French Treaty.

The lobby was not purely one-sided. An English pamphlet, *Our Trade with France*

Under the Cobden Treaty 1859 – 1880 (1881), the cover of which proclaimed Britain's adverse trade balance with France over the period as £480,463,630, produced statistics to show the way in which French wine imports into Britain had risen, from a mere £559,304 in 1859 to no less than £3,283,091 in 1880. In fact, after the initial post-treaty burst they did not exceed £1 million until 1866, but then advanced to £2 million in 1871, and £3 million in 1873, thereafter varying between about £2½ million and £3 million until the 1880 total quoted above. That is if these barbed statistics are reliable. Most of these imports will have come from Bordeaux.

After some hard bargaining the Anglo-French Treaty was renewed in 1873 but finally lapsed, when no further agreement could be reached, in 1882. However, by then so far as the British drinker of Bordeaux was concerned, the treaty had done its job, and until the outbreak of the Second World War the duties on French wines were no serious impediment to their consumption.

In the latter part of the last century it was the wine industry, dependent on exports, which had led all others in demanding the reduction of French tariffs, and Bordeaux had benefited particularly from the reduction of English duties on light wines, for those of some other French wine districts were often alcoholic enough to incur the higher rate of duty.

However the drop of wine production in the 1880s led to an insufficiency of wine for domestic consumption. As a result, for the first time in French history, wine was imported on a large scale. Whereas in the 1870s, before the phylloxera, no more than 50,000 hectolitres of wine entered France annually, in the 1880s the totals surpassed first 1 million hectolitres and then 2 million. Even in the 1890s when the vineyards with their grafted vines had more or less recovered, imports still fluctuated between 1·2 million and 2·3 million hectolitres. Although in the period leading up to the First World War they dropped to an average of three-quarters of a million hectolitres, no return was achieved to the pre-phylloxera trickle.

Much of this wine came from the new vineyards in Algeria, whose abundant supplies of inexpensive, robust wines were for the next three-quarters of a century as welcome to the French wine merchants as they were hated by the growers of the extensive vineyards of the Midi, whose wines often lacked the body of those on the other side of the Mediterranean. Even after Algerian independence in 1960, its wine was allowed to be called French wine; a blend of Algerian and Bordeaux could legally be described as French – though not as Bordeaux. This situation lasted until 1967 when the protests of the southern French wine growers led to the admission of Algerian wine only under licence and the withdrawal of its status as 'produce of France'. Such restriction benefited Bordeaux, which could sell its lesser and off-vintage wines to the Midi producers, giving local wines quality if not body.

It was not only the Algerian wine growers who were stimulated by the drought of French wine in the 1880s. An impetus was given to wine growing and marketing in Italy, Spain, Portugal and other Mediterranean countries, who at the cheaper end of the wine list, increasingly became France's competitors instead of her customers. Moreover Spanish and Italian wines were widely imported into Bordeaux for blending and supplementing its own thin wines in short supply.

From this period too stems the use of French wine-district names by growers in other countries competing in world markets. 'Graves', 'Sauternes', and even 'Claret-Type' appeared on wines originating far from France, let alone Bordeaux. At the time the growers of Bordeaux and elsewhere were too poor, too unorganized and perhaps too indifferent to fight the misappropriation of what were later to be called their *appellations d'origine*. Since then they have had cause to regret their negligence.

Perhaps the French wine shortage also encouraged the development of wine growing in the United States too. For whereas in 1874 the total imports of French wines amounted to 218,000 hectolitres, thirty years later they were down to 28,000, and dropped further thereafter, until Prohibition in 1919 gave them a knock-out blow from which they took many years to recover even after Repeal in 1933.

It should be mentioned, perhaps, that although the top ranks of Bordeaux wines were temporarily affected by natural disasters and economic difficulties, demand for them did not drop; it was the lesser wines, the *crus bourgeois*, *crus artisans* and *crus paysans* that suffered, for it was these which had to face competition from other wine-growing countries. As in the Côte d'Or, some marginal areas, particularly the *palus* vineyards, marginal in more than one sense, were not re-planted, although in Bordeaux the decline in vineyard area really began in the present century; by 1911 it was down to 136,000 hectares.

Meanwhile in the arduous Eighties the Bordeaux merchants embarked on a lengthy agitation for the reduction in the number and value of the internal taxes on alcoholic drinks, whose yield had doubled from 223 million frs. in 1870 to 450 million frs. in 1880. They were also concerned over a minor economic war which had broken out between France and the United States of America, following the prohibition in France of American salt pork. As in the 'chicken war' of a few years ago when the import of American 'broilers' into France was stopped, this led to American retaliation, which clapped extra duties on French wines, so that wines in bottles carried a duty of 14 cents (7d.) and champagne no less than 60 cents (2s. 6d.). Wines imported in cask were also penalized. The Bordeaux merchants, who suffered specially from this warfare, were quite willing at least in theory to eat humble salt pork pie, and urged their government to lift the ban and to make a commercial treaty with America, as they had done with Britain, to the great profit of both; but without any immediate result.

The shortage and consequent high prices of wines in France resulted in falsification and sophistication which led to scandals. In particular these were exposed by the Paris municipal analysis laboratory. The consequence was a questioning of the quality of French wines in importing countries, including Britain, Germany and the United States, much in the same way as recent *appellation contrôlée* and 'non-beaujolais' disclosures in Britain shook public confidence. Then as now, voices were raised to protest that such scandals should not be made known publicly as they 'harmed the reputation' of French wines.

The flood of foreign wines, particularly from Spain and Italy, made the French wine trade in general go over to advocating tariffs against them, but the Bordeaux commerce was by now so deeply involved in the cheap, blended wine business, that it raised an outcry when the government introduced the Meline tariff in 1892. All the advanced countries were now becoming tariff-minded, not least the U.S.A., whose McKinley Tariff Act of 1890 helped to set the pace. Of course the countries on whose wines France levied duties proceeded to protect their own wine industry.

The French Government softened the blow to the Bordelais by establishing a local 'free port' area, supervised by the Customs, in which imported wines intended for blending and re-export only were kept duty-free. This was satisfactory enough for the merchants, but much less so for the growers who claimed, with justification, that the shipment of blended, non-Bordeaux wines was harmful to the reputation of Bordeaux. So in 1897 these facilities were restricted to wines intended for countries outside Europe – on the grounds presumably that the 'natives' (including Australians and Americans) would never notice. In 1899 these 'free ports' were finally closed. The following year the government, moved partly by the wine trade's representations and partly because of the heavy spirit drinking in France, decided that wine consumption should be encouraged. Taxes were considerably reduced and all were removed except a single tax, the *droit de circulation*, which was fixed at 1·50 frs. per hectolitre.

Nevertheless the period between 1900 and 1914 was a hard one for Bordeaux, particularly for the growers. Prices tended to drop over the years. According to figures given in the Chamber of Deputies, the average price of a *barrique* of Bordeaux wine fell from 142·5 frs. in 1905 to 105 frs. in 1910. While exports were quantitatively lower than in the 1880s (when the totals probably included foreign wines blended in), prices were even lower still. Whereas in 1890 Gironde wine exports to the United Kingdom totalled nearly 212,000 hectolitres, from 1900 to 1914 they averaged 110,000 hectolitres.

The pattern of Bordeaux exports and their relation to other French wine exports in the period before the First World War is illustrated by statistics for the year 1910 quoted by Jan Salavert in *Le Commerce des Vins de Bordeaux* (1912):

	Exports in cask	Exports in bottle	Total other French wine exports
Great Britain	100,881 hl.	9,096 hl.	42,764 hl.
Germany	221,159	1,810	193,407
Belgium	110,408	2,282	186,836
Holland	89,780	1,047	10,757
U.S.A.	5,798	4,962	1,271
Argentine	87,958	1,355	32,415

Value of Bordeaux exports in cask–57,760 million frs.

Value of other French wine exports in cask–51,716 million frs.

Value of Bordeaux exports in bottle–7,872 million frs.

Value of other French wine in bottle–4,959 million frs.

It will be observed that two out of every three bottles of French wine imported into Britain in 1910 came from the Gironde. These figures also show not only the predominance of Bordeaux in the French wine export trade, but also the vital importance of the German market, which bought the cheaper wines; when it collapsed after the First World War it meant the decline and disappearance of many of the *crus bourgeois*. Moreover the above export totals were a sad falling-off compared with the pre-phylloxera, pre-slump years. Whereas in 1875 the Gironde exported 1½ million hl. the quantities dropped steadily, and by 1912 they had fallen by exactly 50 per cent – to ¾ million hl.

For although the Edwardian era is now looked back on in some quarters as a golden sunset before the carnage and social upheavals of the First World War, this was not a period of prosperity for any but the upper strata of society. It is perhaps significant that the turnover of the International Exhibition Co-operative Wine Society, founded in London in 1874 and in 1900 composed of about 2,000 members drawn from the professional classes, scarcely advanced. It was about £16,000 in 1900 and £19,000 in 1913, although the membership had risen by a thousand. Wine prices remained unaltered over the years in a manner scarcely credible today, while British wages and salaries scarcely moved between 1896 and 1914.

In France economic conditions did not favour wine drinking, and there was a decline in consumption; indeed some doctors were suggesting publicly that wine was not all that good for the health. Salavert summed up the situation sorrowfully:

'In *bourgeois* circles the number of drinkers of water and milk are growing; on the most lavish tables the good French wines are often replaced by bottles of insipid and disagreeable water, which is thought to be harmless; whereas formerly it was a luxury to have a well-furnished cellar, today one prefers to have an automobile, and rely by chance on the merchant when one wants to drink a good bottle. In working class circles wine is being replaced by spirits.'

So the pre-1914 era was not quite the golden period of discriminating connoisseurs and splendid, inexpensive wines as it is sometimes made out to be. The latter at least was to come later.

Nor, as already mentioned earlier, did the developing United States help much. The average annual imports of wine from the Gironde between 1900 and 1914 were only 11,400 hectolitres.

Bordeaux was not as badly affected as some other areas, owing to its reputation for good quality wines, to the exertions of its merchants in overseas markets, and the fact that the red wines at least could be kept for a time. However, the growers could not hold stock for four or five years; they had to unload, thus accelerating the drop in prices. Often the money they received from the merchants was less than the cost of production, and bitter feeling developed between growers and traders, the former accusing the latter of being responsible for the low prices.

One cause at least of the crisis was over-production. Whereas in the five years ending in 1892 the average Bordeaux output was 2·13 million hectolitres, it rose steadily, reached 3·7 million in the quinquennium ending in 1902 and 3·99 million in the following five years. There was no real delimitation of the Gironde *vignoble* and no control of production; much of the wine was inferior and badly made; this was made worse by the poor vintages. After three disastrous crops in the first three years of the century, 1901 – 3, there was not one outstanding year up to 1914, the best being 1906.

This over-production had been made worse by *chaptalisation*, or sugaring of the must, to raise the alcoholic strength of the weak wine. In 1890 sugar used for vinification was de-taxed, and this was not reversed until 1907, when it had become such an open scandal that a heavy tax was imposed, in order to drive the producers of 'artificial wine' out of business. However as this tax did not apply to purchases of small quantities of sugar under 25 kilograms, the wine 'manufacturers' were not very effectively deterred, although it is claimed that not much sugaring was practised in the Gironde after 1903. However it was not uncommon for producers to sell more wine than they had made by watering it, a highly illegal operation known as *mouillage*.

In such conditions recriminations were exchanged between growers and merchants. The growers blamed the merchants for selling 'imported' wine, to which the latter replied that if they did not do so, their foreign competitors would do so direct to Bordeaux's customers; another exculpatory argument heard since. The growers alleged that the high price of the wine to the consumer was because it passed through too many hands.

From this unsatisfactory state of affairs in the French wine area two developments stem: first the formation of growers' co-operatives, although in the Gironde they only started in the equally difficult Inter-War years. There are now over 60 Gironde co-operatives and they produce 20 per cent of the total Bordeaux output. The other change was direct-selling to customers. This latter trend has not stopped since, with the result France has never had a body of good retail wine merchants as has existed in Britain, the Low Countries and even to some degree in the United States. Not only the growers but also the merchants sell direct to private customers. One large Bordeaux firm told me a few years ago that they had 3,000 private clients inside France. Throughout the country direct grower-consumer sale has expanded greatly in the past few years.

The misuse of French wine names in other countries spread further. At the Paris Exhibition of 1900 the jury judging the wine section found on display many foreign wines bearing French names. They refused to examine them. However that did not prevent the marketing of such items as Californian 'Mâcon', Crimean 'Lafitte', Bessarabian 'Médoc', Caucasian 'St-Emilion' or 'les Lur-Saluce, Le Château Yquem of the Crimea'. This last item was no doubt retrieved from the siege of Sebastopol!

Salavert, quoted above, also took a side-swipe at America and attacked Russia on similar lines. 'Everyone knows that in the United States one finds wines carrying French labels with no kind of authentic origin; one sees the "Bordeaux" and the "Mâcon" fabricated entirely in California or other parts of the United States; also in Russia one finds the Lur Saluces, the Château Yquems, the Château Margaux of the Crimea, the word Crimea being dissimulated in a corner of the label; one finds Russian wines under the names of Sauternes, Haut Sauternes, Chablis; Bessarabian wines under the names of Saint Georges, Graves, Médoc; Crimean wines under the names of Bordeaux, Lafite, Muscat de Lunel, Sauternes and even in the restaurants bottles labelled "Saint Emilion of the Caucasus".'

After this who can deny progress over the years in the matter of *appellation d'origine*?

One result and positive gain from this unhappy period was the delimitation of the vineyard area of the Gironde department on 18 February 1911. Outlying districts such as Arcachon and parts of the Lesparre commune at one end, and sections of Castelnau, St-Symphorien and Bazas at the other end of the region, were no longer permitted to call their wines Bordeaux. This was the first step that was eventually to lead to the institution of *appellation contrôlée* in 1935.

The war years of 1914 – 18 were marked in Bordeaux by a continuation of the poor vintages of the previous decade, along with large-scale requisitioning of wine for the army. This no doubt brought in a good deal of trade, and 810,000 hectolitres of the 1917 vintage, nearly a quarter of the crop, were requisitioned. But it was not very profitable business and clearly unpopular in Bordeaux, for as soon as the war was over the representations of the local senators and deputies in January 1919 secured the end of this requisitioning. The war years also marked a further decline in the vineyard area, since the *bourgeois* growths were cut off from their principal market in Germany. By 1917 the area under vines was down to 130,000 hectares.

Immediately after the war, conditions temporarily improved with the expected post-war boom. This was backed up by a series of splendid vintages unparalleled since the Seventies; and more wine was produced in the Gironde than at any time in its history. Unfortunately the boom petered out under the influence of the ensuing economic difficulties. Trade was poor during the second half of the Twenties and disastrously bad in the Thirties, following the onset of the World Slump in 1929. Germany, the source of much of Bordeaux's bread-and-butter business, was in a state of collapse, and when the Nazis took power in 1933, for political and autarchy reasons they almost prohibited the import of French wines. As a result the lesser *bourgeois* and other minor growths were even worse hit than they had been in the pre-war period. How small most of the growers were is shown by the fact that in 1923 there were 60,000 wine producers in the Gironde, and four-fifths of them owned less than 3 hectares apiece; only 385 owned more than 30 hectares. From the Inter-War years, and particularly from the 1930s, dates the decline of the small estates and the contraction of the whole Bordeaux *vignoble*, which had once more expanded after the First World War. By 1939 it was only 131,000 hectares.

As in the 1900s, difficulties in selling Bordeaux wines were accentuated by the huge production. It has been mentioned that in the five years ending in 1907 average annual output was $3 \cdot 99$ million hectolitres. Yet from 1919 – 29 the average was $4 \cdot 8$ million hectolitres and from 1930 – 9 it was 4 million in a world that could often not afford bread let alone wine.

Part of the trouble during this period was the poor standard of much Bordeaux wine, with quality sacrificed to quantity. In 1919 the system of named *appellations* was introduced throughout France, but no question of quality entered into it. This proved so inadequate that further legislation in 1927 did provide considerations of quality: no hybrid vines were allowed and only areas suitable for wine production could carry an *appellation*. Nationally this did nothing to stop the increase in production and little to stop the spread of vineyards, although this last did not apply to

Bordeaux. So in 1929 a law was passed forbidding additional planting on any property over 10 hectares; and growers producing more than 400 hectolitres (roughly 44 *tonneaux*) were not permitted to sell more than a proportion of their crop with *appellation*.

The negative results of these three pieces of legislation on output can be seen from the figures. The total quantity of French wine declared with *appellation d'origine* rose from 5 million hectolitres in 1923 to 9·95 million in 1931 and 15·7 million in 1934. Then in July 1935, largely as the results of long agitation by Jean Capus, former deputy and senator for the Gironde and one-time Minister of Agriculture, a law was passed setting up the *Comité National des Appellations d'Origine* to administer a strict system of *appellation contrôlée*. The result of the Loi Capus, as it is appropriately known, was the establishment of the *Institut National des Appellations d'Origine des Vins et Eaux-de-Vie*, which had the immense task of providing, in effect, a complete wine map of France, with strict de-limitation. Also the correct *appellations* for every area entitled to them had to be fixed, along with permissible grape varieties, conditions of culture, minimum alcoholic strengths for all *appellations* and maximum permitted quantities that could be sold with these fixed *appellations d'origine*. It was an immense task that was not completed until after the Second World War.*

In Bordeaux the new control operated from 1936 and the amount of *appellation* wine fell off dramatically, although until 1942 the total was swollen by *appellation simple* wines, whose right to their names stemmed from the 1927 law. In 1947, the first peace-time year of relatively normal conditions, the Bordeaux *AC* wines amounted to 2·77 million hectolitres out of a total French wine harvest of 39 million hectolitres and an *AC* total of 5·5 million. In the last ten years the amount of *AC* wine has tended to rise. In 1967, a very plentiful year, Bordeaux produced 3·35 million hectolitres out of a national *AC* total of 9·66 million.

During the 1930s the château owners were all losing money and the merchants were not doing much better, although trade improved from 1937 onwards. Under such conditions it was, of course, a wonderfully cheap time for buying fine wines; for those who had the money and the taste – the latter being more prevalent than the former. English wine merchants could buy splendid wines at very low prices. Ronald Avery of Bristol has told me that he bought Latour 1920 at opening prices for 110s. a case duty paid and Latour 1929 at 76s. In the mid-1930s, the Wine Society paid £12.5s. a *barrique* for 50 *barriques* of Beychevelle 1934. Thirty years later the 1964 wine of this château was first offered at £150 a hogshead.

Indeed in the 1930s claret and white Bordeaux were cheaper than they had ever been, and in fairness to growers and merchants one must hope that relatively they will never be so cheap again. On the eve of the Second World War it was possible in Britain to buy fine 1920, 1924, 1928 and 1929 château-bottled clarets for between six and eight shillings a bottle. In 1940 I paid 7s.10d. for Latour 1929. Now it would be difficult to find a bottle of this distinguished wine under £10.

In the Second World War, after the 'phoney war' period of 1939 – 40 when it was

---

*A list of Bordeaux *appellations contrôlées*, minimum strengths in degrees (Gay-Lussac), and maximum output per hectare is given in Appendix D.

generally 'business as usual', the problems of Bordeaux were largely those of shortage of manpower to look after the vineyards and of chemicals to keep the vines free from disease. There was a steady black market in copper sulphate. The châteaux were occupied by German troops who had strict instructions not to loot the cellars, which on the whole they did not. The Nazi authorities wished to keep on good terms with the French *bourgeoisie*. They made an agreement with the Vichy Government by which they undertook to buy a certain quota of ordinary French wines, but would purchase the finer Bordeaux (and Burgundies) only from those merchants who had sold to Germany prior to the war. This certainly protected French-owned fine wine from confiscation and major pilfering, but in view of the way the Nazis behaved elsewhere in France, it is not surprising that after the war questions were asked about the trade, and punishment demanded. In the end all the Bordeaux firms that had made profits on these deals were required to refund them to the government.

Some 'enemy-owned' wine was confiscated by the Germans, but often was paid for, as at least one English wine merchant discovered after the war, when he found a tidy balance in his firm's name lying in a Paris bank; but by then he would rather have had the wine he had bought but not shipped before the fall of France.

Since the last war, after the initial post-war difficulties were overcome, the Bordeaux trade has enjoyed a period of prosperity unequalled since the Second Empire and pre-phylloxera epoch. At first the growers did less well, as prices rose substantially only in the mid-1950s when the châteaux' proprietors began to see some return on their expenditure; and then estates became reasonably profitable. The prosperity has been unequal. As in other fields, it has been the best-known properties and the biggest merchants who have fared best. Most significant of all has been the great increase in the prices of the four *premiers crus*, and Mouton-Rothschild, Cheval-Blanc and Pétrus. Since the mid-1950s their opening prices have risen from four to nearly seven times, drawing well away from the rest of the well-known red Bordeaux properties, whose prices have not on average increased more than two to three times, although some of the leaders have been able to follow in the wake of the top seven.

The principal reason for this has been the substantial re-entry of the U.S.A. into the Bordeaux market. After the repeal of Prohibition in 1933, the average annual Gironde exports to the U.S.A. up to 1938 were only 8,700 hectolitres, little more than a fifth of Britain's declining imports. From 1947 to 1959 the rate of U.S. Bordeaux imports was only double the pre-war one, but they began to rise sharply in the 1960s, with 25,600 hectolitres in 1961 and 47,900 in 1967. They have now more or less reached parity with British imports, which between 1947 and 1959 averaged only 36,000 hectolitres (there were import restrictions for some years after the war), and in recent years have fluctuated, with a maximum of 54,000 hecto-litres. The difference in the pattern of imports of the two countries is that practically all the American imports are in bottle, while the majority of Bordeaux reaches Britain in cask, as has always been the custom.

This prosperity has not been extended to the sweet white wines nor to the lesser *crus bourgeois* which were the backbone of the Bordeaux trade up to 1900. Yquem is the only Sauternes whose price has at all marched with the increases of the top claret growths. World taste has for the time being turned against sweet white table wines, and Bordeaux has suffered, though – as explained in the chapter on sweet white Bordeaux – neither growers nor merchants are blameless for the decline. On the other hand the medium quality white Graves and other sound white Bordeaux have found ready markets abroad, particularly in Germany, though overall at the expense of the lesser red wines. It is estimated that the output of the sound *crus bourgeois* and *crus artisans* is now not 10 per cent of what it was at the beginning of this century.

The Bordeaux *vignoble* has also been contracting sharply. In 1948 it was rather larger than in 1939, and totalled 134,000 hectares. Helped by government grants to marginal producers who agreed to pull up their vines, by 1960 it was down to 112,000, and by 1967 to 109,000 hectares, the smallest in its modern history. However, owing to improved methods of cultivation and increases in permitted yields there is no shortage of Bordeaux wine; average production between 1962 and 1967 has exceeded 3·1 million hl.

The number of growers in the department of the Gironde is now 40,000, compared with 58,500 at the end of the last war.

Evidence of the increased prosperity of Bordeaux has been the purchase of châteaux by outsiders, including British, American and returned French colonists from Algeria. There has also been extensive re-planting and the extension of existing vineyards, reminiscent of the boom period in the 1860s. It may be questioned whether this has not gone too far.

In Bordeaux the trade has had to face new problems, many of them arising from the growth of powerful purchasing groups, notably the British brewery-owned wine concerns and other large amalgamations less concerned with the traditional methods of wine commerce than with buying as cheaply as possible, and as near to the growers' prices as feasible. Also the American market, on which most Bordeaux merchants now have their eyes fixed – as their predecessors a century ago had on the British market – presents its difficulties, with big names, marketing skill and novelty rather than quality perhaps over-dominant. Nevertheless the growth of wine drinking in America and a level of interest among dedicated *amateurs* unequalled anywhere outside Britain should provide excellent long-term prospects in the U.S.A. for the unique fine wines of Bordeaux.

There are other potential markets too. Before 1917 there was a steady Bordeaux trade with Russia; and up to 1939 there was good business done with countries in Central and Eastern Europe. It would be surprising if the rising standard of life in these countries did not in time lead to renewed demand for the red and white wines of the Gironde.

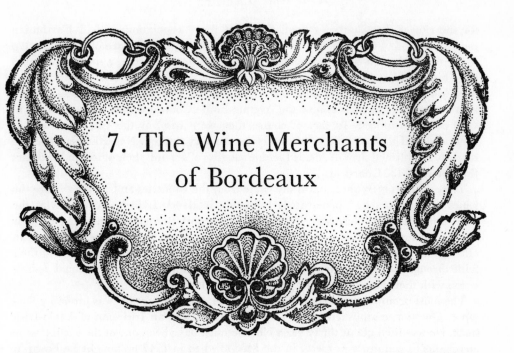

7. The Wine Merchants of Bordeaux

Although in the earlier historical chapters some survey of the Bordeaux wine trade in modern times has been given, this book is not a history of the wine trade in the Gironde. I lack occasion, knowledge and space here to write one, although this is a striking subject awaiting a delving author. However, while the châteaux and sometimes their proprietors receive a good deal of prominence and attention, the wines of Bordeaux owe so much to the merchants (*négociants*) and their enterprise, and they are so entwined in the history of Bordeaux's growth and production as well as their sale, that to give them in this work no more than the passing attention they have received so far would be inadequate as well as ungenerous.

The earlier story of the wine trade has been sketched in among the previous chapters dealing with the history of Bordeaux. Here we are concerned with the firms who have been associated with the modern Bordeaux trade, which began in the seventeenth century, but like the development of the châteaux really dates from the eighteenth century. The arrival of the Dutch merchants, who took up permanent residence in or just outside the city, has been mentioned. One of these was the founder of the oldest existing firm in Bordeaux today: Jean-Simon Beyerman who arrived from Rotterdam in 1620 and began trading in wine. Today the firm, like Barton & Guestier, is in the Cours Xavier Arnozan, formerly known as the Pavé des Chartrons (but changed in 1928 and named after a well-known doctor), and the head is Henri Binaud.

The significant fact about the Bordeaux merchants was that, as in other wine exporting regions such as Oporto, they were mostly foreigners. As such in earlier times they were not permitted to reside within the city walls, and this partly accounted for the rise of the Chartrons area, so called from association with a Carthusian monastery; today the Chartrons still remains the traditional centre of the trade. Up to the end of the last century it was considered inconceivable that a merchant should have his cellars and offices anywhere else than by the Quai des Chartrons, for there they would be conveniently near the docks and the brokers. When in 1899 Eschen-auers moved out to what is now the Avenue Emile Cournord they were regarded as very eccentric indeed. In fact of course they were wise, as the Chartrons area is congested and the possibilities of expansion are very limited. Nevertheless when the recently established firm of Alexis Lichine sought cellars and then offices in Bordeaux they set up on the Chartrons.

These foreign merchants naturally came from the countries and regions where the wines of Bordeaux had penetrated: England, Scotland, Ireland, Scandinavia, the Low Countries and Germany. They came to export Bordeaux wines first to their own countries and then elsewhere. Some carried on an import-export business in other goods as well. Many of these merchants were Protestants and maintained their faith through succeeding generations, although religious as well as national assimi-lation with their French Catholic neighbours also took place.

The most prominent merchant house in the eighteenth century was probably Bar-ton & Guestier, established in 1725 by Thomas Barton, an Irishman of Anglo-Irish stock. He was then about thirty years old. He must have been one of the earliest wine merchants to acquire a property in the Médoc when in 1747 he bought Le Boscq in St-Estèphe. By the time he died in 1780 he had amassed a considerable fortune. Barton was the largest buyer of the first growths. For example in the middle of the eighteenth century he is described in contemporary documents as the normal buyer of Lafite's crop. This was one of Bordeaux's periods of prosperity, although not on account of the wine trade with England, which was at a low ebb owing to the dis-criminatory duties, but through demand from the Low Countries, northern Germany and the developing French colonies.

In 1764 there was a great commotion on the Chartrons arising out of an edict of the local Parlement forbidding the blending of Bordeaux wines with those outside. This arose from the seizure of several English merchants accused of this practice. Led by Thomas Barton, the most important Anglo-Saxon merchant, his fellow-country-men drew up a protest, in spite of the fact that some Dutch and Irish merchants declared themselves perfectly satisfied with the new decree. However it is fair to say that the leading Dutch houses along with the principal French exporters rallied to the English cause. Among the signatories were Cornelis Beyerman, Schröder & Schÿler, J. Lynch and other firms of foreign and French origin.

The protest pointed out that some years previously a body of twenty-four Irish merchants and bottlers had complained that Bordeaux wines were mixed with Span-ish. However there were 'at least a thousand wine merchants in Ireland who all mixed the wines of Bordeaux with the wines of Spain'. More recently such concoctions had taken place at lower cost in Bordeaux, and this had increased the consumption in Ireland, where it was much to the local taste. It consisted of adding 10 per cent Benicarlo with a 'pot' of unfermented Bordeaux wine must. This created a new fermentation and apparently made the wine clear and bright. The Bordeaux brew was so successful that it put the Irish 'brewers' out of business. The merchants then brought forward the wonderfully specious argument which has by no means exhausted its value today, that if blending, on which foreign taste insisted, was prohibited it would go on just the same, but by merchants abroad who would be more shameless about the operation, and this would be a serious detriment to the Bordeaux trade. *On ne cuit bien que chez soi*!

Further, while the Dutch took a great deal of white wine from the Entre-Deux-Mers they chose to improve and strengthen it with a quarter to a fifth of Barsac and Sauternes. Also the Spaniards liked to lighten the colour of their red wines from the *palus* by adding some white wine; while the Irish and the Scots preferred to toughen the red Graves and Médocs with wines from Queyries and Montferrand. Anyhow, protested the merchants, in bad years in the region it was a good idea to improve their wines with those from outside.

After an interval the merchants more or less got their way, but these accusations contributed to the loss by the Bordelais of their famous 'privileges', removed briefly in 1776, restored again and then finally abolished under a more radical regime in 1790.

Jefferson, the American Minister in France, in his southern France tour notes of 1787, stated that 'the principal English wine merchants at Bordeaux are Jernon, Barton, Johnston, Foster (Forster), Skinner, Copinger and McCartey (MacCarthy). The chief French wine merchants are Feger, Nerac, Brunneau, Jauge and du Vérget. Desgrands, a wine broker, tells me they never mix the wine of first quality: but that they mix the inferior ones to improve them. The smallest wines make the best brandy'.

The American envoy clearly had no great respect for the merchants for elsewhere he had written to a friend, warning him to buy direct from the best vineyards, 'and can assure you that it is from them alone that genuine wine is to be got and not from any wine merchant whatever'.

A little later on there is evidence from the Latour archives that the merchants were no more popular with the growers. Most of the firms mentioned above were regular customers of this château, as well as Fennwick and Chalmers. About them and particularly about the brokers (*courtiers*) the Latour *régisseurs* were consistently scathing. Lamothe, manager for the first quarter of the nineteenth century, wrote, 'Yesterday I had the visit of M. Pierre François Guestier, surnamed Pierre the Cruel, but no matter, he is solid' (i.e. financially sound). He particularly distrusted the 'inexorable' broker Lawton and also Merman. 'The rapids of Cordouan are not more dangerous for ships than these two personages are for the proprietors'.

The rapids of Cordouan lay at the mouth of the Gironde, and were caused by some partially exposed rocks near the left bank of the estuary. To mark them a lighthouse was built on a rock in the reign of the French King Henri II (1519–59), and still exists today after many restorations. Over the centuries the rocks have sunk into the river bed, but on occasions when the water is exceptionally clear they may still be seen from the air. However big ships still pass to the north of the lighthouse.

Thomas Barton's son William was born in 1723, joined his father in the business and died in 1791. Unlike most of the other foreign merchants the Bartons have always maintained links with their country of origin, and some of the family continued to return to Ireland to live and work. So it was William's fourth son Hugh, born in 1766, who carried on the firm with his French partner, Daniel Guestier. Hugh Barton married Anna Johnston, daughter of another merchant of foreign origin, Nathaniel Johnston. In the Revolution Hugh Barton was imprisoned in 1794 as an alien, but with the help of his wife he escaped and, it is said, burnt the local guillotine en route for Ireland. In his absence Daniel Guestier ran the business. Barton later returned but died in Ireland. In 1830 his son, Nathaniel, born in 1799 and Daniel Guestier's son Pierre François, were admitted as partners. Nathaniel died in 1867, also in Ireland, being succeeded by his son Bertram Francis (b. 1830), who in his turn was followed by his son Bertram Hugh (b. 1858), the father of Hugh Ronald Barton, the present head of the firm, and uncle of Anthony Barton, whose father took no part in the wine business. Ronald Barton (b. 1902) is the owner of Langoa and that section of the Léoville estate bearing the Barton name. The last of the Guestier family was killed in a car crash some years ago, and Barton & Guestier is now owned by Segram's, the large Canadian concern. In 1969 Ronald Barton resigned as head of Barton & Guestier though maintaining a connection with the firm. Both the Bartons and the Guestiers used part of their substantial profits to buy Médoc châteaux.

Unfortunately records of these Bordeaux firms are very scanty, and little remains of Barton & Guestier's archives. They possess, however, an interesting account book, including records of the purchase in 1790 of the 1788 vintage vines. This shows clearly the way in which Bordeaux wines were blended. The firm bought 56 *tonneaux* of Lafite 1788. Some was sold to Dublin and some to London. Then they bought another 10¾ *tonneaux* of 'Lafitte peur', along with 41¼ *tonneaux* of Latour, plus 10¾ *tonneaux* of 'Latour peur'. As the account books were kept in English 'peur', of course means pure. Also bought were 13 *tonneaux* of a wine named Casterede, and 3 per cent of this was blended into the Brane-Mouton, Margaux, Larose, Léoville (spelt Lehauville), Listrac, etc. Also 'Ermitage' 1788 was used half and half with Casterede for blending. Elsewhere in the accounts is a note of the purchase of 2½ *tonneaux* of that erstwhile notorious Spanish blending wine, Benicarlo, mentioned in connection with the blending charges in 1764 and much denounced by English writers on wine in the nineteenth century. It gave colour and body.

An interesting later note also in this account book is an early reference to La Mission-Haut-Brion, with the record of the purchase in 1793 of 7 *tonneaux* of 'Lamission graves', and also 20 *tonneaux* of 'Leauville' 1791.

The 'hermitaging' of red Bordeaux was an accepted practice, the alleged purpose being to strengthen these delicate wines for the voyage abroad. It was implied that the pure wine usually went to the British Isles, and it was the Netherlanders, Belgians and Germans who liked their wines 'filled out' with a dollop of something stronger and fruitier. One may take leave to doubt whether only the best came to Britain, as may be judged below.

The letter-books of Nathaniel Johnston, quoted by H. Warner Allen in his *History of Wine* (1961), show what was done. Of the Lafite 1795 (a fine year), he wrote that 'made up with Hermitage (it) was the best liked of any of that year'. Only the finer wine had Hermitage added, for it was expensive; the cheaper had Benicarlo and Alicante blended in. For himself he ordered some 'neat Lafitte' of the celebrated 1798 vintage, and when dealing with the well-known London wine merchants, Barnes, who had a great reputation for claret, he recommended that their wines 'should be neat or very lightly made-up'. It must be remembered that there was no *égrappage* in those days, the stalks went into the fermenting vats with the grapes, and the wines were very hard and tannin-ridden. The softer, if fuller wines from the Rhône and Spain mollified them.

However Henderson in his *History of Ancient and Modern Wines* (1824) stated 'there is a particular manufacture called *travail de l'Anglaise* which consists of adding to each hogshead of Bordeaux wine three or four gallons of Alicant or Benecarlo, half a gallon of stum wine, and sometimes a small quantity of Hermitage.' This of course was long before the days of Algerian wine and East Anglian blending. In the *Manuel du Sommelier* (third edition, 1826) A. Jullien wrote: 'The wines of the first growths of Bordeaux as drunk in France do not resemble those sent to London; the latter, in which is put a certain quantity of Spanish and French Midi wine, undergo some preparations which give them a taste and qualities, without which they would not be found good in England'. Somewhat ironically to us today, Jullien dedicated his book to Chaptal.

Even later a writer on wine in the seventh (1842) edition of the *Encyclopaedia Britannica* complained 'it is plain that few of those who imagine they are drinking the first growths of Bordeaux can even be drinking the second'. The sceptical contributor also wrote, 'The most extensive operations of this nature (blending) are carried on at Bordeaux with the wines we now call Claret, but not one-thousandth part of which are of good quality, or unmixed in some way, and the one half of which, perhaps, are not French, but Spanish wine'. Although other writers bear witness to the fact that this was an era of wine sophistication, the envenomed tone of the encyclopaedist suggests that he was a confirmed drinker of port.

To return to the merchant families, the Johnstons, already mentioned, came originally from the Scottish Border but William Johnston was sent to Northern Ireland by the English Government and the family became part of the Protestant Ascendency there. In 1716 William Johnston, grandson of the first Irish settler, went to Bordeaux to learn French, did business in Holland and after returning to Ireland to marry an Irish girl, settled in Bordeaux in 1729 and worked in the firm of Pierre Germe. After the death of his principal he set up on his own in 1734. The firm dealt not only in wine, but were general merchants and continued in this mixed trade for many years. A price list of the 1820s shows they imported everything from cotton, sugar and coffee to incense, oil (castor, whale and cod), and exported apples, liquorice and walnuts, as well as brandy and wine. The last was divided into 'Red common cargo', 'Red East-India ditto', 'White cargo', 'Red in bottles comm.', 'Ditto in bottles better' and 'Good Médoc'.

The firm became William & Nathaniel Johnston in 1765, and in the same year their cellars and stock were partly transferred to Blaye and the rest to Guernsey.

This move was dictated by fear of blending being prohibited in Bordeaux and of increased taxes. Later on they moved back to the Rue de Pessac in Bordeaux.

The Johnstons always had good connections with America, and when trade with England was severely hindered in the Napoleonic wars, the Johnstons did their best to increase their American business. In 1807 a member of the family sailed for New York, armed with an introduction from General Lafayette to General McHenry, an Ulsterman who became secretary to George Washington and Secretary of War (1796– 1800). By 1809 the Johnstons had over 1,000 customers for wine in the U.S.A. The firm prospered throughout the nineteenth century and, like other wine merchants, branched out into château-ownership, members of the family becoming proprietors of Ducru-Beaucaillou, Dauzac, and La Maqueline (a *palus* estate), but unlike some of the other foreign merchants the Johnstons took French citizenship and eventually became Roman Catholics. Today the firm of Nathaniel Johnston has an association with the firm of Dourthe. Another Johnston family ran a pottery in Bordeaux. David Johnston was its head, and his work included plates bearing charming transfer pictures of leading châteaux.

Another very old firm is Schröder & Schÿler, which opened its doors on 1 January 1739 at exactly the same address as its occupies today: 97 Quai des Chartrons. The two original partners came from Germany, although the Schÿlers had been Dutch, and this is said to account for the unusual *umlaut* on the 'y' in their name. They soon built up a big trade with north Germany. Like Hugh Barton they were arrested at the Revolution and brought before the Military Tribunal. However they were acquitted on the grounds that they had 'never shared the ideas of those greedy speculators who, for too long, have grown fat upon the substance of the people'. This throws a light on conditions in the Bordeaux market as well as on the integrity of the Schröders and Schÿlers. The last Schröder was killed while serving in the French Army at the Battle of the Marne in September 1914, but M. Marc Schÿler and his son M. Jean-Henri Schÿler still run the firm, while they own Kirwan in Cantenac. The firm's fine arched stone cellars on the Chartrons date back to the early eighteenth century, and are nearly 100 yards in length. While being general wine merchants the firm has been associated with branded wines, of which the dry white Graves Rosechâtel is the best known. For many years they had the monopoly of the sale of the wines of Carbonnieux. M. Guy Schÿler, another well-known Bordeaux personality, who has his own firm, Alfred Schÿler, and is also associated with publicity for Lafite, is a cousin.

A neighbouring Chartrons firm (at No. 60), founded in 1740, is Tastet et Lawton, the famous *courtiers* or brokers, to whose incomparable records of vintages and prices this book owes no little. Abraham Lawton came from Cork, and the family took French nationality just before the Revolution. Guillaume Lawton retired in 1825, and M. Tastet was taken into partnership in 1830. The present head of the firm is Daniel Lawton, whose wife is the sister of Christian Cruse. Indeed all the wine families are so connected with each other by marriage that a Jewish family gathering has nothing in the way of kinship on a large dinner party of the Bordeaux wine trade. Daniel Lawton is also renowned in Bordeaux as holding the expectatorial record. It is said to be 2 metres 31 centimetres. His son, also Daniel Lawton, is in the firm too.

Their records of the vintages since 1795, and the quantities produced and the opening prices attained by the leading wines since 1830 are unique. Jean Lawton, a cousin, is head of the firm of Lalande, mentioned below, and was proprietor of Cantenac-Brown until its sale in 1968.

Also founded in 1740, but across the river in Libourne, was the house of Beylot, whose offices by the river are on the same site as they were then. Among some pre-Revolutionary documents in their possession is a letter dated 1 September 1782 in which M. Beylot *père* informs his customers that he has taken his son into partnership, and asks them to accept as being equally valid as his own, the appended signature of Beylot *fils* on wine transactions. In the past the firm dealt in Cahors and other Haut-Pays wines, but today they are largely concerned with the wines of St-Emilion, Pomerol and Fronsac, with family properties in the area, including Moulinet in St-Emilion and Junayme in Fronsac. The head of the firm today is M. Conynck.

A French house founded just before the Revolution and still in business is Dubos Frères. Jean-Baptiste Dubos began business in 1785. It was principally an export house, and in particular was concerned with selling wine to Canada. At one period it was the sole supplier to the Quebec Liquor Board, but also had connections in the U.S.A., and in northern Europe. Part of the firm now is the old house of Cunliffe, Dobson who began business at the beginning of the nineteenth century in the Cours Balguerie Stuttenberg. Later on Mr Dobson achieved a financial coup by buying a large amount of wine just before the phylloxera at the end of the 1870s and selling it thereafter. At the beginning of this century the firm was amalgamated with Dubos, but it still trades under the name of Cunliffe, Dobson in the British market.

Most of the early Bordeaux merchants had special associations with certain overseas markets, often the countries of their origin. Beyerman, for example, were for centuries associated with the Dutch wine trade, and the firm possesses the passport issued by the mayor of Leiden, 'in the name of Napoleon, Emperor of the French', to Jean Henri Beyerman, wine merchant of Bordeaux, in April 1811, allowing the latter to circulate freely in the district during the ensuing year. Jean Henri died in 1835 – after being part-owner of Haut-Brion – and the firm became Henri & Oscar Beyerman. Then in 1899, Robert Binaud, great-grandson of Jean Henri, took over and his son Henri Binaud now runs the firm, as well as being joint-proprietor of Cantemerle, whose produce the Beyermans were long accustomed to sell in the Low Countries. The firm used to have its premises in the Chartrons, but is now in the adjacent Cours Xavier Arnozan, where Barton & Guestier have their offices. Henri Binaud has long been prominent in Bordeaux wine trade affairs and in matters of national wine concern.

Another industry associated with the Bordeaux wine trade was started by foreigners: glass bottle manufacture. At the beginning of the eighteenth century the bottles were imported, but the first bottle glass works in Bordeaux was founded in 1723 on the Chartrons by an Irishman, Pierre Mitchell. The second was started two years later in Bourg by a German named Fouberg. These two pioneers secured certain privileges which for a time gave them a monopoly, but in 1748 two more glass factories were opened in Libourne, another followed in Bordeaux in 1751, and several others when the original privileges lapsed. By 1789 there were three glass-works for bottle-making in Bordeaux and five others not far outside the city. Altogether they were making 3,200,000 bottles a year.

After the restoration of the Bourbons in 1815, a number of firms prominent today began business. The earliest chronologically was Mestrezat. Domeine Guillaume Mestrezat was a Swiss citizen from Geneva who became Swiss Consul in Bordeaux. The firm was actually founded in 1814, the year when Napoleon was exiled to Elba, but operations as general exporters and importers began the following year. The family was prominent in Bordeaux affairs in the nineteenth century. D. G. Mestrezat, himself was an administrator of the Bordeaux-La Teste-Arcachon Railway, one of the earliest in France. Like other railways it was not as successful as expected, and Mestrezat and his firm were only rescued from bankruptcy by his banker parents in Geneva. Later, fortunately, the local line was bought out by the main line railway from Paris to Bordeaux. D. G. Mestrezat's son Paul was also Swiss Consul. He married Anna Jackson, whose family came from England. His nephew Willy became an oenologist and colleague of the celebrated Ulysse Gayon, director of the *Station Oenologique* in Bordeaux; later he joined the Pasteur Institut in Paris. Paul's son James was the last Mestrezat in the firm, for his son, also James, was killed in the Battle of the Somme in 1916. The elder James died in 1925, but his daughter had married Jacques Anglivel de la Beaumelle, whose family has directed the firm ever since, the present head being René de la Beaumelle. However in 1926 the firm and chairman of Preller, M. L. Preller, joined Mestrezat and since then the combined concern has borne the name of Mestrezat-Preller. Three other directors today are Jean-Pierre de la Beaumelle, Edouard Lawton of the well-known family, and Georges Roullet. The firm has always had the same premises, but now bearing a different street name, in the Cours de la Martinique. It has long conducted a world-wide export trade. The family has not gone in for château-owning, but at one period around the end of the last century and the beginning of this one, it used to purchase the whole crop of Haut-Bailly.

In 1816 Léon Hanappier arrived in Bordeaux from Orléans and began his career as a wine merchant. There have been four generations of the family in the firm since, and the present representative is M. Michel Hanappier, who is Swedish Consul in Bordeaux, as his father and grandfather were before him. His family was joined by the Peyrelongue family in the Inter-War years, Pierre and Gérard Peyrelongue having been grandsons of Charles Hanappier of the second generation of the family. Both of them left sons now in the business. Hanappier, Peyrelongue besides having a good wine export trade, particularly in Scandinavia and Belgium, has been unusual in having a distillery in the Rue du Jardin Public, where they produce liqueurs and, alas, whisky from imported Scottish malt. The Peyrelongue family are joint proprietors of Calon-Ségur with the Gasqueton family, the two ancestors of the present generation having bought it on an equal financial basis in 1895. Their premises are in the Cours du Médoc, near the Quai des Chartrons. In 1968 the firm made certain commercial and technical arrangements with Calvet, but retained its independence.

The most patriarchal firm and prolific wine family in Bordeaux is that of Cruse. The first of them was Herman Cruse, born in 1790 in Schleswig-Holstein, then part of

Denmark. He came to Bordeaux and began trading in 1819. Cruse had a very large trade with north Germany, and the firm was Cruse and Hirschfeld before it became Cruse et Fils Frères in 1850. Two or three years before that the family fortunes were established by Herman Cruse's daring speculation on the 1847 vintage. The output was very large and the quality excellent although light. However the whole trade was thrown into confusion by the rumblings and then the Revolution of February 1848, when Louis-Philippe fled to England. Moreover the series of revolutions in Germany, one of Bordeaux's best customers, made things worse. Consequently prices slumped, many merchants were unable to meet their obligations, and in some cases a moratorium on debts was declared.

In these adverse conditions Herman Cruse bought at very low prices enormous quantities of the abundant 1847s, particularly the *crus bourgeois*. Whereas the leading wines of this class in the excellent 1844 vintage had sold for up to 800 frs. a *tonneau*, Cruse paid as little as 300 frs. in January and February 1848. In April he bought 35 *tonneaux* of Cos d'Estournel for 350 frs. and thereafter 50 or 60 *tonneaux* apiece of Rausan, Léoville-Barton, Pichon-Longueville and Durfort at 525 frs. and 150 of Léoville-Las-Cases at the same knock-down price. In September 1848 he acquired 140 *tonneaux* – just about all the crop still unsold – of Lafite at 1,025 frs. He was still buying these '47s in 1849, with 24 *tonneaux* of Margaux at 1,000 frs., 12½ *tonneaux* of Yquem at 700 frs. and 29¾ *tonneaux* of Suduiraut at 675 frs. To compare prices, the '44 first growths had been in the 3,000 – 4,000 frs. range, and the seconds about 2,500 – 2,800 frs. Later the '48 Lafite was back at 2,800 to 3,000 frs. Altogether Cruse bought 13,650 *tonneaux* from more than 130 growths. A proportion he sold off on the Bordeaux market to Barton & Guestier, Johnston & Clossmann, and these bottled their purchases. It is interesting to note from the full list that nearly all the red wines came from the Médoc, and nothing of importance from St-Emilion or Pomerol.

Like other successful merchants the Cruses moved into château-proprietorship. In 1852 Herman Cruse bought Laujac in Bégadan in the Médoc from one of the Cabarrus family, and it is still in the Cruses' possession. In 1865 they acquired Pontet-Canet for 700,000 frs. and Giscours in 1875 for 1,000,000 frs. They also bought du Taillan on the border of the Médoc nearest to Bordeaux. When Adolphe Cruse, son of Herman and inheritor of Laujac, died in 1892 he left 30 million francs. The prosperity of the Cruse family is a symbol of the most affluent period for the Bordeaux wine merchants. This prosperity is reflected even today in the charming antique furniture, decoration and ornaments which adorn the châteaux and merchants' houses throughout the Gironde.

The Cruse firm's offices have always been on the Quai des Chartons (No. 124). The Cruse family is prolific. The doyen of the existing partners is Christian Cruse, who for over fifty years visited Britain to sell Bordeaux wines. With an unrivalled memory of the past events, personalities and vintages, he has been of immense help over many details in this book. Throughout his life he has taken a keen interest in wine affairs, and for long was on the Council of the *I.N.A.O.* Today many of his travelling activities are taken over by his son Edouard. However the senior member of the Cruse family is Christian Cruse's brother Roger, who married a de Luze and was a partner in the Cruse firm for over sixty years. The other pillar of the Cruse firm for many years was Christian Cruse's brother, Emmanuel, proprietor of Issan and one of the keenest commercial brains in Bordeaux, as well as a most charming personality. He died in June 1968. If in the 1847 speculation the firm paid scant attention to the wines of St-Emilion and Pomerol, today the firm of Cruse has made something of a speciality of these attractive wines; Edouard Cruse has always taken a special interest in these. Apart from Britain, Cruse have always had special connections with Scandinavia, and more recently with the U.S.A., where they have a very important share of the trade in Bordeaux wine.

Two years after Herman Cruse arrived in Bordeaux, Louis Eschenauer left Strasbourg, and opened his doors on the Chartrons in 1821. He ran an expanding business, particularly with Germany, until his death in 1873. Eschenauer also had a good domestic trade inside France. Louis Eschenauer was succeeded by his son Frédéric, who took into the firm his third son Louis and his nephew-cum-son-in-law Louis Lung. After Frédéric's death in 1899 these two directed the concern, with Louis Eschenauer concentrating on the German, Scandinavian and Russian markets, and Louis Lung on Britain. It was in the year of Frédéric's death that the firm moved from the Chartrons to the present huge premises in the Rue Emile Counord. It has no less than 20,000 square yards of cellar space, including a private cellar in which I have seen such pre-phylloxera wonders as magnums of Lafite '74. So far as seeking vineyard properties went, the Eschenauers turned not to the Médoc but to the Graves. Camponac in Pessac near Pape-Clément was their chief property, although now the name is used as a brand only. The three other vineyards associated with them are Smith-Haut-Lafitte, Olivier and La Garde.

Louis Lung died in 1913 and Louis Eschenauer became sole director, and remained so until his death in 1958 at the age of eighty-eight. 'Oncle Louis' was one of the great personalities of the Bordeaux wine trade. If, probably mistakenly, during the German occupation in the Second World War, he maintained connections with those whom for many years he had been accustomed to do business, it is also fair to say that he was no little responsible for the Germans leaving Bordeaux intact, and particularly its famous Pont de Pierre, when they withdrew in 1944. After his death the firm was sold to John Holt & Co. of Liverpool. In 1969 Holts themselves were acquired by Lonrho, a big group with trading interest in Africa. The actual running of Eschenauer's since has still remained in French hands.

Another firm founded in this period of new wine merchants was de Luze, who began business in 1820 at 88 and 89 Quai des Chartrons where they still have their offices and cellars. The de Luzes were of French origin and had emigrated to Germany, but the founder of the firm, Alfred de Luze, was brought up in Switzerland with his brother, Louis Philippe. Together in 1817 they set off for New York and established an import business there. Three years later Alfred, the younger brother, returned to Europe to help organize trade with the New World, and in order to do so set up in the convenient port of Bordeaux. However, by 1824 he had decided to concentrate on wine, including Burgundy and cognac as well as Bordeaux. Alfred became Consul-

General for the Grand Duke of Hesse, and for that service was made a baron, a title still in the family. In 1862 the family bought Château de Paveil and added their name to its own. Since 1964 they have also administered the vineyard of Domaine de l'Ermitage Lamourous, belonging to the Sisters of Mercy, in Le Pian, near Ludon and Macau. In 1961 de Luze absorbed a firm which was one of the leaders in the last century, Clossman. This very old firm had been founded by a German immigrant in 1785, and was a well-known buyer of classed growths. The de Luze firm has always had a special connection with Scandinavia, and particularly with Denmark, whose Royal Court they supply.

New firms were, of course, always springing up in Bordeaux, but this short survey is principally concerned with those who have survived. After the four houses that opened their commercial doors in the early Restoration period, there is a gap, and the next important concern was Lalande, who began business in 1844, five doors along from the de Luzes, at 94 Quai des Chartrons. They are still there. Armand Lalande the founder was also prominent in Bordeaux affairs, becoming a Deputy for the Gironde. Yet another Lawton – Henry Lawton – was his grandson, who died in 1933 and the latter's son, Jean, is now head of the firm and owned Cantenac-Brown until 1968. At one time or other members of the Lalande family have owned Léoville-Poyferré, La Couronne and Senilhac. Eighty per cent of their trade today is export, particularly with Britain and northern Europe.

A well-known broker who flourished at this period, but whose firm no longer exists was Merman, a partner in the firm of Merman & Baguenard, and already mentioned adversely by the *régisseur* of Latour. He owned the curiously named Le Crock in St-Estèphe, which one passes on the main road from Pauillac to the Bas-Médoc; also Marbuzet in the same commune and now owned by Ginestet. He was one of the jury judging wines at the 1862 International Exhibition in London, at which Cheval-Blanc was awarded a bronze medal. In Bordeaux he lived at 29 Pavé des Chartrons (now Cours Xavier Arnozan). The Merman family were one of the earliest Protestant Dutch families to settle in Bordeaux. They arrived there in the sixteenth century but for a long time their principal interest was in shipping.

As might be expected the period of prosperity in the 1860s encouraged the formation of new wine merchants' businesses, and three firms well known today were established: Delor, Calvet and Kressmann.

Delor was founded in 1865 by Alphonse Delor, and soon became one of the big 'names' in Bordeaux. They specialized in business with South America. Their extensive premises were in the Rue de Macau, but at the beginning of this century these were gutted in probably the most spectacular fire in a wine merchant's premises until Calvet's establishment in the Cours du Médoc was seriously damaged in 1966. The Delor family were at one time owners of Durfort-Vivens. They were one of the houses well known for carrying large stocks of bottled wines, including the classed growths. In 1955 they bought the whole crop of Lafite '55. In 1962 Harveys of Bristol acquired a majority share in the firm.

Unlike many of the Bordeaux merchants, the Calvets were French, and Octave Calvet was born in Tain l'Hermitage on the Rhône. Indeed when he first came to

Bordeaux in 1870, it was with the somewhat suspect-sounding purpose of selling Hermitage to the Bordeaux trade. However, even then many of the foreign markets, notably Belgium, Scandinavia and the Hanseatic cities of Germany still liked their Bordeaux *hermitagé*. Calvet set up his premises in the Cours du Médoc, the broad avenue which runs down to the Chartrons and the river. Here very large cellars were constructed and remained the headquarters of this leading firm until the disastrous fire of 1966. These premises have since been re-built. Jean Calvet special-ized in the British market, and he used to spend about half of each year travelling his wines in Britain. The original family home was Château Tauzia in the Graves, and today this is the name of their branded claret. Unlike many other Bordeaux merchants they had no ambitions to be classed-growth château proprietors. Like Delor they had an extensive business in South America, and opened a branch in Buenos Aires in 1886. Calvets have never restricted their interests to the wines of Bordeaux; they have a substantial Burgundy trade in Beaune, and they also market Cognac. The senior partner today is Jacques Calvet, son of Jean.

The third firm of substance dating from this period, Kressmann, was of German origin. Edouard Kressmann first came to Bordeaux in 1858, but worked in other firms until 1871. He then began well with a speculation reminiscent of Herman Cruse's with the 1847, and Kressmann's was also linked with a period of social upheaval. He bought at bargain prices the initially disregarded vintage of 1871, including 163 *tonneaux* of Lafite and Carruades de Lafite. The first wine of Lafite cost only 1,800 frs., and Kressmann paid but 1,400 frs. for Mouton-Rothschild. These prices may be compared with 4,500 frs. and 3,000 frs. respectively for the 1870 wines of these two growths; and for the next good vintage of 1874 Kressmann paid 4,200 frs. for Mouton which had produced a record crop of 190 *tonneaux*. The purchase and successful sale in England, Holland and North Germany of these '71s set up the house of Kressmann. They are known for their La Tour-Martillac in the Graves, discussed in the chapter on that district.

It is surprising to find any firms setting up in the unpropitious Eighties which have survived, but that is when Sichels started. They opened their premises in 1883 on the Quai de Bacalan, a continuation of the Chartrons, and they are still there. They were a branch of the Mainz firm of Sichel. However when the First World War began, Herman Sichel in Bordeaux formed a completely separate French company. After that war Allan Sichel and his brother Herbert joined the firm, while the German firm set up its own Bordeaux house, which only re-united with its cousin firm in 1966. Allan Sichel become one of the best-known wine shippers in England where he lived until his death in 1965. He was a dedicated, outspoken *amateur* of Bordeaux wines, with a mischievous pleasure in being controversial. Many lovers of claret in Britain today remain in Allan Sichel's vinous debt. The firm also deals in Burgundy, and has considerable connections in the United States as well as in Britain. They are associated with Palmer and Angludet. In the latter lives Peter Sichel, son of Allan and head of the firm in Bordeaux.

Another firm, now part-owners of Palmer, began in the 1890s, Mähler-Besse. They are of Dutch origin.

The next important firm to open was that of Ginestet which began in the auspicious vintage years of 1899, setting up at 132 Quai des Chartrons. Fernand Ginestet faced a difficult period ahead, but did succeed in building up a large trade in the north and west of France, and later began to develop an export trade with the Low Countries and Britain. In 1916 he joined with another merchant, Latrille, and the firm was Latrille & Ginestet until they separated in 1929. Meanwhile Ginestet had begun to purchase vineyards. In 1919 he acquired Clos Fourtet and Cos d'Estournel, and in 1925 was a member of the syndicate which bought Château Margaux. After the last war he relinquished control of Clos Fourtet in order to become sole owner of Château Margaux. His son Pierre, a prominent figure in Bordeaux wine circles, is now head of the firm, which in addition to the properties it owns also controls the sole sale of seven lesser red and four white growths in the Graves, Sauternes, Premières Côtes and Bourg districts. A few years ago the firm moved its premises to the Cours St-Louis. Bernard Ginestet, son of Pierre, is the third generation in the firm.

A smaller but distinguished house is that of Woltner. Around the turn of this century Frédéric Woltner, who had already served his wine apprenticeship in a Bordeaux firm, opened an office in Paris but also maintained cellars on the Chartrons. Not long before the last war these were moved round the corner to the Cours du Médoc. His two sons, Fernand and Henri, joined the firm in 1926, and these two are now the sole partners. Although they have a general wine merchandising business, and were for long the agents in France of Pol Roger champagne, their best-known activities are connected with their three properties in the Graves: La Mission-Haut-Brion, La Tour-Haut-Brion and Laville-Haut-Brion, to be described in the Graves chapter.

One of the largest Bordeaux firms today is Cordier. Desiré Cordier had founded his business at Toul in 1877, but opened a Bordeaux branch during the First World War. The firm was to some extent involved in supplying wine to the French Army during that war. Like Ginestet, Cordier began to buy châteaux when peace arrived, securing Gruaud-Larose, Talbot and later on five other growths. The firm nowadays has a substantial domestic trade, particularly with northern France. Since 1953 all wines from the Cordier châteaux have been sold through agents at home and abroad and are not offered on the Bordeaux market. Jean Cordier, the present head of the firm, owns one of the most attractive eighteenth-century houses in Bordeaux, Labottière, built by the architect Laclotte.

Two firms which have come to the fore since the last war but which had their origins earlier are La Bergerie in Pauillac and J-P. Moueix in Libourne.

La Bergerie actually dates from as long ago as 1904, as the commercial outlet of Mouton-d'Armailhacq, and it was included in the sale of that property to Baron Philippe de Rothschild in 1933. Thereafter it began to develop under the name of the Société Vinicole de Pauillac, until the present name of La Bergerie was adopted in 1954. The premises in the middle of Pauillac include a charming eighteenth-century house with a courtyard. The firm is basically concerned with the brand wines of Baron Philippe's concern, including the best-selling Mouton-Cadet, but it also carries on a general wine merchandising business, buying from other estates, including of course the two Moutons. It has a large American trade. The young, energetic managing director is Philippe Cottin, a source of much information on Bordeaux wines.

The expansion of the house of Moueix is one of the features of post-war Bordeaux. Jean-Pierre Moueix has built up his business since the 1930s largely by acquiring the production or marketing rights of important châteaux in the St-Emilion and Pomerol area, also buying control or part-ownership in local châteaux. In St-Emilion his firm owns Magdelaine and Fonroque, and in Pomerol La Fleur-Pétrus and Lagrange. In addition he is co-proprietor of Pétrus itself. The company is responsible for 'farming' several properties, including Latour-Pomerol and La Clotte, and has exclusive selling rights of nine well-known estates in the two districts, including Pavie, Clos Fourtet and La Fleur. Further it sells a third of the crop of Ausone and a quarter of Cheval-Blanc, as well as important parts of a number of other leading growths in the neighbourhood. The firm also controls the old Libourne house of Danglade, which was founded in 1780. Both Moueix and Danglade have their offices on the quayside in Libourne. The head of Danglade now is Roger Danglade. His father René was the first Bordeaux merchant I met, and who welcomed me on my first visit to Bordeaux in 1939.

The most recently established firm of size in Bordeaux is that of Alexis Lichine, the Russian-born American who has done much to publicize French wines in America since the last war. Following the purchase of Lascombes and Prieuré by American syndicates with which he was associated, he began a substantial merchandising business in Burgundy and Bordeaux. More recently he concentrated all his stocks of French wines in Bordeaux, where on the Chartrons the firm has cellars that formerly belonged to Cruse. At one time his offices were in the old château of Lascombes in Margaux, but they too are now on the Chartrons. A feature of these cellars, like others in the locality, is their great length and narrow width. They run back from the Quai des Chartrons for 365 metres, with bins placed at right angles to a central *piste*. In order that the staff may move quickly from one end of the cellars to the other bicycles are provided, and these dash to and fro along the *piste*, summoned often by a public address system originating in the office. Lichine claims to have the biggest trade in château-bottled wines with the U.S.A. In 1965 his business was bought by the British brewery group of Bass-Charrington. This was yet another example of the influx of foreign capital and control into Bordeaux in recent years. Lichine is no longer actively concerned with the firm.

There are other substantial wine merchants in Bordeaux whom I have not mentioned because they are little associated with the type of Bordeaux wines familiar in Britain or America. In general the wine merchants are not so dominant in Bordeaux as they used to be, owing to the advent of big foreign groups. The role of the Bordeaux wine merchants is that of middle-men, between the growers whose wine they select with the aid of brokers who receive 2 per cent commission on sales, and their trade customers. In addition to the broking firms in Bordeaux, there are individual brokers in every district whose business it is to know the quality of the wines throughout their area. They are the link between the local growers and the merchants.

I have only mentioned the brokers *en passant,* as they are little known to the general public, to whom the merchants' names may be familiar. But in addition to those referred to, well-known names include Damade, Chauvot, Moreau (briefly the owner of Ch. Margaux), de Rivoire, associated with the great Paris concern of Nicolas and a former president of the Syndicat des Courtiers en Vins de Bordeaux, and Daniel Lacoste, who was the principal white wine broker of his time.

In times of prosperity as recently, the role of the merchants with the leading growths in short supply is little more than that of brokers, but for the mass of wines they have considerable responsibilities in buying wines and holding them. Often they have arrangements with particular growers, whom they have to support through bad vintages as well as good. Most Bordeaux wine merchants nowadays in addition to supplying the home and export trade with wines bearing château names, are concerned to develop the sale of their own brands, as a safeguard for the future. With the exception of Mouton-Cadet and perhaps one or two other brands, these so far have proved more successful at home than abroad.

8. The Médoc I

Pauillac and St-Estèphe

To the *amateur* of fine claret the Médoc is surely the Holy of Holies. I yield to no one in my admiration of an outstanding St-Emilion like Cheval-Blanc of a great year, or of the voluptuous qualities of a rich Pomerol like Pétrus or Vieux-Château-Certan; and the leading Graves may fairly consider themselves the peers of their historically junior rivals to the north. I cannot follow a distinguished Médoc château proprietor who said he found Graves not to his taste and St-Emilions and Pomerols 'common wines'; but as to the latter pair I see what he means. They lack the elegance and distinction of a great Médoc.

The late Maurice Healy who wrote as engagingly and enthusiastically about claret as any man, and who sharpened my early knowledge and appreciation of Bordeaux, yet proved an apostate at the last jump. In his *Stay Me With Flagons* (1940) he wrote: 'For let there be no doubt about it: Burgundy at its best overtops claret at *its* best.' He added that one would only drink four or five bottles of truly first-class Burgundy in one's life, and be lucky to find so many; he had only come upon three. They were Volnay Caillerets 1889, La Tâche 1904 and Richebourg 1923.

One cannot argue about wines that one has not drunk, but I would claim to have drunk with fitting appreciation more than three bottles of top rank Burgundy. They would include . . . but this is a book about Bordeaux. It comes down to the kind of taste and flavour one ultimately prefers. There is no need to denigrate Burgundy – to me the second of red wines – to express a preference for red Bordeaux. There is more flavour, more variety and distinction about claret; it is a more interesting wine than Burgundy; a violin compared with a trumpet, a baritone as against a bass. But then some prefer basses.

Maurice Healy went on to admit that one may drink claret of the highest class several times in the year, and this is certainly true. This also makes it that much more difficult to pick out the peak bottles. What claret team can I select from my experience to match Healy's Burgundies? It is not so easy. For one thing Burgundy is usually drunk rather young, and it is rare to open one more than fifty years old – although I have drunk a splendid 1865 Musigny from the Comte de Voguë's estate. Burgundy can seldom compete in antiquity with Bordeaux. Yet with an aged perhaps a pre-phylloxera claret, it is difficult not to be influenced by its seniority, by the dusty, often hand-blown bottle, by the fine nose and fruity flavour of old wine still in possession of its faculties. Unconsciously one may make allowances. Yet age is not enough to win laurels. The oldest bottle of claret that I have ever drunk and ever expect to drink was in Bristol at the table of Ronald Avery in April 1967. It was Lafite 1803, re-corked in October 1957 at the château and is described on page 113.

Much of course depends on memory, the circumstances as well as a touch of nostalgia. A wine may have made such an impression that no other can erase it; and I wonder if that happened to Maurice Healy with his three Burgundies. I cannot put in an opening pair, but I would include in my team, in ascending age order Ch. Margaux 1953, Cheval-Blanc 1947, Lafite 1945, Léoville-Poyferré 1929, Léoville-Las-Cases 1929, Pichon-Longueville-Baron 1929, Latour 1929, Léoville-Las-Cases 1928, Cheval-Blanc 1921, Latour 1920, Cheval-Blanc 1920, Latour 1899, Haut-Brion 1899, Mouton-Rothschild 1878, Lafite 1875, Langoa 1870 and Grand-Puy-Ducasse 1868.

In the reserve team I might include Léoville-Barton 1948, Cheval-Blanc 1948, Pétrus 1947, Pontet-Canet 1929, Cheval-Blanc 1928, Haut-Brion 1920 and others of this year now past their best. Among the very old wines that have left a great impression are Branaire-Ducru 1899, Mouton-Rothschild 1895, 1880 and 1870, Lafite 1870, and Latour 1865.

No doubt there are firmer favourites for other people's selection, but one cannot drink everything. One thing, however, will be noted: most of the wines are Médocs. In a 'colts' team I would spread my net wider, including perhaps La Mission-Haut-Brion 1948 and Vieux-Château-Certan 1947, along with other lesser Pomerols and more than one Cheval-Blanc, but greatness surely implies a certain survival, and although I have put several post-war wines in my two leading lists, their inclusion may be premature.

But I do not doubt the primacy of the Médocs. Being rather harder and firmer wines than the St-Emilions and Pomerols, they take more time to come round, while the latter may often make more agreeable bottles when young. A Médoc of a fine vintage, as Ronald Barton, part-proprietor of the Léoville vineyard and sole owner of Langoa has observed, should not be drunk until it is ten years old.

Physically the Médoc is triangular in shape, with the Atlantic and the Gironde enclosing it on the two long sides and Bordeaux on the short, southern line. The vineyards lie on the eastern side of the triangle, forming a narrow strip only three to six miles wide and about forty-five miles long. The general aspect of the country is flat, and the best vineyards lie on slopes that are never more than 150 feet above sea level and fall gently towards the estuary. Although now well drained there is some marshy land; with occasional little streams, known here as *jalles*, slipping down into the broad river. The best known of these is the *Jalle de Blanquefort*, for that forms near Bordeaux the 'frontier' between the Médoc and the Graves.

The soil, washed down by the rivers, is gravelly and sandy, and the visitor can only wonder that so many fine wines are produced from such poor ground. It has to be fertilized moderately to give of its best. The sub-soil varies, from chalk and clay to iron and sand; but even the top soil varies imperceptibly and this is what accounts for the astonishing variation in the wines made from adjoining properties. The Bas-Médoc is more sandy and has clay, which results in a greater output but a lower quality than in the Haut-Médoc. One reason at least for the difference in style between Latour and Lafite is that the former has a shallower top soil than the latter, so that the roots more effectively penetrate the chalk sub-soil, thus giving a rather fuller, harder wine. To produce a *tonneau* of wine in the Médoc the grapes from about four thousand vines are needed; so a big château vineyard includes over half a million vines to be cared for.

A century ago the Médoc *vignoble* extended to 25,000 hectares, (2·47 acres = 1 hectare) or about 62,000 acres. However today it is little more than a quarter of that area, owing to the successive crises that have hit Bordeaux from the 1870s onwards. In recent years, however, prosperity has led to re-planting, while production is increasing; too much so, some say. Total annual output of the Médoc is now averaging between 220,000 and 250,000 hectolitres, of which three-quarters comes from the Haut-Médoc. The six communes entitled to their own *appellation*, as listed below, produce about 120,000 hectolitres a year.

Nearly 150 years ago, in 1824 Franck gave the total Haut-Médoc and Bas-Médoc output as 286,000 – 346,000 hectolitres, of which the Haut-Médoc accounted for between 243,000 and 293,000 hectolitres. St-Estèphe was the most prolific producer, averaging 40,500 – 45,000 hl., followed by Pauillac with 31,500 – 36,000 hl. Neither of the other two qualitatively important communes, St-Julien and Margaux, produced as much as a third of these totals; and Macau production was double either of them, while Blanquefort equalled each. A quarter of a century later A. d'Armailhacq in 1850 estimated total Médoc output as 364,000 hl., of which 41,000 hl. came from the *crus classés*. Today the average output figures for St-Estèphe and Pauillac are roughly 40,000 hl. and 30,000 hl. respectively. The big drop in output has been owing to the great shrinkage in the *crus bourgeois* and the disappearance of the *palus* wines.

Evidence of recent increased production of the *crus classés* is that in March 1965 the permitted quantity per hectare for the Médoc *appellations* was raised by the *Institut National des Appellations d'Origine (I.N.A.O.)*. The maximum *rendement* per hectare now allowed to be sold with the appropriate *appellation* is as follows:

Pauillac	40 hl.	St-Julien	40 hl.
Margaux	40	St-Estèphe	40
Listrac	40	Haut-Médoc	43
Moulis	40	Médoc	45

These maxima are liable to variation according to the vintage (in the poor year of 1968 the Pauillac *A.C.* crop was reduced to 25 hl. and such variations are an integral part of the system), but contrary to what some growers will tell one, I am assured that greater quantity can only be at the expense of quality. Nevertheless production surplus to the above figures may, on appeal, often be permitted the *appellation*. In 1966 *AC* production throughout the whole Médoc area was 223,000 hl., in 1967 it was 303,000 hl.

There are twenty-six communes in the Haut-Médoc in which wine is produced and, as can be seen from the above, only six are entitled to an *appellation* of their own. The rest are only allowed to label their wine Hau t-Médoc. In the Bas-Médoc (*appellation* Médoc) there are fifteen wine-producing com munes.

Although the Médoc resounds with 'big names', there are in fact remarkably few large estates. However these do produce between two-fifths and one half-of the total quantity of wine. The largest of these probably is Lafite with a vineyard area of 80 hectares. I write 'probably' advisedly, and would like to warn readers that throughout this chapter such figures, and the totals of output, may be approximate rather than accurate. For they vary not only with time and vintage but from source to source. In many cases the figures have been given me by the proprietors, their *régisseurs* or *maîtres de chai*; otherwise from official returns or standard works of reference. They seldom all agree with each other. It may be that a vineyard has been extended since the official figure. For example it was M. André Portet, *régisseur* of Lafite, who gave me the total of 80 hectares, but the latest official figure is 78 hectares. No doubt there has been some additional planting in the meantime. The same applies to the composition of the vineyards, in nearly all cases given me by the men on the spot. Sometimes I have been mildly surprised by the percentage precision with which a *maître de chai* or a *chef de culture* has replied to my question with some such formula as: Cabernet-Sauvignon 53 per cent, Cabernet-Franc 24 per cent, Merlot 21 per cent and Petit-Verdot 2 per cent. How do they measure up those few rows of Petit-Verdot? However, it does not matter, and such accuracy is possible. The significance of such figures is to give the balance of the vineyard, which may give a clue to the style and quality of the wine we drink; few of us are going to lose much drinking time if the percentage of Petit-Verdot is in fact 1 per cent or even 3 per cent. It is there in the vineyard, and the juice of its grapes is in the bottle.

Sometimes the acreage and output given me at the château have seemed rather large in relation to other sources, and perhaps they owe a little to proprietorial pride; although growers in the Médoc and elsewhere in the Gironde are usually more reliable about their own property than about their neighbours. In such cases where I suspected a little rounding-off of the totals, I have done my best to take account of this.

To return to the Médoc, in addition to the big estates, which do not much exceed fifty in number, there are about 450 small growers making their own wine and accounting for roughly one-sixth to one-eighth of the total, and fourteen co-operatives making the balance of total production. These co-operatives are nearly all in the northern part of the district and half of them in the Bas-Médoc. The

The 1855 Classification of Red Bordeaux

Premiers Crus		*Troisièmes Crus (cont.)*	
Lafite	Pauillac	Marquis d'Alesme-Becker	Margaux
Latour	Pauillac	Boyd-Cantenac	Margaux
Margaux	Margaux		
Haut-Brion	Pessac (Graves)	*Quatrièmes Crus*	
		St-Pierre-Sevaistre	St-Julien
Deuxièmes Crus		St-Pierre-Bontemps	St-Julien
Mouton-Rothschild	Pauillac	Branaire-Ducru	St-Julien
Rausan-Ségla	Margaux	Talbot	St-Julien
Rauzan-Gassies	Margaux	Duhart-Milon	Pauillac
Léoville-Las-Cases	St-Julien	Pouget	Cantenac
Léoville-Poyferré	St-Julien	La Tour-Carnet	St-Laurent
Léoville-Barton	St-Julien	Lafon-Rochet	St-Estèphe
Durfort-Vivens	Margaux	Beychevelle	St-Julien
Lascombes	Margaux	Le Prieuré-Lichine	Cantenac
Gruaud-Larose	St-Julien	Marquis-de-Terme	Margaux
Brane-Cantenac	Cantenac		
Pichon-Longueville	Pauillac	*Cinquièmes Crus*	
Pichon-Longueville-Lalande	Pauillac	Pontet-Canet	Pauillac
Ducru-Beaucaillou	St-Julien	Batailley	Pauillac
Cos-d'Estournel	St-Estèphe	Haut Batailley	Pauillac
Montrose	St-Estèphe	Grand-Puy-Lacoste	Pauillac
		Grand-Puy-Ducasse	Pauillac
Troisièmes Crus		Lynch-Bages	Pauillac
Kirwan	Cantenac	Lynch-Moussas	Pauillac
Issan	Cantenac	Dauzac	Labarde
Lagrange	St-Julien	Mouton-Baron-Philippe	Pauillac
Langoa	St-Julien	Le Tertre	Arsac
Giscours	Labarde	Haut-Bages-Libéral	Pauillac
Malescot-St-Exupéry	Margaux	Pédesclaux	Pauillac
Cantenac-Brown	Cantenac	Belgrave	St-Laurent
Palmer	Cantenac	Camensac	St-Laurent
La Lagune	Ludon	Cos-Labory	St-Estèphe
Desmirail	Margaux	Clerc-Milon-Mondon	Pauillac
Calon-Ségur	St-Estèphe	Croizet-Bages	Pauillac
Ferrière	Margaux	Cantemerle	Macau

See map of the Médoc on page 139.

most southerly is at Arcins in the Haut-Médoc; Bégadan in the Bas-Médoc is the largest.

In discussing the wines of the Médoc there are two possible ways of covering them; by geography and by classification. Either method on its own has obvious short-comings, so I decided to combine them as far as possible; and I have followed this procedure in the other districts with classified or outstanding wines. In the case of the Médoc, where the order of the 1855 classification had meaning, I have described the classed growths in sequence commune by commune.

So far as the history of the older growths is concerned firm facts are by no means easy to secure. In many cases it is surprising how little is reliably known about the past, and often fact is difficult to disentangle from fiction, or perhaps tradition. Several important-looking French books published in the heyday of the Médoc in the 1860s and 1870s are inclined to 'write-up' the châteaux they describe, and when it comes to the earlier history they sometimes contradict one another as to events, proprietors and dates. This is often owing to a paucity of solid information. When Latour passed into English hands a few years ago, the new proprietors were dis-appointed to find how little could be discovered from the château's own records.

Then there are certain legends which probably arose through some skilful public relations work of the time. For example it is said that Marshal Richelieu, when Governor of Guyenne, was advised by his doctor to drink Lafite as being the most powerful and most agreeable tonic. Thereupon Louis XV (1715 – 1774) compli-mented him on looking twenty-five years younger. The Marshal explained why, gave the king some bottles and the fortunes of Lafite and its proprietor M. de Ségur were made. It is also said to have been equally appreciated by Mesdames de Pom-padour and Dubarry. All this may be taken with a pinch of salt, particularly as the later French kings were always having thrust on them 'favourite wines', invariably with tonic qualities. Such stories are often told about more than one growth.

Pauillac

Accordingly I begin with the Haut-Médoc, starting – a shade arbitrarily perhaps but arguably without difficulty – in Pauillac. To enter the Médoc on paper by crossing the *Jalle de Blanquefort* would entail a dull, prosaic progress, while to land at St-Estèphe might be logical topographically but ill-balanced vinously. No doubt partisans of Ch. Margaux and St-Julien would have no difficulty in pressing their claims for 'first footing', but whatever the merits of the 1855 classification, discussed later, it does include more growths from Pauillac than any other: eighteen in all, after various sub-divisions of properties. They tend to cluster at the top and bottom end of the five classes, with two *premiers crus*, three *deuxièmes*, one *quatrième* and no fewer than twelve *cinquièmes*.

With exceptions to be noted, this range is justified, for the sumptuous leading growths near the estuary are worlds away from the small, farm-like properties lying inland amid the woods and rather scrubby land of the thinly populated 'outback' towards St-Laurent and the forest of the Landes. So far as the vineyards are concerned, the commune of Pauillac is really split into two: north and south, with the little estuary town of Pauillac in between. In the northerly section lies Lafite (which adjoins Cos-d'Estournel in St-Estèphe), Mouton-Rothschild and the attendant Mouton-Baron-Philippe (formerly Mouton-d'Armailhacq) and Pontet-Canet. To the south-west of these stretch such growths as Grand-Puy-Lacoste and Lynch-Bages. There is a cluster of smaller growths around the town, among them Duhart-Milon, now owned by Lafite, Haut-Bages-Libéral, part of which has been incorporated into Pontet-Canet, and Grand-Puy-Ducasse, whose château, though not its vineyard, is on the river front.

Then there is something of a gap, as one proceeds south on the famous *Route-des-Grands-Crus (D.2)*. Indeed Latour, on the river side of the road, is only marginally a Pauillac and at one time was registered as being in the hamlet of St-Lambert. The other two major growths, Pichon-Longueville-Baron and Pichon-Longueville-Comtesse-de-Lalande, whose châteaux stare across the road at each other (rather sultrily I always fancy) are similarly placed, and at one time the *appellation contrôlée* authorities insisted on part of the latter being labelled as St-Julien. This, however, was carrying bureaucracy a little too far, and has now been stopped, but it demonstrates the distinct physical position of these 'southern' Pauillacs.

The commune as a whole has a fairly heavy gravelly soil, with a stony sub-soil and then iron below. To some extent Pauillac is the wine capital of the Haut-Médoc, with the *Maison du Vin* there, and the headquarters of the *Commanderie du Bontemps*, the publicity organization promoting the wines of the Médoc and the adjacent Graves.

In discussing the Pauillac growths, I deal with them in the order of the 1855 classification, since the approximate class sequence is widely known and less confusing than if the estates were considered only on a geographical basis within the commune. This pattern I have adopted for the other communes and districts. For reference purposes the 1855 classification is printed on page 108.

First in Pauillac, therefore, comes Lafite, whose claim to first-growth status is long-lived and unchallenged. Even its immediate neighbour at Mouton-Rothschild would not aspire to more than parity of esteem although not perhaps averse to stealing an occasional priority of price in the open market. However, I have yet to meet a proprietor of a classed-growth Médoc who does not publicly or secretly believe that on the day – or in the evening – his wine is the peer of any other.

As mentioned earlier, in the Christie's sale in 1788 of the cellar of the retiring French Ambassador, Count d'Adhémar, his Lafite fetched the high price of 66s. a dozen, compared with 49s. for the Margaux. No vintage was listed in either case. In these early years Lafite's name was often spelled in varying ways, sometimes with two 'f's, and often with two 't's, variations not unknown in print even today. In the eighteenth and the first third of the nineteenth centuries it was occasionally called La-Fite or La-Fitte.

As with other Médoc estates, the date when the vineyard was established as an entity is not known; it was probably around the turn of the seventeenth–eighteenth centuries, when many of the Médoc growths began to take shape but it may have been earlier. Lafite then passed to the important vineyard proprietor, the Marquis de Ségur, who also owned Latour and Calon, now named after him. He was a Président of the Parlement of Guyenne, the regional assembly which met in Bordeaux. At the time of the Revolution it belonged to a later Président, M. de Pichard. He along with the owners of Ch. Margaux were perhaps the only important vineyard proprietors of Bordeaux actually to be guillotined in Paris. At Lafite the estate was confiscated owing to the emigration of his daughter. It had been greatly improved by Ségur and its fame may be gauged by the printed notice of sale which may be seen inside the château today. It was described as being the property of 'La Fille de Pichard emigrée'. Maybe if she had not emigrated she would not have lost the property, for as already noted it was emigration that chiefly led to confiscation.

The sale was notified as being in the Fifth Year of the Revolutionary calendar (1796 – 1797), and the property was described as '*La domaine de Lafite, premier cru du Médoc, et produisant le premier vin de Bordeaux*'. Whether or not the last remark was an example of auctioneer's enthusiasm, it is interesting to note that it was described as a first growth. This is amply confirmed in the chapter on the classification of the Médoc. It was valued at the large and precise sum of 1,286,606 frs. 25 c. The notice states that the vineyard did not suffer from frost and was well maintained throughout. It was sold on 2 September 1797 to a Dutch syndicate who resold it in 1803 to M. Vanlerberghe, who had made his pile by supplying the French Army, and might fairly be described nowadays as a war profiteer. He paid 1,200,000 frs., a little lower than the valuation of six years earlier.

Later there was some mystery as to the real ownership of Lafite at this period. For in 1818 it was bought for 1 million frs. by Mme Rosalie Lemaire – the former wife of M. Vanlerberghe – and, ostensibly at least she sold at the same price in 1821 to the London banking firm of Sir Claude (later Samuel) Scott & Co., who later amalgamated with Parrs Bank, which in turn became part of the Westminster Bank. The nominal owner was Samuel Scott, who became Sir Samuel Scott on the death of his father Sir Claude Scott, Bart. in 1830. One French writer (Danflou) says that under Scott's regime the wine became so expensive that it was too dear for the French and most of it was drunk by the British nobility. According to Franck in 1824, average production was 100 *tonneaux* of the first wine, 20 – 30 of the second.

Sir Samuel Scott and his son, also Samuel, continued in apparently unchallenged possession of the property until the death of M. Vanlerberghe's son in 1866. It then appeared that ownership had never left that family, but the property had been transferred to avoid confiscation for debt nearly forty years previously. The heirs had come to terms with the state in 1856, and after the death of the younger Vanlerberghe they put the property up for sale.* It was keenly fought for between a Bordeaux syndicate who wanted to avoid it falling into the hands of 'outsiders', but was finally acquired by Baron James de Rothschild for 4,140,000 frs. plus 300,000 frs. for the Carruades vineyard; roughly the equivalent at present day values of nearly a million pounds or over two and a quarter million dollars.

---

* For much of this information on a matter hitherto obscure I am indebted to Cyril Ray, who generously allowed me to read in advance of publication the ms. of his *Lafite: The Story of Château Lafite Rothschild* (1968).

After the château had been sold, there was an auction in November 1868 of som of the old vintages from 1797, the date of the establishment of the famous *Vinothèqu* mentioned on page 113. Seven bottles of this wine fetched only 12 frs. apiece (25 frs to the £), and 60 bottles of the celebrated 1802 went for 11 frs. Of the 1803 there were 69 bottles offered, and they fetched 13 frs. each. The real interest lay in 21 bottles of the already mythical 1811, the *Vin de Comète*. M. Delhomme, proprietor of the Café Anglais in Paris, had come down specially for this sale and he started the bidding for the 1811 at 50 frs. But he had an opponent in M. Gremailly of the Hotel des Princes in Bordeaux. When finally it was knocked down to the latter for the enormous price of 121 frs. a bottle, the victory for Bordeaux caused the locals to cheer. The price, equal to £5 at the time, would be at least the equivalent of £25 today.

Later vintages were also sold at this remarkable auction. The celebrated 1815 made 31 frs. for each of 35 bottles, and the 1823 – a vintage with a poor initial reputation but a fine one in later life – reached 60 frs. for each of 33 bottles, while 47 of the excellent 1834 made 70 frs. apiece. The fine 1847 was not offered, but 191 bottles of the robust 1848 went for 65 frs. each. The effect of the oidium scourge could be seen in the price of the 224 bottles of the 1854 – 18 frs. a bottle – while the first fine post-oidium year of 1858 made a high price for a ten-year old wine: 195 bottles for 36 frs. each. The already renowned 1864 made 20 frs. apiece for 274 bottles, and a similar quantity of the château's second wine went for 10 frs. while six *barriques* of the 1865, still in cask, achieved between 2,850 and 3,200 frs. each.

Maybe there was an element of auction room fever in some of these prices, for at about this period at Christie's in the doubtless more restrained atmosphere of St James's, the 1858 Lafite, château-bottled and 'bought of M. Goudal in 1864' (M. Emile Goudal was the manager of the château) fetched no more than 105s. a dozen, while the 1848 from the same source had gone for 126s. and the young 1864 had made only 68s. Nevertheless these were high prices for claret at the time.

In the French Rothschild family Lafite has remained ever since, the branch particularly associated with the bank in Paris being the chief shareholders, with generally a third or a sixth share in the château. Today there are five proprietors, with Baron Guy the major shareholder but Baron Elie taking the chief administrative burden. Each of the proprietors is given annually *gratuit* two *barriques* of the new wine. The charming château, with its corner turret and terrace made familiar by one of the most elegant, unassuming Bordeaux labels, is furnished in the Second Empire style current when the house was acquired by the Rothschilds: a little heavy and bourgeois perhaps, but with the solid lavishness of a rich nineteenth-century family. In fact the furniture mostly came from Ch. Ferrières, the family mansion east of Paris where the terms of the Franco-Prussian Treaty were drafted at a desk now at Lafite. It was the Rothschilds who made possible the speedy payment of the 5 billion frs. indemnity, intended by the Prussians to be crushing, and the ink stain on the desk's surface is said to have been caused by Bismarck thumping it in fury at the quick payment by the Rothschilds. Around the walls of the reception rooms are comfortable-looking family portraits, many of the men bearing an unmistakable kinship; and up on the roof, is a weathercock bearing the familiar five Rothschild arrows.

Below stairs lies the celebrated *Vinothèque* of Lafite. Here rest the wines of one vineyard in a collection whose only rival is that of Schloss Johannisberg in the Rheingau. It was started by the manager, M. Goudal *père* in 1798, the year after the public sale, and there are still eight bottles of the 1797 vintage, reputedly a poor thin year, lying in the rectangular trays that house the older wines. There are two bottles of the much finer 1798 vintage, and then follow varying numbers of the succeeding twenty years or so; of some vintages there are none, and of the famous 1811 'comet' year only one bottle remains. This was the wine served at the château on a famous occasion in 1926 and declared to be in perfect condition by the 300 guests to whom it was offered.

This alas was before my time, but I can claim to have drunk a Lafite senior in vintage and older in years. Towards the end of the 1950s the château for some reason decided to sell off a small quantity of unwanted wines. Most were of poor years, but there were one or two good vintages put in as *bonnes bouches*. Ronald Avery, the Bristol wine merchant, chanced to be in Bordeaux at the time, and he bought a mixed two dozen bottles, including the 1897 and three bottles of the 1803. This had been re-corked at the château in October 1957. I was privileged to share in the last of these three bottles, in April 1967, the others being Ronald Avery and his son John, W. E. Newton a director of the firm, André Simon and George Rainbird. Although not surprisingly the colour was tawny, rather like that of a fine old Madeira, the aroma was very fine as it developed after being decanted immediately before being poured out. There was no doubt from the 'nose' and the flavour that this was claret. It had great distinction and for its age was surprisingly fruity; that it had maintained this fruitiness for just on 164 years was extraordinary. Only after half an hour in the decanter did the wine begin to show some sign of decline, but not much even then. The previous two bottles had both, I was told, been excellent too. It was the oldest bottle of claret that André Simon, then aged 90, had drunk. The bottle itself, curved in shape rather like the bottle now used for Haut-Brion, was pitted. The 1803 vintage was average in quantity, and although good in quality, it had not been the equal of 1802, a rival of the exceptional 1798. After that there was not to be another really fine vintage until the fabled 1811.

It is worth digressing slightly here to mention that until well into the nineteenth century, vintages did not have the importance they have assumed since. There were the outstanding vintages which were known to wine drinkers, such as 1798, 1802, 1811, 1815 and 1819. When a first growth of one of these years turned up, the vintage would be mentioned. For example at Christie's in 1811, some Ch. Margot (*sic*) 1798 was sold and described as of 'celebrated vintage, bottled at London in 1802'. Four years earlier the same château's 1802 wine had been listed. Otherwise the wine would generally be sold as from Lafite or one of the other first growths, without a vintage date. Quite often it would be described purely as 'first growth claret'. There were exceptions as when the ordinary vintage of 1804 was mentioned at a sale of Lafite in 1814, but that was at the end of the Napoleonic Wars when claret was very hard to come by in England, and it fetched the good price of 80s. a dozen.

Vintages also came to the fore with the rise of the other classed-growth châteaux.

No doubt in Bordeaux both growth and vintage had *réclame*, but so far as England was concerned it was not until well into the nineteenth century that any but first-growth clarets were sold by the name of the growth. Instead they relied on the names of the wine merchants who imported and bottled the wines. These were described as 'Barnes's Claret', Plasket's, Payne's, etc.

In May 1967 there was an outstanding sale of ancient wines at Christie's in London, and among these were some notable clarets from the cellars of the Earl of Rosebery. These included bottles and magnums of Lafite 1858, a single magnum of Lafite 1864, triple and double magnums of Lafite 1865, bottles of Lafite 1871, magnums and bottles of Lafite 1874 and two magnums of Lafite 1878. I was invited to taste a small selection of the wines before the sale, and one bottle of the famous Lafite 1858 was opened; it was drinkable but in decline, and nothing like so good as a bottle of Latour 1874. The top price was £155, given for a triple magnum of the Lafite 1865, but on a per-bottle basis the record item was the magnum of 1864, which fetched £82. The quantity of wines was as remarkable as the prices. There were 19 magnums of the 1858, as well as six bottles,* 12 double magnums of the 1865 and no fewer than 40 magnums and 60 bottles of the 1874. Nearly all were declared to be in good condition, i.e., with good corks and not ullaged. The only other clarets were a few bottles of Latour 1874 and Pichon-Longueville of unknown vintage. This also I tasted and it had a firmness that might have suggested an 1870.

Some of the Lafites of the 1870s were château-bottled but for many years, from the 1885 vintage in the phylloxera period until the 1906, it refused to accord château-bottling to the purchasers of its wine. It was only in 1925 that Lafite decided henceforth to bottle the whole of each *récolte*. Château Margaux and Haut-Brion had started bottling the whole crop in 1923, Mouton-Rothschild followed in 1924 with its revolutionary 'modern art' label by Carlus, and Latour did the same in 1925.

The refusal of Lafite to allow château-bottling was perhaps occasioned by the fact that although part of the 1884 crop had been bottled at the château, the buyers found the wine not up to standard and brought an action against the proprietors. Not until over twenty years later when the whole crop was bought by two Bordeaux merchants, Lebègue and Rosenheim, did Lafite again consent to château-bottling. (Château-bottling for part of the crop of the finer wines of Bordeaux only became general shortly before the First World War, about 1910 and 1911. At first it was regarded as an accolade of quality bestowed by the château only in good years, but this aspect has long since been abandoned.) Many years later Lafite also had trouble with a vintage. This was the 1928, which the Bordeaux merchants who had bought it declared not up to sample, and it had to be taken back after a court case. It was said to have been pasteurized.

Like the other leading growths Lafite has many other fine wines in its private cellar, for it was the practice of the château proprietors each good vintage to exchange a few cases with each other and still is. In the Lafite *caveau*, for example, I noted

---

* It is interesting to note that in the sale at Christie's in 1867 already mentioned magnums of the 1858 'bottled on the estate' went for 150s. a dozen.

Mouton-Rothschild 1869, Larose 1870, Smith-Haut-Lafitte 1878 and Léoville-Barton 1899 – a bin of about 15 dozen of this last wine. There was also some Carruades de Lafite 1907.

As already stated, the vineyard of Lafite is one of the largest of the classed growths, with an area of 80 hectares (about 200 acres). However not all the production of this area is sold as Lafite. There is the plateau known as Carruades, which in fact runs across into Mouton-Rothschild, and at one time only the wine from this area was sold as Carruades de Lafite. However for many years now this name has been applied to wine from the younger vines – under twelve years, according to the *régisseur*, M. André Portet. The Carruades, therefore, is the second wine of Lafite, but that does not imply any degrading inferiority. Nowadays it is all château-bottled. The Carruades '53 was an admirable wine at a time when the Lafite '53 was considered to lead the Médoc field. In good years there is also a third wine, Moulin des Carruades, all château-bottled and normally reserved for sale only inside France by the Paris firm of Nicolas.

However, about 200 *tonneaux* of wine are sold as Lafite, which is much more than the other first growths. In 1967 a record total of 335 *tonneaux* was made, including the Carruades. Lafite is generally rather a delicate wine for a Pauillac, much less robust than its neighbour at Mouton or at Latour. This is partly to be ascribed to the soil, partly to the composition of the vineyard which is said to contain more Merlot than its neighbours, and partly to the method of vinification. At the château I was told that the vineyard was two-thirds Cabernet-Sauvignon, one-sixth Cabernet-Franc and one-sixth Merlot. In successful years Lafite is the acme of fine claret, well-balanced, elegant and supple with a delicious aroma. Its 1945 is generally regarded as the top wine of the vintage, although this might be contested by those who like a more full-bodied wine. In less good vintages it lacks the stamina of Latour and may be rather thin and disappointing. In recent years its opening price has risen astronomically. Whereas the highly esteemed 1953 was first offered to the British and American trade at the equivalent of £100 or less a hogshead, the 1964 went for £572 and the 1966 for £695. The 1967 was sold for the same price in francs as the 1966, but owing to sterling devaluation in November 1967 the price in Britain was nearly £800. Mouton-Rothschild '67 was the same price. These extravagant prices are the result mostly of a world-wide and particularly an American demand for the first-growth clarets, but partly also to the well-known rivalry between Lafite and Mouton-Rothschild.

Latour has a longer history than Lafite, more dramatic in the earlier times, less eventful or less well-chronicled later on. According to the *Histoire Militaire de Bordeaux* (Ribadieu), in the early days of the English occupation of Gascony the chatelains of Latour were pro-Plantagenet, a record that may be considered satisfactory by the present British owners. The Tower was one of a line of fortifications, erected as a kind of pre-Martello line, against the ocean-going pirates. It is said that this particular link in the chain lay to the south of the existing domed tower, whose appearance owes more to the evocative quality produced by the name of the wine than to any great distinction of its own. Apparently the Latour proprietors did not hesitate to take tribute from the Bordelais navigators as well as from the more suspect Breton mariners who ventured up the Gironde. At some point it evidently passed into French hands, as Jean de Neuville, described as lieutenant of the English king in Gascony, took it from the French in 1378, but in 1444 it was re-taken by Bertrand de Montfaucon. Then the pro-English Gaston de Lisle, Baron de la Brède, recaptured it a few years later. How it finally passed into French hands is not clear, but it is said that Latour saw pass beneath its walls the remnants of Talbot's English army after Castillon in 1453. Possibly it was confiscated after the emigration of its owner, as often happened in the Médoc during the French Revolution, for it is believed that Latour belonged to the Sire de Larsan who was on the English side, and that when he was defeated he sought refuge in England, while the manoir was sacked and burnt. In 1477 the property was owned by Gaston de la Touche, and in 1606 by Denis de Mallet. In 1670 it was bought by M. de Chavanas, passed in 1677 to the Clauzel family and then by marriage to the Ségur family. Nicolas de Ségur, Président of the Parlement of Guyenne and already mentioned as proprietor of Lafite, passed it on to his three daughters, one of whom, the Comtesse de Miromesnil, seems to have inherited most of the estate, and her husband did much to improve the vineyard. Their two daughters, Mme de Beaumont and Mme de La Pallu inherited this part. The rest of the property still owned by the Marquis de Ségur had been confiscated on the latter's emigration during the Revolution and was not re-acquired by the family until 1840. Two years later the estate became a company, entirely owned by the family. At this time it was valued at 1½ million frs., and in the prosperous 1860s the wine sold for much the same price as Lafite. The manager was M. Roug, a notary and mayor of Pauillac. The vineyard was then said to be in excellent condition. It was the Beaumont family who took the lead in administration until in 1962 the property was sold to an English company representing the family interests of Viscount Cowdray. This company took 51 per cent of the shares, Harveys of Bristol, the well-known wine merchants, acquired 25 per cent and the remaining 24 per cent of the shares stayed in French hands, with Comte Hubert de Beaumont, the former chairman, and Comte Philippe de Beaumont representing them on the board. The English buyers are said to have paid over £900,000. This sale did not go through without some protest from those who thought that control of so famous a first growth should not pass into foreign hands. However it was pointed out that Haut-Brion had been American-owned for many years, and General de Gaulle to whom the matter was said to have been referred is alleged to have remarked that the English company could scarcely remove the soil.

When wine was first made at Latour under the estate name is not known, but certainly it was in production early in the eighteenth century. Latour was the first *premier cru* château to be listed with vintage date in a Christie's wine auction. This was the Latour 1785 of which 500 bottles were sold in a trade sale in 1792. The top price was 44s. per dozen in bond. Later, in 1824, its output was given by Franck as 70 – 90 *tonneaux*.

It is interesting that when the present owners of Latour took over they found small parcels of the vineyard in the hands of peasant proprietors. These totalled several hectares and were gradually acquired from them. Only in 1790 did Latour come into the commune of Pauillac; previously it had been in St-Lambert.

The vineyard of Latour, much smaller than Lafite, and also seldom subject to frost, comprises 58 hectares of Cabernet-Sauvignon (80 per cent), Cabernet-Franc (10 per cent) and Merlot (10 per cent); and it produces an average of about 160 *tonneaux*, although output is increasing as the vineyard, which until a few years ago had too high a proportion of old vines, comes into full production. In the exceptionally prolific year of 1964 the production was 216 *tonneaux*. A second wine, similar in status to the Carruades de Lafite, will shortly be marketed under the name of Les Forts de Latour, and it will be made from the younger grapes.

Latour is a powerful wine of a style largely derived from the high proportion of Cabernet-Sauvignon – 80 per cent – in the vineyard. That this has always been its characteristic may be gauged from the comment of Franck in 1824 that Latour had 'more body' than that of Lafite but needed to be kept a year more in cask; also a chemist, M. Faure, in his *Analyse Chimique des Grands Vins de la Gironde*, quoted in Danflou (1866), and stated that the wines of Latour had a stronger nose and a more pronounced flavour than those of Lafite and Margaux. Its character no doubt also arises from the soil, situation and vinification, for the proportion of Cabernet-Sauvignon at Mouton-Rothschild is no less, but the wines are quite distinct in type.

So powerful and strong, almost coarse, is Latour in youth that it is difficult to taste and even not very agreeable, particularly in fine years. In any tasting of fairly mature first growths, Latour is almost invariably the most backward. Good examples of this are 1945, 1949 and 1953. On the other hand Latour has wonderfully fruity qualities, and if it lacks the elegance of Lafite, the concentration of Mouton and the charm of Margaux, it has a splendid depth and richness of flavour. This can still be seen in the 1920 and 1929 wines, and the former surely remains as it always has been, the best wine of the vintage.

Moreover Latour usually makes exceptionally good wine in off or indifferent vintages. A few years ago a special tasting of off-vintage Latours was arranged for me at the château. They started with '63 and continued with '56, '54, '51, '46, '44, '41, '40, '39 and '33. The last was not by any means an off-year, but it was put in as a *bonne bouche* at the end, and to show the lasting power of Latour in a light vintage. Otherwise these years were not only generally poor, but the older wines of most other growths would long since have died. However with Latour only the '56 was non-agreeable, but that was an exceptionally bad vintage. The '39 was definitely on the way down, but who could blame it a quarter of a century after such a deplorable harvest? The wartime examples were brown in colour but perfectly drinkable. I picked out the '40; but my choice of them all was, unexpectedly to me, the '46 which was surprisingly full and well-balanced. It is fair to say that M. Metté, the *maître de chai*, gave his vote to the '51, an excellent wine for its year which I have drunk a number of times. On this occasion the '58 was not on show, but that is still another excellent Latour in a lightweight year.

The virtual reconstruction of the *cuvier* and *chais* in the last few years included the installation of fourteen stainless steel fermentation vats, each capable of holding

200 hectolitres and costing £1,500 apiece. The only other château in the Gironde to install stainless steel vats has been Haut-Brion, although they are different in design from those at Latour. Naturally these have caused controversy and head-shaking in Bordeaux, but at Latour they state that better control can be secured during the fermentation, cold water can be poured over them to reduce temperature and the fact that the vats are of stainless steel is irrelevant; the wine is normally only in them for ten to fifteen days and thereafter is matured in wood. They were first used in the 1964 vintage, in which Latour came out particularly well; so time alone will show.

For consistency over the years, I am inclined to think that Latour leads the first growths (with which I must in this and other contexts include Mouton-Rothschild). It is not always so distinguished a wine as the others at their best, but it has fruit and quality. In any one fine vintage it may be beaten by its rivals: by Lafite in '45, Mouton in '49, and by several in '53. Yet overall its record is impressive, and faced by the need to select one bottle from all the leaders in a vintage unknown to me or of lesser repute I would certainly select the Latour. But of course I could be wrong.

The actual château of Latour is a small, post-Tuileries Second Empire building which has now been redecorated by its English owners. The interior is as charming and comfortable as a small English country house, and to its dark-papered dining room are brought up notable bottles from the small private cellar below. From the windows is a fine view of the Gironde, the only first growth with such a prospect.

The small *caveau privé* of Latour is notable for the representation of its own wines, but not so much as the other leading châteaux for a general collection; the reason being that in the past Latour did not exchange so regularly as the others. The earliest Latour is the 1863, an off-vintage in that remarkable decade, and there were thirty bottles in the bin when I saw it. This wine had not been tasted recently. There were also eighteen bottles left of the famous 1865, and this was proclaimed remarkable in the year of its centenary. It was no less remarkable when I was privileged to drink it at the château three years later: an amazingly full-bodied, fruity wine. Further comments will be found in the chapter on Bordeaux vintages. There are many gaps, but of the great 1899 I noted 100 bottles, and many more of less ancient years, including several hundred of the 1929, of which no fewer than ten dozen were sent to London for André Simon's ninetieth birthday banquet in February 1967. A curiosity is a number of glass-stoppered bottles full of wine and of age unknown; to open them it would be necessary to remove the neck. I believe that elsewhere examples of glass-stoppered Lafites have been found.

At the Rosebery sale in 1967, already mentioned, the highest price reached for old wines in bottle, rather than in magnums or larger sizes, was for 13 bottles of Latour 1874. All were bought by Harveys at 6200s. a dozen, or £25.16.8 a bottle. This was one of the wines which I sampled in advance of the sale; it was in excellent condition and showing no sign of decline.

In the last century Latour was particularly popular in Britain and, according to the 1853 edition of Franck's *Traité sur les Vins du Médoc*, in favourable years the English were the largest buyers. In those days it averaged between 70 and 90 *tonneaux* a year, compared with 100 to 150 for Lafite.

The chairman of the board of Latour today is David Pollock. By an odd coincidence, facing the title page of Michel's *Histoire du Commerce et de la Navigation à Bordeaux* (1867) is a long pull-out English map of the siege of Blaye in 1592. The places on the Médoc side of the estuary are marked and Pauillac is spelled Pollock.

The controversial question of Mouton-Rothschild and its standing in the classification is discussed elsewhere, but there is no doubt that Mouton, its image and its ambience, add a good deal of colour as well as quality to Bordeaux and the repute of fine claret. There are those who disapprove of what they would call the publicity-consciousness, the restlessness which insists on a new label, designed by a well-known artist, each year. When I first visited Mouton over twenty years ago the richly furnished *salle de réception* with its visitors' book covered with the large-scale signatures and gushing praise of American visitors, and the indirectly illuminated Mouton arms at the end of the great *chai*, struck an unusual note among its fellows. To visit Lafite afterwards was like entering a monastery. But now nearly all the leading châteaux and some minor growths have *salles de réception*; most of them designed with far less taste and skill than at Mouton.

This growth is presided over by one of the great 'committed' proprietors of Bordeaux. All the vineyard owners are proud of their wine, but some whom I have met have a special attachment, differing widely in expression. Among these I would place Henri Binaud of Cantemerle, Ronald Barton of Léoville and Langoa-Barton (though more quietly as befits an Anglo-Saxon), Henri Woltner of La Mission-Haut-Brion, Raymond Dupin of Grand-Puy-Lacoste, and above all Baron Philippe de Rothschild. Although his father, Baron Henri, was the proprietor before him, the former was more interested in literature and the theatre. Philippe, brought up in Paris, scarcely visited Mouton before he was grown-up. His grandmother ran the estate, efficiently but perhaps without special flair, from the death in 1881 of her husband, Baron James, to 1920. For many years the labels bore the name of the actual director, Baron de Miollis. The Baroness's name was Laura Thérèse and she came from the Frankfurt branch of the family. When in 1920 the Baroness James was seventy-three she partly handed over to her son but within two years he had passed the property on to the twenty-one-year-old Philippe, who ran it on his own from 1922 onwards. There is no doubt that he has transformed the estate and its reputation.

As mentioned earlier the name Mouton has none of the ovine significance to which the heraldic supporters of the arms give credence. A *motte de terre* is an eminence, and indeed in relation to the slightly lower ground towards the estuary, it is such. The growth seems to have been established as an entity in the reign of Louis XV, when it belonged to the Brane (or Branne) family, later associated with Brane-Cantenac, and previously with a link to Haut-Brion. Baron Hector de Branne was one of the great improvers of the Médoc vineyards, like his neighbour A. d'Armailhacq, and together they are said to have been responsible for introducing the Cabernet-Sauvignon to the Médoc. If so they largely made claret what it has become. The wine of Branne-Mouton had a reputation in Bordeaux, but it was not widely known before the Revolution. The first mention I can find of it in a Christie catalogue was in 1834, alongside Lafite and Latour, and all without vintage date. It was noted again in 1842 and some eight dozen Branne-Mouton, bottled 1835, were in one of the mammoth sales of the cellar of Crockford's Club in 1852. It fetched the moderate price of 59s. a dozen. But even at this time named clarets were the exception, and they were still mostly sold under such merchants' names as Randolph Payne or Maxwell & Keys. In fact after Branne sold Mouton in 1830 to M. Thuret it appears to have been somewhat neglected, which is partly why Baron Nathaniel Rothschild, a member of the English branch of the family, was able to buy it in 1853 comparatively cheaply and for less money than M. Thuret had paid for it (*see* page 69). However, the Mouton production had been considerable, and was given in 1824 as averaging 120 – 140 *tonneaux*.

The other reason was probably the current oidium then ravaging the Médoc; and it was five years before the new owner could harvest a good vintage. The vineyard was greatly improved by the manager, M. Galos, and he planted it with Cabernet-Sauvignon. Previously it had not been an entirely united vineyard, having strips detached from the rest, a not uncommon situation in the Médoc. To this day the two of the three parts of the Léoville vineyard are somewhat intertwined, and below the walls of Ronald Barton's château of Langoa lie parts of Poyferré's portion.

What there was not at Mouton was a château or house of any size; merely a farm. Baron Nathaniel was more interested in improving the property than in building a house, and it was his son Baron James, succeeding his father in 1870, who in the middle of the *chai* courtyard in 1880 – 1883 built the small, period-charming, Second Empire style house now known as Petit-Mouton. Here the family lived until a few years ago, when the first floor of the adjacent stable buildings were converted into a series of splendid apartments, including an open-beamed library and a long gallery overlooking the vineyard. In this gallery are assembled and skilfully placed an ingenious variety of eye-catching *objets d'art*, including an Italian Renaissance painter's wooden model of a horse.

Petit-Mouton, still used for guests and occasional meals, is also full of interesting *objets*, including a collection of English needlework pictures, assembled by Baron Philippe when he was in England during the last war. However, vinously the most interesting item is a fine French carpet presented by Napoleon III to Queen Victoria in 1860. The design shows a slim Napoleon holding one end of a scroll inscribed, 'THE TREATY OF COMMERCE – A further proof of our FRIENDSHIP'. The other end is held by Queen Victoria, less kindly depicted as already somewhat generous in girth. In the side panels are 'N' and 'V' and across the bottom is written '*LA RECIPROCITE EST LA BASE VRAIE ET DURABLE DE LA PAIX.*' For some reason this curious carpet was ejected from the Royal household and subsequently bought by Baron Philippe; it is highly appropriate that this memorial of a treaty which did so much to increase the Bordeaux trade with Britain should find a place in the Médoc.

Under the Rothschild régime, production was increased and by 1865 140 *tonneaux* were produced, and 170 in the following year. There were by then 55 hectares under vines, nearly as many as today.

Mouton is unusual for the high proportion of Cabernet-Sauvignon in the vineyard, perhaps as high as 90 per cent, with 7 per cent Cabernet-Franc and the balance Merlot. Its output is now about 160 *tonneaux*. The wine is distinguished for its fullness and concentration of flavour. It is a rich wine, and more than once I have mistaken it for one of the top Pomerols such as Pétrus. Sometimes almost Burgundian in its power, it is probably the most individual of all the Médocs. As already mentioned, the classification problem is discussed in Chapter XVII, but if a Bordeaux classification is to mean anything Mouton-Rothschild must be in the top class. A very different style of wine is produced at Mouton from its neighbours, but no serious wine drinker can doubt the exceptional quality or the record of fine vintages in the last hundred years. Mouton is said to have *un goût de capsule*, but I have never captured this, although on occasion its other alleged point of individuality, an aroma of cedar-wood, or lead pencils, has come home to me. The special quality of Mouton must lie in the soil and in the method of vinification. The *cuvier* with its seventeen large fermenting vats all made of oak, is built on the traditional two-storey principle, with the vats being filled from above. This is also to be seen at the neighbouring Pontet-Canet. When the fermentation is over the wine stays in the *cuves* for another fortnight before being transferred to brand new oak casks. One of the sights of Mouton and of the other leading châteaux are the carefully-aligned ranks of new oak casks for the new wine. Only the top growths can afford these days to have entirely new casks every time, for they cost about £14 apiece. To spend nearly £10,000 a year on new casks as they do at Mouton even for a bad vintage is a formidable outlay. They must certainly make some difference to the style of the wine, for young oak does give a flavour quite distinct from the rather disagreeable taste of a wine which is 'casky'. Mouton like all the fairly large châteaux has several cellars: one for the first year's wine, and another for the second year's. Save in very poor years, the leading growths do not normally bottle until the winter or spring of the third year after the vintage. In this case the older wine generally stays in the second-year cellar.

The vineyard of Mouton-Rothschild is 75 hectares in extent, but only 61 are in production. To the north it is separated only by a cart track from Lafite. Elsewhere it adjoins Mouton-Baron-Philippe, and to the south-east it marches with Pontet-Canet.

Mouton, like Latour, often makes good wine in off-years, but this is less true of the other top growths. At tastings at Mouton I have sampled such vintages as '60, '58, '56, '54, '51, '50, '46 and '44. The best of these were the '58, '51 and '46. The '60 was very fair and so was the '54, and only the '56 – a terrible Bordeaux year – and the '50 were unattractive. The '44 had a fine nose but lacked fruit, while the '46, also so good at Latour, was remarkably round and fruity for very much of an off-year.

Mouton has always been more publicity- or sales-conscious than the other châteaux, although this is now considered less 'bad form' than it used to be. One aspect of this was close attention to the design of the labels. The first one which broke away from a traditional style was the brightly coloured design by Carlus, employed from 1924 – 1926, and distinctly advanced for its time, with the famous Rothschild arrows prominent. In 1934 the idea was hit upon of inscribing on the label the number of bottles produced in each size, and numbering each. For example the label of the famous 1945 reads:

Cette récolte a produit
24 jeroboams numérotés de A à Y.
1475 magnums numéro. de M 1 à M 1475
74,422 bout. et ½ bout. numér. de 1 à 74,422
2000 Réserve du Château marquées R.C.
Cette   bouteille porte le No. . . .
Philippe de Rothschild

The 1945 was a small vintage but in 1959, for example, the number of bottles and halves was given as 151,744 and the proportion between the two was probably much the same as before. There were 2,091 magnums and 116 '*Grands Formats*', which is the formula now used to include double magnums, jeroboams and impériales. There have been several large vintages since. The number reserved for the château varies, but it is never less than 2,000; in 1947 it was 4,000, and 3,000 in 1955. The only year when the numbered label has been omitted was 1953 the centenary year of the Rothschild acquisition of Mouton. That carried a medallion of Baron Nathaniel, ovals containing the names of the two following owners, and underneath signed by Baron Philippe, a dedication of the vintage to three family predecessors. Fortunately Mouton made excellent wine that year.

It was in 1945 that Mouton started its custom of inviting a different artist every year to design the label for the vintage, in the form of a strip at the top. The first was 1945 – *Année de la Victoire* (a year when even Lafite unbent sufficiently to emboss the year's date on the bottles, but whether this was to commemorate the victory over the Germans or the fine vintage is an open question). Since then many distinguished artists have been commissioned to provide this decoration, including Jean Cocteau (1947), Marie Laurencin (1948), Dignimont (1949), Braque (1955), André Masson (1957), Salvador Dali (1958) and – a compliment to an English artist – Henry Moore (1964).

From here it is appropriate to pass to Mouton's other positive contribution to the relation between art and wine: the *Musée du Vin*. This remarkable collection, open since 1962 to all who care to apply in advance to the secretary of the château, is assembled in a former cellar, lying between the *cuvier* and the other *chais*. This is a book devoted to wine and not to the arts, but here surely is one of the most brilliantly conceived, collected, arranged and displayed small museums in the world. Every object, whether a fourteenth-century B.C. Mycenaean *krater*, a James II silver cup; a series of fifteenth-century Rhine Valley tapestries, on work in the vineyard, re-united here after being as far afield as the U.S.A. and Italy; a Picasso gouache or an ingenious eighteenth-century Italian painting whose strips turn to display the Three Ages of Man; all have a vinous association. It is wonderfully uncluttered and every piece is of the highest quality in its genre. Even the warm terracotta coloured floor in the main hall and the black tiles of a side room all contribute to produce a closely considered effect. The placing of the articles is superb and the lighting spectacular without being obvious. For example, engraved glasses are lit from below and this sharply shows off their design. The assembly and planning of this museum took the Baron and Baroness many years, and the planning and design was done by the

Baroness Pauline, the American-born wife of Baron Philippe. Her artistic knowledge and sensibility are also very evident in the living apartments on the other side of the gravelled courtyard where white doves wheel and beat the air with their wings. Mouton, relaxed and almost informal, provides a strange contrast to the tightly buttoned up *Deuxième Empire* period charm of the other Rothschild mansion just across the way at Lafite.

The *Musée du Vin* has steps leading down to another museum – the private and reserve cellars of wine. There is no wine in the Mouton cellar so old as that at Lafite and the oldest Mouton vintage in the private cellar is 1859, but there is a greater collection of old wines of its own and from other châteaux than any other, not excepting the fine collection at Château Margaux. There are 20,000 – 30,000 bottles in one cellar, 100,000 in another. The specially locked and segregated cellar of Mouton wines has a 'reference library' of twenty-four bottles, five magnums and two jeroboams of each vintage. In the older bins lie, like elephants half-submerged in a sea of mud, ancient jeroboams and magnums encrusted with a dark kind of fungus which has almost to be chipped off when the bottle is taken out for its appointed day of opening. To the visitor the wealth of wine is inebriating without a bottle being opened. For example, I observed fifty-nine bottles, two magnums and two jeroboams of the famous 1870; but it would be difficult to call in vain for any vintage not lying there in considerable quantity. These bottles are re-corked and if necessary topped up from the same wine every 25 years; the last occasion was in 1957.

Mouton has always been a great exchanger and buyer of other châteaux wine. Indeed it is the custom there, as in other Médoc châteaux, always to open for another proprietor invited to lunch or dine a fine bottle of his own wine; and at Mouton very often it may be something that he lacks in his own cellar. The second cellar consists of a 70-metre long 'corridor', with all the first growths on one side, among them a fine selection of the vintages of the 1870s. The wines are not confined to the Médoc, and there are some enviable modern vintages of Cheval-Blanc, Pétrus and various other Graves, St-Emilions and Pomerols. There is also a section where the reserve stock of Mouton is kept. After a conducted tour by the taciturn though amiable chief *maître de chai*, M. Pierre Blondin (his voluble brother Raoul is the other), who may have dropped the remark that the best '*vieux Moutons*' are the 1870, 1878 and 1899, one emerges dizzy into the sunlight.

The next two stars in the Pauillac galaxy of classed growths are the pair of Pichons, which once were one. Jacques Pichon Baron de Longueville was the first Président of the Parlement of Bordeaux in the seventeenth century.

If there is less to be said about the past of these distinguished châteaux and indeed hereafter about nearly all the other classed growths, it is because neither they nor their wines have captured the attention and imagination as the leaders have. Nor have many of them preserved much historical material. Some of them were long in the hands of old families like the Pichons, Barons de Longueville, who held their châteaux for two hundred years, but as wine-makers they lacked wide *réclame*.

This can be gauged from the already quoted Christie's wine catalogues. The first mention of a non-first growth Médoc château that I could find was in 1829, with some Léoville 1820 shipped by Barton & Guestier, a firm already well known in the British market. Probably for that reason they put on the label the name of the vineyard, which Hugh Barton was partly to buy in 1821. Otherwise the nearest to a name was usually a wine sold as St-Julien. In 1832 there is mention of Cantenuc (*sic*), and in 1834 La Rose and Mouton are listed. Apart from these three growths, catalogued occasionally thereafter, I can find no other until Rauzan 1845 in 1848, Cos-Destournel (*sic*) 1848 in 1860, and Pichon 1841 in 1861, when Barton & Guestier's Langoa (1857), an English club favourite, also appeared. In 1862 Pontet-Canet 1841 from Cruse et Fils Frères was offered. Slowly then the other well-known names began to appear before a conservatively minded-public. For the nobility drank either one of the first growths, with Lafite predominating and Haut-Brion rarely seen, or they drank their wine merchants' claret, *tout court*.

The first time I came across Pichon-Baron, so-designated in the sale lists, was the 1851, which fetched 78s. a dozen in 1867. The Baron had a mother born Lalande, and when the estate was divided before the 1855 classification, in the proportion of two-fifths and three-fifths, the larger, 'feminine' part of the château took its name from a Comtesse de Lalande, *née* Pichon-Longueville. At one time the Baron enjoyed the wider repute, although the smaller of the two, and its 1929 was one of the best wines of the vintage. Today it is owned by M. Bouteiller, also proprietor of Grand-Puy-Ducasse and Lanessan. Until recent years it seemed much less distinguished and often rather a hard wine. The vineyard is 60 per cent Cabernet of both varieties and 40 per cent Merlot. Its area is only 18 hectares, compared with 31 for Lalande, which has always struck me as a lighter wine. This may be accounted for partly by the fact that strictly speaking two-fifths of the vineyard lies in St-Julien (and was at one time obliged to label part of its *récolte* as a St-Julien) and partly by the composition of the vineyard. It is about 40 per cent Cabernet of both varieties, 40 per cent Merlot, and the balance Petit-Verdot, the late-ripening grape which produces a powerful wine, rich in alcohol. For its size Lalande often makes a good deal of wine, but the hazards of the Bordeaux producer may be gauged by the fact that whereas in a good year Pichon-Lalande will produce up to 150 *tonneaux*, in the fine but short vintage of 1961 its total output was only 30 *tonneaux*. Today the production of Pichon-Baron is about 90 *tonneaux* annually, and the quality is probably improving.

The proprietor of Pichon-Lalande is the energetic young M. William-Alain Miailhe, who also owns Siran and in 1966 bought Dauzac. In recent years a good deal of work has been done in the vineyard and *chais*, and in 1966 a new cellar was completed, with a terrace on top which looks down on the vineyard of Latour – if such condescension be permitted of a second growth to a first. Although now superior to the Baron I have yet to be struck greatly by a Pichon-Lalande, good wine though it is, but perhaps in a few years we may see a difference.

After this galaxy of *premiers* and *deuxièmes* there is a big gap in the Pauillac hierarchy until we come to Duhart-Milon among the *quatrièmes*. Placed partly on the Carruades plateau adjoining Lafite, it is not altogether surprising that Lafite acquired the vineyard in 1962. At one time it belonged to M. Castéja, a lawyer who was elected Mayor of Bordeaux, and it passed to his widow before becoming, like so many of the main Médoc properties, a limited company or *société civile*. The vineyard area, smaller than it once was, is 20 hectares, and the crop has not been large in recent years: around 70 *tonneaux*. One of the clarets of which I had a few bottles in the early years of my wine-collecting was Duhart-Milon 1923, and a very fine wine it was of a vintage not much seen in Britain. But since then I have not come upon a really exciting bottle from this growth; the quality may improve under Rothschild ownership.

Pontet-Canet, which heads the *cinquièmes*, must be one of the best-known châteaux of Bordeaux, particularly in Britain where it has always enjoyed a special popularity. It is named after M. Pontet, who created the vineyard in the location called Canet (spelt Cannet on the stone front of the *cuvier*) and is one of the oldest Haut-Médoc vineyards. It was sold by his heirs in 1865 to M. Herman Cruse, head of the Bordeaux firm of Cruse et Fils Frères. At that time this large vineyard (it had averaged 120 – 140 *tonneaux* according to Franck in 1824) was somewhat split up, with part at Canet, part at Milon and part in Bages. It has long been reunited; and when a few years ago the Cruses bought Haut-Bages, a 9-hectare portion of the vineyard adjoining Pontet-Canet was added to the latter, which now has a vineyard of between 70 and 80 hectares, and produces more wine than any other classed growth. In 1964, for example, the output was 382 *tonneaux* compared with the next largest producer, Gruaud-Larose, which made 349 *tonneaux* from the same area. In the same year Lafite, the largest in area of all the *crus classés* with 80 hectares, made 290 *tonneaux*, including Carruades. These figures are the quantities declared for *appellation*; total production may well have been higher. The vineyard composition is 60 per cent Cabernet-Sauvignon, 12 per cent Cabernet-Franc, and 28 per cent Merlot.

Pontet-Canet is a very attractive, well-run property, and is rare in the Médoc for having very fine underground cellars. The *cuvier*, overlooking the vineyards, is in two storeys so that the grapes can be hauled up and loaded from above into the large vats. The house itself, with fine trees, lawn and flowerbeds in front, is one of the most agreeable and *familial* of the Médoc châteaux, some of which are more remarkable for their architectural eccentricity than for their domestic appeal. Pontet-Canet, on a slight rise, has a wide view of the neighbouring vineyards, looking across to Mouton in one direction and Lynch-Bages, Grand-Puy-Lacoste and the 'outback' of Pauillac in another. It is a château that I have visited many times, and under the guidance of Christian Cruse and his son Edouard have acquired as much information about Bordeaux wines and drunk as many of the best and most interesting bottles as anywhere in this hospitable region. Not least of the latter has been the notable Pontet-Canet '29, an extraordinarily full-bodied, almost rich wine, that stood out even in that fine year. In May 1962 Christian Cruse gave a dinner in London to celebrate fifty years of visiting English wine merchants. For this occasion bottles of Pontet-Canet 1929 and magnums of Mouton-Rothschild 1929 were decanted in Bordeaux into clean bottles, topped up, re-corked and then flown over to London. It was no disrespect to the Mouton, a fine wine but beginning to show its age, that the general view of the assembled company was that the Pontet-Canet was the finer of the two.

Pontet-Canet has one feature shared only by one other *cru classé* – Langoa. It has refused ever to have any of its wine bottled at the château, although a proportion is bottled in Bordeaux under the label of Cruse et Fils Frères, in the same way as Barton & Guestier bottle Langoa. This policy is a subject of controversy, even of suspicion. It is suggested that the absence of château-bottling makes the authenticity of these wines less assured. The fact that both are sold under non-vintage labels in the restaurant cars of the French Railways is also sometimes adduced as a slightly doubtful feature. However I would think this is a useful way of disposing of the embarrassingly large quantities of off-vintage years from so large a property as Pontet-Canet (in the poor year of 1965 it made 420 *tonneaux*), and in any case Ch. Margaux and other growths have decided to sell a blend of their less successful years with a proportion of the better vintages under a non-vintage label. The argument used at Pontet-Canet is that it is more economical for them and their customers to sell the wine in cask. I would not be surprised, however, with the general tendency towards château-bottling, if Pontet-Canet fell into line some day.

Batailley, which lies somewhat inland, has an attractive nineteenth-century château with a *parc anglais* behind, but the estate is much older. The name is said to have originated from the fact that there was a battle here between the French and the English. Later it was owned by an old Pauillac family named St-Martin, and then in 1818 it was bought by Daniel Guestier, of Barton & Guestier. The price was 118,000 frs., but when his heirs sold it in 1864 to M. Constant Halphen of Paris, the sum realized was 500,000 frs. Daniel Guestier, one of many successful Bordeaux wine merchants to acquire a Médoc estate, died in 1847. The present proprietress is the widow of Marcel Borie, of the firm of Borie-Manoux. However since the last war the estate has been divided into two, and the other part, now called Haut-Batailley, whose vineyard is dominated by a Virgin-crowned tower, is owned by the widow of François Borie, the proprietor of Ducru-Beaucaillou and the wine is made currently at Ducru-Beaucaillou, but perhaps not indefinitely. The Haut-Batailley estate is run by Eugène Borie. Batailley comprises 26 hectares and Haut-Batailley 16. Like other 'outback' classed growths, the large, rather sprawling *cuvier* and *chais*, long, low and supported by iron posts, have rather more of a farmyard air than the show-places nearer the Gironde. In my experience Batailley has consistently made sound, rather unexciting wine, often rather on the hard side and inclined to be unyielding in the way Pauillacs can be. Of Haut-Batailley, owned by Eugène Borie's sister, Mme des Brest-Borie, I have had little experience, but they made an excellent 1961. As Eugène Borie has greatly improved the previously disappointing Ducru-Beaucaillou, I would not be surprised to find Haut-Batailley looking up. The vineyard is composed of Cabernet-Sauvignon 68 per cent, Cabernet-Franc 12 per cent, and Merlot 20 per cent.

Next in the hierarchy are the two Grand-Puys: Ducasse and Lacoste. The first of these is unusual in that the château is separated from its vineyard; for the former is right on the waterfront at Pauillac, and the actual dwelling is now Pauillac's municipal *Maison du Vin*, which is worth visiting as it gives an idea of the situation of the estates in the commune and of other wine details. Alongside are the small old-fashioned cellars of Grand-Puy-Ducasse, with the vineyards lying outside the town and split up into three parts. It is one of the smallest of the classed growths, with a vineyard of only 10 hectares and an output of 30 *tonneaux*. The proprietor is M. Bouteiller who also owns Pichon-Baron. The wine is not much seen in Britain, and the one I remember best is the fruity but rather hard 1948. The '64, tasted in cask in the *chai*, seemed light for a Pauillac. But after drinking the 1868 with Christian Cruse at Pontet-Canet I shall always have a soft spot for Grand-Puy-Ducasse. The name came from an *avocat* in the pre-revolutionary Parlement of Bordeaux. It is now a company.

On the other hand Grand-Puy-Lacoste enjoys quite wide esteem, and I have had a special regard for it too, since it was the first château-bottled 1924 claret I ever acquired, as part of a modest consignment bought from a wine merchant in Nantes. Why Nantes? Because the firm had been recommended to me as having supplied Hilaire Belloc, who had a certain reputation for good living, and was then still alive. The Grand-Puy-Lacoste was about fifteen years old, and was probably the first fine mature claret that I had ever consciously drunk. I remember now the wonderful 'nose' of blackcurrants, a mark of well-matured claret; but nowadays it is blackcurrants that remind me of claret.

After that Grand-Puy-Lacoste passed out of my life for many years. I sampled one or two not very exciting post-war vintages at London tastings, but then in October 1965 when in Bordeaux I was invited to lunch at the château. There I met the sparkling, sprightly Raymond Dupin, a short man full of genial enthusiasm for his wine. The château like many others is not regularly lived in or kept up, but there are at least the essentials: a kitchen and a dining room, the latter embellished with oval carved cask ends more familiar in Germany than in France. When I lunched there, on the simply laid table were bottles of the year-old '64, drawn from the cask; but that was only *pour le soif*, and we went on to drink the delicious '53, the remarkably well-preserved '47 (a very uneven Médoc vintage considering its reputation) and a magnum of '43, which was surprisingly full and complete for a year generally by then considered well past its best. Between the dining room and the kitchen run lofty corridors, and to the English guests was allotted the slightly embarrassing role of summoning each succeeding course of the plentiful meal. This involved advancing to the double doors of the dining room, opening them and yelling *fortissimo* 'Antoinette'. This was soon followed by the smiling appearance of a buxom maid and her companions, bearing heavily laden trays. My own vocal performance was as nothing compared with that of a fellow guest, Sir Solly Zuckerman, then Chief Scientific Adviser to the British Government. To adapt Ouida, none yelled louder than he.

The Lacoste part of Grande-Puy assumed its separate identity in the first half of the eighteenth century, when acquired by the Lacoste family, who owned it at least until the phylloxera. The full name has Saint-Guirons added, commemorating another former owner. Judging by old records, in those days it was larger than now, but today consists of 24 hectares, and in a good year produces about 110 *tonneaux* of wine. There is a big proportion of Cabernet-Sauvignon, and this château is today making excellent wine.

Not far away is the even better-known growth of Lynch-Bages, belonging to one of the 'characters' of Pauillac, M. Cazes. Bages is a hamlet. The château was named after its proprietor of Irish descent, Count Lynch, the Mayor of Bordeaux, who in 1814 displayed his Bourbon-like memory in excitedly welcoming the return of Louis XVIII. He also owned Lynch-Moussas and Dauzac in Labarde. On his death in 1835, it passed to his brother the Chevalier Lynch, who died in 1841. After an intervening owner, it was acquired in 1865, the hey-day of the Médoc, by Maurice Cayrou, yet another Bordeaux merchant. After it had passed to his daughter it was acquired by Jean-Christian Cazes and made into a company.

Lynch-Bages is a large estate of just over 50 hectares, and the *chai* buildings have much the same traditional, agricultural appearance as Batailley. Casks are piled three-high, and the typical long, low cellars are dimly lit. I have heard Lynch-Bages described as 'the poor man's Mouton-Rothschild'. However, there is no marked expenditure on electricity in the Lynch-Bages cellars, as may be found at Mouton. But there are some large new concrete fermenting vats, installed in 1965. There is a high proportion of Cabernet-Sauvignon – 75 per cent – with the balance made up of Cabernet-Franc, Merlot and Petit-Verdot. Production in a good year may be as high as 150 *tonneaux*. Lynch-Bages has indeed something of the 'concentrated' flavour of Mouton, but without its distinction; fair enough considering its status. I find it rather a heavy and often over-sweet wine, but at the same time it can be agreeable when not all of its rivals are; for example, in that hard vintage of 1957, Lynch-Bages made a wine now very attractive. The '53 also had the 'size' that some other wines rather lacked. Lynch-Bages is a wine I used to like more than I do now, but it is probably I who have changed rather than the wine, and I am quite prepared to be surprised by picking it out in a blind tasting. It is an easy-to-drink claret.

To reach Lynch-Moussas one really has to penetrate the backwoods of Pauillac, bumping along a very minor road that runs from near Batailley, with only the château signpost, common in these parts, to indicate the destination. It lies tucked away in the woods, to the south-west of Grand-Puy-Lacoste. As the name indicates the vineyard once belonged to the Lynchs, and in the middle of the last century to a M. Vasquez. It is now owned by Jean Castéja, of the family that used to hold Duhart-Milon and still possess Doisy-Védrines in Barsac. It is a small property of 5 hectares producing only 15 – 20 *tonneaux*, the least of all the *crus classés*. Indeed one wonders why it was included, for it is sometimes suggested that the only reason why Ausone, the leading growth of St-Emilion, was not listed, was that its output of about 15 *tonneaux* was so small. Perhaps the magic of the name Lynch secured entry. Not that size is a necessary criterion of excellence, and maybe in 1855 the wine's quality elevated it above its *crus bourgeois* rivals. In recent years the wine has certainly been little seen abroad, and I have never done more than meet it at trade tastings. In fact the vineyard was practically wiped out by the severe frosts of 1956 and nearly the whole vineyard had to be re-planted, a heart-breaking matter for a small proprietor. So the vines have yet to achieve the necessary balance, which is why I found the '64 very strong, when tasted in the *chai*. My arrival was greeted with some curiosity by the small band of *vignerons* who were assisting at the vintage, and with pleasure by the proprietor and his wife; this welcome because an English journalist a few years ago had written that Lynch-Moussas no longer existed! I can testify that it does and shall look forward to tasting later vintages when the *vignoble* is fully restored.

With Mouton-Baron-Philippe we are back among the bright lights. It runs alongside Mouton-Rothschild, with its incomplete classical-style château – the money ran out less than half way along the pediment – standing at right angles to the gravelled, flower-bordered drive up to Mouton-Rothschild and facing across to Pontet-Canet. Until the eighteenth century the two Moutons were one property, and then the lesser part passed to the d'Armailhacq family, of whom the most distinguished member was A. d'Armailhacq, who took an intense interest in viticulture and who wrote a standard work, *De La Culture des Vignes dans le Médoc*, first published in 1850 and which went into several editions. By the 1860s the property was in the hands of the Comte de Ferrand, heir of d'Armailhacq, and from his successors it was sold to Baron Philippe de Rothschild in 1933. The estate had been a large one, the vineyard varying over the years from 60 to 75 hectares, but Baron Philippe gradually cut it down drastically, with the aim of improving the quality. In 1964 the productive area was only 32 hectares, but it is now on the increase again and up to 53, composed of 70 per cent Cabernet-Sauvignon and 30 per cent Merlot. Production averages 100 *tonneaux*. The name was changed to Mouton-Baron-Philippe in 1956. This is in the Médoc tradition, for most of the properties incorporate the name of a proprietor, but it may well have been thought that d'Armailhacq was too difficult a name to pronounce and therefore a deterrent to selling the wine, particularly in the United States.

Although a fifth growth, Mouton-Baron-Philippe, as Philippe Cottin, head of La Bergerie the marketing firm of Mouton, remarked to me, is run on first-growth lines, with the same care of the vineyards, new casks for the whole of each fresh vintage, and careful selection of *cuves* for selling under the château name. A proportion of Mouton-Baron-Philippe goes into Mouton-Cadet, the brand wine mentioned below. This part of the Mouton estate is not yet by Rothschild standards quite at concert pitch, for the war intervened and it takes a long time to improve a vineyard, but it will be very interesting to see the progress of this wine over the years.

As a side-light on the curious way the French wine laws work, it would be quite possible for this lesser part of the Mouton vineyard to have been incorporated in the major one, and the whole production sold as Mouton-Rothschild. Lafite could have done the same with Duhart-Milon. In each case, of course, the overall quality would show a deterioration, but less scrupulous proprietors might be tempted to make even a short-term gain on wines normally sold for a fraction of the first-growth prices. Contrariwise, if a *bourgeois* growth proprietor were to buy part of a classed-growth vineyard and incorporate it into his own, the former would lose its classed status.

Before leaving Mouton it is well to mention Mouton-Cadet, claimed to be the best-selling claret in the world. Some people believe that it is a second wine of Mouton-Rothschild, a sort of Carruades. In fact it is a branded wine which may be drawn from anywhere in Bordeaux, but is claimed to be essentially Médoc. The *appellation* is Bordeaux. It was started in 1933 in the World Slump which was accentuated in Bordeaux by the deplorable quality of the 1930, 1931 and 1932 vintages

– the worst trio in succession that Bordeaux has ever seen. The first Mouton-Cadet was a blend of these three vintages of Mouton-Rothschild, and the Mouton-Cadet 1938 was largely also from the same source. Since then the blend has always included, I was told, some Mouton-Rothschild in it – perhaps wine made from the younger vines – and particularly a proportion of Mouton-Baron-Philippe. Sales started in France, Belgium and Sweden in the Thirties, but the wine spread to the United Kingdom after the last war, and Britain is now the largest buyer, although it is expected that the United States will soon overtake us. The wine is always sold with a vintage label and so far as Britain is concerned it has had two years in bottle before being marketed. I have found Mouton-Cadet an agreeable, consistent but not very distinguished wine, which is much as one would expect. Owing to the fact that it has to bear a trade mark-up, like other such brand wines, it is rather expensive. The chief sale is in hotels and restaurants.

The small estate of Haut-Bages-Libéral, which owes its title to the name rather than the politics of a mid-nineteenth century proprietor, was partly divided in location. Part lay alongside Latour, and another part was on the side of Pauillac adjoining Pontet-Canet. So when the Cruses bought the property a few years ago they incorporated the latter, lesser portion into Pontet-Canet, as they were quite entitled to do. The other part which produces about 40 *tonneaux* from its 20 hectares is still sold under the Haut-Bages-Libéral label, but is not at present château-bottled, although it used to be and this may change. The wine is now made and kept at Pontet-Canet and the old *chai* near the Gironde is not used.

Two of the remaining three Pauillac *crus classés* are small and not very widely known, and both have their *cuviers* and cellars separated from their vineyards. Pédesclaux's wine is grown in an area which adjoins Mouton and near Lafite, by the main road to St-Estèphe. Its extent is 16 hectares, of which 70 per cent are Cabernet-Sauvignon, and almost 30 per cent Merlot, with the balance made up with a little Cabernet-Franc. Output may go as high as 70 *tonneaux*. The *chai* is enmeshed in Pauillac itself, lying between the church and the river. The young wine as I tasted it in the modest cellars seemed supple for a Pauillac. Most Pédesclaux is sold abroad, with the U.S.A. taking 30 per cent of the crop, and Switzerland and Belgium as the next best customers. The name came from a leading broker in the Bordeaux firm of Merman. It is now a company.

Clerc-Milon-Mondon has its cellars in the hamlet of Mousset, which adjoins the village of Pouyalet, on the outskirts of which is Mouton-Rothschild. The present owners are Mlle Marie Vialard, sister of a well-known notary of Pauillac much concerned with the wine trade, and Mme L. Hedon. All the wine is produced in a *cuvier* little larger than a good-sized drawing room. The output averages 30 *tonneaux*, and is sold in its entirety to the Moulis firm of Dourthe. A proportion is sold in Britain. The vineyard of 10½ hectares is, unhappily, divided, part of it being on the slopes between Mouton and Lafite, and the rest fairly near the Gironde, recalling, as Mlle Vialard reminded me, the local saying that 'the wine is good if one can see the river from the vineyard'. The *cépage* is a blend of Cabernet-Sauvignon, Merlot and – unusual in these parts – Malbec.

Croizet-Bages, last on the official list of classed Pauillacs, is better known. It is one of the relatively 'inland' Pauillacs, and it lies to the left of the road from St-Lambert to Pauillac, on the rising slopes around the hamlet of Bages, in which its *chai* lies. It is also near Lynch-Bages. The vineyard is 25 hectares in area, and the composition is unusual for Pauillac: 50 per cent Cabernet-Franc, 30 per cent Merlot and only 20 per cent Cabernet-Sauvignon, although I was told that the proportion of this last is increasing. In a good year 100 *tonneaux* are produced in the small cellars, whose white columns are an echo of the grandeur of Château Margaux's lofty *chai*. Croizet-Bages, named after two brothers Croizet who owned it in the eighteenth century, has no château to speak of. After other owners it passed to M. Julien Calvé in 1853 and remained with the same family until 1930. The present proprietor is M. Paul Quié. The wine is distinctly robust, even coarse when young, but it has plenty of flavour and occasionally I have drunk mature bottles that surprised me by their roundness. Generally it is a typically big, 'gutsy' Pauillac wine, with more body than beauty, and I had this impression of the '66 when I tasted it in cask.

The *bourgeois* wines of this big commune are more numerous than in the neighbouring St-Julien, and some of them find a ready market. A neighbour of Croizet-Bages is Haut-Bages-Avérous, which unlike Haut-Bages-Libéral is not a classified growth. From its 6 hectares are made 25 – 30 *tonneaux* in distinctly old-fashioned premises but none the worse for that. Other well-known Pauillac bourgeois growths are La Couronne, which belongs to Eugène Borie of Ducru-Beaucaillou, Colombier-Monpelou, Fonbadet, Monpelou, La Tour-Milon, Pibran and La Tour-Pibran. There are a number of variations on the themes of Bages and Milon.

One of the best-known lesser Pauillac names is La Rose Pauillac, the wine of the Pauillac Co-operative. This organization, the first of its kind in the Médoc, was founded in the difficult times of 1932. It 'farms' 520 hectares belonging to classed growths and 300 of other properties. It has 180 producing members, who own from three hectares to half only. Output varies from 6,000 – 8,000 hectolitres (666 – 888 *tonneaux*). At one time its wine was sold as Château Pauillac. The wine can be very agreeable and I remember with pleasure the soft 1959 La Rose. Wicked tongues in the district maintain that the Co-operative is a useful source of wine for proprietors who have run low in stocks of their own wine. But then the stock of wicked tongues is perhaps unusually high in the Médoc.

St-Estèphe

I must here confess at once that the St-Estèphes have never been great favourites of mine. It may be that I have been unlucky; certainly I can never remember being offered a really great St-Estèphe, and I have always found them rather strong, sometimes coarse wines, green and stalky when young and full of tannin. I have been told that in St-Estèphe wine is made more in the traditional way than elsewhere in the Haut-Médoc, and certainly most of the properties I have visited have been impressively conservative. Under the *appellation* laws, since 1965 they have been permitted to make 40 rather than 36 hectolitres per hectare. Principally, however, it must be a matter of soil and situation. Cos d'Estournel adjoins Lafite, but the wine is as different as Lafite is from Mouton. The soil is heavier and more fertile, the gravel being mixed with clay over lime. The wines are robust, full-bodied and repay keeping.

St Estèphe boasts two second growths, Cos d'Estournel and Montrose. The first of these has certainly the most curious buildings of all the eccentric structures in the Médoc. Originally the property was just called Cos (pronounced like the lettuce, not like the common abbreviation for 'company'), and it belonged to the Estournel family who sold it in 1811, only to re-buy it in 1821 and then greatly to enlarge the vineyard from 16 to 57 hectares. M. Estournel built a splendid series of *chais* in the Chinese style and today these have the agreeable appearance of a folly. When a passing traveller asked of a worker, 'What is this palace?' the latter replied, '*C'est le parc à boeufs de M. d'Estournel*'.

In giving proper precedence to the vineyard and wine-making this cow-parking proprietor omitted to build a château at all, and he spent so much money on the former that a year before his death in 1853 he had to sell the property to a Mr Martyn of London. The price stated was 1,150,000 frs. but this possibly included Pomys and two other minor estates that this rich Londoner (was he a banker?) acquired simultaneously. He also bought Cos-Labory next door. With the purchase in 1853 of Mouton by Baron Nathaniel de Rothschild, a member of the English branch of this family, and the ownership at least in name of Lafite by the Scotts, there was a period in the 1850s and 1860s when three famous adjoining estates could be said to be in English hands. Mr Martyn, like his neighbour at Lafite, left the affairs of Cos d'Estournel in the hands of a manager. This was the very experienced M. J. Chiapella, owner of La Mission-Haut-Brion. Martyn's money and Chiapella's skill further improved the standing of Cos, so that in 1866 the Agricultural Society of the Gironde awarded the English proprietor its 'prix d'ensemble' for the high standard of the vineyard, of the buildings and the general conduct of the estate. Specially picked out for commendation was a 'free medical service' for the workers. Like many other vineyard owners Martyn remains a somewhat shadowy figure, except that he was apparently generous as well as rich.

A year after Lafite passed to the Rothschilds in 1868, Martyn sold the property, which passed through several hands including the Charmolue family who owned Montrose. In 1919 it was acquired by M. Fernand Ginestet, the Bordeaux merchant and later owner of Château Margaux, and so to his son Pierre Ginestet. Although Cos d'Estournel is usually given the château prefix, in the past at least it was often written without this; possibly because there was no château. Its productive area is about 47 hectares, and the output is considerable: 180 – 200 *tonneaux*. The vineyard is composed of 60 per cent Cabernet-Sauvignon, and 40 per cent Merlot.

Some years ago the 1945 wines, château-bottled, of the three leading St-Estèphes— Cos d'Estournel, Montrose and Calon-Ségur – were opened at a lunch at Christopher's, the Jermyn Street, London, wine merchants. Of the three Cos was certainly the finest, and a very good wine, less 'spiky' than I had expected. Montrose was adjudged second. Cos often produces good wine in indifferent years; its '58 was excellent and among the best wines of that light vintage. It also made a good '55, not an off-year, but sometimes rather a disappointing one. Cos has taken to selling a non-vintage blend, the first being made up of the '63 and '64 vintages. This matter is discussed when Château Margaux is reached.

To enter the low-ceilinged *chai* of Montrose is to give traditionalists a sense of confidence. One may be convinced chemically, statistically and intellectually by concrete or steel vats, but there is something about the old oak wooden fermenting vats that appeals. At Montrose they have a few concrete vats, but most are of wood, extending almost up to the low ceiling. The *cuvier* is lit by attractive brass lamps. The vineyard extends to about 50 hectares and the output may be as high as 130 – 140 *tonneaux*. Here we are in real Cabernet country, and this may account for the heavy tannin content of most St-Estèphes. At Montrose 70 per cent of the vineyard is Cabernet-Sauvignon, 10 per cent Cabernet-Franc, 15 per cent Merlot and 5 per cent Petit-Verdot.

Montrose, in spite of its rather traditional appearance, is not a very old vineyard. It was carved out of the woodlands belonging to Calon and was accepted as a second growth in 1825. For over seventy years it has been in the hands of the Charmolue family, and the present owner is Mme Charmolue, although her son is the administrator. The estate buildings are very pleasantly set on a slight rise overlooking the Gironde, towards which the vines slope. There is a fine avenue of plane trees leading to the *chais*. Montrose is a powerful wine and 80 per cent is bottled at the château. The strength that can make it rather aggressive in successful vintages stands it in good stead in off-years, such as '58 and '60, when Montrose was rated particularly high. The apparently Scottish name is said to earn it a special popularity in Scotland.

Calon-Ségur, lying slightly inland, is a very old estate, which belonged to a M. Gascq in the seventeenth century and then passed by marriage to the celebrated Président de Ségur, who also owned Lafite and Latour. The heart on the château label is said to commemorate the remark of Ségur: 'I make my wine at Lafite and Latour but my heart is in Calon'. He gave his name to the large vineyard, which is now a third growth. The first part of the name is taken from the little river boats that once ferried timber across the estuary. It belongs to the Gasqueton and Peyrelongue families, after having passed through the well-known Médoc family of Lestapis. Calon has an impressive château with a vineyard of about 60 hectares and production up to 220 *tonneaux*. The vineyard is 50 per cent Cabernet-Sauvignon and Cabernet-Franc and 50 per cent Merlot. A hundred years ago a writer described its wines as the most *corsé* (full-bodied) and alcoholic wines of the Médoc. Today they are more rounded than most St-Estèphes, but perhaps a little at the expense of character. Sometimes they have struck me as being rather on the sweet side and a shade dull, possibly owing to the high proportion of Merlot. But they are consistent wines, and if I have never been particularly elevated by a bottle of Calon-Ségur, I cannot remember ever having been let down. The estate has a wide reputation and is certainly among the better-known classed growths.

Lafon Rochet lies on St-Estèphe's vine-crowded plateau. Although a fourth growth, it seems not to have had a very distinguished history, and in recent times at least it

Lafon Rochet

has been one of the more obscure *crus classés*. In the post-war years it was owned until 1960 by a proprietor from the north of France, but in that year it was bought by Guy Tesseron, a well-known Cognac merchant who specializes in selling brandy to the trade rather than to the public. His wife is a member of the Cruse family. In 1965 they decided to re-build the somewhat nondescript, *chartreuse* (one storey) château, replacing it by one on the traditional low-lying pattern of the district. It must be the only new classed-growth château to have been built for many years indeed, perhaps in this century. The *chai* is unpretentious. The vineyard area is 20 hectares (50 per cent Cabernet-Sauvignon, 20 per cent Cabernet-Franc, 25 per cent Merlot and 5 per cent Petit-Verdot) and production up to 100 *tonneaux*. The wine is more supple than many St-Estèphes.

Cos-Labory, which has a nineteenth-century turreted château of modest size, lies over the road from Cos d'Estournel, looking across to the vineyard of Lafite beyond the low-lying marshy ground separating St-Estèphe from Pauillac. It belonged to the same Mr Martyn who owned Cos d'Estournel, passed to a M. Louis Peychaud, was more recently in the hands of the Ginestets, and in 1958 was bought by its present owner, M. François Audoy. Compared with its imposing neighbour, Cos-Labory like many of the other lesser fifth growths has a pleasantly farm-like air, and the proprietor himself runs the estate. The 15 hectare vineyard is made up of 40 per cent Cabernet-Sauvignon, 20 per cent Cabernet-Franc and 40 per cent Merlot, mingled with a trace of Petit-Verdot. The output is 40 to 50 *tonneaux*. Half of this is sold to Great Britain and the U.S.A., and the balance divided between France and Germany. The wine is kept three months in the fermenting vats and bottled after two years.

St-Estèphe is great *cru bourgeois* country. It abounds in large properties producing between 50 and 200 *tonneaux*, and based for the large part on rambling, old-fashioned traditional wine buildings. Ch. de Pez is a good example, with a vineyard comprising 65 per cent Cabernet, and the balance mostly Merlot with a little Petit-Verdot thrown in for its strength. It is owned by Mme Bernard, a cheerful widow proud of the 400 hogsheads of wine she makes in a good year. In 1965 the Merlot rotted so badly that the wine was made only from Cabernet-Sauvignon, and as a result was surprisingly fruity for such a poor year. The old *chai* is long and lofty, with *barriques* lying in three tiers. The wine is typical St-Estèphe; fruity, and rather coarse in youth.

Meyney which like Montrose lies near the river, is rather more modern in appearance, with concrete vats and virginia creeper-covered buildings lying round a neat square courtyard. From its well-cared-for 50 hectares as much as 250 *tonneaux* can be produced, but 200 is more the average, as in 1966. A peculiarity is that the wine is aged in very large oak casks, each of which holds the equivalent of 20 *barriques*, or 4,500 litres. The purpose is to save ullage by evaporation, which is much less in big casks. However this does slightly retard the development of the wine, so after the first year the wine is transferred to the normal casks. A few of these are also filled during the first year, in order to make comparisons. Meyney belongs to Jean Cordier, proprietor of Gruaud-Larose and Talbot.

There are many other St-Estèphe properties with more than a local reputation. This is partly perhaps because their wines are inexpensive by Médocain standards, and so have found customers abroad, including Britain. On nearly every reputable wine merchant's list will be found some bourgeois growths from this broad commune, which normally produces more than any of the other five appellation-named Médocs. These will include the handsome Marbuzet, belonging to Pierre Ginestet of Cos d'Estournel, Phélan-Ségur (once the property of the Martell family of Cognac), La Tour-de-Marbuzet, Le-Boscq, Beauséjour, Capbern, Canteloup, Ormes-de-Pez, Tronquoy Lalande, owned by M. Quié of Rauzan Gassies, Pomys and Plantier-Rose. There are a number of others. In recent years some St-Estèphe estates in order to sell their large crops more easily have labelled part with subsidiary names which most of them own; very confusing for consumers. More than a hundred of the small proprietors sell their wine to the St-Estèphe co-operative, which markets its wine under the name of Marquis de St-Estèphe. The commune's total output averages nearly 40,000 hectolitres. In the large village, which in one direction looks out over the adjoining Bas-Médoc there is a Wine Museum.

9. The Médoc II

St-Julien, St-Laurent and Margaux

St-Julien

Retracing our steps through Pauillac, we are in the splendid commune of St-Julien, which unhappily advertises its produce by a huge, hideous bottle placed prominently on a corner of the main road. Otherwise it is an inconspicuous enough village, with a church whose nineteenth-century Gothic spire contrasts with the classical tower of Pauillac. The commune is straggling. For some reason St-Julien is a name that has caught on and is a Médoc *appellation* known to those who know no other; not even that it is a Médoc. This is usually just as well, for very few of the bottles labelled 'St-Julien' in British off-licence windows can contain a high proportion of wine from this commune. For one thing there are too few small proprietors who would find it profitable to sell their wine under the commune label only, and for another, it is far too expensive a wine to be sold as a sort of superior Bordeaux *vin supérieur*, roughly what it was in the old pre-*AC* days. The basic wine was sold as Bordeaux and one up the scale was Médoc or St-Emilion. The next step, with perhaps an infusion of the real thing, was St-Julien, or for the more knowledgeable, St-Estèphe or Margaux. You paid your money and got your worth. Nowadays the maximum quantity of *AC* St-Julien is 40 hectolitres per hectare.

St-Julien contains no fewer than 11 classed growths, ranging from seconds to fourths; more than any other commune bar Pauillac, and with more second growths than any other. St-Juliens at their best are perhaps the quintessence of claret. Grown on a fine gravelly soil with iron in the sub-soil, shallower than in Pauillac, they have less body and 'power' than most of the latter, but more than the Margaux and Cantenacs. They combine fruit with delicacy and have a splendid aroma when fully developed. According to Franck, the St-Julien wines with more colour and vinosity than the Pauillacs took a year longer to achieve maturity, and he stated that they required five to six years in cask. This seems excessive even by the standards of a hundred years or so ago. Today certainly the St-Juliens do not stay more than two and a half years in cask and often less than two years. One wonders if they used to be quite different in style.

Unfortunately all too many of the classed growths of this great commune have not been making consistently the quality of wine that their classification and reputation imply. This no doubt was partly owing to a long period of unprofitability for the Médoc properties until about the mid-1950s. This may be surprising to those who know only the proud reputation of these classed growths; yet several château proprietors have told me how small until recently was their return. Since the 1955 vintage they have secured much better prices, and there has been now something of a boom, comparable with but not probably as great as in the 1860s. The leading châteaux are said now to earn 8 per cent on their capital, and there has been until recently at least no lack of buyers for any classed-growth Médoc château of good repute that may be in the market. The last big purchase was that of Latour in 1962.

These poor profits may explain why some of the St-Julien growths have over the last thirty or forty years not made such good wines. Another factor is the personality, interest and experience of the proprietor, and equally of his *régisseur* or *maître de chai*. The latter posts may be almost hereditary in some estates, and the reputation of a château may well vary according to the skill and expertise of these key men. A *maître de chai* without a suitably equipped son to follow him means a problem in store for the proprietor. In St-Julien there is also the question of site to be considered. As in Pauillac there is a wide difference between the vineyards near the estuary and those in the backwoods towards St-Laurent and the Landes.

In the eighteenth century the Léoville estate must have been the largest in the Médoc, comprising as it did the three separately owned vineyards of Las-Cases, Poyferré and Barton that exist today. It was originally known as Mont-Moytié – another example of the Médocain propensity to make mountains out of little more than molehills in this flat country. M. Moytié, a merchant of Bordeaux, had created the estate in 1638. Then a century later it was re-named after another Président of the Parlement of Bordeaux, M. Léoville, who died in 1769. He was a member of the Abbadie-Léoville family. In the Revolution the Marquis de Las-Cases-Beauvoice, who owned a quarter of the great vineyard, emigrated and as a result the whole property was sequestered. The rest of the family who had not emigrated demanded the restoration of the remaining three-quarters and this was granted. The emigré's portion was eventually sold to Mr Hugh Barton, of Langoa and the firm of Barton & Guestier, partly in 1821 and partly in 1826. Another quarter came into the hands of the Baron Poyferré, who sold it in 1866 to Armand Lalande, a Bordeaux wine merchant and the proprietor of Cantenac-Brown. This portion is now owned by Cuvelier. The rest of the estate remained in the Abbadie family's possession, represented by the Marquis de Las-Cases, who inherited it from his father in 1815. For many years now this has been a limited company. At one time the Poyferré château was equally divided between the owners of the Poyferré and Las-Cases vineyards.

Las-Cases is much the largest of the three portions, with a vineyard of 60 hectares, compared with about 36 for Poyferré and 35 for Barton. Its composition is 80 per cent Cabernet-Sauvignon, 5 per cent Cabernet-Franc, 12 per cent Merlot, and 3 per cent Petit-Verdot. The average *AC* output of Las-Cases is about 250 *tonneaux* (227 in 1967), as against 100 each for the other two. The Las-Cases vineyard is not parcelled but Poyferré and Barton are very much intermingled. Also Ronald Barton told me that among the lines of his part of Léoville run some vines officially designated as Langoa. The low-built Léoville château, neglected-looking nowadays, belongs to Poyferré. Las-Cases has no château, but the Bartons have Langoa, which they bought with the vineyard in 1821. The charming mid-eighteenth century château is built on one-storey only, with cellars below. This style of building, common in these parts, is known as a *chartreuse*. Until the latter part of the last century all three wines were customarily sold just as Léoville.

Poyferré, once so fine, is one of the St-Julien growths that I now find disappointing. After making superb wines in the 1920s, and possibly the best '29 of all, then some good wines in the disappointing 1930s (particularly the '34 and '37), since the last war the wines have all too often seemed green and pinched. It is frequently said that the wine is improving, and in view of the long time required to raise the standard of a vineyard, this may well be true. I hope so, for Léoville-Poyferré is one of the great names of Bordeaux. The vineyard make-up is quite different from Las-Cases; 50 per cent Merlot, 30 per cent Cabernet-Sauvignon, and 20 per cent Cabernet-Franc. Production averages 180 *tonneaux*.

Las-Cases too had a long bad patch. Again they made wonderful wines during the 1920s, with the '28 leading the Médoc field, and the '29 in the front rank. But there was a similar decline to Poyferré's, possibly owing to the fact that the wines were made by the same management. Year after year in trade and other tastings I used to look for better things in Las-Cases, but was disappointed. The '48, '49, and even the almost universally good '53 were thin, ungenerous wines, and the '53 remains so today. But things have looked up in the last few years, and '59, '62 and '64 have a good reputation. From time to time they make a second wine called Clos du Marquis, sold with a vintage date. It is made from the younger vines. In 1968 fourteen new cement *cuves* were installed in the *cuvier*.

On the other hand Léoville-Barton has come much to the fore since the war. Until 1929 they refused to bottle at the château, and that particular vintage suffered from not too good corks. In England I have found it rather disappointing on the few occasions I have drunk it, but at the château it has sometimes been delicious. This may have been owing to the defective corking of some bottles sold, or to the fact that the wine at Langoa had never been moved. Ronald Barton has assured me that his stock is no different from that sold, yet although in Bordeaux châteaux the wine

THE MÉDOC

138

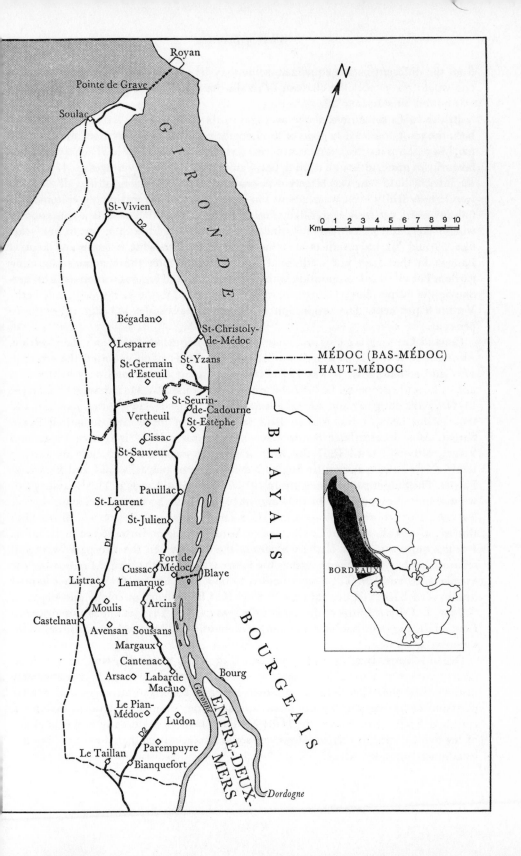

Royan

Pointe de Grave

Soulac

G I R O N D E

St-Vivien

D1 D2

Bégadan

Lesparre

St-Christoly-
de-Médoc

St-Germain
d'Esteuil

St-Yzans

St-Seurin-
de-Cadourne

Vertheuil

St-Estèphe

Cissac

St-Sauveur

Pauillac

St-Laurent

St-Julien

D1

Fort de
Cussac Médoc

Listrac

Lamarque

Blaye

Moulis

Arcins

Castelnau

Avensan Soussans

Margaux

Cantenac

Arsac

Labarde

Bourg

Macau

Le Pian-
Médoc

Ludon

Le Taillan

D2

Parempuyre

Bianquefort

Dordogne

B L A Y A I S

B O U R G E A I S

E N T R E - D E U X - M E R S

Garonne

0 1 2 3 4 5 6 7 8 9 10
Km

·—·—·—· MÉDOC (BAS-MÉDOC)
- - - - - HAUT-MÉDOC

BORDEAUX

from the different vats is equalized, some may be more equalized than others, and one would not expect the château to retain the worst casks. In this case I think it was not an outstanding '29.

In the 1930s sometimes above average, in the post-war era Barton has certainly been the most consistently good of the Léovilles. The 1945 is very fine, and the 1949 too, but perhaps its greatest recent success was its 1948. This year has been a particular favourite of mine, although coming between two such famous vintages as '47 and '49, the intermediate year was largely overlooked. Barton '48 was firm, like all '48s, but wonderfully fruity even when about ten years old, and it remains the epitome of a full-flavoured yet truly claret-like wine of its age. Ronald Barton is a conservative wine-maker, and in off-years his wines are sometimes a little thin, but in fine years like '59 and '61 his products are among the best. The wine is made and kept at Langoa in the clean but traditional *chais* abutting upon the château's charming garden. The vineyard composition both of the Léoville and Langoa sections is Cabernet-Sauvignon 62 per cent, Cabernet-Franc 9 per cent, Merlot 21 per cent, and Petit-Verdot 8 per cent. The proportion of Cabernet-Sauvignon is being raised to 70 per cent.

Gruaud-Larose is a handsome stone château, lying rather back from the riverside. At one time it was known as Fond-Bedeau, but M. Gruaud acquired the estate in 1757 and re-named it. It was 116 hectares in extent and second only to the then united Léoville property. In 1787 the growth was bought by M. Larose, who married M. Gruaud's daughter and added his name to his father-in-law's. After his death and those of his heirs, it was sold in 1812 to a group of three men, including Baron Sarget. After several later deaths the vineyard was divided into two: Faure and Sarget, although until 1867 the wine was made together, producing an average total of 110 – 120 *tonneaux*. In England the wine was generally sold and known as Larose. The Sarget part was bought in 1918 by M. Désiré Cordier. The two vineyards were re-united by purchase in 1934 and since then have been sold as Gruaud-Larose *tout court*. The proprietor today is Jean Cordier, grandson of Désiré, who owns both this, as well as Talbot and other vineyards in Bordeaux and one in Sancerre on the Loire. I drank quite a number of the vintages of the 1920s when the two parts were still separate, and my view then was that the Faure was rather the better. I remember the excellent '20 and '29. The Sarget tended to be a little lighter. On the other hand I drank a '24 Sarget at the château in 1966 that had plenty of colour and depth of flavour, and showed little of the decline obvious in most '24s; yet a magnum drunk in London the previous year was much more obviously on the way down; as usual wines unmoved keep best.

Gruaud-Larose is a big fruity wine and is probably made that way, as is Talbot. Nearly always an agreeable, acceptable claret, I have never found it a particularly distinguished one. This depends, of course, on one's taste, and although I am always prepared to be beguiled by the heavy brigade from Pauillac, I tend to look for a certain delicacy in the rest of the Haut-Médoc; one does not usually find it in either of the two Cordier *crus classés*. However, some like them for their fullness; they are usually well-rounded wines.

Gruaud-Larose with an area of 70 hectares, is said to contain 80 per cent Cabernet-Sauvignon and sometimes produces more wine than any other classed growth save Pontet-Canet, averaging 250 *tonneaux* but often making more. In June 1965 it suffered a very bad fire, and no fewer than 547 *barriques* of the 1964 vintage were lost. Fortunately the crop was exceptionally large and over 800 casks survived. As a result some of the cellars have been rebuilt. The *cuvier* is very long, with large wooden vats on one side and glass-lined vats opposite, as at Talbot, although the properties are operated completely separately so far as work in the vineyard and making the wine are concerned. At Gruaud-Larose the wine is transferred from the fermentation vats immediately after the fermentation into the wooden vats opposite, where it is left for one or two months before being racked into the normal-size *barriques*. At Talbot, however, the wine is kept in big casks for eight months. The difference between wine in big and little casks, Jean Cordier told me, was the difference between wines in magnums and bottles. All the Cordier properties are immaculately kept and at Gruaud-Larose there is a first floor cellar whose eastern wall made of glass faces across to the Gironde.

Not far from the river Ducru-Beaucaillou's architecturally somewhat grandiose near-classical style building is familiar from its label. One reason for its size is that the cellars lie beneath the house, which is near the Gironde. The property is of medium size, with 35 hectares of vines, and produces about 150 *tonneaux* a year. It was once called just Beaucaillou, but a M. Ducru did the common thing of adding his name, and then in 1866 his descendants sold the property to the wife of Nathaniel Johnston, of the prominent Bordeaux wine family, for 1 million frs.

Not long before the First World War the Johnstons who owned Ducru-Beaucaillou began to make a sparkling wine. At first it was made from a blend of wines of St-Julien and neighbouring communes, but later on production was transferred across the river to Bourg, where it continued until about 1933. As at first the marketing company was situated at Ducru-Beaucaillou it seems likely that the wine was sold under that label. Certainly the International Exhibition Co-operative Wine Society of London sold sparkling Ducru-Beaucaillou from 1912 until the 1930s, although I am now assured that it contained none of the wine from the famous *deuxième cru's* vineyard. Since The Wine Society has always enjoyed a reputation for probity, I may assume that this curious labelling was permitted. I never tasted the wine, but this is one of the lesser alcoholic regrets of my life.

Johnston's heirs sold the property in 1928 to M. Desbaraats but since 1941 the Borie family has owned it and Eugène Borie runs it. Ducru-Beaucaillou is another St-Julien property that was distinctly disappointing for many years but has now made a fine recovery. I suspect that in the latter years of Nathaniel Johnston's proprietorship, matters were not too good financially. Even the 1929 was generally poor in that fine year, though I had a fair bottle as late as 1967.

Since the early Fifties, the wines have steadily improved; the '53 is a delicious glass of wine and the '59 and '61 show great promise. It is one of the Médoc properties to watch. The vineyard make-up is Cabernet-Sauvignon 70 per cent, Cabernet-Franc 7 per cent, Merlot 18 per cent, Petit-Verdot 5 per cent.

Lying far back in the commune and near the boundary with St-Laurent lie the massive buildings of Lagrange. From 1791 to 1842 it was owned by the Cabarrus family, a famous name in Revolutionary Bordeaux, as a Mlle Cabarrus married a famous revolutionary, Tallien, and is said to have saved many people from the guillotine. Then Lagrange was bought by Comte Duchatel, minister of King Louis Philippe. At that time it was the largest of all the Médoc properties, 300 hectares in extent, with 120 under vines, and it had the biggest output of all the *crus classés*: 250 *tonneaux*. Nowadays it is much reduced with a *vignoble* of 40 hectares or less, and a production in a good year of 100 *tonneaux*; yet in the prolific 1964 it made only 80. The vineyard is almost half Cabernet-Sauvignon, with a little Cabernet-Franc, and half Merlot. The lines of solid buildings look as if they might have been the stables of a demolished palace. Opposite the Lagrange *cuvier* is another inscribed outside with the names of growths no longer in existence: Ch. St-Julien and Ch. Latour Rauzan; a sad reminder of the *crus bourgeois* that went out of production either after the phylloxera or between the wars. The cellar at Lagrange is dark, low and old-fashioned like so many of these establishments. The proprietor now is M. Cendoya. I must confess that I have never drunk a Lagrange of real distinction although a 1926 opened in 1968 was fruitier than I anticipated. Indeed I have drunk very few bottles at all of Lagrange. Nearly all the wine is château-bottled, which may be one reason why it is seldom seen in Britain.

However the next third growth, Langoa, is a particular favourite in Britain as well as in Ireland, and this no doubt can be ascribed partly to the nationality of the proprietor, Ronald Barton, who has contrived to support Irish origin, English education and French domicile. In 1940, when the Germans arrived at Langoa and began to pillage the cellar, as belonging to an enemy alien in England, it was Ronald Barton's 'neutral' Irish nationality that saved most of the precious contents of the private *cave*. By that time the 'neutral' was in the British Army.

Langoa is made in the same *cuvier* and kept in the same cellars as Léoville-Barton, but there is no confusion, and Ronald Barton maintains, as the only proprietor of a second and a third growth, that he can demonstrate the superiority of the former over the latter. Each year he makes both as well as he can, but the Léoville always wins; it is a slightly softer, more rounded wine with greater 'flesh'. Yet the Langoa can be very good, and in particular the '53 which Barton says is the best Langoa he has ever made. Nevertheless to the outsider, the difference in quality between wines made on very similar ground is one of the fascinations of claret. Like Pontet-Canet, the wines of Langoa are never château-bottled. This is partly at least, as with the Léoville, because Ronald Barton finds it an additional 'chore', for which his property is not regularly geared. He admits, however, that the proportion of his Léoville, for which the purchasers insist on château-bottling, is increasing. The production of Langoa is now around 50 – 60 *tonneaux*.

The one-storey *chartreuse* style château of Langoa is one of the most charming in the whole Médoc. It was built and owned by a judge, M. Pontet, in 1758. He had exchanged his old holding in St-Laurent for the much more promising site in St-Julien. It was bought by the Barton family in 1821, and thus provided them with a home and a *chai* for the portion of the Léoville vineyard they soon acquired. In the pre-phylloxera period Langoa was said to fetch more money than any other third growth, and among its well-known successes was the 1846. The château in its central part is only one room deep, and in plan not unlike that of the rather grander Beychevelle. It is curious in having the main floor, the *piano nobile*, leading off a first-floor terrace, so that the private cellars and kitchens are on the ground floor level. Behind it is a *jardin anglais* and a *potager* which have more than a whiff of England. Both Langoa and Léoville-Barton are the personal property of the Barton family.

The two St-Pierres, Bontemps and Sevaistre, are now one, although a section of Bontemps is said to be included in the *bourgeois* growth of Gloria. St-Pierre owes its name to a baron of that name who bought it in 1767. In 1832 the property was divided among his descendants, part being kept by Colonel Bontemps-Dubarry, the rest going to his daughter, who became Mme de Luetkens. That part was sold in 1892 to M. Léon Sevaistre. It now belongs to a firm of Antwerp wine merchants, Van den Bussche Fils. For this reason the wine is frequently to be found in Belgium. The vineyard is fairly small, about 13 hectares, but it generally makes sound enough wine to make an interesting fourth growth. For a period it was unusual in not blending its wine from the Cabernet and Merlot grapes, and they were sold separately. At a time when the '49s were generally rather hard and edgy, the St-Pierre-Sevaistre was an agreeable soft wine; clearly the Merlot wine. This separation stopped about 1955. The '53 was light and attractive too.

It is curious, in a way, that St-Pierre heads St-Julien's *quatriémes*, as it is certainly the least known of them today. Not far from the disfiguring publicity bottle of St-Julien is the entrance to Branaire-Ducru, once known as Duluc, and before that as Bergeron, after an earlier owner. The charming low house, two storeys high, was built in 1770 and like Langoa is only one room deep. The attractive staircase in the hall mounts between columns and behind the house is a pleasantly rural garden and a fine orangery that has seen better days. M. Mital and his successors owned Branaire from 1880 to 1952, when they sold it to M. Tapie, who died in 1969.

Brainaire, as it is now called, is a growth that used to make fine wine and then fell on bad times. I remember their 1899 of which I once had a few bottles from Averys of Bristol; they were superb in the 1940s. I cannot remember an exciting bottle of any vintage since, but that may have been my misfortune. Certainly in the post-war period this château, with a considerable vineyard of 34 hectares that can produce 130 – 140 *tonneaux*, made rather thin wine. However its last proprietor was enterprising. The composition of the vineyard is two-thirds Cabernet-Sauvignon and Cabernet-Franc and one-third Merlot. M. Tapie had introduced new methods of vinification, which owe something to Algerian systems. Nor should this put anyone off for some very enlightened viticulture and wine-making has been practised in Algeria. Moreover at Branaire they have now gone in for producing a non-vintage wine, like Château Margaux and Cos d'Estournel. I sampled the first blend in the autumn of 1966. It was made from the light, elegant '64 which I had tasted on its own, and the definitely rather slight '63. Certainly the result was much more drinkable than the '63 on its own, and it was said that the blend would be drinkable by

1969. It is easy to shake a purist head at such things, but what is a classed-growth proprietor to do with his off-vintages like 1963 and 1965?

Talbot, not a little assisted by its name, is a popular wine in Britain. Named after the English commander who fell at the Battle of Castillon in 1453, any direct connection with him is legendary. It used to be called Talbot d'Aux, because at one time it was owned by a marquess of that name. In 1919 it passed into the hands of Georges Cordier, who had an English wife and was the son of Désiré Cordier, who bought Gruaud-Larose. It now belongs to his son, Jean, who also owns Gruaud-Larose and other châteaux, as well as a large merchant business in Bordeaux. Talbot has always been a very big property, running behind the Léoville and Langoa vineyards, and to the north of Gruaud-Larose. A hundred years ago it was producing 120 – 130 *tonneaux*, and today in a plentiful year it can make 300 *tonneaux* from its 85 hectares, one of the half-dozen largest classed growths. The house has something of a comfortable English nineteenth-century appearance but the extensive *chais* are very much up-to-date. As already mentioned in connection with Gruaud-Larose both have glass-lined fermentation vats, and large wooden casks for maturing the young wine. Talbot, like Gruaud-Larose, is said to contain 80 per cent Cabernet-Sauvignon, with the other grapes common in the Médoc making up the balance. Although all the Cordier properties in the Bordeaux area are under one *régisseur*, M. Humbert, each château is responsible for making its own wine under his general supervision. Nevertheless there seems to me a family resemblance between Talbot and Gruaud-Larose; both are rather full and fruity wines, agreeable, dependable but seldom very exciting. The backbone that Talbot sometimes slightly lacks makes it very drinkable in rather tough years like 1952 and 1957, and a very mellow wine was produced in 1948. The 1953 was, and indeed is, a very charming round wine.

To me one test of a château's reputation is the Unknown Wine List. Upon inspecting the wine list of a restaurant, hotel or club, it can happen one knows none of the wines. It is therefore necessary to pick by vintage and/or château. Assuming that the really expensive first growths and the like are out, then I would certainly short-list Talbot, as well as Gruaud-Larose, and if I would not hope for a surprise, as I might with some others, I would expect and almost certainly drink a well-rounded and sometimes slightly rich wine by Médoc standards.

Talbot produces about 20 *barriques* each year of a white wine known as Caillou-Blanc, which of course is rather like a white Graves in style.

The long line of St-Julien classed growths ends with one of the best known: Beychevelle. This fine eighteenth-century château, basically built on one storey only, like Langoa and perhaps by the same architect, lies beside the main *D.2* road which passes so many Médoc châteaux. From its terrace looking across the vineyards and meadows, there is an excellent view of the estuary, and this explains the theory that the name comes from '*baisse voile*', because the autocratic Admiral d'Epernon demanded that all passing ships should dip their sails. At any rate this story gave the château an opportunity to put a ship on its label and so achieve a suitably nautical touch in a district which is inclined to be introspective from a label point of view. To pass Beychevelle by road is to enjoy one of the not too common architectural pleasures in the Haut-Médoc; and horticultural too, as the parterres are splendid. So is the garden on the other side of this well-kept and beautifully furnished house, which contains one fine room after another opening on each other.

Beychevelle has usually enjoyed well-off owners. It was the property of the Abbadie family in the first half of the eighteenth century, but they neglected it. The château itself was built in 1757 by the new owner the Marquis de Brassier, but the property was lost in the Revolution because his son, the Baron de Brassier, killed an opponent in a duel; he was exiled and the property was sequestered. However the family contrived to win it back, only to sell it to M. Conte, a rich '*armateur*' or shipowner of Bordeaux. In turn he sold in 1825 to his nephew, P. F. Guestier, connected with the wine firm of Barton & Guestier who during a bad time for Bordeaux wines held it until trade improved as a result of the Anglo-French Commercial Treaty in 1860. In 1874 he sold out to M. Armand Heine for 1,600,000 frs., who left it to his daughter, mother of the present owner, Achille Fould, Minister of Agriculture in one of the pre-war French governments and whose son is Deputy for the Gironde. The area under vines is 48 hectares, the property is productive, and in 1964 made over 200 *tonneaux*. Beychevelle is one of the classed growths particularly well-liked in Britain and is common on wine lists here. In the post-war period it appears to have suffered some decline, with wines less fruity than one would expect. It is said that Beychevelle has been an 'early picker' with a consequent lack of stamina. Possibly the vinification methods were varied, and certainly the casks containing the young wines were turned over with their bungs on the side rather than on top earlier than in other châteaux where the top position is normal for the first year. This would appear to indicate that the wines were brought on earlier. However that might be, Beychevelle certainly returned to form with the 1964, where a very elegant wine was made and generally agreed to be among the best of the vintage in St-Julien.

St-Julien is almost certainly the claret name most taken in vain in Bordeaux and abroad, and the outsider might imagine large stretches of vineyards in the commune, which are most happy to sell their wine under the sole *appellation* of St-Julien. Nothing could be further from the reality. The classed growths occupy nearly all the available vineyard area, and the eleventh edition of Cocks et Féret's *Bordeaux et ses Vins* (1949) mentions a mere 25 *crus bourgeois* and *crus artisans*, which together only account for about 350 *tonneaux*. In addition there is a note of fifteen small proprietors who make between 1 and 5 *tonneaux* apiece. Any growers who thought it worth while to sell their wine under the commune name only would certainly demand a price that would put it well above the price of 'commercial' St-Julien; so the wine would have to be sold under a château label. The vineyard area is about two-thirds of Pauillac's acreage. Output averages about 25,000 hectolitres, similar to Margaux and its associated communes.

The best known *bourgeois* growth in St-Julien now is certainly Gloria, owned by Henri Martin, who is also the manager of Latour and a prominent figure in Bordeaux wine affairs. It includes part of the old vineyard of St-Pierre-Bontemps, and is now over 31 hectares. The wine is full, perhaps a little sweet for some tastes, but usually makes an agreeable glass. The 1953 was notable for being drinkable very early.

Production is now well over 100 *tonneaux* and in 1967 was just on 140. Another *bourgeois* St-Julien is de Glana, an imposing if perhaps rather out-of-place mansion near Langoa and opposite the vineyard of Ducru-Beaucaillou; the wine used to be better known than now. In the village there is a Ch. Médoc – a name one would think less than genuine on a bottle were it not for the fact that it truly exists – which belongs to Eugène Borie, and is partly used for bottling wines of his châteaux. There is also an equally suspicious-sounding but actual Ch. Grand St-Julien.

Motorists travelling from Pauillac to the main *D.1* road at St-Laurent will probably have passed the massive, deserted buildings bearing the name Larose Trintudon. This was once a well-known vineyard planted on land that had formerly belonged to M. Larose of Gruaud-Larose, and later to one of his heirs. It was reckoned as a fourth growth and produced about 25 *tonneaux*. This vineyard, now owned by M. Forner, is being restored. Beside it, once belonging to M. Lahens, was Perganson, which was much larger and made from 50 to 80 *tonneaux*. Both were classed as St-Laurent wines and fetched rather less than the St-Juliens. They were the victims of the post-phylloxera slumps and on this marginal land for vines long ago passed out of production. The empty château and the outbuilding were for long a grim reminder of the problems that even growers in the favoured Médoc have had to contend with.

St-Laurent

Inland from St-Julien lies the commune of St-Laurent, centred on the village of that name on the straight *D.1* road, the *Crus Classés* by-pass which runs direct to Lesparre, the Bas-Médoc and the Pointe de Grave, where a car-ferry crosses the mouth of the Gironde. St-Laurent has an attractive, spired church and also three classed-growth châteaux: a fourth and two fifths.

It has no *appellation* of its own, but the wines bear the Haut-Médoc *AC* and the maximum *rendement* with this qualification is 43 hectolitres per hectare, 3 hectolitres higher than for the six Médoc communes entitled to their own *appellations*. The soil is gravelly towards the St-Julien side, where the best wines are produced; on the west it shades off into the sand of the Landes.

La Tour-Carnet really has a tower, a rectangular medieval one that puts Latour's affair to shame; there is a moat too. The vineyard, a very old one, once belonged to Jean de Caranet or Carnet. In the eighteenth century it passed to a Swedish family, de Luetkens, and remained in their hands for about a century. Then after several changes it became a private company, but a few years ago was acquired by M. Lipschit, who has embarked on a re-planting of the vineyard and a renewal of the cellars. When I visited it, in the *cuvier* were five brand new oak vats and two others. The whole estate, including the house and gardens, has had a thorough renovation, and this is indeed to the good, for it is a growth that has to some extent fallen out of public notice. In 1962 it had produced only 5 *tonneaux* instead of the 70 credited to it by Cocks et Féret. But by 1966 the total had been increased to over 30 *tonneaux*. The vineyard make-up is unusual: 45 per cent Cabernet of both varieties, 40 per cent Merlot and 15 per cent Petit-Verdot. La Tour-Carnet is one of the growths now selling non-vintage blends of good years and less good. Although La Tour-Carnet has not often come my way, I always have had a soft spot for it, because it was one of the wines that introduced me to the 1920s. Early in the last war the distinguished old Bath grocery firm of Cater, Stofell & Fortt – originators of the Bath Oliver, one of the best biscuits to go with cheese and claret – had some of its own bottling of La Tour-Carnet as well as Pontet-Canet. Priced at 6s.6d. a bottle and very good too, it was a real bargain at a time when wines doubtfully labelled Liebfraumilch were already fetching £1 or more.

Belgrave is rather better known or more widely distributed. Until the present proprietor, M. A. Gugés, took over in 1955 the property was run together with La Tour-Carnet. It is a real backwoods property, tucked away in St-Laurent on the poor soil that yields rather slender crops. It adjoins the St-Julien boundary, behind Lagrange, and I was told that at one time Belgrave was counted as a St-Julien and part of it was a fourth growth. The untraditional *chai*, built in concrete in 1934, has vats of the same material and after the fermentation the wine is left in these vats for three months. The more traditional-looking cellars were, on my visit in 1966, full of the odour of ripe apples as well as of wine, for the estate also grows apples for the market. The *vignoble* is 33 hectares and at present produces 120 *tonneaux*. The vineyard is 40 per cent Cabernet of both types, 40 per cent Merlot with the balance Petit-Verdot and Malbec. In the cellars was a large bottle stock of 1961, 1962 and some 1959, which probably demonstrates the problems of marketing that face these smaller properties. I have often found Belgrave a sound claret in the good Médoc tradition, fruity but not very refined. I remember a good 1953.

Camensac must be a rare wine outside France, unless there is a special call for it in some foreign market. It lies on a plateau not far from La Tour-Carnet, but the rectangular old farmhouse in a square courtyard gave the impression of being far from anywhere as I drove up after bumping along a minor road. As I got out to the barking of a farm dog I could not recall that I had ever tasted a Camensac. I still have not, for the *maître de chai* was away, and no one else had the key of the *chai*. The owners were the firm of Cuvelier, but are now two Spanish brothers, named Former and Merlaud. The area is but 13 hectares and current production about 35 *tonneaux*. I was glad to see one side of the courtyard recently spruced up, as this may indicate a new broom. St-Laurent contains a fair quota of *bourgeois* and lesser growths, but none strikes a chord with me. In spite of its three honoured estates, St-Laurent is something of a vinous backwater.

Margaux

With Margaux, however, we are again in the main stream. Such, indeed, is its *réclame* that a number of the neighbouring vineyards in Cantenac, Soussans, Arsac and Labarde are now allowed to sell their wine under the *appellation* Margaux, which carries a 40-hectolitre to the hectare *AC* maximum. Those who look at a map of the Haut-Médoc are often surprised by the gap in the famous vineyards between St-Julien and Margaux. After one leaves Beychevelle on the outskirts of St-Julien no great 'name' greets one until Lascombes hoves in sight, with its line of flagstaffs and flags representing, no doubt, Alexis Lichine's customers in many countries. The reason for the gap lies in the poor quality of the land: heath and marsh much of it. The Bordelais vineyards are often on marginal land, and in the thirsty gap between the two world-famous villages great wines are impossible, although reputable crops are produced in Cussac, Arcins and Soussans. Up until 1914 the gap was much smaller and less thirsty for there were many *bourgeois* growths on the now vine-deserted stretches.

Although Margaux possesses a nominal eleven classed growths, the commune is dominated by its celebrated *premier cru*, Château Margaux. To wine drinkers of many generations it has symbolized fine claret, and the name of commune and château alike have been familiar to those who could not readily give, let alone pronounce, the name of the commune of Lafite and Latour. Judging by the prices of the first growths in Christie's wine auctions, Margaux seemed the most sought-after during the first half of the nineteenth century. It had the advantage of being sold as Château Margaux, to distinguish it from a wine of the commune, while the other wines seldom had this prefix until well on into that century.

Margaux has undergone so many changes and had so many owners that to recount them would be valueless. It used to be called La Motte or Lamothe, and was said to have been the property of Edward II. It is also alleged that English soldiers ravaged the vineyard at the end of the fourteenth century, so presumably by then it was in French hands. The owner commonly thought to have enlarged the vineyard and planted it with top quality vines in 1750 was M. de Fumel, also owner of Haut-Brion. There is a story that the next owner, the Comte d'Hargicourt, the godson of Mme Dubarry, the mistress of Louis XV, attracted the attention of that sovereign by wearing buttons of unusual lustre. The king said that to wear such stones he must be the richest man in his kingdom, whereupon the owner of Château Margaux replied, 'I am wearing the diamonds of my soil'. These were the plain stones of the Médoc, cut and polished. Whether true or not (the anecdote is also told of Latour) this public relations story stood the estate in good stead. In the cellar of Count d'Adhémar, Louis XVI's retiring Ambassador to the English Court, in 1788 there was some Ch. Margeau (*sic*).

The Comte d'Hargicourt acquired Margaux by marrying in 1768 the daughter of the Marquis Joseph de Fumel and during the Revolution both were guillotined, so that Château Margaux like Lafite was sequestered by the state. In 1802 the *régisseur* of Latour estimated that Margaux was worth 1,200,000 livres, the same price for which Lafite had been sold five years earlier, but it was bought by the Marquis de la Colonilla the same year for 651,000 frs. and the old building was pulled down without him even seeing it. From that year dates the splendid classical First Empire building whose colonnaded portico is so familiar from the label. The architect was J. Combes, a pupil of Louis. In 1836 the château was acquired for 1,300,000 frs. by M. d'Aguado, Marquis de Las Marismas, who also bought the little port of Margaux on the estuary. The Aguados were the first of a number of bankers who acquired Médoc châteaux in this period; others were to include the Rothschilds, Pereires and Foulds. In 1879 it was transferred to the Comte Pillet-Will for 5 million frs., and his name across the label may be remembered by those who have had bottles of Margaux prior to 1920, when a company acquired it. The owner after Pillet-Will was his godson, the Duc de la Tremoille. The present proprietor is M. Pierre Ginestet, whose father began to buy shares in the company in 1925 and the son completed the purchase in 1949. To do this he sold Clos Fourtet in St-Emilion. However, he still owns Cos d'Estournel as well as Petit-Village in Pomerol. He has furnished Margaux with great taste in the First Empire period of the building, and the décor makes an interesting contrast with that of the Second Empire furnishings of that other first growth, Lafite.

The cellars of Margaux are among the finest in the Médoc, particularly the lofty building, supported by a line of white pillars, where the young wine is kept for its first year. Adjoining this is the splendid private cellar, in the form of a long gallery built at the same time as the château of stone from the Charente. The stone bins, three rows high on either side, can each hold 50 dozen, the contents of two *barriques*. There are 60,000 bottles there, including the wines of other leading châteaux. This long gallery-cellar makes a fine sight, but Pierre Ginestet says it is no longer big enough and another is planned. One of the reasons for this is that Château Margaux is large and conveniently near Bordeaux to make it an attractive place for celebrations and the visits of distinguished persons. These may make calls not only on the private cellars but on the young wines still in cask. When the late Chancellor Adenauer visited Bordeaux he was taken officially to Margaux with his suite and French hosts. In the course of the day it is said that two *barriques* of samples of the young wine were consumed by the visitors! During the month of August alone, when tourists descend in coach-loads, no fewer than eight *barriques* may be emptied in this way. Expensive publicity.

Fortunately Margaux is a big estate, although only a relatively small part is planted with vines: about 55 hectares, with an average production of 150 *tonneaux*. The composition of the vineyard is 50 per cent Cabernet-Sauvignon, 10 per cent Cabernet-Franc, 35 per cent Merlot, and a small balance of 5 per cent of Petit-Verdot, which is providential in a wet year, as it provides the acidity and backbone that will be lacking, especially in the Merlot. The soil is gravelly, except in one part where it is soft water chalk, rare in the Médoc. This is where the white wine, sold as Pavillon-Blanc de Château Margaux, comes from: 50 *tonneaux* of it on average. The *cépage* is 50 per cent Sauvignon and 50 per cent Sémillon. It is a pleasant, dry wine but does not aspire to be in the same class as Haut-Brion-Blanc. Quite a number of minor Médocain proprietors make a little white wine, which cannot be too easy to sell, as it can only be marketed as plain Bordeaux Blanc and lacks the slight cachet that the *appellation* Graves gives. Pavillon-Blanc, of course, relies on the cachet of Margaux. The soil of the commune is very thin, a coarse gravel with lime sub-soil. The average yield is small. Ch Margaux used to market a second red wine as Pavillon Rouge.

The wine of Château Margaux is noted for its fine bouquet and the delicacy of its flavour. At a blind tasting of young first growths it may often be picked out by its 'nose'. On the whole it is a wine particularly successful in fine years, but sometimes correspondingly disappointing in off-vintages; although the excellent 1950 is an exception to this. Yet, for example, the 1953 is outstanding, and the 1961 already has a high reputation. Although it is early days yet, the 1966 seems very good, yet the 1964 so far shows poorly. Over the past half century the château has had its ups and downs, and for a period was making wine well under its class. With Haut-Brion it was the first of the first growths in 1923 to establish compulsory château-bottling. But in 1930 this rule was abandoned and for 20 years Château Margaux could be bought in wood, the only one of the *premiers crus* to whom this applied, (1949 was the last year it shipped in wood, but later at least one cask appears to have got away. For Château Margaux 1952, bottled by Skinner and Rook of Nottingham was sold at Christie's in February 1968). No doubt this gave the wine some competitive advantage in the difficult Thirties, but good vintages were rare then and in the intermediate post-war period the wine was not very inspiring, but the 1950 was first-class. The last really good old Margaux that I have tasted was the 1924, a perfectly balanced wine and probably the best Château Margaux of the decade. Part of the 1929 was excellent too, but some was thin and poor, owing, I believe, to problems during the fermentation.

Château Margaux is a difficult wine to taste young, and this applies to other wines in the neighbourhood. For they tend to taste astringent and thin, lacking the 'flesh' of the Pauillacs and the fruit of the St-Juliens. When first offered, it is usually the least dear of the *premiers crus*, although these days that is but a relative term. When Château Margaux is successful, this is, one may feel, the essence of claret – fine, delicate but fruity – and its rivals up there in Pauillac can seem a little heavy-footed. But when it falls short, even in a reasonably successful year like 1955, it is not a very attractive glass of fine claret, except to those who value refinement above fruit.

To solve the problem of off-vintages, in 1966 Pierre Ginestet decided to produce a non-vintage wine on his properties, including Margaux and Cos d'Estournel. This is a blend of young vintages, good and indifferent, and the first batch, of about 10 *tonneaux* so far as Margaux was concerned, was to be a blend of 1963 and 1964. When I first tasted the blend it had not been in bottle many months, but it was certainly better than the 1963 on its own. This move has been the subject of controversy, and at first thought it seems somewhat below the dignity of a *premier cru*, and even of lesser classed growths, to market their wine like this. As recently as 1936 Lafite sold most of its crop of that year as Pauillac *tout court* and even today proprietors sell off part of their crop not considered good enough to be sold under the château name, although it does not cost any less to produce a bad wine than a good one. There was no wine produced at Château Margaux in 1965 sold under the château label, and if sold as plain Margaux or even as Bordeaux rouge, it secures a fraction of the price of the wine sold as a château wine. In 1963 there was not a Médoc proprietor who did not lose money, and 1965 was even worse.

However even a blend of years requires some bottle age, and I would feel happier if the wine were not offered until it was reasonably mature; otherwise there is nothing to prevent it being sold, opened and drunk when far too young. If this system develops there will be a series of Château Margaux without vintage date on wine lists; whereas with a vintage label one has some idea of drinkability, when a wine has no such age guide one will assume it is ready for consumption. Accordingly I think that these non-vintage wines should have at least a bottling date on them; and I confess to some doubts about non-vintage wine from leading châteaux.

Rausan, along with Léoville and Larose, were probably the first named growths outside the *premiers crus* to establish a reputation abroad. Originally this Margaux vineyard was united and belonged to the Mesures de Rausan family, merchants, one of whose descendants M. de Rausan, was a member of the Bordeaux Parlement in the eighteenth century. The story goes that, dissatisfied with the price offered for his wine in Bordeaux, he chartered a ship which he loaded with casks from two good vintages and sailed for London. Using his ship in the Thames as an office, his initiative brought him both publicity and orders. Unfortunately he still did not consider the price high enough, so he announced that unless he secured what he considered a fair price, he would throw the casks into the river, barrel by barrel. After four casks had thus been jettisoned the onlookers could stand it no longer and surrendered to the vendor.

Later on the vineyard was divided, with two-thirds remaining to the Baronne de Ségla, born a Rausan. In 1866 this portion passed to M. Eugène Durand-Dassier, the father-in-law of M. Frédéric Cruse, for 505,000 frs. The Cruse family owned it until 1956 and turned this charming, low-built house into a kind of private museum, with rooms furnished in the style of various French epochs. In one room, I remember, there was a replica of the curious bath in which the unfortunate Marat was murdered. Other rooms were more comfortably adorned and the house was of considerable interest. The Cruses sold it for 36 million old frs., and after an intermediate owner, M. de Meslon, a descendant of the Rausan family, it passed at an advanced price, after much re-planting, in 1959 into the hands of John Holt & Co., the Liverpool firm of West African merchants, who thus began their growing involvement in the wine trade.

The vineyard of Rausan-Ségla now lies compactly in front and at the side of the low château buildings, but – an illustration of the parcelization of Bordeaux vine-yards – until 1933 it was divided into no fewer than 240 strips. In particular it was deeply mixed up with its neighbour, Rauzan-Gassies, but in 1933 an exchange was made with them and other neighbours, and it is now contained in only 16 'parcels'.

As a wine Rausan-Ségla had a particularly distinguished record in the 1920s, and the '29 was outstanding for its balance of fruit and delicacy. Meanwhile the vineyard and its output had been allowed to fall. Whereas in 1899 and 1900 it had produced 62 and 122 *tonneaux* respectively, this was down to about 20 *tonneaux* in the 1930s, and the vineyard area had dropped sharply to only 34 hectares. Re-planting took place in 1934, but even in the post-war period the crop was small: 30 *tonneaux* in 1945, a very short vintage, and only 44 in 1953. By the time the Cruses disposed of the property, the active area was again reduced to scarcely 20 hectares, and in 1959 only 35 *tonneaux* were made. However, much re-planting with a large proportion of Caber-net-Sauvignon took place under de Meslon and this continued under Holts, so that it had risen to 95 *tonneaux* by 1962, although the general shortage of the '61s is demonstrated by the production of only 35 *tonneaux*. Now the vineyard area is 42 hectares and the average crop about 70 *tonneaux*. Since 1961 when the château celebrated its tercentenary of being known as Rausan with a special label for this vintage, the wine has been bottled in a newly designed, embossed bottle. Rausan-Ségla was the last Bordeaux estate of importance to tread the grapes; it ceased after 1956, with the transference of ownership. A curiosity by which I remember Rausan-Ségla is its *vin rosé*, known as a *vin de goutte*. In common with other properties, they occasionally made a few hogsheads of this wine for domestic consumption; the wine is taken off the skins after passing through the *pressoir foulior* and fermented in hogsheads, so there is little contact with the skins. Only a few years ago the '47 was still delicious. Ronald Barton has also made a *vin rosé* periodically at Langoa, and Alexis Lichine has commercialized this in recent years at Lascombes. The most interesting *vin de goutte* I have tasted was the remarkable Léoville-Poyferré 1898, referred to in the vintages chapter.

Rauzan-Gassies – whose variation in the spelling of the first part of its name, called after a seventeenth-century owner, is often mis-rendered in wine lists – was sold in 1866 to M. Charles Rhoné-Péreire. It is much smaller than its neighbour, consisting of 22 hectares, but relatively produces quite a large quantity: about 110 *tonneaux*. Perhaps too much. Rauzan-Gassies has one of the most attractive labels, but almost consistently I have found the wine thin and disappointing. A few years ago I shared in a splendid magnum of 1920, but otherwise I have been unlucky, and years ago even the 1929 was lacking in fruit. It is unfortunate that one of the pair that top the *deuxièmes* after Mouton, which has long since shrugged off this ascription, should not be better. It is fair to add that the '61 is the most promising wine from this growth for many years.

Although Durfort-Vivens stands high in the 1855 classification, this has not been a prominent wine in the last generation. It has hardly ever come my way, although once I had some 1934 from the Wine Society which was softer and more agreeable than most of the Médocs of that hard year. Originally named after a proprietor, M. Durfort, the next owner, M. Vivens, added his own name when he acquired it in 1824. In 1866 his great nephew sold out to MM. G. Richier and E. de la Mare for the considerable sum of 500,000 frs. At that time it was 30 hectares in extent and produced 50 – 55 *tonneaux*. Towards the end of the century Durfort-Vivens was the property of the family and firm of Delor, who disposed of it during the difficult times in the 1930s. After that it was owned by Pierre Ginestet until 1963 when he sold the vineyard, the *cuvier* and the name, but not the château, to Lucien Lurton, the owner of Brane-Cantenac, another second growth. Pierre Ginestet told me that he sold it because he did not want to own adjoining first and second growths. The château, with its name on the wall is on the outskirts of the village of Margaux, and is now occupied by Pierre Ginestet's son Bernard. For some time the area of the Durfort vineyard was much reduced, but is now said to be on the increase, perhaps with the transference of part of the large Brane-Cantenac vineyard. The output is about 60 *tonneaux*.

It must be understood that these château names are in effect brand names, and can be used at will inside a commune, but without violating the gap between classified and non-classified vineyard areas, already mentioned. A classed-growth proprietor cannot buy a *bourgeois* vineyard and add the production to his own, but he can acquire another classed growth and use the name and/or the vineyard. This is what Palmer has done with Desmirail.

Margaux's fourth *deuxième*, Lascombes, was yet another highly-placed classed growth that somehow had not shone for many years, until in 1952 it was bought by a large American syndicate headed by Alexis Lichine, an American of Russian origin who has certainly created a name for himself and an increased market for French wines in the United States. The price is said to have been very low; only a five-figure sum in dollars, but much money had to be spent on the property. Lascombes was named after the Chevalier de Lascombes, and then it passed into the hands of the Johnston family, and later to that of M. Petit who owned it a century ago. At one point it was well known for its 1847 and 1848, but the production was small, and during the present century it has had many masters, which no doubt accounted for often disappointing wines. The original château was a charming small eighteenth-century building, still standing, but in the last century a rather ugly if more imposing building was erected, and this has housed both annual exhibitions of pictures associated with wine and a shifting flock of young wine students. Alexis Lichine when in Bordeaux lives in the smaller, more domestic Le Prieuré.

Lascombes has a common Médoc vineyard make-up, with 55 per cent Cabernet-Sauvignon, 15 per cent Cabernet-Franc, 25 per cent Merlot and 5 per cent Petit-Verdot, yielding an output of about 180 *tonneaux*. Although it made a better than average '52 when the new owners were scarcely in possession, there is no doubt that the wine has greatly improved since and should continue to do so. I remember the '64 as being attractive when tasted after a year in cask. Most of it, not surprisingly, now goes to America.

It is convenient to take Malescot St-Exupéry and Marquis d'Alesme-Becker together, for both have been under the same ownership for many years. Malescot – which at one time enjoyed, I am told, a certain popularity in Canada when pronounced as Male Scot – was named after Simon Malescot, *procureur* in the Bordeaux Parlement, who bought the property in 1697. In 1827 it passed to the Comte de St-Exupéry who added his name, and the estate changed hands again in 1853, being acquired by M. Fourcade. At that time the vineyard was very large, amounting to 77 hectares, producing well over 100 *tonneaux*, but this diminished over the years, and now production is much smaller, yielding 50 – 60 *tonneaux* from 12 hectares. Becker, said to be one of the three oldest Médoc vineyards, on the other hand was always one of the smallest classed growths, and a century ago was making only about 7 *tonneaux*. Now the figure is 25 – 30 from 8 hectares. For a period this pair of estates was English-owned because in 1919, after being in German control, they were acquired by the London wholesale wine firm of W. H. Chaplin, best known for their connections with the Australian wine trade. Soon after the last war they sold out to Seager Evans, the distillers, who in their turn in 1955 sold the two Margaux growths to Paul Zuger, who had been running the estate on their account. The handsome house, associated with the St-Exupéry family, stands in the middle of Margaux. The former Becker château is elsewhere in the village. Paul Zuger has done a good deal of re-planting and worked very hard to improve his property. The *cuvier* adjoining the château is on two floors, as at Pontet-Canet, and contains five wooden vats and four concrete type. Both wines are made in the same *chai*, and the vineyard composition of each is similar: 40 per cent Cabernet-Sauvignon, 20 per cent Cabernet-Franc, 30 per cent Merlot and 10 per cent of Petit-Verdot. There is no Malbec. Neither wine is now much seen in England, but the '48 Malescot has been an outstanding example of that vintage. Malescot has the style and elegance associated with Margaux; Becker is rather more *corsé*. The estate also has a second wine, Domaine-du-Balardin, which has the *appellation* Bordeaux Supérieur.

By one of the many irrationalities of the Médoc, Boyd-Cantenac is indeed a third growth Margaux, and was entitled to this *appellation* in 1855. A hundred years later its now associated growth, Poujet, a *quatrième* in Cantenac, also became entitled to sell as a Margaux. Of the two, Poujet is the older property and used to belong to the monks of Le Prieuré. Mr Boyd must surely have been of Irish or Scottish origin but this is not clear, although the present owner believes that this gentleman lived in the time of Napoleon III. Boyd-Cantenac used to belong to the Ginestet family and was bought from them in the mid-1930s. Both are owned by Pierre Guillemet and his energetic wife, who won my heart when I called to taste their wines, by insisting that I preserved my health from the ravages of young wines by eating bread and cheese at the same time. Together the two properties form 25 hectares and produce 100 *tonneaux*. After the vintage the best *cuves* are set aside to be called Boyd-Cantenac, the less good are sold as Poujet. (Another example of the brand element in these wine names.) The vineyard is 70 per cent Cabernet-Sauvignon, 10 per cent Cabernet-Franc, 15 per cent Merlot and 5 per cent Petit-Verdot. The reason why these wines are not very widely known is that the Boyd part is normally sold to one or two wine merchants only, while the Poujet goes exclusively to private clients. I thought the Boyd-Cantenac in particular a soft, supple wine in good years.

Margaux seems somewhat the home of lost châteaux. Desmirail has disappeared as a vineyard, Durfort is divorced from its vineyard, Ferrière has been somewhat marginally active recently, and Dubignon-Talbot, a classed growth in 1855, no longer exists.

Of these Ferrière is the senior in the classification lists. It was named after Gabriel Ferrière in the mid-eighteenth century, and was in the hands of that family until 1914. The production was always tiny, and in 1867 was given as only 6 *tonneaux*. The modest château lies in the middle of the village, and part of the small vineyard is actually walled; the remainder is near Lascombes. In 1962 a fifteen-year lease to Lascombes was arranged, and the wine is made and kept there. There has been re-planting of the vineyard and production, now 10 – 12 *tonneaux*, might rise to 15. It will be interesting to see how the wine develops.

The Château of Desmirail, a third growth like Ferrière, is also situated in the middle of Margaux. Originally the vineyard was part of the large Rauzan estate and was split off when a M. Desmirail married a Mlle Rauzan de Ribail in the eighteenth century. Production of this vineyard was never large, about 25 to 30 *tonneaux*, but it had an excellent reputation. I remember a '28 that was much less hard than many of its peers. Finally, however, in 1957 the property was sold to Palmer, and the vineyard incorporated in that estate. It is now a brand name.

Marquis de Terme, the one fourth growth of Margaux, has its *cuvier* on the outskirts of Margaux near the Rauzan-Gassies vineyard, but the other *chais* are a mile away. The wine is not very well known in Britain, although production can be as high as 200 *tonneaux* from a rather small vineyard of 24 hectares. Perhaps the output is excessive, for a hundred years ago when it was owned by M. Oscar Sollberg the production was given as 50 – 60 *tonneaux*. The present owner is M. Pierre Sénéclauze. Certainly the wine is made unusually in the tile-lined vats in the *cuvier*, for the *maître de chai* told me that, after the fermentation, the wine is kept in these vats for a year and then in cask for a further two years. All the wine is château-bottled. The make-up of the vineyard is unusual too, for it is split up equally between the four main grapes, Cabernet-Sauvignon, Cabernet-Franc, Merlot and Petit-Verdot. There must be a higher proportion of Petit-Verdot at Marquis de Terme than in any other classed growth in the Médoc. The young wine as I tasted it from the vats seemed full and fruity, but I cannot recollect ever drinking a mature bottle.

A former classed growth that has now completely disappeared is Dubignon-Talbot. It ceased production in the phylloxera period, was revived, but about six years ago Cordier bought the brand name, presumably to avoid a rival Talbot to his own, while the tiny vineyard was divided between Ginestet and Zuger.

Margaux *tout court* is a name not infrequently to be found on wine labels, but there can be scarcely enough of such wines from proprietors content to sell them only under the commune label to inspire confidence in most of such bottles; so the contents are unlikely to have originated solely in the district. Of course, some may come from the outlying communes which, as already explained, are entitled in part to call their wines Margaux. These are the whole of Soussans and Cantenac and part of Arsac and Labarde. This first authorization was given in 1955. However the balance of proprietorship can be seen from the fact that thirty large proprietors account for 85 per cent of the wine sold under the *appellation* Margaux, while seventy small owners take up the remaining 15 per cent. Counting the 'satellite' communes, the area under vines is nearly as large as Pauillac and St-Estèphe: about 820 hectares, but on the thin soil average output is much less, about 25,000 hectolitres.

10. The Médoc III

Cantenac and the Lesser Communes

Cantenac

Adjoining Margaux is the leading commune now allowed to sell its wines as Margaux: Cantenac. As a result the name has almost disappeared so far as wine lists are concerned, except for the growths that have the commune name incorporated in their own. The wines of Cantenac tend to be a trifle fuller, less delicate than those of Margaux, although Palmer, whose vineyard adjoins Château Margaux, is somewhat similar in style, with perhaps a little more body, which I find agreeable. The vineyards of these adjoining communes are considerably intermingled.

According to the classification, Brane-Cantenac, a second growth, is the leader of the Cantenacs. It was named after the former proprietor of Mouton, who moved south after his sale to M. Thuret in 1830 and then concentrated his talents on this vineyard, which was once called Gorse-Gui. It then passed through various hands rather quickly, including those of M. Roy, owner of Issan. Today it is the property of François Lurton and is situated rather back from the river and near the woods. Behind the small château, one storey high except for a central upper room, lies a very 'green' lake. The aspect of the wine buildings is traditional but the vineyard is large, with some 65 hectares producing well over 200 *tonneaux* a year. The vineyard is comprised of 75 per cent Cabernet-Sauvignon, with the balance made up of Cabernet-Franc, Merlot and a very small quantity of Petit-Verdot. Brane-Cantenac is a big, sometimes rather coarse wine, with a good deal of fruit but not overmuch delicacy; or that has been my experience. But I remember one or two splendid wines in the 1920s, notably the 1924 and the 1928. The latter, in a vintage which has remained hard longer than any vintage should, is an exceptionally well-balanced wine.

Again in 1948 it came up trumps and is one of the leading successes of the vintage in the Médoc. A big estate like this is doubtless a heavy responsibility for all but proprietors of considerable resources or other connections. Brane-Cantenac, like its Brown neighbour, is notable for its resplendent black and gold label.

Ch. Kirwan (is the name Irish in origin?) is something of a curiosity. At one time it must have made distinguished wine and in the 1855 classification Kirwan was placed at the head of the third growths; a position of note. About this time the estate was owned by M. Godard who became Mayor of Bordeaux, and when he died about 1882, he left it to the city of Bordeaux. No doubt this was intended as an act of civic piety, but as in similar cases one may suspect that the gift was an embarrassment, for although municipally-owned vineyards are not unknown in Germany and Switzerland, they are not part of the Bordeaux scene. So in 1885 the well-known firm of Schröder & Schÿler made a contract to buy the whole crop every year, and for a long period the wine was sold as a *monopole* without vintage date, although a small part of the crop was disposed of with a vintage year on the label. Then I remember the wine being listed on a pre-Second World War list of Avery's of Bristol as 'ten years old'. In 1904 the city of Bordeaux divested itself of the property and sold it to two other well-known wine merchants Daniel and Georges Guestier. Alfred Schÿler married Daniel Guestier's daughter and when his father-in-law died in 1924 Schröder & Schÿler acquired the property whose crop they had been marketing for about forty years. It used to have a considerable sale in Germany, where much of the firm's business lay. The eighteenth-century château and its gardens, somewhat tucked away behind the Médoc railway line, are particularly attractive. The vineyard is 25 hectares in extent and now makes 80 – 100 *tonneaux* of wine. After a bad period the wine is now improving again. In the 1956 frosts 100,000 vines out of 250,000 were lost. Nowadays the wine is sold with a vintage label.

With the exception of Ch. de Lamarque in that commune, Issan could almost be described as the only original old château of the Médoc, complete with towers and moat. The oldest part dates from about 1600. It lies between the *D.2* Médoc road and the river; down on the flat land which is almost a drained marsh, with dykes. Much of the vineyard, however, is on a slightly higher ground, not far from Château Margaux and opposite Le Prieuré. Its early days are associated with those of the last of the English in Bordeaux. For after the capture by Dunois in 1451 of Blaye across the river, the English had to evacuate the country and fought a skirmish at Issan on their way out. The legend is that they succeeded in extricating some of the local wine as well as themselves and carried it off to England where the wine of Issan became known. More recently there was apparently a special demand for Issan in Britain in the last century. In 1848 it belonged to M. Deluc, whose family sold it to M. Gustave Roy, also owner then of Brane-Cantenac. The wine had a high reputation in the nineteenth century – and its label motto had been *Regum Mensis Arisque Deorum*. It was said to be a favourite of the Austrian Emperor Franz Josef; particularly the 1899. But from the middle of the 1920s it declined, under the proprietorship of M. Grange who also owned Giscours. The estate certainly passed through not very good times in the first third of this century, but was purchased just after the war by the late Emmanuel Cruse, part owner of Rausan-Ségla. Restoration was not taken in hand until after the sale of the latter in 1956. A great deal of money has been spent not only on the charming château, with its fine rooms and furniture, but also on the cellars and vineyards. One of the *chais* has timber rafters, recalling an old dining hall, and is registered as an historic monument.

The vineyard area is not much above 10 hectares, situated on the higher ground near Margaux, and its composition is now 68 per cent Cabernet-Sauvignon, 8 per cent Cabernet-Franc and 24 per cent Merlot. Production is about 50 *tonneaux*. At present the wine is not château-bottled but, like the Cruses' other château, Pontet-Canet, is shipped in cask or bottled in Bordeaux. At one time there used also to be a wine from the neighbouring *palus*, sold as Moulin d'Issan; as much as 200 *tonneaux* used to be made in the days when large quantities of wine were made in the riverside strip which runs up to Cussac. Moulin d'Issan was said to be particularly liked by the Protestants of Paris, as the proprietor was of that faith. But it has not existed for many years.

Cantenac-Brown was formerly called Brown-Cantenac, but no doubt the confusion and pronunciation problems arising from the adjacent Brane were too much, and the name was reversed. Mr Brown was a Bordeaux merchant, and a century ago his vineyard was very large, running to 70 hectares under vines, compared with about 20 – 25 today. It was bought in 1860 by the owner of Léoville-Poyferré, M. Armand Lalande, from a banker, M. Gromard, who had let the property run down. M. Lalande set to work to erect a large and curious-looking brick and stone château, which in the 1860s was described as 'one of the architectural beauties of the Médoc'. Whether nowadays this looks more out of place than some of the other Médoc châteaux is a matter of opinion, but I would not have been surprised to come upon it equally incongruously placed in some Highland glen or forming the back-drop for *Lucia di Lammermoor*. This house belonged to M. de Wilde, whose father owned du Tertre in Arsac, and was for a long time divorced from the vineyard; another that had been in the doldrums for a long time, although one sees it now and again on British wine lists. Yet it made one of the outstanding '29s that I remember. The proprietor was Jean Lawton, head of the firm of Lalande, but in 1968 it passed to Comte Bertrand du Vivier, on behalf of the Bordeaux firm of de Luze, of which he is chairman and managing director. The price was said to be in the neighbourhood of 1,800,000 new francs. At present the vineyard composition is 40 per cent Cabernet-Sauvignon, 20 per cent Cabernet-Franc, 30 per cent Merlot, and 10 per cent Petit-Verdot, but it is proposed to increase the proportion of Cabernet-Sauvignon at the expense of the Merlot. Cantenac-Brown has been due for a revival, and with a new proprietor and a vineyard with a good proportion of old vines, it will be interesting to see how the wines show in future.

Palmer, on the other hand, is commonly accepted as one of the most successful châteaux of its class and the wines among the most distinguished in the Médoc. Before the Cantenacs were permitted in 1955 to call themselves Margaux, Palmer was known as Palmer-Margaux and this seemed fair enough, for the vineyards adjoin those of Château Margaux, and its wines are similar in style. By some they are also considered to have an affinity with Lafite, perhaps because both are soft wines and have a fair proportion of Merlot in their vineyards, although Lafite claims to have much less than Palmer.

Even by Médoc standards the vineyard is not very old, having been constituted by General Palmer, who is said to have taken a liking for the Médoc and its wines when the English army occupied the region in 1814, near the end of the Napoleonic Wars. He bought what was then called Château de Gascq from the family of that name and energetically expanded the property, including a somewhat remote part called Boston. Unfortunately the general's resources or commercial acumen did not match his enthusiasm, and in the 1840s he went bankrupt without even building a château. However he had been successful enough with his wine to establish it as a *troisième cru*, and this was confirmed in the 1855 classification. Two years previously it had been bought by one of the great Second Empire banking families, the Pereires, who gave their name to the Place Pereire in Paris. At one period they were rivals of the Rothschilds. The Palmer property, badly ravaged by the oidium and entirely re-planted, was bought for 425,000 frs. and in 1856 the present château was erected, built in what may be called the 'château style', with some affinity with Pichon-Longueville-Baron. The château today bears the initials of Emile Isaac and Isaac Rodrique Pereire, whose descendants in 1938 sold out to a consortium of three. The biggest shareholder is the Bordeaux firm of Mähler-Besse, and the balance is held by Sichel & Co. of Bordeaux and M. Alain Miailhe, proprietor of Pichon-Lalande and other growths. Until his death in 1965 the late Allan Sichel largely represented the English interest of Palmer. I have already referred to him. He was one of the most enlightened, enthusiastic, downright and fluent exponents of Bordeaux. His geese were never mistaken for swans, and if he thought that his beloved Palmer had produced a disappointing vintage he never hesitated to say so, and to dissuade, if possible, his customers from buying the wine. To illustrate the difficulties that faced even well-known châteaux until a few years ago, he once told me that Palmer made no money from the time it had been acquired just before the last war until after the 1953 vintage. Baron Philippe de Rothschild has more than once said the same about Mouton, except that his first profitable year was 1955.

On the top of the steep roof of the château, which the French call *'Pal-Mehr'*, flies the Union Jack along with the French Tricolour and the Dutch flag, representing the other two proprietors, and they look across the vineyards to the Union Jack flying from Rausan Ségla. Allan Sichel's son, Peter, now lives at Angludet in the same commune.

The vineyard of Palmer is about 38 hectares, having been increased slightly by the accession of Desmirail, which was bought in 1957 and absorbed. The reason for this incorporation is that wine can be sold more advantageously under the Palmer label than under that of Desmirail, and this is quite legal. However in the poor year of 1963 the whole Palmer crop with *appellation* was sold under the Desmirail 'imprint'. Otherwise Palmer, hemmed in as it is by surrounding vineyards, has not expanded like some other châteaux; and this may partly account for its fine quality. The composition of the vineyard is 38 per cent Cabernet-Sauvignon, 10 per cent Cabernet-

Franc, 35 per cent Merlot and 17 per cent Petit-Verdot; in the last few years the proportion of Cabernet-Sauvignon has been increased appreciably. The normal output is just over 100 *tonneaux*. Yet in that fine but short vintage of 1961 they only made 30 *tonneaux* of a splendid wine. In off-years it is sometimes a little thin, like its neighbour, Château Margaux, although it produced an exceptionally good 1960. There is little doubt that Palmer is under-classed. Some of its successful vintages are mentioned in the chapter on vintages. A hundred years ago the first Pereire was ambitious to make it a second growth, and so it should be.

Also foreign-owned is Prieuré-Lichine, whose charming little square-built eighteenth-century château looking more English than French is approached through an archway on the main road. It was indeed once a priory, and the house almost touches the parish church of Cantenac. Always a small property, a hundred years ago it belonged to a M. Rosset, and the output was 15–20 *tonneaux*, but now from 15 hectares it produces about 60 *tonneaux*. The vineyard is 50 per cent Cabernet-Sauvignon, 10 per cent Cabernet-Franc, 35 per cent Merlot and 5 per cent Petit-Verdot. It was bought in 1952 for about 150 million old francs (equal to 1·5 million new francs) by Alexis Lichine and, although nominally owned by a company, it is essentially his property. The vineyard was re-planted and is certainly now producing more distinguished wines. The small château, in which I have stayed, is attractively furnished and decorated. In the converted kitchen, with its fine scrubbed farmhouse table and galaxy of copper cooking utensils, the serious business of the day takes place when the American proprietor is in residence.

One of the lesser Cantenac châteaux not very widely known is Poujet. This, in fact, is run in harness with Boyd-Cantenac, as already mentioned on page 154.

That ends the classed growths of Cantenac, but certainly Angludet, which belongs to the Sichel family, deserves promotion. It claims to have had classed-growth status up to the Revolution, when it acquired the temporarily topical name of La République, but was split up when the 1855 classification was being considered. This low, friendly-looking château lies out in the country from the village; both vineyard and wine-making have improved since the war. The '53 Angludet is still a delicious wine. The vineyard contains 20 hectares made up of 40 per cent Cabernet-Sauvignon, 20 per cent Cabernet-Franc, 30 per cent Merlot, and 10 per cent Petit-Verdot, and production is around 50 *tonneaux*. There are few other Cantenacs of wide repute. There is Martinens belonging to Mme Dubos, and another is Pontac-Lynch. The lesser growths are sold as Margaux.

Arsac

It is convenient to mention here the wines of those neighbouring communes who harbour *crus classés* and are entitled in whole or in part since 1955 to sell their wines as Margaux. Arsac boasts one classed growth in its territorially large commune, which lies inland and broadly south of Cantenac. This is du Tertre, a fifth growth. It is a vineyard which had considerable *réclame* in the nineteenth century, and when it was bought in 1870 by M. Koenigswater he paid 530,000 frs. A later owner was

Achille de Wilde, whose family had owned Cantenac-Brown. In recent years the property certainly fell into some decline, but it has now been bought by the Gasqueton family, co-proprietors of Calon-Ségur, and considerable re-planting of the vineyard, remote on a plateau, has taken place. Otherwise the Arsac wines are not very well known, although there are those who say that they can be very good.

Labarde

Labarde adjoins Arsac and Cantenac, on the river side of the former, and has two classed growths, Giscours and Dauzac. Here again the story is one of a fine earlier reputation but more recent decline. Giscours is a large vineyard, and at the Revolution its owner, M. de Saint Simon, joined the emigrés, so his estate was confiscated. It was sold to a Mr Michael Jacob who, oddly enough for the period, had two American merchants as associates, John Gray and Jonathan Davis, but this partnership did not last long, and in 1825 the property was sold to M. Marc Promis, a Bordeaux merchant, whose family name is incorporated in the Sauternes growth of Rabaud-Promis. In 1847 he in turn sold to a rich Paris banker, M. J. P. Pescatore, and when he died in 1855, his nephew took over. The latter sold Giscours to M. Edouard Cruse, great uncle of Christian Cruse, for 1,000,000 frs. Cruse restored the vineyard and château. The Cruse family owned the estate for many years before selling it to Monsieur E. Grange. Since then it has changed hands a number of times. It was making excellent wines in the 1920s, particularly the '24 and the '29. Then came a drop, but about ten years ago it was bought by M. Tari from Algeria and he set to work to improve its status and increase the vineyard, which has now risen to 75 hectares, with about 65 per cent Cabernet-Sauvignon and Cabernet-Franc in equal proportions, 30 per cent Merlot, and the balance Petit-Verdot. Whereas fifteen years ago production was a mere 15 – 20 *tonneaux*, it is now no less than 300. Extensive renovations have been made of the large mid-nineteenth-century château, which has something of the air of a seaside or spa hotel, and of the *chais*, which were all too small for current production. As with other proprietors having Algerian experience, M. Tari has imported some modern methods of vinification. When the balance of age in the vineyards has been established, Giscours is expected to return to its old form.

Dauzac has also had its ups and downs. The estate lies on the Gironde side of the commune, and the vineyards touch those of Giscours. At the Revolution it was owned by the celebrated Count Lynch, Mayor of Bordeaux at the Restoration. When he died in 1835 it went to his brother, Chevalier Lynch, but he died in 1841, and with one intervening owner the property passed in 1863 to Nathaniel Johnston of the Bordeaux family. It was at Dauzac that Bordeaux Mixture, which successfully combated the mildew in the 1880s, is said to have been devised. But it is also alleged that it had originally been used by Johnston to colour unpleasantly blue the grapes near the road which might be eaten by the local children. At one time a great deal of wine was made at Dauzac, and the 1900 crop was no less than 1,000 *tonneaux*, although most of this was sold as La Maqueline. At one time the prolific Dauzac had its own railway line; but in the Inter-War period this fifth growth fell on hard times and production declined. Recently the average was about 40 *tonneaux* only. However in 1966 M. Alain Miailhe, owner of Pichon-Lalande and of Siran, which adjoins Dauzac, bought the property and set about its complete re-modelling. In a few years' time it should again be an interesting wine. Sparkling Ducru-Beaucaillou has already been mentioned. Nathaniel Johnston also used the wines of Dauzac for making sparkling wine, which was actually produced across the estuary in Bourg.

Next to Dauzac is Siran. M. Miailhe has in recent years put a great deal of money and effort into his properties so that the whole establishment now looks very well. Production at Siran is increasing and runs at about 120 *tonneaux* a year. The soil tends to be sandy and the wine is light and fine, in the Margaux style. I remember a particularly good '53, when the wine was already in its 'teens. It is certainly one of the châteaux that would be included in any new classification of the Médoc.

Not the least remarkable feature of Siran is behind the old two-storey house: the garden filled with cyclamens. Many of the Médoc châteaux have the charming little white and pink varieties in their gardens, but nothing approaches the display in the early autumn at Siran, where they grow as thickly in the long grass as bluebells in an English wood in spring. Siran is a first Soussans-growth for cyclamen.

In this part of the Médoc now entitled to the *appellation* Margaux there are some of the best-known and respected *crus bourgeois*. In Margaux itself there is a series of three growths with a variation of the name Labégorce. They are de Labégorce, L'Abbé-Gorsse-de-Gorsse and Labégorce-Zédé, and to rival such complexity one probably has to go to Germany. This cannot assist their distribution. The third of these extends into Soussans and is said to be the best, but some favour the first, which has an agreeable Louis XVI château. It produces 70 *tonneaux* of wine, exclusively sold by Dourthe of Moulis. In Margaux also is the curiously named La Gurgue, whose name is pronounced as if the last two letters were omitted and not like the noise the last of the bath-water makes as it disappears down the plug-hole. The only time I drank it I found it rather a hard wine.

The area includes two of the somewhat curious six or seven *crus exceptionels*. Curious because although some but not all of them are rather more widely known than most of the *bourgeois*, they have not benefited much from this promotion. Also the list is a shifting one. The two candidates in the Margaux fold include Angludet, already mentioned, and Bel-Air-Marquis d'Aligre, a splendid name, whose length is little calculated to secure its success in foreign markets, although said to have enjoyed popularity in the Low Countries. Though the production is now small, it heads the list of Soussans wines.

Much better known, however, is La Tour-de-Mons. This excellent property, lying out in the country towards the estuary and named after a Belgian family who bought it in 1623 (M. Pierre de Mons also owned Angludet), is run by Bertrand Clauzel, grandson of Pierre Dubos, who was the owner of Cantemerle for so many years, and relative of Henri Binaud, who married Dubos's daughter and now directs Cantemerle, although Bertrand Clauzel controls the wine-making there too. The large *chai* is traditional in appearance, and production varies from about 80 – 100 *tonneaux*. The vineyard is 55 per cent Cabernet-Sauvignon, 5 per cent Cabernet-

Franc, 35 per cent Merlot, and 5 per cent Petit-Verdot. The wine has been consistently good and the '53 was one of the most distinguished Médocs in an outstanding year. It has a good proportion of old vines, including some Merlot planted in 1898.

Another Soussans growth of repute is Paveil-de-Luze. The first word is a derivation of *pavillon*, as there is an old seventeenth-century tower attached to the low-lying vineyard buildings. In the eighteenth century it belonged to a M. Bretonneau who married a daughter of the Chevalier de Rauzan, but in 1862 it was bought by a member of the Bordeaux firm of de Luze. Today its chief owner is Baron Francis de Luze. Production, in a vineyard which is 35 per cent Cabernet-Franc, 30 per cent Cabernet-Sauvignon, 30 per cent Merlot, and 5 per cent Petit-Verdot, is not large, around 50 – 60 *tonneaux*, but the wines are particularly well known in Denmark. A bottle of '24 was still sound and fruity if showing its age in 1968. A little white wine is made, bearing of course the *appellation* Bordeaux Blanc. Its composition is 50 per cent Sémillon and 50 per cent Sauvignon.

There are not many other well-known *bourgeois* properties in the area permitted to sell their wines as Margaux. In Labarde, Rosemont used to be fairly well known in Britain, but its production is now very small. Arsac, already mentioned above, is vinously a small commune, but adjoining it is the more important one of Macau, whose best known growth is Cantemerle.

Macau and Ludon

Those who point to the inadequacy today of the 1855 classification often mention the fact that Cantemerle is the very last of the fifth growths, whereas most people would certainly put it much higher. From 1579 until nearly the end of the last century the property was owned by the Villeneuve family, and a hundred years ago the proprietress was the Baroness d'Abbadie de Villeneuve de Durfort, which must have been quite a formidable name to announce when she went visiting her neighbours. I suspect that the low rating in 1855 was owing to the fact that at that period its sale was almost exclusively confined to Holland, and compared with other growths the wine was therefore hardly known in the Bordeaux market. The special popularity of the wine in the Low Countries continued until a generation ago, but nowadays its best export market is probably Britain, where it is highly esteemed. Certainly the quality has been rising ever since 1892 when Pierre Dubos's parents acquired the château for 770,000 frs. Curiously enough Cantemerle was bought by Calvet for 600,000 frs. – the only moment when the Calvet's were classed growth château proprietors – but a fortnight later it was bought by Dubos. Dubos junior ran the property for over sixty years and was famous for the detailed weather records that he maintained over the years. He was one of the most expert and charming of the last generation of Médoc proprietors. When I visited the château after the 1966 vintage Henri Binaud was able to show me that the weather conditions that year had closely resembled those of 1920 – no bad omen for the '66s, which have yet to prove themselves. The château, in parts very old, is approached by a long avenue. The *chai* buildings are exceptionally extensive and solid with a fine stone facade.

Henri Binaud, also head of Beyerman, the ancient Bordeaux merchant firm of Dutch origin, may be counted as among the most extrovertly enthusiastic of Bordeaux château proprietors. When at a private dinner in London a few years ago Latour '53 and Cantemerle '53 were both served blind, and the Cantemerle was judged the finer wine, the latter's director was not only gratified; he clearly felt that the judgment could only be correct. Cantemerle is generally well thought of by the other Médoc proprietors, and I have heard Baron Philippe de Rothschild say that his choice after Mouton would be Cantemerle.

Cantemerle has one advantage over some of its classed neighbours to the north. The *appellation* is Haut-Médoc and therefore entitled to the extra 3 hectolitres per hectare more than the vineyards in the Margaux 'consortium' of communes limited to 40 hectolitres. This of course also applies to the other growths in Macau and the adjoining Ludon. So while Binaud at classed-growth Cantemerle may make up to 43 hectolitres from each of his 17 hectares, on *cru bourgeois* La Tour-de-Mons, with which his family is associated, permitted *AC* production under the Margaux label is 40 hectolitres. It must be emphasized here that, from vineyard to vineyard and vintage to vintage, the maximum is by no means always reached (at Cantemerle the average is only 27 hl.), and even when it is the proprietor may not declare all his wine with the *appellation*. He may prefer to de-class a proportion to maintain a high quality for his wine. On the other hand in plentiful years, and 1967 was an example, some châteaux have been making quantities far in excess of the permitted maximum, and this cannot be for the good of their reputation or the quality of their wines. The maximum as increased in recent years is agreed by most growers and merchants to be generous enough. Yet it is not uncommon for part at least of the excess production to be allowed the top *appellation*.

In Macau we are near the end of the fine wine area of the Médoc, and on the road to Bordeaux only one classed growth is nearer the city: La Lagune. It is surprising, therefore, that Cantemerle in semi-isolation is so distinguished. The composition of the vineyard is 45 per cent Cabernet-Sauvignon, 15 per cent Cabernet-Franc, 30 per cent Merlot and 10 per cent Petit-Verdot, and the average production about 85 *tonneaux*. The wine is fairly full-bodied and rather 'bigger' than the Margaux wines. As it has been regularly listed since the last world war by the Wine Society in London, I have drunk a considerable amount of Cantemerle, which often contrives to make good wine in off-years, such as '58 and '60. The '53 was one of the most successful Médocs. I have also drunk older vintages of Cantemerle, back to the excellent '16 and '20 and the still fine '06. Château Cantemerle must not be confused with *Cru* Cantemerle across the Dordogne in the commune of St-Gervais. (There is also another Château Beychevelle nearby on the same river.) Not many other growths in Macau are well known, but an inexpensive wine sold under that commune label is Beau-Rivage. In view of the old association of Cantemerle with Holland it is interesting to note that in the first edition of Franck's work in 1824 he makes the comment about Macau wines that their roughness depreciates them in Holland, where they only like soft wines. This remark was omitted in later editions.

The last of the important Médoc wine communes now is Ludon, with its third growth La Lagune. The vineyard was originally planted about 1724, to the extent of 50 hectares. The production has varied very much. A century ago it was 70 – 80 *tonneaux*, but until recently it had dwindled, coming down to as little as 15 *tonneaux*. Indeed the whole vineyard was very run-down, but in 1957 it was purchased by a company which re-planted nearly all the vineyard in 1958 and 1959; ever since production has been increasing, so that it is now about 250 *tonneaux*. The *chai* has also been reconstructed on the most modern lines, with series of steel pipes running from the vats along above the rows of casks. If this all looks a little factorial to those accustomed to more traditional cellars, conditions are certainly changing in Bordeaux, and it is the results that as elsewhere will count at La Lagune – which now likes to be known as Grand La Lagune. Another break with tradition is a female *régisseur*, Mme Boirie. The vineyard is beautifully kept, as can be seen from the road. The proprietor now is M. Chayoux, who is also a champagne merchant. La Lagune used to be regarded as a particularly long-lived wine and indeed took time to come round. It used to be popular in Britain and made an excellent '26, which I have drunk a number of times. Since the re-planting the wines have usually seemed to me excessively sweet, as if it had been necessary to add sugar to mask the green-ness of the young vines. Indeed more than once I have mistaken the '61 for a Burgundy, and a rather suave, velvety one at that. It will be very interesting to see the La Lagune vintages of the 1970s when the vineyard is more mature.

The only other Ludon wine known to me is the *bourgeois* growth of Nexon-Lemoyne. Its production is small, about 10 *tonneaux*, and the wines that I have tasted have been rather hard.

The Lesser Communes of the Haut-Médoc

As Bordeaux is approached the soil becomes more like that of the Graves. At one time a good deal of *bourgeois* wine came from the communes of Blanquefort, Parempuyre, Le Taillan, and Le Pian-Médoc, but most suffered with the decline of these wines; and the city has been advancing into the vineyards. At Blanquefort is the local School of Agriculture, in Château Dillon, where some wine is made on an experimental basis. Before the last war at least it used to be sold in England. At Le Taillan is the very fine Château du Taillan, which belongs to the Cruse family. In addition to the red wine, there is white wine produced, which can only be called Bordeaux Blanc Supérieur, as it is a mile or so from the edge of Graves. So Cruse sell it as La Dame-Blanche. At Parempuyre is another substantial mansion, built during the palmy days of the Bordeaux wine trade in the last century and known as Château de Parempuyre. Durand-Dassier, a connection of the Cruses, had it built, and it belongs to the same family. Centuries earlier this was the territory of the Pichon family. At Blanquefort also is the not unknown Maurian, but broadly speaking this is not now the wine area it once was.

This leaves to be mentioned a number of communes in the Haut-Médoc, lying between the best-known districts and the Landes, and possessing no classed growths. The most important are Moulis and Listrac, and these alone have a wider reputation. These two communes produce about 6,000 – 10,000 hectolitres of *AC* wine annually. They were among the 11 communes stretching from Le Taillan to Cissac called by Franck in 1824 Le Derrière du Haut-Médoc.

Moulis, indeed, boasts in Chasse-Spleen one of the *grands crus exceptionnels*, with an output of about 120 *tonneaux*. As with other Moulis wines I have tended to find the vintages of this growth that have come my way to be rather hard and astringent. However at the *Ban de Vendange* dinner in the great pillared *chai* of Château Margaux in September 1967, the '61 Chasse-Spleen was served, and was an admirably fruity wine with more roundness than normal. In recent years there have been renovations at Chasse-Spleen, including a new, semi-underground cellar. It also boasts ambulant peacocks. The Moulis wines are entitled to their own *appellation* and a number of them incorporate the name Poujeaux in their frequently long titles. There are Pou-jeaux-Castaing, Gressier-Grand-Poujeaux, Poujeaux-Marly, Poujeaux-Theil and Dutruch-Grand-Poujeaux. Poujeaux is a gravelly sub-area of Moulis, and generally regarded as the finest. The best of these that I have had some experience of is the Dutruch, which can be rounder and less austere than many Moulis wines, which have an inner core of firmness, also associated with the Listracs. Among other Moulis growths of repute – and the estates are quite considerable – are Pomys, Mauvezin, Duplessis, La Closerie, Renouil-Franquet and Maucaillou.

About a dozen years ago La Closerie gave me an object lesson in how quite minor growths can on occasion produce outstanding wine. Some cases of the 1920, 1929 and 1934 vintages then became available in London and I tasted them all several times and acquired a few bottles of the '20. This was a splendidly round and complete wine, and at a time when the '20s of far greater repute had passed their best. The '29 was also good, and the '34 very fair for that hard, tannin-struck year. These were all château-bottled stock released by the proprietor. In youth the '49, bottled in England, was good, but latterly it turned somewhat acid. Maucaillou is owned by the firm and family of Dourthe, who from Moulis run a wine business which specializes in the exclusive sale of the wine of a number of Médoc and other châteaux. Maucaillou itself produces 120 *tonneaux* and is a very sound wine.

Moulis wines are for the long haul, unless one overlooks their firmness and drinks them young as fruity, youthful claret; and much the same applies to the Listracs, except that no very interesting bottles have come my way. The soil is gravel with some clay and sand. It was from this and surrounding areas that came the red Bordeaux *crus bourgeois* which were purchased in great quantities by pre-Nazi Germany. They were bought in the spring following the vintage and carried off at once to be matured in the Hanseatic cities. When Hitler seized power the trade dropped, and has never been resumed on anything like its old scale; nowadays the Bordeaux which the Germans overwhelmingly buy is white.

The Listrac wines which are perfectly respectable if rather hard come from such growths as Fourcas-Dupré, Fourcas-Hostein, Clarke and Pierre Bibian. There is also a co-operative, founded in 1935, which sells its wines under the title of Château Grand Listrac. Moulis and Listrac *AC* output is limited to 40 hectolitres per hectare as two of the six named Haut-Médoc communes.

To the south of Moulis is the small commune of Avensan, which contains another of the *crus exceptionnels*, Villegeorge, whose vineyard, but not the château, belongs to M. Pecresse. Its production is under 20 *tonneaux*. I have only tasted it when very young and it has seemed to me a sound but not exciting wine. Much larger is the only other widely-known Avensan growth, Citran-Clauzel which makes over 60 *tonneaux* and is owned by Jean Miailhe. A century ago its production was between 250 and 325 *tonneaux*, an indication of the scale of *cru bourgeois* production in that period. There are a scattering of other growers in Avensan.

Further north and nearer to the estuary, on the *D.2* Médoc road is Arcins on the edge of the 'thirsty gap' in the vineyards of quality. Between St-Julien and Soussans-Margaux near the river, and St-Laurent and Listrac further inland is a considerable area of scrubby, plantation-filled country, looking about as infertile as a rather neglected piece of English common land. It demonstrates the essential role that the soil and situation play in viticulture. A stranger visiting the Haut-Médoc for the first time might reasonably expect an almost uninterrupted stretch of vines from Blanquefort to St-Estèphe and beyond; and if aware of the high value of good vineyard land in the Médoc he might think it extraordinary that the frequent, extensive gaps in the vineyards have not been put under vines. In fact there used to be reasonably well-known wine made in Lamarque, now best remembered for its ferry to Blaye, and Cocks et Féret still lists some growths now. Properties such as Lamarque, Cap de Haut-Lamarque and Malescasse made wine in considerable demand in Germany up to 1914. According to Christian Cruse, the area of the *crus bourgeois* here and elsewhere in the Médoc occupies little more than 10 per cent of what it did early in this century. Over 400 *crus bourgeois* recognized in the Médoc less than forty years ago are now reduced to about 100. The others have gone out of production or sell their grapes to the co-operatives. Much the same decline applies to Cussac, although that still retains two fairly familiar châteaux, Beaumont and Lanessan, mentioned below. Yet in relation to the market demand as it has existed for many years the land here is as marginal as in the *palus* once so productive, adjoining the Gironde. Even if wine were grown on a large scale in this thirsty gap it would not secure a higher *appellation* than Bordeaux Supérieur, and the price would be correspondingly low as well.

Arcins (the 's' is pronounced as is common with a final 's' in these parts) is a very small area, and the best known of its few *bourgeois* growths is probably La Tour-du-Roc, but there is also a Ch. d'Arcins and a co-operative which uses the name Chevalier d'Ars. The village has also the distinction of having a small estate in English hands. For Nicholas Barrow has been cultivating Courant since 1964, using traditional methods. He produces about 20 *tonneaux* and he deserves well.

Moving up the Médoc, Lamarque, as already indicated, need not detain us, but Cussac on the main road is more of a wine village, with one or two houses notable for the mid-nineteenth-century exuberance of their architecture. Lanessan is a large estate with a reputation which is rising. It provides another example of the fact that not only the greatest names make fine wines. For several years I have had a few bottles of Lanessan '29, which had been lying in a central London cellar since before the

Second World War. With one or two exceptions, owing probably to the cork rather than the wine, they have been deliciously fruity, strong-flavoured and complete. One cannot say the same about a number of the leading '29s.

Lanessan lies in a large 'park', and is approached by a long avenue from the *D.2* road. The substantial *chai* buildings indicate that it was once a very large estate. Nowadays the vineyard runs to 30 hectares, two-thirds Cabernet-Sauvignon and one-third Merlot and produces 125 *tonneaux*. It has a certain fame in the district for having a small carriage museum installed in one of the old *chais*. There is a mail coach and nine carriages, including an odd-looking four-wheeled '*Americaine*' with canvas hood and an open '*Break de Chasse*'. There is a fine display of horse equipment and a stable in whose opulent marble feeding troughs 'Darling', 'Tommy' and 'Whisky', according to their inscribed names, once regaled themselves.

One Cussac estate mentioned above that used to be famous in the popular *bourgeois* claret trade was Beaumont, but its production is now much reduced. Better known is Lamothe-de-Bergeron.

From there northwards we are again in the belt of famous châteaux but from the north-west of Pauillac there is a small string of lesser Haut-Médoc communes running round to the estuary and mostly adjoining the Bas-Médoc. These are St-Sauveur, Cissac, Vertheuil and St-Seurin-de-Cadourne. They are the last communes entitled to the *appellation* Haut-Médoc before the descent to the Bas-Médoc. In the first of these is the very extensive Liversan, producing well over a hundred *tonneaux*, and at one time well known in Britain. Nowadays Peyrabon, which makes a well-balanced wine, has a wider reputation. St-Sauveur also has a co-operative, which calls its wines Ch. St-Sauveur. Cissac has a château of that name as well as a cooperative, and there is a Lamothe here too, as well as La Tour-du-Mirail. The Vertheuil wines are not much known under their own names, but I have come across Le Bourdieu. There are co-operatives both here (the brand name is La Chatelerie) and at the neighbouring St-Seurin, which is a little more prominent in wine annals. There are Coufran, owned by Jean Miailhe, who also owns Citran in Avensan, Verdignan, Bel-Orme, Sénilhac and Sociando. Most of these are considerable producers on large rolling vineyards, many of them adjoining St-Estèphe.

The wines from these communes have something of the quality of St-Estèphe but with less distinction. They can make excellent, inexpensive bottles. Coufran stands out in my mind as the last château of the Haut-Médoc. Physically the epithet 'Haut' in this flat country is strictly relative, but in fact on passing Coufran, still on the *D.2* which has given us so much vicarious wine pleasure since we joined it before Blanquefort, one does descend a hill to the Bas-Médoc. The contrast is emphasized by a little international rivalry. For in the vineyard of Coufran there is a small tower from which waves the *tricolor*, and this looks down physically as well, no doubt, philosophically, on the first estate in the Bas-Médoc, which happens to be Loudenne, in English hands ever since it was bought by the Gilbeys in 1875. This too has some towers in its vineyard, constructed in what one might call Victorian Flamboyant. On one of these facing Coufran, as well as on the château terrace overlooking the Gironde, flies the Union Jack.

The Bas-Médoc

Nowadays the word 'Bas' is more or less discarded, for to foreign ears and eyes it suggests inferiority. For the same reason the *départements* of Loire Inférieure and Charente Inférieure were constrained to change their names to Atlantique and Maritime respectively. The Bas-Médoc's geographical name is now Médoc Maritime but is seldom used. It so happens that a Bas-Médoc wine is likely to be inferior to an Haut-Médoc one, though this is not the case in the Armagnac country, where the Bas-Armagnac is the best. However there is not necessarily much to choose between the lesser *Hauts* and the better *Bas*. With all respect to Coufran, whose wine I have drunk with pleasure, a good Loudenne is likely to be at least as good. Nevertheless the term *Haut* is worth something in terms of cash, even if the plain Médoc *appellation* allows two more hectolitres to the hectare.

A hundred years ago they were not so class-conscious on the lower levels of *appellation*, and when, as mentioned earlier, Alfred Gilbey and his colleagues bought Loudenne in 1875 they were probably looking for a source of good, sound, inexpensive wines as well as a base for their Bordeaux operations. So I do not suppose that they cared much that their estate lay in the Bas-Médoc commune of St-Yzans just across the way from Coufran in St-Seurin in the Haut-Médoc.

Indeed it is clear from the splendid series of diaries of the visits of the proprietors, their associates and their friends still preserved at Loudenne, that the Gilbeys were delighted with their acquisition.

The Gilbeys could scarcely have bought at a more unfortunate time, for not only did a general depression develop – a factor now forgotten when the classic vintages of the period are recalled – but within four years came the phylloxera scourge, dealt with earlier. In the diary for 1878 there is reference to the large vintages of '74 and '75, with the statement that production was far ahead of consumption and that many of the Haut-Médoc proprietors had three vintages in hand, owing to 'the general depression of commerce through Europe'. In the following year is the first reference to the phylloxera in the Médoc, although it was already well established in the Charente and the Midi.

Nevertheless Gilbeys consolidated their position at Loudenne and built the extensive brick and stone *chais* still in use today, and a good example of what has now been upgraded to 'industrial architecture'. Down by the waterside they constructed a small 'port', once used for shipping their wines, but long since disused. In recent years the charming château has been restored and re-decorated, and externally is pink-washed. It has welcomed many visitors from Britain, including myself, and at one meal I drank a Loudenne '24, which although showing its age after more than 40 years was still fruity and surprisingly good for a lesser growth. At the same meal, David Peppercorn, then my host and a most serious-minded *amateur* of claret as well as being a professional wine merchant, opened a bottle of Château Margaux of that 'over-productive' year of 1875 when the Gilbeys became owners of Loudenne. The wine was almost *rosé* in colour and very light, but not entirely gone.

Loudenne now makes white as well as red wine in considerable quantities and the quality is good. The white of course is only entitled to the *appellation* Bordeaux. The red part of the vineyard is 49 per cent Cabernet-Sauvignon, Merlot 39 per cent, Cabernet-Franc 9 per cent, Malbec 1·5 per cent, and Petit-Verdot 1·5 per cent.

I do not propose to give a château-by-château account of the Bas-Médoc for two reasons that appear relevant. First, with a few exceptions the wines are not widely known in the Anglo-Saxon world, and secondly, my experience is limited. The low-lying level country, intersected by drainage channels and with English-looking church spires standing up against the sky-line, has something of the appeal of Lincolnshire. Although well cultivated, and in recent years fruit farmers have been developing the region, this part of the Médoc has a rather lost, back-of-beyond air. History seems to have passed it by, and Bordeaux, some 40 – 50 miles down the straight *D.1* which by-passes most of the Médoc vineyards, seems in a different country.

The chief town of the Bas-Médoc is Lesparre which, with its suburb of St-Trélody, appears quite large and animated after the silence of the surrounding countryside. It has a pleasant eighteenth-century town hall. Lesparre was of course in English hands in the Middle Ages and the fine old churches of the area, mostly much older than those of the more recently developed Haut-Médoc, show that it had a prosperous past. The Romanesque apse of the church at Bégadan is particularly fine.

The region's wine growing has never quite recovered from the effects of the phylloxera and the following slump in the lesser wines of the Médoc. Abandoned and ruined buildings here and there testify to this. The proportion of Cabernet-Sauvignon grapes tends to be smaller, and that of the Merlot and Malbec larger. The permitted output per hectare is 45 hectolitres compared with 43 in the Haut-Médoc. Most of the wine properties lie towards the base of the area, thinning out near the sea, but there are even a few vineyards in the commune of Soulac, which abuts on to the Atlantic. Many of the growers make white as well as red wine in properties which often produce altogether no more than 10 *tonneaux*. In the good vintage of 1966 the output of red Bordeaux entitled to the *appellation* Médoc was 52,538 hectolitres, compared with 41,073 for the Haut-Médoc. The first figure omits the white wines, as they are entitled only to a Bordeaux *appellation*, and the second does not include those wines from the six communes allowed a higher *appellation*. In the same year St-Estèphe produced 37,699 hectolitres and Pauillac 27,499 hectolitres so the relatively limited production of the large Bas-Médoc can be seen; it is less than 25 per cent of total Médoc output.

The chief wine communes are Bégadan, St-Germain d'Esteuil and St-Christoly-de-Médoc. Bégadan contains Laujac, a large property bought in 1852 by M. Herman Cruse and still in the family. It now makes 100 *tonneaux*, but used to produce much more: 1,000 in 1901. There are also Cru Patache d'Aux and La Tour-de-By. In St-Germain the Livran estate was familiar in England as it was owned by an English firm, Denman; du Castéra is also known. The main communes all have co-operatives. For example, that at Bégadan sells under the name of Ch. Bégadanais.

To complete this record of the Médoc it is worth mentioning the wines of those Girondin isles which are near the shore of the Médoc. They are not now entitled to the *appellation* Médoc as they used to be, but are Bordeaux or Bordeaux Supérieur. Those on the other side are Bourgs or Blayes. At one time a good deal of wine was grown on these islands, but now the most important is the Ile Patiras, and one growth that is seen on British wine lists is Valrose, a pleasant light wine. Both red and white wines are made.

To end this tour of the Médoc in mid-stream seems incongruous, although it will be the first view of those who cross on the ferry from Blaye to Lamarque. Little shows among or above the trees except the occasional church spires, the riverside bastion of the Fort de Médoc and the inland white water tower of St-Julien, less offensive to the eye than its black bottle. Few travelling the length of the Gironde estuary from the Pointe de Grave to the Bec d'Ambès and the Garonne would guess that behind the fringe of mud, projecting fishermen's huts and green trees lay perhaps the greatest red wine vineyard district in the world; certainly the most varied. Such glimpses as one has – the terrace of Loudenne, the half-deserted waterfront of Pauillac, the modest-looking château of Latour, the wider splendour of Beychevelle – hardly reveal much of the energetic, competitive yet friendly world of wine beyond. A world of such fine distinctions of commune, soil and individual growth, that one is hard put to it indeed to describe them. The variations are much greater than in the other districts that make up the Bordeaux *vignoble*. This variety is the chief attraction of the Médoc for dedicated claret drinkers, and even in cases where my comments have been less than enthusiastic, I am always more than willing to review the situation by way of practical application.

11. The Graves

The Graves district was the wine cradle of Bordeaux. In the Middle Ages wine was grown in the suburbs and gradually spread nearly all round the city. It is not a coincidence that Haut-Brion was the first known of the *premiers crus* and perhaps the first Bordeaux château wine to be mentioned in English literature. On 10 April 1663 Samuel Pepys recorded that he 'drank a sort of French wine called Ho Bryen that hath a good and most particular taste that I never met with'. The vineyard of Haut-Brion possibly existed from the beginning of the sixteenth century when it was owned by Jean de Ségur. Once well outside the city in Pessac, it has now been more or less engulfed, as has La Mission-Haut-Brion across the road in Talence.

Thomas Jefferson, American Minister in France from 1785–1789, whose comments on the Bordeaux red wines are given in the chapter on the classification of the Médoc, said of the white wines, 'those made in the canton of Grave are most esteemed at Bordeaux. The best groups are 1. Pontac, which formerly belonged to M. de Pontac, but now to M. de Lamerl. He makes 40 *tonneaux* which sells at 400 l. new. 2. St. Brise belonging to M. de Pontac, 30 *tonneaux* at 350 l. 3. De Carbonius, belonging to the Benedictine monks who make 50 *tonneaux*, and never selling till 3 or 4 years old, get 800 l. the *tonneaux*.'

Throughout the last three centuries many Graves vineyards have fallen to the house and factory builders, some of them in recent years. Much of Merignac has been swallowed up by the airport of Bordeaux and the military airfield although at least one good growth remains: Pique Caillou. In theory, however, the Graves begins where the Médoc ends at the *Jalle de Blanquefort*.

To most people Graves indicates a fairly dry white wine, and indeed there is much more white than red. Average production in recent years has been 20,000 hectolitres of red wine and 60,000 hectolitres of white. Yet the region was originally basically a red wine area, and today in those communes nearest to Bordeaux the red wines predominate. Certainly they are more important than the whites, although there is a small band of fine white wine vineyards; and as will be seen a number of the growths contain both red and white.

As the name indicates the Graves soil is gravelly and sandy. It produces quite a distinct type of red wine from the Médoc, although some declare that the wines of the communes nearest to the Graves, such as those from Ludon and Macau, resemble the Graves. The difference is not at all easy to detect, although the Graves red wines have a certain *goût de terroir*, a slightly earthy taste, often more easy to recognize when one knows that the wine is a Graves than beforehand. They are often rather drier, more austere than the Médocs although in style the Graves are nearer to the Médocs than to the St-Emilions and Pomerols, but I know at least one Médoc proprietor who declares his lack of liking for Graves; for many of the Médocains, of course, the St-Emilions and Pomerols are beyond the serious wine pale as well as across the two rivers. I am inclined to believe that nowadays at least many of the red Graves do not last so well as the Médocs.

For the red wines the best soil is a mixture of pure gravel which on its own produces rather light wines, with a somewhat heavier mixture of heavy gravel and clay. Upstream the gravel becomes heavier and the soil contains more clay. There the white wines are sweeter. Indeed in the three communes of Cérons, Podensac and Illats those white wines made in the Sauternes way, the grapes picked as they become ripe and achieve the *pourriture noble*, are entitled to the *appellation* Cérons; those made in the usual way, with one picking through the vineyard, have a Graves *AC*. The Graves area goes even beyond Sauternes and ends in the Bazadais at St-Pierre-de-Mons and St-Pardon. Consequently there are really two styles of white Graves: the dry and the fairly sweet. Only about 30 communes produce wine on any scale, including the three around Cérons just referred to. As mentioned earlier the two chief grapes are the Sémillon and the Sauvignon. In the less distinguished wine communes the former predominates, and up to 5 per cent of Muscadelle may be found. The permitted quantity per hectare is 40 hectolitres compared with 43 hectolitres in most of the Haut-Médoc and 40 in the named Haut-Médoc communes. The minimum strength for red Graves, however, is the same: 10 degrees. For white Graves it is 11 degrees, and 12 degrees for Graves Supérieures.

I should say here and now that for white Graves my enthusiasm is limited. I can enjoy the few at the top, and on occasion – not too frequent an occasion – I can pleasantly employ the modest near-anonymous Graves Supérieures well cooled, to wash down an equally modest meal in summer. For one thing nearly all white Graves seems to smell of sulphur, used to keep the wine stable and pale; and that applies to many of the sweeter white Bordeaux too. Though perhaps more the fault of the wine-makers than of the wines, this takes much of the fresh, flowery even honeyish aroma out of them and deadens the flavour too. Often too they are rather sweet and that does not provide the suitable prelude to a dry red wine that a white Burgundy affords. Much dry white Graves strikes me as rather dull, and although I am assured that this is at least owing to the way they are made nowadays, I have my doubts. Yet they are often very moderately priced; except for the top flight, some of which in my view are often over-priced. So if some of my succeeding comments on various white Graves appear a little hard or tepid, I hope some allowance will be made for my lack of enthusiasm and my sulphur-conscious nose. Others enjoy them with abandon.

Classed Growths of the Graves

Red Wines (classified in 1953)

Château Bouscaut	Cadaujac
Château Haut-Bailly	Léognan
Château Carbonnieux	Léognan
Domaine de Chevalier	Léognan
Château Fieuzal	Léognan
Château Olivier	Léognan
Château Malartic-Lagravière	Léognan
Château La Tour-Martillac	Martillac
Château Smith-Haut-Lafitte	Martillac
Château Haut-Brion	Pessac
Château La Mission-Haut-Brion	Pessac (Talence)
Château Pape-Clément	Pessac
Château Latour-Haut-Brion	Talence

White Wines (classified in 1959)

Château Bouscaut	Cadaujac
Château Carbonnieux	Léognan
Domaine de Chevalier	Léognan
Château Olivier	Léognan
Château Malartic-Lagravière	Léognan
Château La Tour-Martillac	Martillac
Château Haut-Brion	Pessac
Château Laville-Haut-Brion	Pessac
Château Couhins	Villenave d'Ornon

Pessac

The senior commune of the Graves is Pessac. Not only is Ch. Pape-Clément probably the oldest single vineyard of Bordeaux (although it did not at first bear that name, or so far as I know any prior title in the Middle Ages), but Pessac includes the only red Graves admitted to the 1855 classification: Haut-Brion. It also heads the official classification of 13 red Graves made in 1953.

Haut-Brion has had many owners, perhaps 25 since the beginning of the sixteenth century, when it was in the hands of Jean de Ségur. In 1525 it passed to Philippe de Chabot who was a mayor of Bordeaux as well as being an admiral. A few years later it was transferred to the daughter of a mayor of Libourne, de Bellon, and she married a Pontac, a family which intermittently owned or were connected with the château for the ensuing 200 years.

According to another story, Jean de Pontac, a property owner, was the real creator of Haut-Brion as a vineyard, by buying it in 1533 from Jean Duhelde, a Bordeaux merchant of Basque origin, for 2,650 livres. The currency used in Bordeaux was the *livre tournois*, until supplanted at the Revolution by the roughly equivalent franc. According to Malvezin's *Histoire du Commerce de Bordeaux* (1892), the value of the livre fell by nineteen-twentieths between the reigns of Louis XV (1715 – 1774) and Louis XVI (1774 – 1793). Either way the Pontacs became large landowners, including proprietors of vineyards, throughout the Bordeaux region, among them several in the Graves communes and in St-Estèphe. Even today Ch. Myrat in Barsac is owned by the Comte de Pontac. Pontac was indeed the familiar name for Graves in seventeenth-century England. In the eighteenth century Haut-Brion was certainly sometimes known in England as Pontac, although Pontac was also a white wine.

In 1748 Haut-Brion passed into the hands of Catherine de Fumel, née Pontac, and the Fumel family owned the property until the Revolution. The first Fumel, Comte Louis, managed to acquire a fine assortment of first-growth titles, for not only was he Seigneur of Haut-Brion, but also of Margaux and Baron de Pauillac. He it was who in 1749 divided the estate into two parts: the château and one portion of the vineyard, and another smaller part known as the *Chai-Neuf*. In 1770 the latter part passed to the Marquis de Latresne and was detached from the rest of the property until 1840.

The Revolution produced a complicated situation for the rest of the château, as part was confiscated by the state owing to the emigration of Joseph Fumel, but his brother J. P. Fumel and his sister, Mme Branne, owned the other two-thirds and did not leave France. The brother acquired the confiscated portion for 237,666 frs. and 50 centimes (no less!) and bought out his sister. In 1800 he sold the whole to Talleyrand, who thus added the role of vineyard proprietor to that of his many other profitable callings from bishop onwards. He paid 255,000 frs., but in 1804 it was bought from Talleyrand, then Foreign Minister, by a banker, M. Michel, for 300,000 frs. He in his turn sold it twenty years later to M. Beyerman, the well-known Bordeaux merchant, and M. Comynet, a stockbroker of Paris, for 525,000 frs. The former ran the estate and paid his partner a rent of 25,000 frs. This arrangement appears not to have worked very satisfactorily, for there was a lawsuit and the property was once more put up for sale. The notice of the sale on 12 March 1836 can be seen in the château. It was valued then at 250,000 frs., but in fact at the auction it fell to M. Eugène Larrieu for 296,000 frs. In the sale notice the area of that part is given as 91 hectares, of which 40 – 50 were under vines, a similar total to that existing today in the whole, for it is now about 42 hectares.

In 1840 M. Larrieu succeeded in reuniting the portion of the vineyard which had been split off in 1770 and paid 60,000 frs. for it; and the property has remained one vineyard ever since.

The estate remained in the Larrieu family until a few years after the First World War. Prior to that war Cocks et Féret recorded Haut-Brion as producing 100 *tonneaux* of first wine and 20 of second. This second wine used to be sold under the label of Château Bahans-Haut-Brion with a vintage, and this name is still used today, as a non-vintage wine. Output is from 20 – 30 *tonneaux* and the wine is mostly sold in French restaurants, although it may be found in the U.S.A. and Britain.

In the earlier part of the eighteenth century Haut-Brion was still probably the leading red wine of Bordeaux, but thereafter it certainly declined, perhaps as a result of the division of the property. Although clearly it had a high reputation just before the Revolution, as exemplified by Thomas Jefferson's high praise of it, quoted in the chapter on the classification of the Médoc, little more than thirty years later Franck in the first edition (1824) of his book was writing about it: 'for several years it has lost its reputation because too much manure is used. It cannot be put in bottle until six or seven years after the harvest, although other first growths are drinkable at the end of five years'. Haut-Brion's lack of *réclame* may be shown by the fact that up till the middle of the nineteenth century its name appeared far less in the Christie's auction catalogues than the other *premiers crus*. Then it improved, after the re-unification in 1840, and the wine had an excellent reputation in the latter part of the nineteenth century. In the great vintage of 1899 Haut-Brion's opening price of 2,600 frs. a *tonneau* was 400 frs. higher than Margaux, 600 frs. above Lafite and Latour, and 800 frs. above Mouton. It is generally agreed that the quality of Haut-Brion fell off later. From 1907 to 1916 the sale of the first wine was the monopoly of the Bordeaux firm of Richard et Muller, a by no means uncommon practice at that time when prices were steady for good quality wines. Under the next proprietor the house of Rosenheim bought all the 1929 crop.

In 1923 the château was bought by M. André Gibert, who made it into a company. This was not a happy period for the château, and in 1935 it was bought by Mr Clarence Dillon, the American banker, with Mr Seymour Weller as the president of the company. It is said that not only was Haut-Brion then in the market but also Cheval-Blanc and Ausone. Mr Dillon could have acquired Cheval-Blanc for half a million francs, but on the day he visited St-Emilion the country was swathed in fog. So he decided not to buy Cheval-Blanc, but instead acquired Haut-Brion for 2 million francs. It is an open question which would have turned out the better buy, but in those days Cheval-Blanc's international reputation was less than now. In 1958 the property became the Domaine Clarence Dillon, S.A.

Production has remained fairly constant over the last century at around 100 *tonneaux* of red wine although in 1966 the crop made 150 *tonneaux*. The vineyard is composed of 55 per cent Cabernet-Sauvignon, 22 per cent Cabernet-Franc and 23 per cent Merlot, a higher proportion of Cabernet and a lower one of Merlot than a few years earlier.

GRAVES

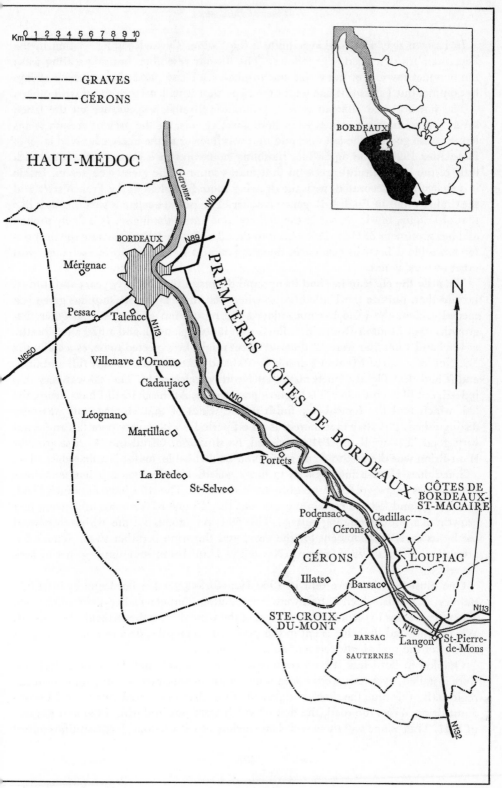

Km 0 1 2 3 4 5 6 7 8 9 10

—··—··—··— GRAVES
—·—·—·— CÉRONS

HAUT-MÉDOC

Garonne

N10

BORDEAUX

N89

Mérignac◇

Pessac◇

Talence◇

N113

PREMIÈRES CÔTES DE BORDEAUX

N650

Villenave d'Ornon◇

Cadaujac◇

N10

Léognan◇

Martillac◇

Portets◇

La Brède◇

St-Selve◇

Podensac◇

Cérons◇

Cadillac◇

CÔTES DE
BORDEAUX-
ST-MACAIRE

CÉRONS

LOUPIAC

Illats◇

Barsac◇

STE-CROIX-
DU-MONT

N113

N113

Langon

St-Pierre-
de-Mons

BARSAC

SAUTERNES

N132

N

In its own way Haut-Brion is quite a 'big' wine. Cyrus Redding writing in the Beyerman era described it as follows: 'The flavour resembles burning sealing wax: the bouquet savours of the violet and raspberry.' These parallels are nearly always lost on me, but I pass this one on, in the hope that it will strike a chord with others.

The fine turreted château is widely familiar from its appearance on the label, surely one of the most attractive in Bordeaux; or was, for the present version seems to me not so good as the last one, and that was inferior to the finely engraved label of the earlier 1920s. The agreeable, rambling house lies in a grassy *parc anglais* with little of the horticultural precision that marks some of the greater châteaux. Inside it is charmingly decorated, with the drawing room furnished in the French style and the dining room in English Regency lacquer. The private cellar is small, rather like that of Latour, but leads out of the *chai* and not under the house. It is finely arched and has specimens of Haut-Brion back to the 1890s but, perhaps because the proprietor has seldom been in residence, there appears to have been little exchange with other owners' wines.

Vinously the château has had its ups and downs in the last forty years and it must be said that, outside the United States where its American ownership has given it a special cachet, the wine has not enjoyed the reputation of some of the other first growths or of Mouton-Rothschild. Earlier on it was splendid, and I had a few bottles of 1899 and 1900 that were all that old claret might be expected to be, especially the '99. Not long ago at Mouton I drank the '08 and that was surprisingly full and firm, and it had that slightly burnt taste that Redding referred to. The '20 was very fine indeed, but like most other '20s has now passed over. At the château I have drunk the '26, which had the typical dry finish of the wines of that vintage, but was very distinguished. But after that there was an off period – with a very poor '28 and a not very good '29 – until the 1945 retrieved the situation. Of all the '45 first growths Haut-Brion was the first to come round and be drinkable, and it is a first-class wine.

Since then Haut-Brion appears to have varied. In off-vintages it has sometimes struck me as over-sweetened, notably the '50 and '60. The '49 I have not much liked, but the '52 and '53 are certainly good, and the '55 one of the more interesting first growths of a not outstanding vintage. The '59 is very good, but the '61 has impressed me by its early development for the year, and the wine is rather sweet. The '62 is attractive, but also very forward. Nowadays Haut-Brion sometimes seems to lack 'weight'.

One must mention here that in 1960 Haut-Brion startled Bordeaux by installing stainless steel vats, which Latour were later to adopt, but of a rather different pattern. The purpose was to secure better control of the wine during the fermentation period. When fermented the wine is left in the vats for two months, during which time part at least of the malo-lactic fermentation takes place.

Opinion in Bordeaux is both conservative and critical, and when these steel vats were installed, eyebrows were raised (an exercise much practised and enjoyed in the region). By this time the shock had passed of the enamel-covered vats of La Mission-Haut-Brion across the road, the first of which were put in during 1926 and the rest in 1951. Time alone will show with Haut-Brion, as with Latour, but scientific control of the fermentation should be easier under such circumstances, and who would deny that it is desirable?

Another small change at Haut-Brion was the design of a new bottle, with a longer neck and a more rounded body, very much in the style of earlier claret bottles. This was first used for the 1958 vintage.

Haut-Brion is also known for producing one of the leading white Graves, Haut-Brion Blanc, although oddly enough in the 1953 Graves classification it was not included initially. Production is small – from 8 to 15 *tonneaux* – and the wine is much sought after, particularly in the United States. I first came upon it in the 1949 vintage, when part at least was shipped in cask and bottled in England. That and succeeding vintages were fine, honey-nosed wines with a good deal of flavour and distinction. In recent years, however, all château-bottled, it has seemed to me to be over-sulphured, although when I have sampled the young wines in cask, including the '64 and the '66, this has not been apparent. Now very expensive for a dry white Graves, this would not be my first choice.

The second wine of the district and in recent years something of a rival to Haut-Brion is La Mission-Haut-Brion, which lies just across the main road to Arcachon. Although the reference books place it in Pessac, in fact La Mission is in Talence, for 13 of its 16½ hectares are in that commune and only 3½ in Pessac. The agreeable château, with at one end the seventeenth-century chapel that contributes to the estate's name, is also in Talence, but in view of its accepted status, it is convenient to include the wine here among the Pessacs.

The Mission was one conducted by the order of St-Vincent-de-Paul, and the interior of the charming little chapel is full of objects of interest. So indeed is the château, including a collection of holy water stoups and a splendid assembly of superb Delft dishes brought by the Dutch merchants who came to collect Bordeaux wine. The *cuvier* and the cellars are impeccably kept.

La Mission-Haut-Brion was owned in the last century by M. Chiapella and then by M. Coustau who sold it in his old age in 1918 to Frédéric Woltner, father of the present owners Henri and Fernand Woltner. The active partner here is Henri Woltner, certainly to be classed as one of the most infectiously 'committed' Bordeaux château owners. In my time I have had my share of meals at which on sitting down an array of glasses has faced one like sentinels, but I can remember no comparable number at a private lunch as on a notable occasion at La Mission; in front of the four places at table, there were ten apiece for M. and Mme Woltner, his manager and myself. First we had four white Graves, two of them different vintages of his own Laville-Haut-Brion but not including the neighbour's across the road – then five red wines, and a Barsac to end up with. That did not include, of course, the bottle of Pol Roger (the Woltners used to have the French agency) beforehand or the glass of cognac afterwards. Fortunately we were not expected to finish all the bottles, although it was not easy to refuse replenishments of such wines as La Mission '47 and Cheval-Blanc '47, and La Mission '29 and '20 (these last two at my request, and very fine too).

However one can certainly drink safely in Bordeaux much more than in London, and any soporific tendency was checked by Henri Woltner's enthusiastic discourse. For he is certainly a man with a mission; not a religious one, but for his *'fermentation froide'* system of vinification.

During the period of fermentation the main aim of a château's *maître de chai* or *régisseur* is to secure a continuous vinification without extremes of temperature. If this falls too much the fermentation may stop and be difficult to re-start, leaving danger-ous unfermented sugar in the must. If the temperature rises too high – the danger point is variable but 35 degrees C. (95 degrees F.) is very near it – the wine may turn to vinegar.

In M. Woltner's vitrified steel *cuves* at La Mission the temperature may be more easily controlled than in wooden vats, and this obviates the exhausting manual work and watching that may be necessary if the temperature is running too high. Thus at La Mission the temperature never goes above 30 degrees C. (85 F.), and is more likely to run at 27 C. or 28 C. (80·6 – 82·4 F.). Had it not been for the Second World War, all the vats would have been replaced long before 1951 when the change-over was completed. The stainless steel vats at Haut-Brion and Latour are designed for the same purpose, although one may suspect that Henri Woltner believes his own to be more satisfactory, as well as being a good deal less expensive. It can be seen that the term *'froide'* is a relative one, and does not imply any degree of refrigeration. After the vinification in the vats is finished, the wine is transferred to oak casks, and norm-ally bottled about two and a half years after the vintage. This operation takes place not at the château, but in a specially authorized annexe of the firm's cellars in Bordeaux. This authorization enables the label to bear the usual *'mise du château'* inscription.

M. Woltner's system is not to the taste of some other proprietors, and of course it involves considerable capital outlay, but there can be no doubt that La Mission produces splendid, fruity wine. At a blind tasting of comparable vintages of Haut-Brion and La Mission a few years ago, the weight of opinion was on the side of La Mission. The latter is sometimes a better balanced wine, but we have yet to see the full results of Haut-Brion's new vats. Among exceptionally good vintages of La Mission that I have enjoyed are '48 and '53. By careful selection M. Woltner often makes sound wine in indifferent years.

The composition of the vineyard is 65 per cent Cabernet-Sauvignon, 10 per cent Cabernet-Franc and 25 per cent Merlot. Output is 80 – 90 *tonneaux*.

Henri Woltner also owns two other vineyards: La Tour-Haut-Brion, a red wine growth of Talence, and Laville-Haut-Brion, which is devoted entirely to white wines. The composition of the former is identical to that of La Mission; the latter is 60 per cent Sémillon and 40 per cent Sauvignon. La Tour is a small vineyard with an area of only 4 hectares, and an output of 10 – 12 *tonneaux*. Although it has not the distinc-tion of La Mission, the wine is fruity and well balanced, and made in the same *chai* as La Mission. The white wine growth is also in Talence and output is about 20 *tonneaux*. Laville-Haut-Brion is certainly in the first flight of dry white Bordeaux. Indeed along with Domaine de Chevalier I would put it top on current showing. La Mission secures a higher price for its wine than any other red Bordeaux under the first-growth level, selling for about 75 per cent of the price of the more moderate of the latter. I include in the first-growth category Mouton-Rothschild, Cheval-Blanc and Pétrus.

The next most important Graves of Pessac is Pape-Clément, whose archiepiscopal origin has already been mentioned. It belonged to the Church until the Revolution, when it was sold to a wine merchant in 1791. In the 1824 edition of Franck the proprietor is given as Jarrige and the output as 30 – 40 *tonneaux*. This château has a long tradition of excellent wine-making, and not least in the 1920s; the '20, '24 and '29 were splendid wines. Then the property fell into some eclipse, and indeed it was rumoured that the estate had been sold to builders. Certainly production dwindled and was at a very low ebb after the last war. The vineyard was re-planted, but not until 1953 did the wine recover its old form. Both in that year and in 1955 the wine was excellent, although the latter did not keep well. There was a very fine wine in 1961, when only about 20 *tonneaux* were produced instead of a normal 50. Compared with the growths discussed above the wine is made very traditionally at Pape-Clément. It tends to be a lighter, more delicate wine than its neighbours, but keeps reasonably well and is once again a wine of good repute.

One Pessac vineyard that has been swallowed up by the bulldozers is Laburthe-Brivazac, which sixty years ago ranked high among the wines of the commune. M. Brivazac was a councillor in the eighteenth-century Parlement. A few years ago it was sold, but Ronald Barton bought for his firm a stock of several thousand bottles of the fine 1929. I acquired a few bottles, and although the wine is a little dry at the end, it is still very fine and enjoyable. There is something a little melancholy in drinking wine from a vineyard no longer in existence.

With the remaining small collection of Pessac growths I can claim no acquaintance. The best known is Camponac, which was bought by Frédéric Eschenauer in 1875, but is now used as a brand name of the firm. Several of the other growths manage to weave the magic words Haut-Brion into their name, but they have no wide reputation. It may be noted that the *appellation* throughout the red Graves villages is Graves and does not include a village name as in the more important parts of the Haut-Médoc.

Léognan

Talence need not delay us apart from the growths already mentioned and the next important Graves commune for red wines is Léognan, which includes six of the thirteen classified growths.

First in general standing is Haut-Bailly. Its reputation was established in the last century by a proprietor, Bellot des Minières, a famous grower known as '*le Roi des Vignerons*'. According to the firm of Mestrezat, which used to buy the whole crop around the turn of the last century, one at least of the 'secrets' of Haut-Bailly's success was that he 'cleaned' out his *cuves* before the vintage with a few litres apiece of Grande Fine Champagne cognac. This drop of spirit at the bottom of each vat was conveniently 'forgotten' when the grapes were shovelled in, and the result in the wine was nothing but beneficial. Fortunately or not this no longer takes place. Like Pape-Clément in Pessac, Haut-Bailly had a splendid reputation and then temporarily rather lost it. In the Inter-War years some splendid wine was made, notably a fine '28 and a supple, fruity '37, no mean feat in that hard year. After the Second World War it had two disastrous years in 1959 and 1960, owing to frost. In the former, production was 10 *tonneaux* only, instead of a normal 50, and in 1960 was down to 1·5 *tonneaux* – six hogsheads. Fortunately the château made a very sound '64 in that uneven year. The Graves vineyards tend to lie among woods off the main roads and are difficult to find. More than once I, and even Bordeaux merchants with me, have lost the way in the small cross-country roads. Haut-Bailly is one of these remote-seeming châteaux, although not in fact very far from Bordeaux. The 15-hectare vineyard is about 45 per cent Cabernet-Sauvignon and Cabernet-Franc and 40 per cent Merlot with the balance made up of other varieties. If it escapes frost, Haut-Bailly should turn out some excellent wine in the vintages ahead.

Equally high if not higher in repute is Domaine de Chevalier, whose white wine carries an equal renown as the red, and is certainly among the top three or four white Graves. Like Haut-Bailly, the Domaine de Chevalier is tucked away in the countryside, and its modest appearance can be gauged from the photograph on the old labels. The property is a small one, with a vineyard area of 15 hectares. Production averages 30 *tonneaux* of red and 10 *tonneaux* of white wine.

At one time Domaine de Chevalier was very much of a connoisseur's claret, for production was small and the growth was not widely known; being a domaine in a country of so-called châteaux did not altogether improve the sales prospects. Although dating back well into the last century, I am inclined to think that the Chevalier's more than local reputation dates from this century only. The estate was founded by M. Ricard in the last century, and today his grandsons of the same name cultivate the property. In between came a relative of the first M. Ricard, M. Gabriel Beaumartin, who ruled over the domaine from 1900 until his death in 1942. André Simon in *Vintagewise* (1945) includes the 1899 among the fine wines of that vintage which he had enjoyed, but I never came on it anything like so early; not even the 1907 which he reckons to have been the best wine of that very light vintage, nor the 1909, which was generally another uncertain year.

Yet Domaine de Chevalier really introduced me to the red Graves. During the last war I bought from Justerini & Brooks some excellent bottles of the '24, domaine-bottled I suppose one must say. They had a great deal of elegance, but plenty of fruit and were fine true claret right up to my last bottle in 1952. The '23 was a notable wine of Chevalier, but this I did not drink until a few years ago, when it was going downhill. Nevertheless I did drink the '28 in its prime and, along with Léoville-Las-Cases and Cheval-Blanc, it was certainly the best '28 that has ever come my way. Indeed the Chevalier '28 was a wine with a considerable reputation in Bordeaux, for it lacked the hardness of most '28s. The '29 I only drank once, but remember it as good, and so was the '34. I have even heard tell that a very fair wine was made in that deplorable year '31, and again in '35, but I have never sampled them. Another success in a generally disappointing vintage was the Chevalier '37, which I bought not very long after the last war, and finished with regret early in the 1960s. It was wonderfully supple in that hard year, and even better than Haut-Bailly.

Gabriel Beaumartin must have been a particularly fine wine-maker, for he triumphed when others failed. One reason for his success was that he was also a timber merchant with a large labour force. At the vintage he waited until he believed the moment of full maturity had arrived. Then at once he brought in his workers and cleared the relatively small vineyard in two or three days instead of the more normal ten to fourteen days. He was also very selective with his grapes, eliminating any that were unripe. Whatever art he added to nature, the result was a success. Unfortunately in 1945 much of the vineyard was wiped out by frost and had to be re-planted. The wine was certainly disappointing in the next few years, but showed signs of revival in 1953. I confess to having tasted it seldom since, but the '58 – a year in which Beaumartin might have pulled something out of the bag – was thin and disappointing. The '62 is agreeably fruity.

The white wines have kept a more consistent path and were good in the Inter-War years. I had bottles and half bottles of the '37, which were excellent after nearly 20 years. Later came a beautiful 1947, followed by fine wines in the Fifties. The '64 Chevalier was certainly among the best of the white Graves. I hope that the more recent red Chevaliers will exhibit the old form of this vineyard, for they rank among the most expensive of the non-first-growth clarets.

The four other classed Léognans are Malartic-Lagravière, Carbonnieux, Fieuzal and Olivier. All four also make white wine. I have drunk the red Malartic several times, but apart from an ageing but fine '26 recently have found it rather a hard and not altogether well-balanced wine; yet I may have been unlucky, for Alexis Lichine places it high. I have found the white '64 excellent. The vineyard area is only 10 hectares.

Carbonnieux, once the most famous dry white Graves and as a red wine on a line with the top Léognans, has generally disappointed me. Perhaps in view of its famous reputation I have expected too much. The property once belonged to the Abbey of Ste-Croix in Bordeaux. Here I may repeat the famous story that in order to fool the innocent, wine-forbidden Turks, the not so innocent, not so scrupulous Benedictine monk-exporters labelled their wine as *Eaux Minérales de Carbonnieux*. Later, in the last century, Carbonnieux rather unusually took to growing a wide variety of grapes taken from all over Europe, although the main vines in the vineyard were the normal Bordelais types, Cabernet-Sauvignon, Verdot, Malbec and Merlot.

Nowadays the red wine is seldom seen in Britain, and on the only occasions that I have drunk it, including the '48 and the '59, I was not much impressed. Nor is the white wine, once more famous than the red, on the level of the best dry Graves; I find it too heavy. The vineyard of 48 hectares is large by Graves standards, and bigger than Haut-Brion. The great majority is planted in white grapes, and total production is about 75 *tonneaux*.

I cannot recollect ever tasting Fieuzal, another small vineyard with 14 hectares. The wine is seldom seen in Britain and probably little exported, for it is not easy to sell red Graves, simply because they are not numerous and not well publicized. Fieuzal mostly produces red wine, but there is a little white also.

Olivier is certainly much better known, but mostly for its white wine, which has been sold as a monopoly by the owners, the firm of Eschenauer. Some red wine is made there but much less than white. Olivier is not in the top class of white Graves, but is a sound, reliable wine well above the average. The moated château, owned by M. P. de Bethman, is very picturesque, but the vineyard property is rented to Eschenauer. It extends to 25 hectares. Since Eschenauer was bought by the Liverpool merchant firm of John Holt a good deal of money has been spent on all their estates, including those in the Graves.

There are a number of other quite well-known Léognan estates, including Larrivet-Haut-Brion, whose red wine I have enjoyed in the past, but not seen recently; and La Louvière, best known for its white wine.

Martillac

The next best-known red Graves commune is Martillac, which adjoins Léognan, and includes two classed growths: Smith-Haut-Lafitte and La Tour-Martillac. The former is another Eschenauer property, and one always well known in Britain, initially perhaps because the first of its three names had a familiar ring to the not so knowledgeable and the last suggested quality to the rather more sophisticated. I remember a very fair '29. Like other Graves it seemed to decline or merely not sell over here for a long period, but with the arrival of new owners, there have been fresh developments, including a special bottle, which in Bordeaux is sometimes the outward and visible sign of change within; others content themselves with a new label. The area is 30 hectares, and an average of 90 *tonneaux* of red wine is made. In 1968 white wine production started. The château is separately owned, and the wine although made on the spot is then transferred and kept in Eschenauer's cellars in Bordeaux. The fruity '61 has turned out well, and the '66 when I sampled it in cask was a supple wine with plenty of colour. I would place the estate among the good, second-rank red Graves, which might well improve in the next few years.

La Tour-Martillac is an exceptionally interesting small property, for it includes what must be among the oldest vines producing grapes for wine in Bordeaux today. If the estate were not run by one of Bordeaux leading wine enthusiasts, Jean Kressmann, knowledgeable about the history and background of Bordeaux, one can imagine that these ancient white wine vines would have been dug up; for they were planted in 1884, in the middle of the phylloxera, and were grafted on to immune American stocks. Throughout his vineyard, which also produces red wine, the average age of the vines is 30 – 40 years, which must be nearly twice the normal average. How little old vines yield may be seen from his production. From 4 hectares of white wine grapes, including the 1884 plantation, he secures only 20 hogsheads of wine, whereas the 8 hectares under black grapes yield 112 – 120. But the old vines give the quality, and Kressmann is justifiably proud of them, although the oldest section must soon be re-planted. Jean Kressmann is also proud of the careful way he makes his white wine, and says it is unnecessary to use sulphur – the bane of so much white Bordeaux. Indeed I have heard it suggested that since the recent prohibition in the United Kingdom of the use of sorbic acid in white wine, the application of sulphur has increased. The wine is kept in Bordeaux before bottling in the cellars of the firm of Kressmann. The tower which stands before the charming small château was apparently built by an ancestor of Montesquieu.

There is yet another Eschenauer property in Martillac, La Garde, which seems particularly tucked away in the woods. A rural-looking establishment with a fine two-storeyed stone *chai*, this is predominantly a red wine vineyard, producing about 50 *tonneaux*, of which only a few are white, but the proportion of white is increasing, owing to the demand for good quality white Graves and the corresponding difficulty of selling the lesser-known red wines. The red wine that I tasted seemed particularly full-bodied for a Graves, and in 1968 in Bordeaux I was surprised to find the '47 still so fruity, with a slightly strong flavour.

Villenave d'Ornon

Before we reach the white wine area proper there are a number of small communes in the neighbourhood of Bordeaux which make red wines of fairly wide reputation. In Villenave d'Ornon there is Baret, which makes both red and white wine, and Couhins, which is owned by the Hanappier and Gasqueton families, associated with Calon-Ségur. Here they make a well-known *rosé*, which is among the best in Bordeaux. White Baret I have often drunk in England, and it can be very agreeable of its kind. At Villenave also there is Pontac-Monplaisir: its name sufficient to make one order a bottle; a very fair wine. The property formerly belonged to the Pontac family. The estate used to be planted with Riesling vines.

Cadaujac

Cadaujac has the important and very well-cared-for estate of Bouscaut, to be seen from the main road from Bordeaux to the Sauternes country. Until 1968 it was owned by Victor and Robert Place, but was then sold for 450,000 new francs to an American syndicate, Domaine Wohlstetter-Sloan. This vineyard of 40 hectares produces 100 *tonneaux* of wine, of which two-thirds are red and one-third white. The composition of the red part of the vineyard is 40 per cent Cabernet-Sauvignon and Franc, with the majority Sauvignon, 40 per cent Merlot and 20 per cent Malbec. The white wine is made from 60 per cent Sémillon and 40 per cent Sauvignon. When making the white wine the uncommon practice is followed of putting the white grapes into a cement vat for one night prior to pressing. This apparently results in the impurities falling to the bottom of the vat. Thereafter the fermentation of the juice pressed from the skins takes place as usual in the hogsheads. The Places were go-ahead winemakers, and all the property, including the charming château, rebuilt after more than one fire, is in first-class order. Both young red and white wines that I tasted seemed good, the red supple and fairly forward, the white fresh.

Although there is plenty of red wine made in the communes to the south of Cadaujac, more and more the white wines take over. As already indicated at Bouscaut, the two grapes used are Sauvignon which produces an elegant, perfumed wine and the Sémillon which results in wine lighter and less distinguished in aroma and flavour. White Graves is usually bottled after about 16 – 18 months. White wine is normally more difficult to make than the red as it suffers much more from the risk of oxydization and darkening of colour, or *madérisation*. To counteract this sulphur is used, all too often to excess. So a great deal of white Graves suffers from too much sulphur and too little freshness. Contrary to common opinion white Graves is a fairly strong wine, for to be entitled to the *appellation* of Graves Supérieures it must have a minimum of 12 degrees, although the plain Graves *appellation* calls for only 11 degrees. In good years white Graves may be 12 – 13 degrees, while the red will be a minimum of 10 – 11.

One of the show-places of the northern part of the Graves is the Château La Brède, where Montesquieu (1689 – 1755) was born and lived. He took a prominent part in the affairs of Bordeaux, but was also a substantial vineyard owner, both in the Graves, where he owned Rochemorin in Martillac, and in the Entre-Deux-Mers at Raymond in the village of Baron. Both estates still exist. On one occasion Montesquieu said, 'What makes me love being at La Brède is that there it seems to me that my money is beneath my feet'. Nevertheless he was aware of the comparatively low value of his wines, the nearest of which was in competition with the more famous estate of Carbonnieux, whose average price was no more than 215 livres per *tonneau*; although as mentioned at the beginning of this chapter, thirty years later Jefferson gave its price as 800 livres. Although the charming, turreted and moated château is more of a show-place (and open to the public) than a wine-château, a very agreeable white Graves is made there in relatively small quantities and is now all château-bottled. The owner is the Comtesse de Chabannes.

As one travels south in the Graves region, the wine tends to become less distinguished and rather sweeter. There is Graves de Portets which is cheaper and less good than most Graves to the north. In spite of the often resplendent names on the châteaux' gates and in the books of reference, the area becomes largely one of anonymous Graves and Graves Supérieures. Only the local brokers really know the lie of the wine land, whose wine is good and whose is less good. On British wine merchants' lists will usually be found one or two white Graves with unfamiliar château names, and they probably come from this southern part of the district, which in fact extends round and beyond the sweet wine area, down to the town of Langon. There the *appellation* is not Sauternes as might be imagined, but Graves. The whole Graves district is about 60 kilometres long with an average breadth of 10 kilometres.

It should be pointed out here that a wine labelled Graves de Vayres is not a Graves, but in effect an Entre-Deux-Mers, for it lies more or less near the *RN.89* which runs from Bordeaux to Libourne. It is referred to in the chapter on the Entre-Deux-Mers.

12. St-Emilion

Many wine drinkers first 'discover' claret through the St-Emilions. For the fruitiness and earlier maturity of these wines makes them more immediately attractive than the rather drier and when young austere Médocs. Hence the St-Emilions and their neighbours in Pomerol are referred to as the 'Burgundies of Bordeaux', although that simile is unlikely to appeal to either party. The wines are soft and full because the soil is distinctly richer than in the Médoc or the Graves; this is obvious to any visitor. Also the high proportion of Merlot and the presence of Malbec grapes, both of which produce softer wines than the Cabernet-Sauvignon, are factors in the style of the St-Emilions. A variety of the Cabernet is known as the Bouchet in these parts; the Malbec as the Pressac. On the whole St-Emilions mature and decline sooner than the Médocs, though there are exceptionally long-lived examples from the Côtes area.

The Merlot and Malbec are prolific bearers, but the St-Emilion *appellation* permits 42 hectolitres per hectare, compared with 43 in the Haut-Médoc and 40 for the six named communes of that district. As against that the wines must be 11 degrees in strength compared with the Haut-Médoc's and Médoc's minimum of 10 degrees. This is not a factor of concern to the general run of St-Emilion proprietors. The Merlot and Malbec have the further advantage of being early ripeners, so the vintage in St-Emilion normally begins a few days earlier than in the Médoc. However they also have their disadvantages: they are subject to frost, mildew and *pourriture grise*. In unfavourable weather just before or during the vintage, rot can spread through the vineyard with alarming speed, and this is another reason for early vintaging in St-Emilion. The susceptibility to frost was demonstrated in the terrible disaster of February 1956, when the St-Emilion and Pomerol districts were far worse affected than the Médoc. This was partly owing to situation as well as frost, but the result was that a great number of vines were killed outright, and even ten years later the unexpected collapse of apparently healthy vines was attributed to their weakening in the 1956 frosts. The effect of rot was shown at the 1968 vintage, when St-Emilion and Pomerol were devastated after a wet late summer.

St-Emilion is viticulturally a large district by Bordeaux standards. The output of wines entitled to its *appellation* averages 200,000 hectolitres a year from about 700 growths, compared with about 225,000 from the whole of the Médoc. In addition there are five fringe communes attached to St-Emilion which together produce not far short of another 100,000 hectolitres. So there is plenty of St-Emilion available, much of it inexpensive.

Until the coming of motor transport, the local wines were all shipped from the quay at Libourne. Several important firms, including the old house of Beylot, along with Danglade and Moueix have their cellars there yet; and there are still barrels of wine on the quayside. In the pre-1914 days, the Gilbey family and their friends on their way to Loudenne in the Bas-Médoc used to take the steamer from Libourne. If the place is now quieter than it once was, it is a pleasant but by no means sleepy town, known chiefly to foreign visitors as lying at the end of an essential bridge – blown up by the retreating Germans in 1944 in spite of a promise to the contrary – on the way to St-Emilion, Fronsac and to the north.

St-Emilion, which likes to describe itself as 'the pearl of the Gironde' lies four miles inland from Libourne. It is as charming a small wine town as is to be found in France, occupying a splendid position on top of a hill with wide views over the Dordogne valley. There is a famous monolithic church excavated from the limestone, which locally provides admirable cellars for a number of the châteaux, topped by a spire that rises above the town's small main square. There is also the alleged cell of the hermit, Aemilianus, who gave his name to the town, but there is no evidence that he had any wine associations. Nor are the local wine connections of the fourth-century Latin poet Ausonius, Fourth Consul of Rome, clear. It is maintained that he owned a villa – the Château Ausone is said to have been built on the foundations – and that he was born in Bordeaux.

Parts of the town walls still remain, along with a very fine collegiate church which has a finely proportioned cloister and the remains of a monastery. It also has two well-known restaurants in the main square, and is notable for its macaroons, though these cannot be recommended as a suitable accompaniment to the local wines.

The heart of St-Emilion is divided geologically and physically in two: the Côtes and the Graves. The first part, as the name implies is on the slopes, which are in fact the sides of the river valley. The soil is comprised of silica, clay and chalk. The leading growth of these is Ausone, and its vineyard, lying below the château terrace, is sited on a considerable slope. This Côte is not the unbroken line of hillside one associates with the Côte d'Or, but is irregular. Nevertheless most of the vineyards are

ST-EMILION

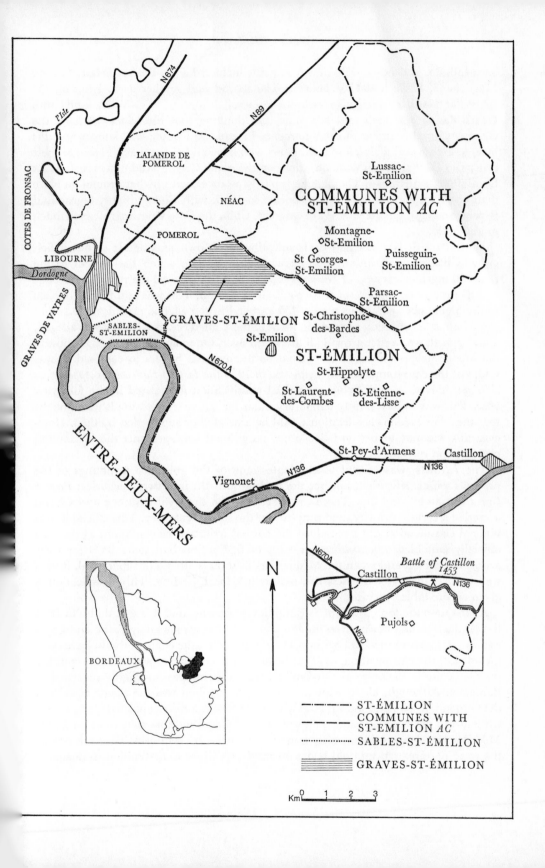

N674

N89

l'Isle

CÔTES DE FRONSAC

LALANDE DE
POMEROL

NÉAC

POMEROL

LIBOURNE

Dordogne

GRAVES DE VAYRES

SABLES-
ST-EMILION

GRAVES-ST-ÉMILION

St-Emilion

N670A

Lussac-
St-Emilion

COMMUNES WITH
ST-EMILION *AC*

Montagne-
St-Emilion

St Georges-
St-Emilion

Puisseguin-
St-Emilion

Parsac-
St-Emilion

St-Christophe-
des-Bardes

ST-ÉMILION

St-Hippolyte

St-Laurent-
des-Combes

St-Etienne-
des-Lisse

ENTRE-DEUX-MERS

St-Pey-d'Armens

Castillon

N136

Vignonet

N136

BORDEAUX

N

N670A

Castillon

*Battle of Castillon
1453*

N136

N670

Pujols

-----·----- ST-ÉMILION
-----·----- COMMUNES WITH
            ST-EMILION *AC*
·············· SABLES-ST-ÉMILION
▦▦▦   GRAVES-ST-ÉMILION

Km 0   1   2   3

on a hillside, and other well-known growths include La Gaffelière, Belair, Canon, Magdelaine, Pavie and Clos Fourtet. The second and smaller area, lying on the fairly flat plateau which also includes Pomerol, has a more gravelly, sandy soil. Hence the name which misleads some into thinking that the wines are from the Graves. Cheval-Blanc is the pre-eminent château, and other well-known growths include Figeac and a clutch of neighbours who have added the name Figeac to their own; also another group with variations on the name Corbin; and others such as La Dominique and Ripeau. The plateau is partly a saucer, with higher ground on more than one side, and this was a frost pocket in 1956, with Cheval-Blanc, Figeac and Ripeau among the most severely devastated, while the Côte vineyards escaped much more lightly.

Until 1955 St-Emilion had a classification of its own making. It sprouted first growths like generals in a military dictatorship, and to soften the descent to the ranks an ingenious system of *deuxièmes-premiers* was devised. All the rest were seconds and there were no *crus artisan* or *cru paysan* troops at all. This was said to give offence to the highly class-conscious men of '55 enrolled in the Médoc classification and to cause immense confusion abroad, not least in the United States where, it was alleged, a first growth was a first growth all the world over. One may doubt whether most of the Médoc proprietors were so put out or the overseas buyers so confused as was said, but the case sounded convincing. So in 1954 the *Institut National des Appellations d'Origine* moved in and set up an official classification formalized in the following year. This was to be a purely temporary affair for ten years, because it was thought that the 1855 Médoc classification would be amended or superseded by then. However this was not to be, and like other provisional arrangements the St-Emilion classification remains in force.

The *I.N.A.O.* was careful to eliminate some of the gold-lace trimmings of the previous self-classification, and set the leading growths into two categories: *Premier Grand Cru* and *Grand Cru*. There are eleven of the first, with Ausone and Cheval accorded a certain priority, and sixty-two of the second category. This official if provisional classification did not reduce the alleged irritation or confusion, as the now officially ennobled seventy-three growths of St-Emilion had some basis for their status, but even if and when the Médoc classification is altered or superseded, it may well be that the other districts will maintain a local grading. This classification is given on the table opposite.

At one time the top growth of St-Emilion was Ausone, and it is said that if in 1855 the production had not been so small – about 15 *tonneaux* for many years, and given as only 8 *tonneaux* in the 1893 edition of Cocks et Féret – the château would have been included in the classification, as Haut-Brion was. I rather doubt this, because in the middle of the last century the St-Emilion wine district was not highly regarded in Bordeaux. Although, along with the Graves, St-Emilion was the senior *vignoble* of the Gironde, it was, and indeed largely remains today, a district of small proprietors, without the development and the prestigious château-building that went on in the Médoc in the eighteenth and even more in the nineteenth centuries. This is shown by the scarcity of reference in old books on Bordeaux wines to St-Emilion châteaux.

The 1953 Classification of St-Emilion

Premiers Grands Crus Classes

A. Château Ausone

    Château Cheval-Blanc

B. Château Beauséjour

    Château Belair

    Château Canon

    Clos Fourtet

    Château Figeac

    Château La Gaffelière

    Château Magdelaine

    Château Pavie

    Château Trottevieille

Grands Crus Classés

    Château l'Angelus

    Château Balestard-la-Tonnelle

    Château Bellevue

    Château Berget

    Château Cadet-Bon

    Château Cadet-Piola

    Château Canon-la-Gaffelière

    Château Cap-de-Mourlin

    Château Chapelle Madeleine

    Château Chauvin

    Château Corbin

    Château Corbin-Michotte

    Château Coutet

    Château Croque-Michotte

    Château Curé Bon

    Château Fonplégade

    Château Fonroque

    Château Franc Mayne

    Château Grand-Barrail-Lamarzelle

    Château Grand-Corbin-Figeac

    Château Grand-Corbin Despagne

    Château Grand Mayne

    Château Grand Pontet

    Château Grandes Murailles

Grands Crus Classés

    Château Guadet-St-Julien

    Château Jean Faure

    Clos des Jacobins

    Château La Carte

    Château La Clotte

    Château La Cluzière

    Château La Couspaude

    Château La Dominique

    Clos La Madeleine

    Château Larcis-Ducasse

    Château Lamarzelle

    Château Larmande

    Château Laroze

    Château Lasserre

    Château La-Tour-du-Pin-Figeac

    Château La-Tour-Figeac

    Château Le Châtelet

    Château Le Couvent

    Château Le Prieuré

    Château Mauvezin

    Château Moulin-du-Cadet

    Château Pavie-Decesse

    Château Pavie-Macquin

    Château Pavillon-Cadet

    Château Petit-Faurie-de-Souchard

    Château Petit-Faurie-de-Soutard

    Château Ripeau

    Château Sansonnet

    Château St-Georges-Côte-Pavie

    Clos St-Martin

    Château Soutard

    Château Tertre-Daugay

    Château Trimoulet

    Château Trois Moulins

    Château Troplong-Mondot

    Château Villemaurine

    Château Yon-Figeac

In the first edition (1850) of Cocks et Féret's *Vins de Bordeaux* thirty-seven first growths and twenty-one seconds were listed. In the third (1853) edition of Franck's then standard work, which describes all the districts of Bordeaux in spite of the short title limiting it to the Médoc, no single St-Emilion château is mentioned in the text as being outstanding, as was the author's custom in most other areas. There is however a classification, the basis of which is not declared. It divides the St-Emilions into wines of the '*premier marque*' and '*seconde marque*' with 42 in the first category and 17 in the second. The first includes Ausone (with an output of 12 – 15 *tonneaux*), Beauséjour, Belair, Canon, etc., but Cheval-Blanc (25 – 30 *tonneaux*) and Figeac (40 – 45 *tonneaux*) are only in the second category, although the latter is marked as '*très-bon cru*'. None of the Graves-St-Emilion wines is in the first class, although some of the Côtes, including Gaffelière are in the second. Well-known Graves-St-Emilion growths today like La Dominique and Ripeau do not appear at all, and it would appear that the vineyards in this part of St-Emilion had then little reputation.

Moreover Charles Lorbac in his section on the *Crus Classés* of Bordeaux in *Les Richesses Gastronomiques de la France* (1867) makes scant reference to the St-Emilion wines in comparison with the space given to the Médocs. He states that the wines were then well known, but the demand was so great and the quantity so small that much of it sold as such was nothing of the sort. Wines labelled St-Emilion *tout court* were more often than not fraudulent. True Lorbac goes on to repeat the story that when Louis XIV visited Libourne in 1750 he is said to have compared the wine of St-Emilion with the nectar of the gods; however one may fairly attribute the remark to the publicity-conscious Libournais who had sent a special deputation to ask the king to visit the town. Moreover as *Le Roi Soleil* was at that time but twelve years old, his appreciation of wine must have been rudimentary and his opinion worth little. Anyhow thirty-five years later his savage as well as stupid Revocation of the Edict of Nantes which had given toleration to the Protestants in 1598 showed his mature view of at least the Huguenot citizens of Libourne.

Evidently St-Emilion had a share in the Second Empire prosperity, for by the second edition of Cocks et Féret (1868) the number of first growths had increased to 44, many of them with divided ownership (La Madeleine had four different proprietors), and 26 second growths. Surprisingly, in this edition Bel-Air is placed firmly at the head of the list, followed by Troplong-Mondot, Canon, Ausone and Beauséjour in that order. The editors state Bel-Air had 'always been placed at the head of the first growths of St-Emilion', and include among its earlier owners Ausonius, Robert Knoll, the English Governor of Guyenne, whose name became Frenchified into Canolle, and the Baron de Marignan, who acquired the château as the dowry of a Mlle Léontine de Canolle, and was in possession in 1868. There is no comment on Ausone, but then experienced readers of this bible of Bordeaux are aware that the footnote puffs are not altogether objective and were doubtless paid for. Ausone adjoins Bel-Air, and the alleged Ausonian origin may have been shared. In any case Bel-Air's production in 1868 was given as 20 – 28 *tonneaux*, compared with only 10 – 12 for its neighbour.

By 1868 what are now known as the Graves-St-Emilion were given a separate identity, but only to the extent that they are listed separately, and described as having a special character, lying among the wines of St-Emilion and Pomerol. Figeac is placed top, followed by Cheval-Blanc, and their production appears to have increased since 1853, as they are given as 50 – 70 *tonneaux* apiece.

However the comparative obscurity of the St-Emilion wines was partly at least caused by the traditional jealousy of the then dominant Bordeaux trade. Thus it was the Médocs who stole the show at the 1855 International Exhibition. Mindful of this the St-Emilionnais decided not to be left out in the cold at the next International Exhibition in Paris, to take place in 1867. Accounts differ as to whether the Bordelais refused to include St-Emilions in their display, or whether the St-Emilionnais decided anyhow to act on their own, but the result was a collective stand of St-Emilion wines. According to Cocks et Féret's listing, thirty-seven of the principal growers combined to show their wines, and collectively they won a gold medal. This certainly helped to put St-Emilion on more extensive maps.

What is interesting about this collective exhibit is that the names of the exhibiting châteaux are known, and they include Ausone, Beauséjour, Bel-Air, Canon, Clos Fourtet, Ferrand, Les Grandes-Murailles, Laroque, La Madeleine, Troplong-Mondot, Pavie, Les Trois-Moulins and Trottevieille. The vintages they showed are also known. Ausone, then owned by M. Cantenat, displayed its '47, '48 and '62. Canon the '58, '61 and '62, Clos Fourtet '58, '59 and '64, Trottevieille '59, '61 and '64. A château now little known called Sarpe, in the associated commune of St-Christophe-des-Bardes, showed a '34. It will be noted that the range of vintages on display was considerable. The 1859 vintage in the Médoc was not at all good, and the 1861 like its successor a hundred years later was very small, owing to a notorious frost in May.

The other significant point is the absentees. Cheval-Blanc, Figeac and Ripeau, for example, did not collaborate. Cheval-Blanc at least cannot have been averse from exhibitions, as one of the two medals shown on the château's label to this day is a bronze one won at the 1862 International Exhibition in London (successor to the more famous 1851 one). La Dominique also won an award in 1862. Figeac was of course a well-known estate locally, and indeed at one time had extended all over the present Cheval-Blanc vineyard. La Gaffelière was probably there under the name of Puygenestou, for that was the property of the Comte de Malet-Roquefort, whose family now own La Gaffelière and Puy-Blanquet in the lesser St-Emilion village of St-Etienne-de-Lisse. It rather looks as if the joint exhibit at Paris in 1867 was largely a Côtes St-Emilion affair.

At this Exhibition the Médoc châteaux were not overshadowed by the St-Emilions, for the leading growths were represented and showered with gold medals. Among those thus rewarded were Lafite, with its 1848 vintage, Latour also showing 1848, Margaux with 1825 and 1848, Léoville with 1848, and Haut-Brion, Mouton and Larose, with no vintages particularized.

It seems likely that a good deal of the St-Emilion wines at this period were not well cared for. Lorbac stated that the best wines were made in St-Emilion itself and the adjoining St-Christophe-des-Bardes, St-Hippolyte and St-Laurent-des-Combes, and that between them only 690 *tonneaux* of first quality and 2,100 of second quality were produced. According to Cocks et Féret in 1868, the prices *en primeur* of St-Emilions ranged from 600 – 1,200 frs. for first growths down to 300 – 600 frs. for third growths. However, in the fine year of 1865 the first growths opened at 1,500 – 1,700 frs. and two years later had risen to 2,000 frs. As will be seen by comparison with opening prices of the classed Médocs in the Appendix (on page 305), the St-Emilion leaders fetched less than third growths like Langoa, and were more on the level of the fifths.

Although, no doubt, the status of St-Emilion wines improved after their success at Paris in 1867 – sixty of them went on to win the collective *Grand Prix* at the 1889 Exhibition – their progress was slow. True the 1893 edition of Cocks et Féret lists the prices over recent years as from 1,200 – 2,400 frs. for the first growths, 800 – 1,600 frs. for the seconds, and 500 – 1,000 frs. for the thirds, thus showing a relative advance towards the classed Médoc prices for the vintages of the Eighties and of 1890 as shown in the Appendix on page 305. But the range is so wide that it looks very much as if the top prices referred only to a few wines, such as Ausone, Bel-Air, Cheval-Blanc, and Figeac. For probably a few of the better growths alone had much of an international reputation until after the First World War.

Even then the more esteemed Médocs were so inexpensive in the depression years that the lesser St-Emilions had not much chance of widening their repute. Since the Second World War they have, along with the Pomerols, come into their own; for that extra body and fruitiness combined with their relatively early maturation have proved attractive to many who find young Médocs rather hard and astringent.

Today Cheval-Blanc is certainly the most esteemed St-Emilion – and one cannot imagine the proprietor now being satisfied with a bronze medal at an international exhibition – but there is no doubt that fifty and more years ago Ausone was the leader. A few years back the present proprietor M. Dubois-Challon had been told of some derogatory remarks about the lasting quality of St-Emilion wines. So he organized a small luncheon party at which various old vintages of Ausone were opened, running back to 1869 and even to 1834. Present at this lunch was Ronald Avery of Bristol, who made careful notes on the wines, and later told me that the 1834 was still 'just there'. As recently as 1967 I myself drank a bottle of the not-very-highly regarded vintage of 1880, and the wine was perfectly sound and agreeable, in spite of having been moved several times in its life.

On the other hand, many would agree that for a long time Ausone has not made wine up to first-growth standard. Years ago I remember an excellent '20 and a good '24, but since the last war I have never met an outstanding Ausone. It is true that in recent years a new *cuvier* has been built, with new vats and equipment, including a horizontal cooling apparatus for use during the fermentation. The proportion of Cabernet-Sauvignon has been increased in the 7-hectare vineyard which has been about 50 per cent Merlot and 50 per cent Bouchet, and the composition will henceforth include 60 per cent Sauvignon of both varieties. Over the years production has been increased and in 1964 the output was 45 *tonneaux*, though only 35 in 1966. The situation of the vineyard should be ideal, and behind the terrace above, the fine cellars, excavated from the limestone, are suitably humid, so that the barrels have mould on them. One hopes shortly to find Ausone again at the top.

In these cellars is also kept the wine of the neighbouring Bel-Air, which was acquired by the Dubois-Challon family in 1916. The château itself, a very old building with turrets wedged into the rock, lies along the terrace from Ausone, and the two growths are worked together. The soil here is more chalky and Bel-Air is usually a lighter wine than Ausone but often very agreeable. Output is about 40 *tonneaux*. Its earlier *réclame* has already been mentioned.

On the plateau just above Ausone lies Canon, with a pretty courtyarded château, adjoining an old church and owned by the lively Mme A. Fournier, one of the senior but not least energetic wine-growers of the region. The vineyard area, enclosed some-what uncommonly in these parts by a wall, is 20 hectares in extent. The *cépage* is 60 per cent Merlot, 30 per cent Bouchet and 10 per cent Cabernet-Sauvignon, with a very small quantity of Malbec insufficient to be allotted a percentage. By St-Emilion standards, production is on the high side: about 80 *tonneaux*. The fermentation is carried out in unusually small wooden vats, as Mme Fournier believes this leads to more regular fermentation. One of the leading St-Emilions, it is a big, firm, fruity wine. There was an excellent '37 and a fine '59. However unquestionably the finest Canon I have drunk was the '21, which showed that Cheval-Blanc did not have it all its own way in that famous vintage. This was served in September 1965, appro-priately enough at lunch in St-Emilion, but in fact had been decanted in Bordeaux at 8.45 a.m. and brought out by Edouard Cruse in his car. When drunk at 2 p.m. the wine was remarkably full and sweet-flavoured in spite of a very brown colour, with a firm, almost hard background that no doubt had preserved it. Otherwise Canon is a wine that I have, to my regret, drunk too seldom.

Immediately below Ausone is La Gaffelière, which a few years ago removed the supplementary 'Naudes' from its title. The château was built on the site of an old leper colony and the château name comes from the medieval word for a leprosarium. Until then and for many years the proprietor was the late Comte de Malet-Roquefort, who combined running a vineyard with owning a pack of hounds. He once told me his family was connected with the English Malet family. His wine has long been popular in Britain. La Gaffelière is a medium-sized St-Emilion property, producing about 90 *tonneaux*. It is a well-made, reliable wine, which has now become rather expensive like several other of the classed St-Emilions.

I remember in particular two vintages of La Gaffelière, '34 and '29, and put them in that order, for it was the excellence of the former over a period of more than fifteen years that led me to taste the latter. The '34 La Gaffelière was in the first case of wine that I bought from Avery's of Bristol in the month that the Second World War broke out. It cost 3s.4d. a bottle, and the initial bottle was opened in November 1939 – my note reads, 'a fine bouquet and an almost creamy wine'. The following year, having joined the International Exhibition Co-operative Wine Society, I bought a further quantity for no more than 2s.7d. and continued to buy from both sources when possible, until the last half-dozen from Avery's in 1951 cost 11s.6d.; in all, counting half bottles, over 5 dozen. I do not remember a bad bottle, and that in a year so disappointing in the Médoc considering its fame. This '34 was always a splendidly rounded wine.

Accordingly when I visited the château some years after the last war and the proprietor in his private cellar prior to lunch in St-Emilion asked me what wine of his I would like to try, I thought it would be interesting to see what the vineyard could produce in a really notable year. So I asked for a bottle from the bin of the '29s. I then noticed that the bottling date was on all the bin labels and this was given as August 1934, almost five years after the vintage. Thinking that the wine would be thin I feared the worst until we tasted it an hour or so later; the wine was still wonderfully fruity and showing absolutely no sign of decline. The Count explained that it had been a very big wine and that is why it had been left so long in cask.

I bought or have enjoyed most of the well-known post-war vintages (there was a good, powerful '37 too), and the '50 also was excellent for a moderate year. All have been good though not exceptional. La Gaffelière should not be confused with Canon-La Gaffelière, which has never appealed to me; an acceptable but often dull wine.

The other St-Emilion of renown from the Côtes area is Clos Fourtet, situated on the outskirts of the town, opposite the collegiate church. It has the most remarkable limestone cellars of the neighbourhood, extending under the town. This property belonged for many years to the Ginestet family, but Pierre Ginestet sold it after the last war in order to complete the purchase of Château Margaux. It made a famous 1899 and in the 1920s Clos Fourtet made some remarkable wines: '21, '23, '24, '28 and '29. The most remarkable was perhaps the full, rich '24. Yet since the last war the vineyard's reputation has declined and I have not come upon a distinguished bottle since. This is much to be regretted, for, consistent though many of them are, there are not all that number of really fine St-Emilions. Adjoining Clos Fourtet is Grandes Murailles, named after the ruins of a monastery in its vineyard, and once better known than today.

A neighbour of Ausone that has been making particularly good wine in recent years is Magdelaine which belonged to the Chatonnet family for nearly 300 years but now belongs to Jean-Pierre Moueix, who owns several other châteaux, as well as the firm on the quayside at Libourne. Popular in the Low Countries, perhaps on account of its religious name, it is a soft and fruity wine, which to me has more than a suggestion of Pomerol, in spite of its situation. It produces about 40 *tonneaux* a year. The other classed growths in this part of St-Emilion are Beauséjour, which is divided into two, Pavie and Trottevieille. Pavie, owned by M. Valette, is certainly the largest of the top level St-Emilion vineyards, and extends over a large steep hillside to the south of the town. The cellars are in the very large galleries of an old quarry. Pavie has long been well known in Britain, but had a bad patch, from which it now seems to be emerging, for the '59 was excellent. Production is 120 *tonneaux* and the 36-hectare vineyard is made up of 50 per cent Merlot, 30 per cent Bouchet, and 20 per cent Cabernet-Franc. Trottevieille is about the same size as Magdelaine and also makes very sound wine.

There are so many *grand cru* St-Emilions of the Côtes area that it is difficult to single out those with a particular reputation, or which I know myself. Grand-Pontet, recently acquired by the firm of Barton & Guestier, now seems good, and so does La Clotte, oddly named to English ears. The proprietor, the ebullient M. Chailleau, was pleased to show me the cave in the limestone cliff overhanging his vineyard which was excavated by 'you English'. The reference was not to some recent archaeological 'dig' but to the English soldiery in the days of the English rule of Gascony. La Clotte is a pleasant, supple wine, with an average production of 20 *tonneaux* from 5 hectares. Troplong-Mondot (partly named after S. E. M. Troplong, President of the French Senate in the 1860's, who owned this once more prominent property), Villemaurine and Tertre-Daugay are all to be found on English wine lists from time to time. So are that religious trio Grâce-Dieu, L'Angélus and Le Couvent; and the more secular sounding Clos des Jacobins, although in fact named after a religious order. Just off the main square is the Couvent des Jacobins, whose deep cellars include monastic remains. The average production of its suburban vineyard is 35 – 40 *tonneaux*. I have enjoyed agreeable wines from all of these and other growths lying deeper in St-Emilion's long list. There is a Cheval-Noir, no connection with any other stable in the district, but owned by the Bordeaux firm of Mähler-Besse, and a La Fleur-Pourret belonging to Ginestet. There is also a co-operative in St-Emilion, founded in 1933. It sells its wine as St-Emilion-Royal.

The difference in style of the Graves St-Emilions lies in situation and soil. The growths lie on a plateau which also includes Pomerol. This is prosperous, profitable land and the prospect is entirely vinous, with the lines of vines occupying every piece of ground not lying fallow prior to re-planting. The soil is much more gravelly and sandy than on the Côtes.

The outstanding wine is certainly Cheval-Blanc, which does not mean that it is always the best wine. Over the past couple of generations it has advanced in reputation probably more than any other single property in Bordeaux; the much smaller Pétrus, whose wider reputation is even more recent, is its only rival in this respect.

Cheval-Blanc's reputation, as M. Fourcaud-Laussac, one of the two brother proprietors, confirmed to me, really began with the famous 1921. Not that this was the first outstanding Cheval-Blanc vintage. The '20 was a splendid wine too, and when in the mid-1950s I opened together bottles of the '20 and '21, the majority opinion preferred the '20 as a more complete wine; but I was in a minority at my own table in preferring the '21 for its extraordinary sweetness and depth of taste. The merits of various vintages are discussed in the chapter on Bordeaux vintages, but '21 Cheval-Blanc was as famous as '21 Yquem.

The secret of the special appeal of Cheval-Blanc lies partly in that it is almost a Pomerol. Only the width of a cart-track separates it from La Conseillante in Pomerol, and on the minor road to Montagne-St-Emilion, the vineyard of Cheval-Blanc is on one side and L'Evangile in Pomerol on the other. The rich, full flavour of Pomerols is embedded in Cheval-Blanc, but the rather greater distinction of the best St-Emilions gives Cheval-Blanc a unique quality.

This individuality, showing a fruity, welcoming aroma, and a big rich, almost sweet flavour, makes Cheval-Blanc of a good year, and sometimes an indifferent one also, a very easy claret to drink. A fine Médoc often retains for some years a marked austerity and even astringency, calling for a certain experience to appreciate fully, but the softer St-Emilions in general and above all Cheval-Blanc come out to meet one. Rich but not so experienced wine drinkers, buying by name, often go for wines like Cheval-Blanc '21, '34 and '47, and this inevitably increases demand, in the same way as an international *prima donna* attracts to Covent Garden Opera the not-so-musical as well as the regulars. As an admirer of Cheval-Blanc but not at present prices, I am constrained to misquote a celebrated remark and say, let them drink Burgundy! Cheval-Blanc is at its best a wonderful claret, but it is no more the consistent summit of all clarets than Lafite, Haut-Brion or Pétrus are.

The Médocains would certainly enter a protest at any undue elevation of a non-Médoc wine, and more than one château proprietor would deprecate the integration of St-Emilions in a new classification. Yet it was at Langoa that Ronald Barton opened for me a beautifully rounded bottle of Cheval-Blanc '26. When at Mouton-Rothschild and given a choice of wines, I asked for the '29 to precede a Mouton 1900, the *maître de chai* paid the wine (and me) the compliment of saying it was one of the best wines in the cellar. Although I would not pick a Cheval-Blanc as the finest claret I have ever drunk, I think I have had greater enjoyment of more vintages of this château than any other; the frequency is partly owing to the fact that it used to be inexpensive by first-growth standards.

The vineyard of 33 hectares is, with the neighbouring Figeac and Pavie, one of the three largest in the district. It is composed of one-third Merlot, one-third Bouchet and one-third Pressac (Malbec). However as an experiment some Cabernet-Sauvignon has recently been planted, with the idea of giving the wine more finesse. When I was there one September there were loads of soil from the *palus* by the river being dumped on the vineyard as a form of fertilizer or humus. The production averages 120 – 130 *tonneaux*, but although in 1964 the output was 145 *tonneaux* yet in 1966 it came down to not much above half that total.

I was a witness of the devastation that affected this part of St-Emilion and Pomerol in February 1956, for I visited the area the following June; where there should have been an expanse of green leafage the black stumps of the vines stood bare; it looked like a battlefield. No wonder, for there had been 24 degrees C. of frost. Fortunately fewer of the vines were dead than at first thought, and they sprang up again, although at Cheval-Blanc as elsewhere some died throughout the following decade. The immediate result at Cheval-Blanc was that their crop for 1956 was precisely three *barriques*. The following year it was about 120 *barriques*, or 30 *tonneaux*, and reached 100 *tonneaux* only in 1959. It was not until 1961 that Cheval-Blanc recovered something like its pre-frost quality, but with an output of only 40 *tonneaux*. The '61 is certainly a fine wine and will be better, but I am not sure that any other vintage has come up to the outstanding post-war run that finished with the '52. But that applies also to other St-Emilions and Pomerols.

Visitors to the *chai* at Cheval-Blanc will notice how small it is for the size of the vineyard, and in comparison with other châteaux producing similar quantities. Proportionately the *cuvier*, adjoining the pleasant but modest house, is even smaller, and it is a wonder that the wine can be accommodated for the fourteen-day fermentation in the crowded cluster of vats. One result of this lack of space is that the wine is bottled not at the château but in Libourne in an officially-designated annexe, which, as with La Mission-Haut-Brion in Bordeaux, counts as part of the château for the purpose of château-bottling. Incidentally, Cheval-Blanc is the only growth on *premier cru* level which still sells part of its output in cask. Modest too is the private cellar of this famous growth ranking with the *premiers crus* of the Médoc. It contains no very old bottles, and I could not see any of the famous '21, but there were some bottles of the '29 and '34. The fact is that by Médoc standards Cheval-Blanc and the adjoining Pomerols do not enjoy long life. They tend to go brown early (though not the Cheval-Blanc '21) and after twenty years or so look and taste much older. This applies even more to the Pomerols, whose '45s now show distinctly brown while still tasting well. In my experience the '20 Cheval-Blanc began to 'descend' nearly ten years ago, and the same has happened to the '28, one of the outstanding wines of this variable vintage. So the Fourcaud-Laussac family are probably right not to make too much of a museum of their private cellar, but to drink their wines while still at their best. However, M. Fourcaud-Laussac did tell me that the '93 and the '99 had been wonderful wines which had lasted well, but he had possessed neither for many years.

Adjoining the Cheval-Blanc vineyard is that of Figeac, which in the eighteenth century owned all the estate of its chief rival (which as already indicated it led by a short head a hundred years ago), as well as those other Graves-St-Emilions which have captured the name Figeac with prefixes and suffixes. It is a very old property which in the hands of its present proprietor, M. A. de Manoncourt, has made considerable progress since the last war, although very severely stricken by the 1956 frosts. The vineyard, very stony and sandy in appearance, is unusual in these parts for its large proportion of Cabernet-Sauvignon, which accounts for about one-third of the *cépage*, and no doubt gives Figeac its special quality. The rest of the vineyard of about 27 hectares is taken up by Bouchet (32 per cent), Merlot (30 per cent) and the balance Pressac. When young the wine often strikes me as having an unusual 'smoky' nose and taste which is perhaps a *goût de terroir*. Yet it seems to disappear with maturity. Normal production is from 125 – 150 *tonneaux*. M. Manoncourt is an 'engaged', albeit modest, vineyard owner, and he and his charming family live in a somewhat English-looking late eighteenth-century château with flanking buildings overlooking a courtyard led up to by a fine avenue of trees. The château has been burnt down twice. Although Figeac had a considerable reputation in the last century, greater even than Ausone, so far as international reputation was concerned, later it suffered some eclipse. Apart from the excellent '28 I have not come upon the Inter-War vintages myself, but since the Fifties it has usually been on my buying list. M. Manoncourt told me that the best post-war vintage for him was '53, although I have considerable hopes of the '61. Like several other St-Emilions the price of Figeac has risen sharply compared with twenty years ago, and is now a fairly expensive wine, although much below Cheval-Blanc, which on occasion it can at least equal; an example of this is perhaps '59 and certainly the lesser year of '62. It is a growth to watch.

In the neighbourhood are a number of smaller properties which have been able to adopt the name Figeac. The proliferation was also caused by division of the properties.

For example La Tour-Figeac, split off from Figeac itself in 1879, was sub-divided into three, of which the original château retained 16 hectares. The other two parts were both called La Tour-du-Pin-Figeac, each with vineyard areas of about 8 hectares. One part is owned by M. G. Bélivier, the other by M. Jean Marie Moueix, a cousin of M. Jean-Pierre Moueix, and like him also a wine merchant. The two La Tour-du-Pin-Figeacs make big, fruity wines which can be very agreeable, without having the distinction of Figeac itself. Between them they produce about 100 *tonneaux* compared with 100 from La Tour-Figeac. Yon-Figeac also makes at least 100 *tonneaux*. On the other hand Petit-Figeac, owned by Pierre Ginestet, produces an average of 3 – 6 *tonneaux* only. All these are in the *Grand Cru* class, as is Grand Barrail-Lamarzelle-Figeac, which turns out over 100 *tonneaux* but which is seldom referred to by its full name. There are also Franc-Petit-Figeac and La Grave-Figeac, but I have not met either.

All these growths are near the Pomerol 'frontier' road. Another which also adjoins Chevel-Blanc is La Dominique, whose '55 has much of the character of its neighbour. It is a growth with a good reputation. The vineyard is of 17 hectares, producing an average of 200 *barriques* from a *cépage* which is 50 per cent Bouchet and 50 per cent Merlot. The proprietor, the cheerful M. de Bailliencourt, also owns Gazin in Pomerol. The modest house at La Dominique still showed the scars of the last war when I visited it nearly a quarter of a century after the Germans had left it, the only house in the district which had been fought over. Next along this Montagne road is Ripeau, a fair-sized property but the few bottles I have drunk of it have not impressed me particularly. The road here leaves Pomerol entirely, and on the left side is now Croque-Michotte, a typically full St-Emilion of which I remember the '47 with particular pleasure.

I should here state that for me to pretend to have an intimate knowledge of even all the better known 62 St-Emilion *Grands Crus* and their unclassified peers in Pomerol would be misleading. Few outside the local *courtiers* have, let alone even the Bordeaux merchants. For the latter tend to follow certain growths and perhaps have contractual relations with them. It is virtually impossible to know all the St-Emilions and Pomerols all of the time, and the best one can do is to follow some of them some of the time.

There is, for example, a cluster of Corbins in this part of St-Emilion: Grand Corbin, Corbin d'Espagne, even a Corbin-Michotte, etc. The land is claimed to have belonged to the Black Prince. I have come upon several of these Corbins from time to time, and they have never seemed more than middling wines, but I may have missed some winners. One such excellent wine that came my way not long after the last war was Chauvin '29, which was listed by Nicolas, the famous Paris chain winestores. Since then I have once or twice chanced on Chauvin at some tasting of young wines, and have always paid it special attention in recollection of its '29, but I have never found one that stood out in any way. The property adjoins Ripeau.

The list of Graves-St-Emilions is much shorter than the Côtes, and the 'other ranks' of the old *Deuxièmes Crus* are even fewer.

The third section of St-Emilion which is part of the commune proper and not associated with one of the seven adjoining villages entitled to that *appellation* pure and simple, is the small area of Sables-St-Emilion. This is near the Dordogne on the flat riverside plain, and it begins just outside Libourne on the road to Castillon and Bergerac. There are very few vineyard properties and more than one of these is threatened by the expanding factory zone of Libourne. The best known is certainly Martinet, which has a charming late eighteenth century château, resembling an English country house. It is owned by the family associated with the old Libourne wine merchant firm of H. Beylot, and the wine is light and agreeable.

Near here is the very agreeable Ch. Videlot, not essentially a wine château but the eighteenth-century home of Jean-Pierre Moueix, set in a park extending down to the Dordogne, and looking very English in this ensemble. It is notable for its fine collection of modern paintings, including more than a dozen Dufys, two Picassos, a Derain, etc. There is also a splendid array of modern French illustrated *éditions de luxe*. As a change from vineyard visiting an invitation to Videlot makes a welcome diversion.

The seven associated St-Emilion villages which lie on the east and south of St-Emilion, extending down to the right bank of the Dordogne, once came under the jurisdiction of St-Emilion. Collectively they make a good deal of wine, but little of it has a wide reputation. The districts, with the names of one or two better known properties in brackets are St-Christophe-des-Bardes (Haut-Sarpe), St-Laurent-des-Combes (Larcis-Ducasse), St-Hippolyte (de Ferrand, Lassègue), St-Etienne-de-Lisse (Puy-Blanquet owned by the Comte de Malet-Roquefort of La Gaffelière), St-Pey-d'Armens, St-Sulpice-de-Faleyrens (Monbousquet, Castelot, and Vignonet). The first two of these villages used to include a number of properties of *soi-disant* first growths.

In addition, to the north-east of the St-Emilion plateau and on higher, more undulating ground are five communes entitled to add St-Emilion to their names. These are St-Georges, Montagne (Plaisance), Lussac (Lyonnat), Puisseguin and Parsac. To ease the multiplicity of *appellations* these might well follow the Burgundian custom and call themselves St-Emilion-Villages. Nearly all have co-operative societies, and there are some very large estates as well. Outside the central area of St-Emilion the vine is less ubiquitous and the country becomes more interesting, more rural. The 'montagne' to the north-east of the plateau is not a very considerable one, but it affords a pleasant view of the heart of St-Emilion, with the fine monolithic church spire on the horizon, and Pomerol's church spire prominent in the plateau, as it is everywhere in the neighbourhood. Montagne itself has a church with a fine Romanesque apse, and for those who like a little sight-seeing as a change from wine-tasting, on the outskirts of the district there is Château Monbadon, an historic monument standing rather gloomily on a hill with a fine slope below it. Broadly speaking as the road rises out of the plateau the reputation of the vineyards descends, but the wine though less distinguished may still be agreeable.

One should mention St-Emilion's *Jurade*. As elsewhere this was the assembly of town councillors, but it is now a publicity and propaganda organization to spread the fame of the wines of St-Emilion. It meets several times a year, and enrols candidates who pledge themselves to quaff St-Emilions. It has, however, rather more of an unbroken link with the past than its rivals in the Médoc and Sauternes.

Before leaving the region of St-Emilion a visit is worth while to the site of the Battle of Castillon which effectively put an end to English power in Gascony. This is outside the wine area of St-Emilion, and lies beyond the small town of Castillon. On the hillside above the town, which is on the Dordogne, stand reminders of medieval warfare in the shape of fifteenth-century towers. The busy main road to Bergerac and a railway line run across the battlefield, which is surrounded by a semi-circle of wooded hillsides, partly covered also by vines. The flat valley is described on a notice board as a '*Zone Industrielle*' and there is one token factory to disturb a landscape that only the road builders and railway makers have altered since the Middle Ages. On the river side of the road the land falls away in tree-lined meadows to the fast-flowing stream.

The battlefield on which old Talbot led his army against the French is marked by a monument, sited perilously near the road on which the *camions* thunder past. The monument was erected only 80 years ago by a 'union of patriots' with an evident surge of chauvinist emotion. It reads:

> Dans Cette Plaine
> Le 17 Juillet 1453
> Fut Remportée la Victoire
> ou délivrer
> du joug de l'Angleterre
> Les Provinces Méridionales
> de la France
> et termina
> La Guerre de Cent Ans

As described earlier on, the Bordelais were by no means enamoured at being liberated by their semi-compatriots, and for a period after Castillon preferred the English yoke to the French embrace. But at least we English should have a special regard for the wines of St-Emilion.

13. Pomerol

The finer wines of Pomerol are the most immediately attractive red wines of Bordeaux; even more than those of the neighbouring St-Emilion. They are soft, lacking much of the tannin that marks the Médocs and the Graves when immature and they may be drunk fairly young, a consideration these days when the accent is on quick turnover. Consequently it is no surprise that the Pomerols have won many adherents in the last twenty years; and with demand prices have risen sharply too.

Sometimes one finds Pomerols described as being halfway between St-Emilions and Médocs, with the softness and roundness of the former and the intensity and some of the distinction of the latter. I cannot see this. The really typical Pomerols to me have the intensity of aroma and flavour all right, but to resemble St-Emilions only more so. If the aroma of Médocs often recalls blackcurrants, the Pomerols for me evoke brown sugar.

A fine Pomerol has a wonderful concentration of perfume – and I use the word advisedly here – and flavour which marks it out from other clarets. The wine has a rich, but not an enriched, taste that is seductive. If I cannot follow the late P. Morton Shand – that pioneer writer on wine to whom all serious wine drinkers have been grateful for over forty years – in detecting in Pomerols 'a rich truffle scent, which leaves just a whiff of hidden moss and violets in its wake', this must be because these similies seldom reflect what I seem to smell and taste in wine. In a blind tasting of clarets, Pomerols should be the easiest to pick out although I confess that I have confused them with Pauillacs and vice versa.

Such comments refer to the more successful wines. There are Pomerols which lack this concentration of aroma and flavour, and are merely full-bodied and St-Emilion-like in style. These I find dull and prefer a sound St-Emilion. If all Pomerols are open to some criticism, it is that they tend to lack 'centre'. Whereas a fine Médoc has an inner core which keeps the flavour 'true' to the end, a Pomerol is 'all over one' immediately, and its flavour may slightly 'depart' or soften out at the finish. However this is high-level criticism, and I am particularly fond of fine Pomerols. Owing to their richness they are sometimes rather difficult to accommodate on an occasion when red wines from the other Bordeaux districts are being served. A Pomerol will often 'blanket' a Médoc, as I remember when I served to a Médoc proprietor a splendid La Croix-de-Gay '47, followed by the then outstanding Léoville-Poyferré '29. The finely balanced though fruity '29 had to struggle to surmount the rich concentration of the '47. It succeeded but afterwards my guest remarked, 'Never serve a Pomerol before a Médoc.' This is perhaps an exaggeration, and that distinguished *amateur* of Pomerols, Edouard Cruse, to whom I recounted this remark, strongly disagreed. 'The great thing', he rejoined, 'is to give a vintage of the Médoc corresponding in reputation to that of the Pomerol, and always a considerably older Médoc. The finesse of the Médoc will usually show up better even after a powerful Pomerol'.

Nevertheless a Médoc after a very rich Pomerol can come close to drinking claret after Burgundy. Yet although there is much less variety in the Pomerols than the Médocs, it is always interesting to show a range of vintages from the same growth.

By Bordeaux standards Pomerol is a 'new' district, for up to much less than a century ago the wines were sold as St-Emilions, in the same way as other outlying villages of that area. If then the wines of St-Emilion were not highly considered, those of Pomerol attracted even less individual attention. Being powerful and fruity they were often used for blending with lighter wines. In 1853 Franck dismisses Pomerol in a five-line paragraph, and mentions one growth only: Château de Curtan (*sic*). He says they last well, are inexpensive, and that the wine on the low-lying part is inferior to that on the high ground; true enough today. Moreover the production total he gives of six to seven hundred *tonneaux* is less than a quarter of today's average of three thousand *tonneaux* made by 135 growers. Even in the 1868 Cocks et Féret the list of seventeen principal proprietors is headed '*crus bourgeois et 1ers artisans*'. First is Vieux-Ch.-Certan, followed by Trotanoy and Pétrus. Although Pétrus won a gold medal at the 1878 Paris Exhibition, in the 1893 edition of Cocks et Féret Pomerol was included as part of the St-Emilionnais. In this edition 31 first-growth Pomerols were listed and 25 seconds.

Nevertheless Pétrus's gold medal must have helped it to sell its average output of only 16 *tonneaux*. For it apparently sold the 1879 – generally a moderate year only – for 2,800 frs. per *tonneau* and the 1891 for 1,600 frs., equal to the price of the Médoc second growths.

Much later, in George Saintsbury's *Notes on a Cellar Book* (1920) the St-Emilions are dismissed because he did not care for them; the Pomerols are not even mentioned. Even Alexis Lichine in his valuable *Wines of France*, first published in 1952 but revised recently, gives hardly any space to Pomerol, although some amends

POMEROL

204

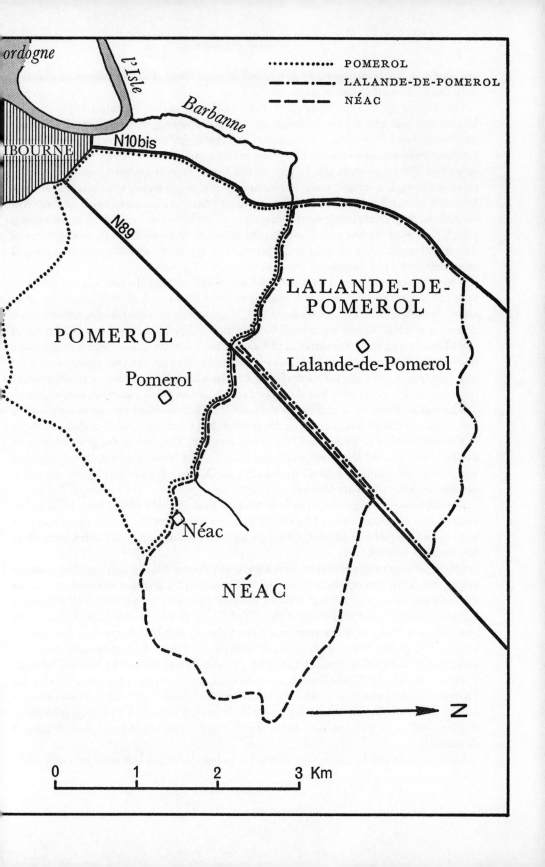

are made in his *Encyclopaedia of Wines and Spirits* (1967). The commune of Pomerol only secured separate delimitation in 1923.

One reason for this earlier neglect is the small size of the properties on the roughly 700-hectare plateau which includes all but the outlying sub-districts of Lalande-de-Pomerol and Néac. For the most part individual production is small, less than 50 *tonneaux*, and the châteaux are little more than farmhouses or villas. Nénin, with an output of 100 *tonneaux*, is the largest of the better known growths, and Pétrus, the most celebrated, averages only 30, including the *vin de presse*, which is usually not included at the *assemblage*. Accordingly these small estates have with one or two exceptions not the quantity or the resources to make much individual mark among wine drinkers. This has not, however, inhibited their proprietors from disposing of their relatively modest crops at good prices. The *appellation contrôlée* output is limited to 40 hectolitres per hectare.

I have already observed that St-Emilions of the plateau do not normally last as long as Médocs, and this certainly applies to Pomerols, which after fifteen years or so generally acquire the tawny colour of age. With one or two exceptions, among them Pétrus, the '45 Pomerols are now fully stretched, whereas this is not true of most of the Médocs; and such Pomerols of the Twenties as I have drunk have seemed older than their Médocain coevals. However this is little cause for complaint, and I do not quite agree with the *maître de chai* of Pétrus, who told me that his wines were at their best at ten years old; but then the French like to drink vigorous, *corsé* wines.

The soil in Pomerol is similar to that of Graves-St-Emilion on the same plateau, but in one part there is some iron in the ground. Yet there are small but sharp changes in the composition of vineyards close to one another. The clay in the gravel accounts for the rather special character of Pétrus, including its fuller, heavier, style compared with the neighbouring Vieux-Château-Certan. On the edge of the plateau the soil is sandier, and the wines are lighter.

The make-up of the vineyards is similar to that of St-Emilion, with perhaps an even greater emphasis on the Merlot, which gives soft wines. A number of the growths have even a majority of Merlot, although a general indication is one-third each Merlot, Bouchet and Malbec.

Of the famous major Bordeaux red wine areas Pomerol is the only one now unclassified, and, as in pre-officially classified St-Emilion, first growths abound as well as second-firsts in front of a small rank of seconds. However an unofficial classification has some support and if and when the *I.N.A.O.* decides to produce an authoritative one, this is unlikely to differ very much from the present list except that it might be longer. This places Pétrus on a similarly slightly elevated level like Ausone and Cheval-Blanc in St-Emilion. Nine or ten other growths follow, including Vieux-Château-Certan, Certan, La Conseillante, Petit-Village, L'Evangile, Trotanoy, Gazin, La Fleur-Pétrus and one or two others according to personal choice. One reason why an official Pomerol classification may be unlikely is that there are so many growths of similar quality in this compact area. Their local 'guild' calls itself the *Hospitaliers de Pomerol*.

Not everyone would agree that Pétrus is the best Pomerol, but none can deny that it is the most famous. Combined with the quality and appeal of the wine itself, this is very largely owing to the efforts of the late Mme Loubat, a woman of great personality who never made the mistake of under-estimating the value of her product. She affirmed that her wine was equal to the first growths of the Médoc, and accordingly should sell for the same price. Personality and perseverance, aided by a limited supply of an excellent wine, won through, and today Pétrus sells at about the same price as Ch. Margaux. From the eighteenth century to the First World War, Pétrus was owned by the Arnaud family, who then turned it into a company. About 1925 M. Loubat bought part of this estate, but after his death Mme Loubat gradually acquired the rest, finally achieving this about 1945. Its rise in reputation is much more recent than Cheval-Blanc's, and although the 1893 was listed at a fair but not first-growth price on the International Exhibition Co-operative Wine Society lists in the later 1890s, it was hardly seen in Britain and the wine was not offered generally before the last war by the two firms in England who had first featured it in the post-war years: Averys and Harveys of Bristol. True it had a special French reputation and in an unofficial classification in the 1920s Pétrus was listed as *premiers des grands crus*, followed by Vieux-Château-Certan and Certan as *grands premiers crus*. The 1906 was first listed in the 1933 edition of the famous special illustrated lists of Nicolas of Paris, who only include notable wines therein. In recent years I have twice drunk Pétrus '20, but the bottles had come from Switzerland. One bottle was good, the other *passé*. No Pétrus is mentioned in André Simon's *Vintagewise* (1945), which describes the wines he and later the Saintsbury Club had drunk over many years.

The rise in the popularity of Pétrus and of Cheval-Blanc in the early post-war years may be demonstrated by their opening prices per *tonneau* in comparison with those of the established *premiers crus*. As such prices vary, the exactness of the figures may be questioned but the trend is clear. Moreover it should be noted that first growth prices include keeping charges while the wine is in cask, but this did not apply to Cheval-Blanc and Pétrus, and this added 15 – 20 per cent to their prices.

1945 Vintage		*1949 Vintage*	
All *premiers crus*	200,000 – 240,000 frs.	All *premiers crus*	*c.* 250,000 frs.
Cheval-Blanc	100,000 frs.	Cheval-Blanc	175,000 frs.
Pétrus	80,000 frs.	Pétrus	225,000 frs.
1947 Vintage		*1953 Vintage*	
All *premiers crus*	*c.* 200,000 frs.	All *premiers crus*	*c.* 300,000 frs.
Cheval-Blanc	130,000 frs.	Cheval-Blanc	200,000 frs.
Pétrus	100,000 frs.	Pétrus	275,000 frs.

Cheval-Blanc '53 was not considered as successful as in some vintages, and this may account for the comparatively low price. Today Pétrus sells for the same price as all but the most expensive *premiers crus*, and in 1966 the Cheval-Blanc opening price was much higher than Margaux and Haut-Brion.

Pétrus is indeed a modest estate, with no very grand château, and one comes on the buildings quite suddenly amid the network of small roads that cross the plateau. The composition of the vineyard, which extends only to 6½ hectares, is 70 per cent Merlot and 30 per cent Bouchet.

As already stated its output is about 30 – 35 *tonneaux* (12 – 15 a century ago) but it suffered as severely as Cheval-Blanc in the 1956 frosts. No wine at all was produced that year.

In succeeding years output was as follows:

Year	Tonneaux	Year	Tonneaux
1957	8	1962	30
1958	24	1964	37
1959	18	1966	27
1960	31	1967	28
1961	17½		

The drop in 1961 when spring frosts again affected the vineyard will be noticed.

These figures were based on the number of *barriques* filled, but evaporation and the resultant topping up will reduce the final quantity of this and other Bordeaux by 10 per cent or more, which strikes hard on a small growth. The best post-war vintage of Pétrus is probably '47, although the fine '61 has yet to show its full paces. There are those who find Pétrus almost too full and rich, too heavy and concentrated and prefer a rather lighter Pomerol such as Vieux-Château-Certan, where the flavour is more subtle. I can see the point of the criticism, but do find Pétrus a splendid wine in a good year. I have drunk the '47 against Cheval-Blanc '47, and found that the latter had more character though not so much concentration. On this occasion I was in a minority in preferring the St-Emilion. The '49 has been very fine too. Until the 1956 frosts Pétrus was sold in cask as well as in bottle, and wines like the '50 (an excellent wine in this variable, lesser year), '52, and '53 could be bought in Britain for 15s. or so a bottle, English-bottled. Now the whole crop is château-bottled, usually about two and a half years after the vintage. The name is of course taken from St Peter, who figures on the excessively old-fashioned label. Since the death of Mme Loubat in November 1961, the property has been owned partly by her family (her niece Mme Lily Lacoste is head of the company), and partly by Jean-Pierre Moueix, who also markets a quarter of the crop of Cheval-Blanc in which he likewise has a financial interest.

Vieux-Château-Certan which lies very near Pétrus is generally accorded now the unofficial first rank given it over 40 years ago. Until 1858 it belonged to the May family and was then bought by M. Charles de Bousquet. In 1893 the average output was only 15 *tonneaux*. The vineyard area is about twice that of Pétrus, but the output is less than double, about 55 *tonneaux*. It is a remarkably full, velvety wine and like its neighbour the château's reputation in Britain has greatly increased in the last twenty years; although this wine has always been sought-after in Belgium, possibly because the owners, the brothers Thienpont, are Belgian wine merchants. In recent years the whole crop has been château-bottled. I myself have only drunk post-war vintages with the exception of a bottle of '28, powerful deep-coloured but with a curious burnt taste, which I drank in Bordeaux in 1967. However the '47 was an exceptionally fine wine, and the '55 was one of the most successful wines in a vintage often disappointing to me considering its early *réclame*. In that year Vieux-Château-Certan may well have surpassed Pétrus.

I have two recollections of visits there. During the vintage I was surprised to see a baboon tethered just out of reach of the vines, which the animal was making strenuous, noisy efforts to reach; and a number of ponies similarly staked. M. Thienpont explained that the pickers were gypsies who came every year, bringing with them their livestock. He then led me in to taste the previous year's wine. At first he seemed uncertain into which cask to insert his *pipette*. This was partly because the *égalisage* had not taken place, so his Merlot was in one cask and Bouchet in another; but also because he wanted me to taste from a good cask. For never, said he, taste from a cask near the cellar door, as the wind gets at it; always taste from a cask in the middle of the cellar. An inside tip.

Just across the road is Ch. Certan, once part of the same estate as its neighbour, and more recently known as Certan-Demay. (There is also a Certan-Giraud and Certan-Marzelle, both less renowned.) This growth is only about a quarter the size of Vieux-Château-Certan in output, but at times it has made some admirable wine, of which the '47 was an outstanding example and the '49 no less so. Since then it seems to have lost a little ground, although the '50 and '53 were both very agreeable; yet I have not come upon a particularly fine post-frost vintage.

There are a number of other claimants to leading rank in Pomerol. Possibly because they are small and perhaps owe their position to one man – or woman – their reputations seem to vary. For example L'Evangile was a Pomerol with a considerable reputation in the 1920s, and its vineyard signs immediately opposite Cheval-Blanc bear the inscription 'L'Evangile Haut-Pomerol', although it would be difficult to say how the situation was any higher than its neighbours. I remember a '24, from Avery's, which though a little tenuous aged twenty years and more was still a wine of distinction. I may have been unlucky but I did not come upon another vintage for many years. Then I drank the '59 several times, and very good it was, although not in the top flight. The growth makes about the same amount of wine as Pétrus.

Another in the same class is its neighbour La Conseillante, which also adjoins Cheval-Blanc. Before the last war this château was one of the best known of all Pomerols, and still today has a good reputation; but once again I have not found it outstanding in recent years, although the '49 was very fine, and the '53 agreeable. Yet it has been surpassed by others which would have been little known a generation earlier. Production is about 35 *tonneaux* and the price is high.

Yet another estate is La Pointe, one of the larger Pomerol growths and prominent to the left of the road from Libourne. As Pomerols went a hundred years ago it was fairly well known and its 1865 was sold at 1,500 frs. the *tonneau*, on a level with fifth growth Médocs. One of the most enjoyable '34s from any Bordeaux district was La Pointe, and, bottled by Avery, it was still good when over thirty years old; a wine of great concentration of flavour. Even in that *annus mirabilis* for Pomerols, 1947, La Pointe stood out. Since then I have drunk acceptable but generally rather unexciting wines from this property, which produces about 70 *tonneaux*. Sometimes the wines have lacked acidity. The '64, however, is said to be excellent.

Many other châteaux are making excellent wine, and often they are growths that used to be little known. One is La Croix-de-Gay, situated in the main street of the village of Pomerol, and directed from a modest enough villa. My attention was drawn to it by a superb '47 bottled by Harveys, and one of the finest Pomerols of that year; although now beginning to show age it still is a delicious wine, and my only regret is that I have never had the chance to drink the château-bottled wine to discover if it were even better. I then acquired the '45, also bottled by Harveys, a beautifully mature claret with a brown tint that makes one at first think it must be a wine of the 1920s. The '43 was very good too, and, coming forward, so was the delicious '49, in this case bottled by the Wine Society. The '52, with that toughness but fullness of flavour that marked the best Pomerols of that year, is also a good wine. I believe the château was less successful for a few years, but I have added the '64 to my collection without regrets. La Croix-de-Gay has always been liked in Belgium.

Another up-and-coming Pomerol has been Clos René, a further Harveian find for me, with the '53 at 9s. a bottle: a soft, but deliciously rounded wine. The '52 was bigger and firmer, and the '61, bottled by Christophers of London has all the flavour one could expect from a Pomerol. I have particularized the English-bottlings here, because one is unlikely to find many château-bottlings of these smaller, less famous Pomerols. Making the wine is their concern, and they would rather sell it in cask. So one quite often comes upon Bordeaux bottlings, not least by Cruse who have made a speciality of interesting Pomerols. With reference to Clos René '61 a comparison between a Bordeaux bottling and one by Christophers gave the palm unquestionably to the latter. Maybe the wine in France had been left too long in cask, a not infrequent occurrence when lesser growths are concerned. Clos René, situated in the village of Pomerol, with a garden round the house, is a typically unselfconscious Pomerol vineyard. The wine, in which there is a large proportion of Merlot and some Malbec, is powerful and well flavoured. Production is now around 60 *tonneaux* and Clos René is no longer the inexpensive wine that it used to be.

Near at hand is a third growth in the same excellent class, L'Enclos, which produces 40 – 50 *tonneaux* from a *vignoble* which is 70 per cent Merlot, 20 per cent Bouchet and 10 per cent Cabernet-Sauvignon and Malbec. This may be regarded as a common Pomerol vineyard make-up. The cellar in which one tastes the wine is below the house itself. The oldest l'Enclos I have drunk was a '29, opened in the company of Cruse's London agents, Rutherford, Osborne & Perkin two or three years ago. Certainly it was showing its age, and the colour was very brown, but the wine was delicious. Much younger, the '45 was another exceptional vintage of this area, while the '53 remains a rival of the Clos René.

There are other Pomerols with no very wide reputation which I have met perhaps only in one or two vintages, and they have then passed me by. One of these has the unwieldy name of La Grave-Trigant-de-Boisset (the three latter words were a former owner's name), whose '55 was another Harvey find in the days when that great claret lover Harry Waugh was their claret scout and buyer. With more acidity than many

'55s, it was that much more successful and agreeable, but I have not met it since. Another '55 in the same class was Lacabanne, just near the Pomerol church with its prominent spire. This is quite a fair-sized property making 40 *tonneaux*; the '55 was excellent but I have not seen it again. Pomerol is indeed an area worth exploring, but one can easily lose the way there amid the jig-saw pattern of small vineyards.

Although Pomerol is a smaller area than St-Emilion, with less than 700 hectares under vines, there appears to be a larger number of fairly well-known vineyards. Of these Gazin is one and Nénin another. These are among the largest Pomerol vineyards and their wine probably the most exported. Each produces between 80 and 100 *tonneaux*. Gazin was particularly badly stricken in the 1956 frosts. In spite of its wide reputation I have usually found Gazin a rather clumsy, sometimes coarse wine, although the '45 has been exceptionally fine. Nénin, which is opposite La Pointe, has always seemed to me rather dull, although the proprietor, M. Despujol, is an engaging enthusiast for his wine. In recent years he has built new cellars and is constantly concerned for the improvement of his vineyard. While being a sound wine, Nénin lacks the appealing concentration of flavour so attractive in the best Pomerols. There is also a Lafleur-du-Gazin which makes very amiable wine; a small growth. It takes its name partly from Lafleur, which is near Pétrus and is owned by the Mlles Robin. Although this small growth, producing only about 12 *tonneaux*, has a good name, apart from a fine '61 I have not found it in any way outstanding. The same applies to Le Gay which is in the same hands.

The swapping of names is no less prevalent in Pomerol than in St-Emilion, and there are a number of combinations, adopting names calculated to bring prestige to less well-known growths. It would be impossible to do this today, as charges of 'passing-off' would soon be made, but these names have the acceptance of tradition. Indeed it is not rare to find that a growth can use several names, and might do so for a second wine. A well-known double name is Lafleur-Pétrus, now owned by Jean-Pierre Moueix. For some reason it has a flag on its label, giving it a shipping-line appearance. The property produces about 30 *tonneaux*, and is well known in Britain. I have in the past found it rather a heavy wine and prefer Trotanoy which is also owned by J-P. Moueix, and produces 25 *tonneaux*. But both are now making fine wine. Trotanoy is normally a rich wine with plenty of flavour, and would certainly rank among the top twelve in the district. Another property is Petit-Village, which belongs to M. Pierre Ginestet. This is certainly one of the finer Pomerols and it made a particularly distinguished '47. In 1956 the 10-hectare vineyard was wiped out by frost. Production is about 45 *tonneaux*, and the wine is one of the more expensive of the area, but certainly one to watch. For these parts it has the unusually large Cabernet-Sauvignon proportion of 55 per cent, with 10 per cent Cabernet-Franc and 35 per cent Merlot.

A Pomerol growth that has confused not a few drinkers is Latour-Pomerol. It has not always been made clear on wine lists that this is a Pomerol, and on occasion it has at least been ordered if not drunk as the more famous Pauillac *premier cru*. It was owned by Mme Loubat of Pétrus, and on those rather few occasions when I have drunk it – aware of the true origin – I have thought it a fine wine. With an output of about 30 *tonneaux*, Latour-Pomerol is one of the better-known wines of this lesser star-studded district. The vineyard is run by the ubiquitous J-P. Moueix.

Indeed there are so many Pomerol wines that have edged into my drinking and then not been encountered again that it is impossible to generalize about them. Among those which I remember are: de Sales, one of the largest but not a very inspiring growth; Plince, a well-known name but not one that has impressed me; Rouget which has produced one or two very agreeable wines; Domaine de l'Eglise, a medium-to-good quality wine; Clinet, a wine with a traditional name but not remarkable in my experience; Bougneuf, a medium wine that can show well in good years, but is not exceptional: Lagrange, another J-P. Moueix property, sometimes mistaken for its namesake in the Médoc, but not striking; La Commanderie, run-of-the mill; Mouli-net, respectable but not exciting. I offer these comments for what they are worth, and would not claim too much for them. There may be other surprisingly good wines among the ranks of *soi-disants premiers crus*, *deuxièmes premiers crus* and *deuxièmes crus* which march across the Pomerol plateau. In the 1949 edition of Cocks et Féret is listed L'Enclos-du-Presbytère. Its production is given as a mere 3 *tonneaux* and its owner 'le curé de Pomerol'. It is to be hoped that his vineyard is a substantial assist-ance with his pastoral problems. How many of his parishioners emerge from the Pomerol presbytery with the comfortable delusion that 'presbyter is but priest writ large'?

One straight main road (*RN.10-bis*, Bordeaux-Paris) runs through Pomerol from Libourne in a north-easterly direction and crosses the small stream named the Bar-banne, which flows from the east to join the l'Isle just before the latter enters the Dor-dogne on the west side of Libourne. Nearly all the better growths of Pomerol are on the east side of the road, with one or two exceptions such as Clos René and L'Enclos. The vineyards shade off into the commune of Libourne. Beyond the Barbanne lie the two associated sub-districts of Pomerol: Néac on the right and Lalande-de-Pome-rol on the left. On the eastern side of Néac is Montagne-St-Emilion, but if one enters this small area by the road from Montagne one notices a difference at once. The anonymity of the vineyards gives way to name-plates, and by a hamlet a notice board announces '*Néac-Ses Grands Vins*'. The country is more broken up and the miniature valley of the Barbanne *en passant* looks agreeably rural and remote, affording some relief from the monotony of vineyards. The village of Néac is by the stream, and then one ascends a slight hill on to the Pomerol plateau, with Pétrus and other well-known names at hand.

The Néac wines are not very well known, although entitled to their own *appellation* until 1954 when they were merged with Lalande. Total output of the two is about 24,000 hectolitres. I suspect many of them dodge under the net and are sold as Pom-erols. There are Tournefeuille, Belles-Graves, Moncets, Siaurac and Moulin-à-Vent, all producing 40 *tonneaux* or more a year, but I claim little experience of them. Siaurac, formerly owned by a deputy of the Gironde is now the property of the Baronne Gui-chard and yields 100 *tonneaux* from 30 hectares. The wine is sound.

Some of the Lalande wines are better known, and among my early purchases before the last war was a delicious Bel-Air '29 – not to be confused with the growth in

St-Emilion. This growth, which in the 1868 Cocks et Féret headed the small Lalande list, still has a good reputation and is near the main road dividing Lalande from Pomerol proper. The district was once the property of the Templars, and the village of Lalande has a twelfth-century church, with a *clocher* over the round-arched west door. There is a sharp change in the aspect of the country and the vineyards as soon as one crosses the main road from the highly cultivated, disciplined-looking commune of Pomerol. Although Lalande-de-Pomerol also proclaims '*Ses Grands Vins*', this is mixed farming country, as in Néac, and the vines are less dominant and concentrated, less well cared-for in appearance. No doubt this reflects not only the smaller reputation of the wines but of the prices they can command. In style the wines of these two lesser communes are rather coarser and with less finesse than the Pomerols. Not far away to the west, beyond *RN.10-bis*, from Libourne to Coutras, lies Fronsac whose 'mountain' overlooking the Dordogne is clearly visible from Lalande; and perhaps the wines slightly resemble each other. In addition to Bel-Air the better-known châteaux selling under the Lalande *appellation* include La Commanderie and Perron. Considering how near Libourne is, this little strip of country is very quiet. A railway line runs through it, and to return to the town one has to summon the keeper of an apparently not too greatly used level-crossing to raise the gates for the car.

The wines of the commune of Libourne are not of great significance and are entitled only to the *appellations* Bordeaux or Bordeaux Supérieur. They are either wines of the *palus* by the river or *sables*.

The reader will have gathered that I have a particular affection for the wines of Pomerol, without in any way wavering in my ultimate allegiance to those of the Médoc and the red Graves. It is common for serious wine drinkers in France to maintain contact with small growers in the various wine areas, and these latter furnish them with regular supplies of their wine. If I lived in France I do not doubt that one of my *petits fournisseurs* would be in Pomerol; and to keep him up to the mark regular visits would be necessary.

14. Fronsac, Bourg & Blaye

Large quantities of wine are made in the lesser districts on the right bank of the Dordogne and Gironde. They amount so far as the local *appellations* are concerned to about 15 per cent of the total Bordeaux production which averages 3 million hecto-litres. Then there are the Bordeaux and Bordeaux Supérieur *appellations* which are not confined to this area, and which altogether account for about one-third of Bordeaux's output. The best of these lesser right-bank wines are red; the Fronsadais have the highest reputation and fetch the best price, while the white Blayais are probably the least good.

As is normal the best wines come from the Côtes and are entitled to a higher *appellation*, whether it be Canon-Fronsac, Côtes de Bourg or Premières Côtes de Blaye. The lower *appellations* are Côtes de Fronsac (there is no plain Fronsac *appellation*), and Blaye or Blayais; but Bourg and Bourgeais rank equally with their Côtes wines.

The Fronsac wines are big and fruity, but by no means coarse, and in style like the lesser St-Emilions; the Canon wines in particular can be very agreeable, though without the finer points of the better St-Emilions. The country is picturesque and the Tertre de Fronsac rises to a high point overlooking the Dordogne and across to the Entre-Deux-Mers. But the vines do not climb as high as the top of this hill. The district begins a mile or so to the west of Libourne, across the little river l'Isle, which here joins the Dordogne, its last tributary of any size. Down by the river are level *palus* vineyards, which produces no more than Bordeaux or Bordeaux Supérieur wines, but as the ground rises the growths are entitled to one or other of the two Fronsac *appellations*.

The whole area of Fronsac consists of between 15 and 20 villages spreading inland from the river across a plateau. On the west it approaches the two long bridges that carry the Bordeaux-Paris railway and *RN.10*, the Paris road. One of these bridges was built by Gustave Eiffel. The best known of the villages apart from Fronsac itself on the eastern fringe are St-Michel-de-Fronsac, La Rivière and St-Germain-la-Rivière. The last named of these is entitled only to Bordeaux and Bordeaux Supérieur *appellations*, but one or two of the other villages, such as St-Aignan and Saillans, which are indeed on the Côtes are allowed the Côtes de Fronsac *appellation*. Part of St-Michel is entitled to the Canon-Fronsac *appellation*. The large output of 50 hectolitres per hectare is permitted under the Bordeaux *appellation*, but this is cut to 40 for the Supérieur, which is 2 hectolitres less than allowed the two Fronsac titles. For these and the Bordeaux Supérieur *appellation* a minimum strength of 10·5 degrees is prescribed, but Bordeaux may be as low as 10 degrees, which is light for a red wine. White wine is only made in the minor Fronsadais areas, and this is only allowed the two Bordeaux *appellations*, with output of 50 hectolitres and 10·5 degrees and 40 hectolitres and 11·5 degrees respectively. Canon-Fronsac produces about 11,000 hectolitres, and Côtes de Fronsac 25,000.

The best-known château is probably Canon in the Côtes Canon-Fronsac area. It must not be confused with the well-known St-Emilion growth, nor indeed with several other adjacent châteaux in Fronsac which have adopted the name. There is even another Canon in St-Michel-de-Fronsac, with a pleasant view over the river. Such a prospect is shared by several of the other attractively placed Côtes châteaux, including Junayme whose conspicuously prosperous nineteenth-century house is enclosed in very fine magnolia trees. The soil is rich hereabouts and the wine correspondingly powerful. Another well-known growth is Bodet, which has given rise to several little Bodets, not forgetting Vrai-Canon-Bodet-La-Tour. Also in Fronsac itself are Gaby, Domaine de Toumalin, La Dauphine, not unknown in Britain, and La Croix. Down by the river is the extremely prolific Château La France, whose name no doubt helps it to dispose of an enormous crop of about 500 *tonneaux*.

Names of Fronsac growths are not of great importance to wine drinkers outside France, but most British wine merchants will have a Fronsac or two early on their claret lists. The first Fronsacs I remember bore the imposing name of Larcheveque and before the last war I bought the 1934 vintage from Berry Bros. at the even then very moderate price of 3s. a bottle. It was a well-balanced, not too strong wine and the late Charles Walter Berry told me that the celebrated and fashionable doctor Lord Dawson of Penn, physician to George V, was so impressed with a trial dozen, that he ordered first another 20 dozen, and then called in at the famous St James's Street premises to secure yet another 20 dozen. He liked a reliable bottle of claret a day. It had been sold to Berry's by M. René Danglade, and when I visited the latter in the summer of 1939, with an introduction from Charles Walter Berry, I was asked if I would like to be shown the source of this wine. It turned out to be a very modest seat for an archbishop.

I must mention M. Danglade's own property, Ch. Rouet, situated high up in St-Germain-la-Rivière. From the terrace of the eighteenth-century château is probably the finest view anywhere in the region, looking across the Entre-Deux-Mers. In a fit of pique the German detachment which occupied the château in 1940 departed from their general policy of being '*toujours correcte*' towards the Bordelais, and burnt the place down. After the war it took M. Roger Danglade, the present proprietor and a wine merchant like his father, many years to restore this charming house. Rouet is a large estate and produces over a hundred *tonneaux* of red wine.

To sum up, Fronsac wines can be excellent and they are often under-appreciated, partly perhaps because of careless vinification in the past; also, because like their neighbours in Bourg and Blaye they are often drunk too young. The best Fronsadais are certainly worth keeping for up to ten years.

North of Fronsac lie the two small communes of Coutras and Guîtres, both in the l'Isle valley, with the former lying upstream beyond Lussac and the lesser St-Emilion villages. In the Middle Ages Guîtres was quite a well-known vineyard area, largely owing to its river communications, as well as being near the Roman road from Bordeaux to Périgueux. It is amusing to note that the Guîtres wines suffered from the same disabilities *vis-à-vis* St-Emilion as did the Haut-Pays production in Bordeaux: they could not be transported by water or road to St-Emilion, including Libourne, until St Martin's Day (11 November).

These wines are not of great importance today; production limitations are those of their Bordeaux and Bordeaux Supérieur *appellations*, and white wine is made in the 24 villages which comprise the two communes. This area is one of those to have suffered a decline in vineyard area over the last twenty years. After the 1956 frosts many growers accepted compensation to pull up their vines.

Also worth mentioning here is a half circle of lesser wine villages, entitled to the two basic Bordeaux *appellations*, which begins in Libourne, runs round the outside of the Pomerol and St-Emilion communes and south of Coutras, and joins the Dordogne at Castillon. There are twenty-two of these communes, all small villages with the exception of Libourne at one end and Castillon at the other. Probably the best known of them, on historic rather than viticultural grounds, is Monbadon, whose château I have already mentioned. Here is produced 120 *tonneaux* of red wine, much more commonly grown in this area than white. No doubt in earlier times the wines from all these outlying parts were sold as St-Emilions.

In and around Castillon there are now two small *sub-appellations* authorized by the *I.N.A.O.* In Castillon itself and eight other nearby communes, the red wines may be labelled Côtes de Castillon after the *appellation* Bordeaux. To the north of Castillon the red and white wines of Francs, Monbadon and three other communes may be labelled Bordeaux Supérieur Côtes de Francs; and the white wines of Monbadon commune are entitled to the same labelling. One of the villages, Les-Salles-de-Castillon, is divided between these two *sub-appellations*, which are not significant enough to have their *récolte* output listed separately; it is included in the Bordeaux and Bordeaux Supérieur totals. The soil in this undulating country is largely lime or clay, with alluvial deposits from the Dordogne. The chief red grape is the Merlot, the most popular white the Sémillon.

FRONSAC, WITH COUTRAS AND GUÎTRES (1)

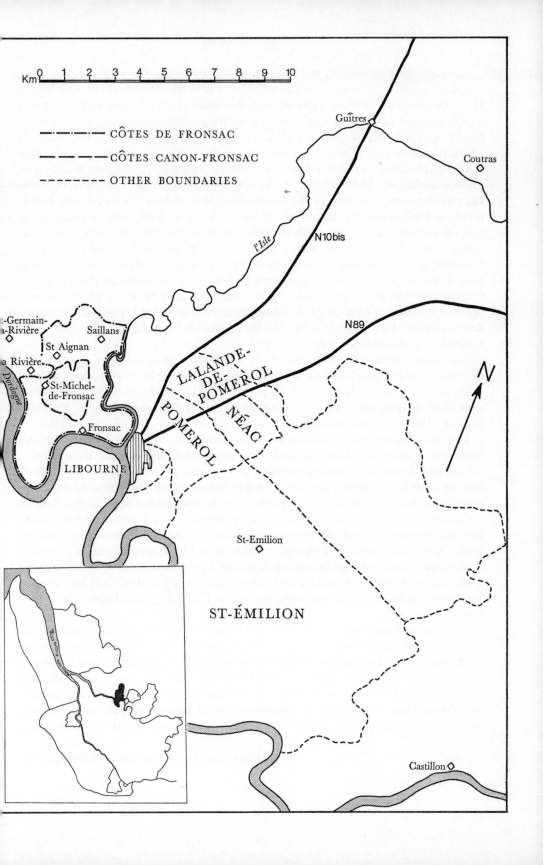

Km 0 1 2 3 4 5 6 7 8 9 10

CÔTES DE FRONSAC
CÔTES CANON-FRONSAC
OTHER BOUNDARIES

Guîtres

Coutras

l'Isle

N10bis

N89

-Germain-
-a-Rivière

Saillans

St Aignan

a Rivière

St-Michel-
de-Fronsac

LALANDE-
DE-
POMEROL

POMEROL

NÉAC

Dordogne

Fronsac

N

LIBOURNE

St-Emilion

ST-ÉMILION

Castillon

Rather more significant is the Cubzadais, which runs to the west of Guîtres and across the north of Fronsac, and the chief town is St-André-de-Cubzac, well known to motorists on the Paris-Bordeaux road. Its wines carry the two basic Bordeaux *appellations*, and large quantities of white wine are made as well as red. The red wines are inclined to be rather 'plummy', but of course they can have that touch of quality which Bordeaux gives. There are nine communes, and the soil is chiefly lime and clay.

In the area there are two well-known properties. The first, Château du Bouilh, is an historic monument better known for its vast though incomplete range of buildings than for the wine. Designed by the famous Bordeaux architect, Victor Louis, for the family of La Tour du Pin, if completed this would surely have been his masterpiece, and on a scale almost comparable with that of Versailles. Only one side of an enormous 'quad' was completed, and a building now known as *Le Grand Pavillon*, but even that was not finished. What is charming is a *'Hémicycle'* of two-storey buildings, with a chapel preceded by columns and pediment in the centre of the half-circle. Other 'works' of this huge architectural conception may be seen. The whole was planned to welcome Louis XVI on a progress that he intended to make in the region. Before this could take place, the Revolution arrived and the building operations were stopped. It is well worth a visit.

The wine is kept in the limestone caves which abound in this area. No less than 300 *tonneaux* of red wine, and 75 of white and *rosé* are made here, and the cellars and ex-quarries are full of casks. Much of the wine here, as throughout the right-bank wine districts, is disposed of direct to private customers throughout France. A proportion is sold in small casks for home-bottling.

The other property is Terrefort in Cubzac-les-Ponts, which is owned and well publicized locally by Marcel Quancard, a substantial firm of wine merchants at La Grave-d'Ambarès. Terrefort produces 100 *tonneaux* of red wine and 50 of white, and the wine is well made. The estate used to belong to the Monbadon family. Two well-known names occur in the Cubzadais. At St-André there is a Ch. Beychevelle and in St-Gervais a Cru Cantemerle. (In Blaye there is a Ch. Cantemerle too.) These produce substantial quantities of wine, but have, of course, no connection with the Médoc properties, although I have seen them offered in Britain; if wine drinkers see these names at surprisingly low prices they had better look at the *appellation* on the label. The wines are by no means bad. I have sampled all of them, but they are not on the *cru classé* level. The vineyard area in the Cubzadais has declined in recent years.

Bourg wines have a wider reputation than those of Cubzac, and the best reds can be very attractive. They are usually more vigorous and with more character than the neighbouring Blayais; the red are certainly better than the white. Franck, writing more than a hundred years ago, says that the Bourg wines were preferred to the Médocs, by which he meant the general run of wines in the latter district, and not the *crus classés*. This was because the Bourgeais wines were fruity and had plenty of body; and Franck goes on to say that the Bordeaux trade would only use Bourg

BOURG AND BLAYE WITH CUBZADAIS (2)

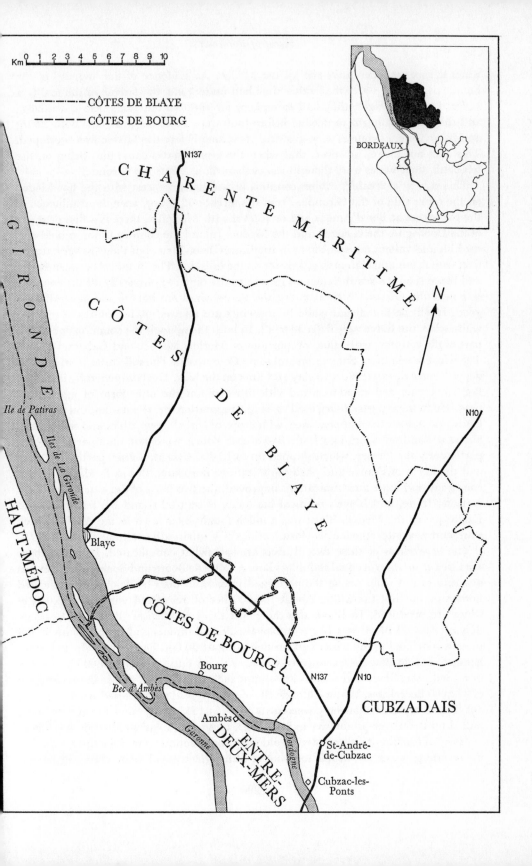

Km 0 1 2 3 4 5 6 7 8 9 10

—·—·—·— CÔTES DE BLAYE
—·—·—·— CÔTES DE BOURG

BORDEAUX

N137

C H A R E N T E   M A R I T I M E

N

G
I
R
O
N
D
E

C
Ô
T
E
S

D
E

B
L
A
Y
E

N10

Ile de Patiras

Iles de La Gironde

HAUT-MÉDOC

Blaye

CÔTES DE BOURG

Bourg

Bec d'Ambès

Ambès

Garonne

Dordogne

ENTRE-DEUX-MERS

N137   N10

CUBZADAIS

St-André-
de-Cubzac

Cubzac-les-
Ponts

wines to mix with the '*petits vins*' of the Médoc. As evidence of the 'bigness' of the Bourgeais, Franck states that unless they had undergone 'the fatigue of the sea' (i.e. suffered a sea voyage), they had to be kept for eight to ten years before drinking; and they did not begin to decline before they were 25 to 30 years old. Both Bourg and Blaye were, of course, wine-growing areas long before the Médoc was developed. This does not mean, however, that when the great estates came into being on the left bank, their wines were thought less of than those across the Gironde.

This is very agreeable, rolling country, providing a contrast with the flat Médoc on the other side of the Gironde. From the terrace of Bourg, near the confluence of the two rivers at Bec d'Ambès and on a level with Margaux, there is a fine prospect of the Dordogne, the Gironde and the Médoc. Inland the country is not so bold and the hills and valleys not so steep as in the Entre-Deux-Mers, but they are very attractive, with farms and *chais* attractively set on the hillsides. The 'frontier' between Bourg and Blaye is only a small rivulet on its way to the estuary; physically all the countryside near the Gironde is similar, but the Blaye wines are lighter and generally less good. It will be noted that while Bourg wines are allowed 50 hectolitres of red and white wine, the Blaye vary from 50 to 42. In both the *cépage* is the common one in this part of the country, with equal proportions of Merlot, Malbec and Cabernet-Franc. The white is Sémillon, Sauvignon and some Colombard. The soil varies from alluvial deposits near the waterside, to clay and lime on the hills. The land generally is rich by Bordeaux vineyard standards and viticulture is not the only form of agriculture practised in these parts. Bourg used to have a reputation for its potatoes, and today the landscape has a varied appearance, with crops of cereals, vegetables and fruit. Until about a hundred years ago both Blaye and Bourg were not unimportant ports, particularly the former, which shipped up to 15,000 *tonneaux* a year, partly to Rouen and the north of France and partly upstream to Bordeaux. But as Bordeaux's influence grew and road communications improved, the two ports of the estuary lost their carrying trade, and Blaye's nautical life today is centred round the ferry across to Lamarque in the Médoc. Blaye was a much fought-over town in the Anglo-French wars, and even later; the massive fortifications of Vauban still overhang the river front.

The *appellations* of these two districts are somewhat complicated. In Bourg there are three *appellations* of equal standing: Bourg, Côtes de Bourg and Bourgeais. An excess quantity of red wine above the permitted maximum may be de-classed and called Bordeaux, but not the white. About 100,000 hectolitres of red wine and 35,000 of white are produced. In Blaye also there are three *appellations*: Premières Côtes de Blaye, Côtes de Blaye and Blaye or Blayais. For all intents and purposes the first of these is restricted to red wine, and produces about 50,000 hectolitres. On the other hand, Côtes de Blaye is exclusively white, with an output of only 6,000 hectolitres in a good year. Blaye and Blayais are almost exclusively white, and make an average of 250,000 hectolitres. White Côtes de Blaye may be sold as de-classed Bordeaux, but not Blaye/Blayais. Following government offers in 1953 of premiums to growers who pulled up their over-productive hybrid vines, these two areas' production has fallen.

Many of the Bourg estates have an old tradition of sound wine. Like the Fronsadais many Bourg wines are drunk too young, although in good years they still have a reputation of lasting twenty-five years or more. Both Bourg and Blaye have a hierarchy of estates without official backing, but this is an indication of relative quality. It runs: *premier cru bourgeois, cru bourgeois, premier cru artisan, cru artisan, en palus*. There is also a *premier cru de Bourg*. In the first rank in Bourg there is du Bousquet, belonging to the de Barry family for well over a century. It produces 150 *tonneaux*. An even larger production comes from another well-known growth, de Barbe, which makes 220 *tonneaux*, mostly red. The composition of that part of the vineyard is 50 per cent Cabernet-Franc, 40 per cent Merlot and 10 per cent Malbec, which can be seen to differ considerably from the norm. This is a typical 'country growth', with a big old-fashioned *chai* on one side of a courtyard reached through an archway. Inside the *chai* are rows of cement tanks. I have found the red wine fruity and 'substantial' and better than the slightly sweet though acceptable white. Among the other better-known estates are Croûte-Charlus, Tayac, Eyquem (does the name confuse anyone?), La Croix-Millorit, Blissa, Rousset, Thau (a romantic-looking fortified castle on a hill), Mendoce and La Tour-Séguy and Mille-Secousses, whose 'shaking' wine was served on the old Great Western Railway to the delight of Maurice Healy. The list is arbitrary and nearly every Bordeaux merchant would produce a different one. Indeed this is unknown country to most of them, and when I have visited Bourg, Blaye and Fronsac growths in their company, they have usually brought with them a broker to act as pilot to estates which lie, outwardly unnamed, up narrow roads and down winding lanes.

The co-operatives play a considerable part in these areas. There are at least five in Bourg and four in Blaye. The one I visited at Tauriac, in Blaye is typical. Situated opposite the derelict Château du Pia, another work attributed to Victor Louis, its large concrete bulk has the factory air common to wine co-ops. This one turns out 16,000 hectolitres of white wine and 12,000 of red, and the variations in quality largely rest on alcoholic strength. There are 180 members, and I found nothing to complain about in the wine, much of which is sold to the Bordeaux merchants for blending.

So far as Blaye is concerned, my own experience of vineyard visiting is even more limited. There is a Barbé, distinguished from the Bourg growth by the elimination of a 'de' and the addition of an acute accent on the final 'e'. I remember a surprisingly good '58 when the wine was about seven years old. I have visited the pleasantly situated and attractively built Lescadre, where M. Paul Carreau makes 150 *tonneaux* of a wine big and fruity for a Blaye. Other well-considered growths include the curiously-named Sociando, Le Virou, Petits-Arnauds and Monconseil. Off-the-main track there is Le Menaudat, associated with the Cruse family and whose wine one may see on an English list. The better-known estates of Bourg and Blaye find regular customers in Belgium and Holland. In the more outlying communes of Blaye white wine increasingly predominates, and only white can be called Côtes de Blaye. North and east they almost reach the departmental border, and beyond that is the Charente-Maritime, where the grapes one sees there will be made into brandy, though not of the finer quality which comes from much further north.

My comments on these right-bank wines have been scattered like the properties themselves. This is charming country in which to wander, and the village restaurants will not fail to provide a satisfying midday meal and a local wine list wherever one happens to find oneself between midday and 2 p.m. With the left-bank red wines now so dear, there is a case for taking a leaf out of the book of the thousands of French wine drinkers who enjoy the wines they order regularly from Fronsac, Cubzac, Bourg and Blaye. In our case it is not wise to order direct but to rely on our wine merchants, who already usually list one or two and may turn more to them. Not distinguished wines, they are however the essential red Bordeaux which for centuries have helped to build the reputation of claret. Just because they are cheap they should not be quaffed young, but kept until they are fully mature. However, they must not be expected to match their rivals across the estuary.

Now that every district has its own dressing-up publicity organization, it is not surprising that Blaye, Bourg and the Premières Côtes de Bordeaux are united in the *Conétablie de Guyenne,* which assembles in the fine château at Cadillac in the Premières Côtes. Even the Bordeaux and Bordeaux Supérieurs have their *Compagnons de Bordeaux.*

15. Sweet White Wines

The Sauternes district lies about 25 miles south-east of Bordeaux, and is generally reached by the *RN.113*, which leads on to Toulouse and to the Central Pyrenees. Just short of it lies Cérons and opposite, on the right bank of the Garonne, are the two small districts of Loupiac and Ste-Croix-du-Mont. To reach them from the left bank, the river must be crossed either from near Cérons to Cadillac, or beyond the Sauternes area at Langon. This left-bank area is a very old one and there is a mention of a vineyard in Preignac in the eighth century A.D. The soil is poor, composed of chalk and stony gravel with a sub-soil containing clay. In Barsac the soil is less gravelly, contains more clay and has a chalky sub-soil. The clay is more prominent on the low hillsides of the district. The Cérons district is more gravelly and flinty, with sub-soil of clay and stones. Across the river on the hillsides the vineyards of Loupiac and Ste-Croix-du-Mont are a mixture of stones, clay and chalk, but rather more gravelly on the top of the slopes.

These lesser districts are allowed to produce with *appellation* more wine than the five Sauternes communes: 40 hl. per hectare compared with 25. While the latter must have a minimum alcoholic strength of 13 degrees, and so must the two right-bank districts, Cérons need only be 12·5 degrees. Throughout, only the sweet wines are entitled to these *appellations*; the dry varieties are Bordeaux Supérieur.

The main grapes throughout are the Sémillon, which accounts for from two-thirds to four-fifths of production, and the Sauvignon, which represents the remainder, except for a certain amount of Muscadelle, as detailed below in referring to the individual vineyards. There is even a little Ugniblanc.

The fine sweet white wines of Bordeaux are currently the most under-appreciated

223

and under-valued table wines in the world. This is not because people do not like them, for I have never known anyone refuse a glass of a fine Sauternes or Barsac at the end of a meal; and the engagingly luscious liquor often elicits more appreciative comment than the red wines that have preceded it. The drop in demand is part of the decline in popularity of all dessert wines, unless we include therein the so-called 'cream' sherries. Also nowadays a bottle of sweet white Bordeaux does not seem so integral a part of a meal as a bottle of dry white wine from Bordeaux or elsewhere earlier on. However genuine Sauternes cannot be among the very cheap white wines, for the method of production is expensive, and at the lower end of the market no doubt many people have fallen for Spanish 'Sauternes', a wine which bears no resemblance to the original except that it is sweet. Finally many of the Sauternes producers have not done their wine much good in the last 30 years by the way they have made it.

Taking this last point first, unfortunately it became the custom on the Bordeaux market in the Inter-War years to buy these sweet white wines by alcoholic strength; the higher the strength the better the price. This still obtains. The minimum strength of a Sauternes entitled to the *appellation* is 13 degrees, but by the use of additional sugar the wine may be forced up to 15, 16 or even 17 degrees. The result is a heavy, unbalanced wine, and the public taste is rightly not in favour of such wines. Further, a good deal of the so-labelled Sauternes has for years been nothing of the kind.

This 'blending', as it is perhaps fairer to call it rather than falsification, has been owing to an alleged refusal of the consumer and the wine merchants to pay for the real thing. So most of the basic 'Sauternes' one sees in off-licences or on wine merchants' lists is a blended wine, with probably a good proportion of sweet Premières Côtes de Bordeaux 'cut in'.

However, in the last few years it is possible that the Sauternais have seen the error of their ways and the desirability of eliminating the errors of others. In 1967 a scheme was adopted according to which there should be a minimum price per *tonneau* for *AC* Sauternes (it was fixed initially at 2,500 francs) in return for which the growers promised to make better wine, to be subject to the tasting approval of independent committees. Further, *en principe*, all Sauternes should be bottled at source. This, however, was seen to be impracticable in the immediate future, so a number of approved Bordeaux merchants were allowed to buy and even to re-sell in cask.

These measures were greeted with some disfavour and scepticism by the Bordeaux merchants. They claimed that there was no improvement in standards of wine making in the next year or so, and that the tasting committees were too apt to pass inferior wines. On the other hand the growers alleged that few merchants were paying the legal minimum. Time alone will show whether the wine will improve before demand increases. Meanwhile, thanks partly to a poor succession of vintages from 1963–5 – and no first-class one since 1961 – the plight of the Sauternes growers is a sad one, and in a number of cases even classed-growths properties are turning over to produce red wine, which only bears the *appellation* Bordeaux Supérieur. Not only is this more saleable, but almost twice the permissible quantity may be produced from a given part

SAUTERNES AND BARSAC

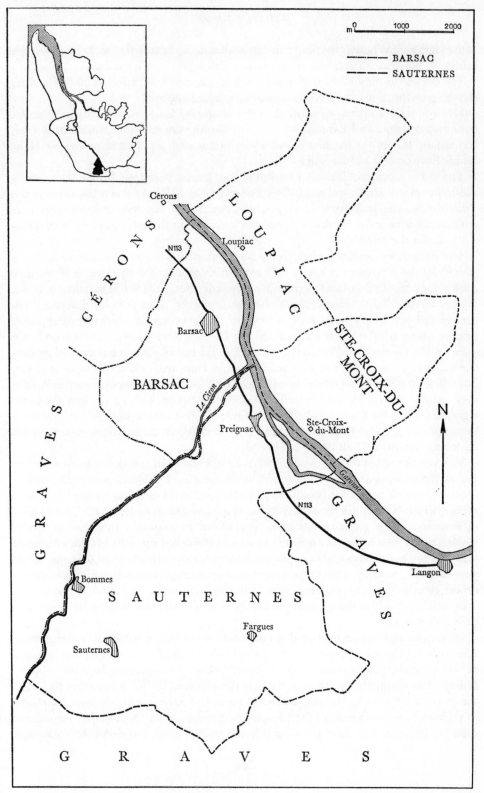

of the vineyard. Whereas the Sauternes *appellation* limits production to 25 hl., often not achieved, Bordeaux Supérieur allows 40 hl., although the price is low.

The decline in the standard of Sauternes has not, of course, affected all the leading classed growths, but most have suffered from the side-effects.

Five communes alone are entitled to the *appellation* Sauternes: Sauternes, Barsac, Bommes, Preignac and Fargues. In addition Barsac may call itself Sauternes-Barsac, but usually leaves out the first name. Descriptions such as Haut Sauternes or Haut Barsac have no official standing.

The soil in Sauternes is similar to that of the Graves, perhaps a little richer, but its sub-soil contains chalk and some clay. For example, half-way down the slope of the Yquem vineyard is a layer of clay which could obstruct the drainage and thus damage the vine roots. So drain pipes have been laid in the sub-soil to carry the rain-water down the hillside.

The particular quality for which Sauternes is esteemed, its aromatic richness, is caused by the *pourriture noble*, or noble rot, which attacks the ripe grapes if weather conditions are suitable from September onwards; but only if the weather is right. Rather warm, slightly humid atmosphere is necessary. This is quite different from the normal rot, or *pourriture grise*, a form of decay caused by excessive damp and against which wine farmers all over the world have to contend. It is, however, the same as the German *edelfäule*, responsible for the luscious *beerenauslesen* and *trocken-beerenauslesen* wines. In a wet year the Sauternes vineyards will suffer from grey rot, but when attacked by *botrytis cinerea* the grapes at first have a slightly rosy hue, then they begin to shrivel up; and indeed look decidedly rotten. However, when one tastes a grape, there is no disagreeable flavour of rot, but instead the juice is sweet beneath the unpunctured withered skin. Under good conditions the *pourriture noble* may set in during the second half of September.

The vintage tends to take place later than elsewhere in the Gironde, in order to ensure the greatest amount of *surmaturité* in the grapes. The picking normally begins about the end of September and may go on as long as six or seven weeks; but if frost occurs, which is rare, the remainder of the crop is picked at once. There is no *Eiswein* in Sauternes! The great estates alone can afford to maintain this slow tempo of picking the grapes only when they are nearly all shrivelled up; a St Martin's Summer is looked for but does not always arrive. At Yquem the vintage may take the better part of three months, with the vintagers going through the vineyards nine or ten times; elsewhere five or six times is usually the maximum. The small growers may wait until as much of the crop as possible is ripe and affected by *pourriture noble* and then pick quickly.

When was the importance of this noble rottenness first discovered in Sauternes? Almost certainly it was known much earlier in Germany. It is said to have originated at Schloss Johannisberg owing to the delayed arrival of a messenger from the princely Bishop of Fulda giving permission to start the vintage. In the intervening fortnight the grapes were attacked by rot, and when picked were kept separate from the others to prevent contamination. In fact, however, the wine from these grapes turned out superbly luscious. The date given for this anecdote is 1716, but certainly Tokay was made from grapes affected by *botrytis cinerea* long before that, and probably as early as the beginning of the seventeenth century, for there was a famous cellar of Tokays dating back to this period in Warsaw until it was destroyed by the Nazis.

The late proprietor of Yquem, the Marquis Bertrand de Lur Saluces, whom I asked about the origin of the deliberate use of rotten grapes in the production of Sauternes, was of the opinion that it began about 1860. He thought also that a German oenologist with experience of the *botrytis cinerea* in the German vineyards helped to develop its acceptance and use in Sauternes. However M. Jean Bureau, *maître de chai* at Yquem, told me that the earliest wine of the château he had ever drunk was the 1845, and he believed that it had been made essentially in the same way as today. The earliest that has come my way has been the 1869. This was but a sample in a medicine bottle and decanted from an ordinary bottle a day or so earlier; the wine was certainly remarkably luscious and deep-coloured.

Yet it is said that there was not much *botrytis* in the district in 1855 when the Sauternes alone were given the distinction of classification alongside the Médocs. There was then as now a certain amount of red wine produced in the district. Nevertheless there is no doubt that the finest wines there were wonderfully luscious, and in the middle of the last century the Russian Tsar's brother Constantine, one of those traditionally sweet-toothed Russian Grand Dukes, paid 20,000 frs. (*c.* £800 then but the equivalent now of about £4,000) for a cask of the 1847 Yquem. In 1861 and 1864, when the first-growth Sauternes sold for the same prices as first-growth Médocs, Yquem made up to 6,000 frs. a cask, higher than for Lafite. In successful years 24,000 frs. a *tonneau* was not infrequently paid for Yquem.

It was in the exceptionally fine year of 1869 that the house of Cruse bought the whole *récolte* from the properties owned by the Marquis de Lur Saluces in Sauternes and Barsac: Yquem, Filhot and Coutet. There was no château-bottling for these wines then, but the whole quantity was bottled by Cruse in their Bordeaux cellars, bearing a label 'Monopole des Crus du Marquis de Lur Saluces'. Most of this was then shipped to the firm's customers in Moscow and St Petersburg. Some indication of the wealth – as well as the taste – of some Russians then was that an important Moscow customer demanded that his Yquem should be bottled in cut glass decanters, with the inscription Château Yquem 1869 engraved in gold on the glass. Although these decanters were corked, they also bore glass stoppers, tied to the neck of the decanter with a silk ribbon.

When comparing the finest Sauternes with the German *trockenbeerenauslesen*, one must bear in mind that whereas the latter seldom attain more than 7 – 8 degrees of alcohol after a long and frequently assisted fermentation – and the same is true of Tokay Essence – the Sauternes may go up to 17 degrees of alcohol quite naturally; often they are 14 or 15 degrees. The German wines, particularly the Moselles, may have more acidity. In comparing them with their French rivals, it should be remembered that while very small quantities of these wines are made in exceptional years (perhaps 100 – 250 bottles), the fine Sauternes are produced in quantity. A celebrated comparison between the two wines in 1867 is mentioned later in connection with Rayne-Vigneau.

The high repute of the Sauternes in the last century is demonstrated by their inclusion in the 1855 classification, when Yquem was placed as the sole *Grand Premier Cru*, eleven châteaux were classed as *Premiers Crus* and twelve as *Deuxièmes Crus*. The list, as amended by subsequent sub-divisions of properties, is below. A hundred years ago Yquem fetched about 20 per cent more than the better first growths, while the seconds sold for 20 – 25 per cent less than these.

The Classification of the Sauternes in 1855

Grand Premier Cru		Deuxièmes Crus	
Yquem	Sauternes	de Myrat	Barsac
Premiers Crus		Doisy-Daëne	Barsac
La Tour-Blanche	Bommes	Doisy-Védrines	Barsac
Clos Haut-Peyraguey	Bommes	d'Arche	Sauternes
Lafaurie-Peyraguey	Bommes	Filhot	Barsac
Rayne-Vigneau	Bommes	Broustet	Sauternes
Suduiraut	Preignac	Nairac	Barsac
Coutet	Barsac	Caillou	Barsac
Climens	Barsac	Suau	Barsac
Guiraud	Sauternes	de Malle	Preignac
Rieussec	Fargues	Romer	Fargues
Rabaud-Promis	Bommes	Lamothe	Sauternes
Sigalas-Rabaud	Bommes		

Yquem was certainly well known in the previous century, for Thomas Jefferson who, as mentioned earlier, visited Bordeaux in May 1787, wrote in French in December of that year to 'M. d'Yquem' asking to buy some of his wine for drinking in France and even after his return to America. 'I know that yours is one of the best growths of Sauterne (*sic*), and it is from your hand that I would prefer to receive it directly, because I shall be sure of receiving it natural, good and sound'. He went on to ask if he could let him have 250 bottles of the 1784, via the American consul, John Bondfield, in Bordeaux.

The Comte de Lur Saluces replied from Yquem on 7 January 1788 that he would draw and bottle the wine desired and hoped he would like it. (The Lur Saluces family had bought this property only in 1785.) Evidently Jefferson did, for in November 1788 he wrote to Bondfield that 'the Sauterne sent me by the Marquis de Saluces turns out very fine'. The following year Jefferson bought five more cases (250 bottles) of Yquem, and these cost 340 livres, including packing and freight.

To judge from Christie's catalogues Sauternes château names were not well known in England. The first mention of Barsac, *tout court*, was in a sale in 1787, and occasionally thereafter, but 'Vin de Sauterne' (with the final 's' omitted as by Jefferson and for American wine today) seemed to appear only in 1808; at 60s. a dozen it was fairly highly priced, but 4s. cheaper than a Barsac. In 1788 there was a 'Prigniac' for sale and the following year a 'Vin de Langon', but entries were infrequent compared with 'Vin de Graves'. However this was in the years of revolution and the wars with France, and the import of all French wines was severely discouraged. Moreover the British devotion to port must have limited the demand for sweet French wines. Certainly they did not appear very frequently at auctions, and the first mention of Yquem itself that I was able to find in the Christie catalogues was in 1862 in the sale list of a large cellar from Herefordshire. No vintage was given, although clarets in the same sale bore dates. Four years later some Yquem '58, described as *'vin de goutte'*, sold for the respectable price of 96s. a dozen. Then the following year Yquem appeared several times, the '47 (120s.), '51 (92s.) and the '58 again (80s.), with the Marquis de Lur Saluces mentioned as proprietor. Up to that date I can find no other Sauternes château named in the auction catalogues.

It is no disparagement to the other leading Sauternes to say that Yquem is the quintessence of these great luscious wines. Its charming setting on a small hill, the courtyard of turreted buildings dating back to the twelfth century and the Renaissance, and the easy appeal of its wine have made Yquem a focal point for visitors to the region. So much so that casual visitors are now discouraged, and appointments must be made; and no wonder, for one must be surprised that M. Bureau and his staff find any time for their work.

The château buildings themselves have the pleasantly old, informal air of a manoir, and the late Marquis, who died aged 80 in December 1968, used to spend most of his time in an attractive house in Bordeaux near the Jardin Public, with a fine music room built by the famous Louis, architect of the Théâtre. But in the base of one of the turrets at Yquem there is a small but fine private cellar, with bottles of Yquem going back to 1892 and of Coutet to 1888 and 1890. The bottles, which include samples of the '21, most famous Sauternes of this century, are re-corked every thirty years. It was odd, it occurred to me as I looked over the bins of old Sauternes, to come upon a purely white wine cellar in France. The present member of the Lur Saluces family in charge of Yquem is Comte Alexandre.

Yquem is as traditional in its equipment as Mouton. Everything that comes into contact with the grapes is of wood, and the pressed juice ferments in new oak casks. During the period of fermentation in these white wine *chais* the whisper of the bubbling wine in the bung-less casks reminds one of a muted apiary. Thereafter the wine remains in wood until bottled three to three-and-a-half years after the vintage. Since 1922 the whole crop has been bottled at the château. When the wine is a year old the *égalisage* or *assemblage* takes place, with the wine from each cask brought together for blending. For the casks will vary, since some will contain wine that may have started its life as long as two-and-a-half months earlier than the wine from the last picking. Each *barrique*, therefore, bears the date of vintaging. Standards are high at Yquem, and they can afford to be, for sometimes as much as 60 per cent of the crop may be de-classified and not sold as Yquem; this in addition to the fact that although the permitted *AC* output is 25 hl. per hectare, at Yquem only about 9 hl. are produced from each of the 100 hectares under production. The vineyard is made up of 80 per cent Sémillon and 20 per cent Sauvignon. Yet over the years the average total production is around 70 *tonneaux* or 80,000 bottles. A century ago its average was higher: 100 – 130 *tonneaux*.

For, as everywhere in this part of the world, the dreaded risks are frost and hail. In 1950 there was only a half crop owing to frost, and because of hail there was no Yquem in 1951 or 1952. Recently a very bad run of vintages has adversely affected all the Sauternes, and there has been no very acceptable year between 1962 and 1966. Yquem, unwisely, did offer some '63 but it was very dark-coloured by the time of its bottling, and grew even darker thereafter; certainly not up to the level of quality that Yquem often produces even in off-years like 1954 and 1958. There was no 1964 Yquem and only a little 1965, for 60 per cent of the crop was sold off as Sauternes. The 1966 and 1967 will bear the château label, and probably 1968 also, owing to late picking in a fine autumn of that generally poor year.

Unlike its peers in the Médoc who bottle the whole of their *récolte*, Yquem is not offered *en primeur*. The wine is not sold until bottled, and then is marketed in three successive portions or *tranches*, in the Bordeaux term. The late Marquis explained to me that it had been his policy over many years to sell each year no more than his average production, or about 80,000 bottles; the surplus in the good, prolific years, made up for the deficit in others. Yquem is the one Sauternes whose price has more or less kept level with those of the red *premiers crus*. Whereas it used to cost only a quarter to a third more than the best of its neighbours, now it is more than double; for their price has remained low.

In 1959 Yquem rather startled the wine world by producing a dry wine, which it called Ygrec. A number of other Sauternes growers have been selling a dry wine, notably Filhot and Doisy-Daëne, but that was mostly owing to the difficulties of selling a sweet wine. The Ygrec has the full, honeyish nose one associates with Sauternes but the flavour is fairly – and to me disappointingly – dry on the palate. The wine is made from 50 per cent Sauvignon and 50 per cent Sémillon, and is not marketed every year. So far the '59, '60, '62, '64, '65 and '66 vintages have been offered. About 20 *tonneaux* are usually made, but the quantity varies from 15 *tonneaux* of the '59 to 26 of the '62.

The hazards and heavy costs of producing Yquem go a long way to account for its high price. So does its unequalled reputation. It is irrelevant whether some of the other fine Sauternes and Barsac châteaux have often produced as successful wine, for world opinion has rated Yquem a consistent first. There have been three particularly outstanding vintages: 1869, 1893 and 1921. These were all exceptionally hot years, and wonderfully sweet white wines were made not only in Bordeaux but also in Germany. If one may count the spoonful of the '69 from a medicine bottle, I have been lucky enough to drink them all. The '93 and the '21 I have actually owned to the extent of two or three bottles apiece, and both came to me in an unusual way.

When Sir Arthur Evans of Knossos fame died early in the last war, part of his cellar was included in the sale of his house on Boar's Hill, near Oxford. By this time Britain was cut off from Continental wine supplies, and prices were rising fast. A friend of mine attended the sale, and while anonymous St-Julien and doubtful Liebfraumilch fetched about 30s. a bottle, six or seven times their pre-war value, some old bottles of Burgundy and Sauternes were largely disregarded and went very cheaply. My friend bought five or six bottles of Yquem '93 for 15s. apiece, and some Clos de Vougeot '98 for the same price. He passed me a proportion of each, and I also shared more than one of his bottles. When I drank the '93s they were either side of fifty years old, the colour was dark, but the flavour wonderfully complete and luscious.

My few bottles of the '21 – certainly the most celebrated Yquem of this century and on a par with the Cheval-Blanc of the same year – came to me soon after the end of the last war from a doctor friend in Swindon. Swindon, a railway town in southern England reminiscent of the industrial north, is not exactly the place where one would expect to find a small cache of Yquem '21, but it had belonged to the departed husband of a patient, who asked my friend to take eight or nine bottles of this precious wine, along with a few other old Sauternes, including Coutet '21 and '24, in settlement of his account. In due course several of these found their way into my cellar, and I drank the last bottle of this Yquem '21 in 1955. It was still pale and in excellent condition, whereas, according to Harry Waugh who shared in this splendid bottle, a number of examples he had had in Bordeaux in previous years had been *maderisé* (Madeira-coloured and having lost its freshness) and past their best. One up for Swindon and its cold climate!

I have drunk Yquem '21 several times since, and the last occasion was in October 1966 at lunch in the London office of Sichel & Co. Although this 45-year-old Sauternes was a little dark in colour, it was far from being *maderisé*; still a wonderfully rich, velvety, deep-flavoured wine.

These three years are not the only vintages in which Yquem had a special *réclame*. Among others in my own recollection were '24, '28, '29, '37, '45, '47, '49 and '55. I remember the 1929 being served at the dinner given in London in May 1962 by Christian Cruse to commemorate his fifty years of 'calling on' his English wine trade customers. When the Yquem was poured out, my apprehensions were aroused, as the colour of this 32-year old wine was distinctly dark. The nose was old too, but the flavour was magnificently full and without any sign of decay.

The '28 has been equally fine, although I have had variable experience of it. The reason is that white wines are much more susceptible to the conditions of keeping than red wines. The most recent bottle I have drunk of the '28 was in Bordeaux in September 1967, when for its age the colour was not particularly dark but the wine was at the top of its form.

The '37 was very fine too, but in this year I consider that the Climens beat it. The '45 Yquem remains a wonderful wine, and I would be inclined to place it at the top of the post-war vintages, but then '49 also had all the richness one looks for in Yquem. The criticism sometimes made of Yquem is that it is too heavy, too liquorous. Even allowing for the number of poor or indifferent vintages recently, I am not sure that Yquem has been up to form in the past dozen years. Yet few would deny that it is always an experience to drink.

Although Sauternes is the omnibus name for all the wines grown in the five privileged communes, there are only five growths within the village area of Sauternes itself. This village lies right at the back of the commune, and considering the fame of the name it is probably little visited, compared with Barsac on the main road. Not that it is a village of any character, being unexpectedly dull and nondescript.

The only *premier cru* in the commune is Guiraud, formerly known as Bayle. It lies on a plateau rather higher than Yquem and to the south. This large estate belongs to M. Paul Rival. The courtyard and *chai* are substantial, with big wine cellars. The vineyard is of 65 hectares, made up of 50 per cent Sémillon, 35 per cent Sauvignon, 14 per cent Muscadelle and 1 per cent Ugniblanc. The average production is 400 *barriques* of sweet wine; but there are also about 12 – 15 *barriques* of dry wine, which has been made for the last ten years, and is sold as Pavillon Sec de Château Guiraud. In addition an increasing amount of red wine is being made, under the label of Pavillon Rouge. This started in 1961 and about 40 *barriques* are now produced annually. The composition of this section of the vineyard is 50 per cent Cabernet Sauvignon, 25 per cent Cabernet Franc, and the balance of Merlot and Malbec. When I visited the *chai* in 1968 I was surprised to find the 1961 and 1962 sweet white wine still in cement tanks, in order to keep them fresh; but the former was already rather heavy. This is symptomatic of the difficult times through which the Sauternais have been passing. It is sad that a first-growth château like Guiraud should have such difficulty in selling its wine. I have had good examples in the past.

It must be borne in mind that the sequence of châteaux within the 1855 classification was significant; those at the top of each class were considered better than those lower down. The three other classed Sauternes were all among the *Deuxièmes Crus* and not particularly high up. D'Arche and Filhot were fourth and fifth respectively and Lamothe was bottom.

Ch. d'Arche, named after a wealthy eighteenth-century proprietor, is on a hill near to the village of Sauternes. The buildings are single-storeyed on three sides of two courts which look across to Lamothe on a hill opposite. The proprietor is A. Bastit Saint Martin, and he owns part of Lamothe too. The vineyard of Arche is 50 hectares in extent, producing 200 *barriques*. The vineyard composition is 20 per cent Sauvignon and 80 per cent Sémillon. The better *cuves* are sold as Ch. d'Arche, the less good as Ch. d'Arche-Lafaurie. It is bottled after two years. The wine is usually well balanced.

Filhot, set in an English-type park, is much grander. Indeed the château, with two projecting wings, is the most imposing in the Sauternes region, and the ensemble has rather an English look. It was the home of the Lur Saluces family, and indeed belonged to them until 1936 when it was sold to the Comtesse de Lacarelle, herself a Lur Saluces. Out of a total property of 320 hectares only 45 are under vines. The soil here is quite different from Yquem, and is a mixture of sand, gravel and clay. Filhot makes a dry wine as well as a sweet one, and total production is about 250 *barriques*. The dry wine is sold as Grand Vin Sec de Château Filhot, and about 10 *tonneaux* only are made. Sémillon is, of course, the predominant grape, and here the grapes are said to ripen later than at Yquem, and it is normal to go through the vineyards five times. No wine of the '63, '64 and '65 vintages was sold as Filhot. Not only is the proprietor of Filhot a woman, but the *gérant* or manager also; Mme Cazeaux Cazalet. These days Filhot seems less to be seen on wine lists than it deserves.

Lamothe, prominent on a crest facing d'Arche, also near the village of Sauternes, is exactly divided in two. M. Bastit St Martin owns 15 hectares and produces about 100 *barriques*, and M. Jean Despujols makes the same amount of wine from an equivalent area of land. Neither is widely known outside France.

There are several other fairly well-known *bourgeois* growths in the Sauternes commune, including Raymond-Lafon, Arche-Vimeney, and Lamothe-Bergey which claims classed-growth status. There is also Lafon, whose wine is exclusively marketed by Dourthe of Moulis.

Adjacent to Sauternes is Bommes, which includes no fewer than seven classed growths, among them La Tour-Blanche, in 1855 placed immediately after Yquem. It is something of a curiosity for it was owned by a Monsieur Osiris, an umbrella manufacturer in Bordeaux and a friend of Pasteur. In 1910 he gave the whole property to the state on the condition that it was used as an oenological and viticultural school. Today there are 50 students who do a two-year course. The vineyard, with a stony soil, is exploited separately, and is of 25 hectares, of which nearly 90 per cent is Sémillon, 10 per cent Sauvignon with a little Muscadelle, but the proportion of Sauvignon is increasing and will be 25 per cent. Production averages 200 *barriques*, and since 1967 a little dry wine has been made. There is a second wine sold under the name of Cru St-Marc. At one time the marketing was done by the firm of Cordier, but nowadays the estate does its own selling; a good deal is disposed of direct to the private consumers, a practice not uncommon in this part of the world where trade is difficult. La Tour-Blanche is not as well known as one would expect in view of its distinguished placing in the 1855 classification. The installations are modern and, unlike at Yquem, the fermentation takes place in concrete vats, on the grounds that the fermentation is more rapid, being completed in about 10 days, that it is more economical and there is less oxydization. Here is quite a different school of thought from the traditional Yquem. They also have a different attitude towards fining, for at La Tour-Blanche it is done two or three times before bottling, while at Yquem the first fining only takes place in the second year.

Lafaurie-Peyraguey, the next Bommes on the list, is a much smaller estate, with a fine château surrounded by an old crenellated wall. Part of it dates from the thirteenth century, and the property, owned by Cordier, is as well kept as his other estates. The vineyard is only 16 hectares, with a composition of 60 per cent Sémillon, 30 per cent Sauvignon and 10 per cent Muscadelle. Average production is 100 *barriques*. The wine is bottled after three years and is an excellent example of the slightly lighter type of Sauternes. I remember a remarkably fine '24. The property, which adjoins Yquem, was owned in the eighteenth century by the Président Pichard, proprietor of Lafite. Like the latter this property was confiscated as a '*bien national*' after the death of its owner in the Revolution, and sold to M. Lafaurie who greatly improved its standing.

Adjoining this estate is the small one of Clos Haut-Peyraguey, originally part of its neighbour and non-existent as a separate entity in 1855. The vineyard is 8 hectares, and in addition there are 4 hectares of a *cru bourgeois*, Haut-Bommes. Both are owned by the company of Pauly Frères. The composition of each vineyard is 80 per cent Sémillon, 17 per cent Sauvignon and 3 per cent Muscadelle and bottling takes place after 2 – 3 years. Average production is 60 and 30 *barriques* respectively. From my limited experience of the wine I would not say that Haut-Peyraguey is in the same class as Lafaurie-Peyraguey, but as one of the smaller Sauternes estates its problems are certainly greater.

Rayne-Vigneau is one of the biggest properties of the district. The large turreted nineteenth-century château is similar to several of those in the Médoc, such as Pichon-Baron, and there are substantial out-buildings including two very big cellars well over 100 yards long. Standing on a slope the château commands a fine view over the Sauternes vineyards and across the river to the hills of the Premières Côtes. For many years the estate was owned by the Pontac family, well known for its association with Haut-Brion, and a hundred years ago was generally considered second to Yquem. In 1961 it was bought by Monsieur G. Raoux, a Bordeaux wine merchant.

A common dispute among *amateurs* of sweet white wine is as to the relative superiority of the Sauternes and the richer products of the Rhine and Moselle. At the 1867 Paris International Exhibition a notable success was scored by the 1861 Vigneau-Pontac, as it was then, when a mixed jury of French and German tasters in equal numbers awarded the palm to the French wine. The triumph of the Vigneau was underlined by the fact that its samples came from the whole, equalized crop, while the German wines, as customary, were from two selected casks of extra-luscious wines out of several hundred casks produced in the vineyards.

The vineyard of Rayne-Vigneau extends to 45 hectares, producing 350 *barriques* from a grape composition of 65 per cent Sémillon, 30 per cent Sauvignon and 5 per cent Muscadelle. The vineyard is notably stony, and at the château I was assured that this contributed to the fine quality of the wine which I have certainly found one of the more delicious Sauternes. Ninety per cent of the wine is château-bottled and this takes place after three years. It is one of the fuller Sauternes.

Rabaud, the last of the classified Bommes, as Peixotto its only *deuxième* in the 1855 classification was later absorbed into this estate, is named after a Mlle Marie Peyronne de Rabaud who married into one of the Parlement families, the de Cazeaus. The family sold it in 1819, and then it was re-sold in 1864 to M. Henri de Sigalas, who in 1903 parted with more than half the estate to M. Adrien Promis. Re-united in the 1930s, they were divided again in 1952. This explains why there are now two Ch. Rabaud wines: Sigalas-Rabaud and Rabaud-Promis. The former is only of 15 hectares, made up of 60 per cent Sémillon and 40 per cent Sauvignon, and the average production is 160 *barriques*. The wine is fermented in concrete fermenting vats, and then kept in concrete tanks for a year before being transferred to wooden casks for another year or so. Bottling takes place between two and three years after the vintage, according to the state of the wine. The proprietor is the Marquis de Lambert des Granges. This is a lighter and generally regarded as a better wine than its neighbour, which is owned by M. Lanneluc. This latter is 30 hectares in extent, of which over 80 per cent is Sémillon, and the rest Sauvignon save for a little Muscadelle.

Average production is 400 *barriques*. The wine is not only fermented in cement vats but also kept in vats until bottled after two years. It does not lie at all in wood, and it is claimed that the wine keeps younger and fresher this way. The variation in practice between the two Rabauds demonstrates the individuality of Bordeaux. Rabaud-Promis has large arched cellars below the house, claimed as a work of Victor Louis. The tops of the *cuves* have covers in the cellar floor. For the 1962 vintage Rabaud-Promis had numbered bottles, but this is not a common practice. The best market lies in Germany.

There are few *crus bourgeois* in Bommes, the smallest of the Sauternes communes, but M. Lanneluc owns the small foreign-sounding Ch. Cameron, which should commend itself north of the Border.

Fargues is the most southerly of the Sauternes communes, but these are so inter-mingled that it is not easy to say at any given moment in which commune one is standing. All are sparsely populated, and it is hard to find one's way about, for few of the châteaux bother to put up a name-plate. Not even the natives are very familiar with the whereabouts of the various growths. A villager of Sauternes when asked the way to Rieussec, replied, '*C'est au Fargues*', with the air of one describing a far away commune of which he knew little. They adjoin!

Rieussec is indeed in Fargues and is the only *Premier Cru*. The wine is distinctly lighter and less liquorous than some of the other Sauternes, notably Yquem on which it abuts. It is an estate of 50 hectares, producing 320 – 350 *barriques*. The vineyard composition is 80 per cent Sémillon, 15 per cent Sauvignon and 5 per cent Mus-cadelle. The soil is decidedly gravelly. Wine considered not good enough to be sold under the château label is marketed as Clos Labère, non-vintage. It is a well-kept property with underground cellars, rare in this part of the world.

The other Fargues *cru classé* is Romer, little known these days, and tucked away among woods, and much nearer the main Bordeaux-Langon road (*RN. 113*) than Rieussec. It is only 7 hectares, and is a real peasant property, with the small *chai* abutting on a little farmyard. The soil here is also very gravelly. The composition of the vineyard is 60 per cent Sémillon, 20 per cent Sauvignon, and 20 per cent Mus-cadelle – a very high proportion of this last grape. The wine is heavy and not very distinguished. It is sold exclusively to Calvet.

Preignac, nearer the Garonne, is a much larger commune but also with only two classed growths, of which the sole first growth is the Ch. de Suduiraut. The fine old turreted seventeenth-century château lies at the end of a long drive and avenue of trees, with no prior indication of the identity of the large house. For, unlike in the Médoc, as already mentioned, few of the owners identify their properties by signposts, and in view of the need of publicity for Sauternes this is surprising. Although the local wine growers' association has devised a '*Circuit du Sauternais*' which is alleged to pass deviously by all the leading growths, my experience of château-visiting in the district takes me back to that hazardous, halt-provoking, diversion-creating nursery game, Peter Rabbit's Race Game. Amid the obscure, winding, unpopulated roads one always seems to overshoot the mark, to be two roads away, if not in the wrong commune and heading straight for the Landes or the Garonne!

To return to, or rather arrive at, Suduiraut, whose hard-to-pronounce name cannot be a sales asset in, say, Texas or Manchester, the house itself is a classified building of historical interest and has been owned since 1940 by M. Léopold Fonquernie, a wealthy industrialist from the north of France, who has devoted a great deal of attention and money to improving the property, which for many years previously had been sadly neglected and made little wine. From the courtyard with buildings on both sides, one passes into the château, which externally is rather severe, but agreeably furnished within. Beyond a finely panelled hall lie formal gardens said to have been laid out by Le Nôtre. The cellar buildings are thick-walled and traditional, but there are concrete vats. For although the wine is made in the traditional way, with the vineyard traversed six or seven times, the young wine is transferred after about eight months from wood into concrete vats, in order to keep it fresh and to avoid oxydization; a practice already noted elsewhere. Of course development is also delayed or prevented, but the results seem good when the wine is bottled three years after the vintage. The *maître de chai* told me that Suduiraut has a micro-climate warmer than its neighbours. As a result the vintage usually begins earlier. The wine is rich and luscious even by Sauternes standards, and fairly high in alcohol. Sémillon forms almost two-thirds of the vineyard, Sauvignon one-third, which is rather high, and Muscadelle the small balance. Production ranges from 300 to over 400 *barriques*, and all the wine deemed worthy of the château label is bottled on the spot. In the past the reputation of Suduiraut suffered from lack of care, but since about 1955 onwards the wine has been reckoned among the best in the region.

The other classed Preignac, de Malle, is also a classified historic building and certainly the finest in the district. Dating from early in the seventeenth century it has a courtyard in front, and round pepper-pot towers on each flank. At the back is a very formal Italian garden. The interior is open for public visits and well worth seeing. There is a splendid panelled hall with a marble floor, and the Italian influence can be seen. Most attractive is a seventeenth-century round chapel in one of the towers. The Duke of Wellington stayed here during his campaign against Napoleon. For many years de Malle belonged to the Lur Saluces family and the last owner of that name was Comte Pierre, but by marriage it has descended to the young, energetic Comte Pierre de Bournazel, an electronics engineer who devotes all his spare time – and his spare cash too, one would hazard – to restoring both château and *chai*, and to improving the quality of this *deuxième cru*, which lies very near the border of Barsac and also of the Graves. Nearly all the vineyard had to be re-planted after the savage winter of 1956, and is now 36 hectares in extent. Half of this is planted in white grapes and half in red. Until the last century the château always made red as well as white wine, the former being entitled to the *appellation* Graves, as part of the vineyard is in Graves. This red part is made up of 80 per cent Cabernet-Sauvignon and 20 per cent Merlot, while the white is 65 per cent Sémillon, 30 per cent Sauvignon and 5 per cent Muscadelle.

The red wine is made by the method of carbonic maceration, as described at the Cave-de-Bel-Air in the Premières Côtes. It is bottled within the year and sold under the label of Ch. de Cardaillan. The wine is for early drinking, and up to 400 *barriques* are made. Of the rest, 200 *barriques* of sweet wine are produced, and bottled after about 18 months, while 150 *barriques* are made of a dry white wine, fermented out. Both sweet and dry white wines are fermented in cask for a week and then as the fermentation slows up the wines are transferred into concrete tanks. The dry white is sold under the name of Chevalier de Malle, having been bottled after 18 months. The *appellation* for this is Bordeaux Supérieur. It will be seen that the young Count is enterprising in these difficult times for the Sauternes. The sweet wine is on the light side, the dry is fresh and clean-flavoured.

In Preignac there are quite a large number of *crus bourgeois* and the best known is Bastor-Lamontagne, which produces about 250 *barriques*. There is also the Domaine du Mayne, and Domaine de Lamothe, Ch. des Remparts, so-named to distinguish it from the other Lamothe in Sauternes. It is very near the little stream, the Ciron, which divides the Sauternes communes from Barsac.

This last is much the largest of the fine sweet wine communes, producing about 35 per cent of the total crop, averaging 16,000 hl. The total production in the five Sauternes communes is about 45,000 hl. Barsac is probably the best known. 'A nice bottle of Barsac' has provided many drinkers of tender years with their introduction to wine. The Barsacs are generally considered a little heavier and a trifle less distinguished than the best growths of the other villages. No doubt the lesser properties of which there are several dozen are more plebeian, but this certainly does not apply to the leading châteaux among whom Coutet and Climens certainly stand out.

In the 1855 classification, which included eight Barsac growths, but which subsequent division has increased to ten, Coutet leads Climens, although over the years many people would place the latter first. Climens is rather a fuller wine than Coutet, but both can be excellent. In its best years Climens can be a challenger of Yquem. A celebrated Climens was the '29, often reckoned the best Sauternes of the vintage. Early in the 1950s I had bottles and halves of the '37 of both Yquem and Climens, and I thought that the latter had the edge on its rival, being rounder and fuller. The last time I have drunk Climens '37 was in 1965. The wine had the tint of a well-coloured cognac, but the flavour was complete and clean, whereas Suduiraut of the same vintage opened in the same year was well past its best. Climens '47 was another outstanding wine; but then so in its own style was Coutet '50, delicate and fruity.

To visit, the two châteaux afford a marked contrast: Coutet spick and span, with a well-kept garden beside the small turreted château, and a very neat *chai*; Climens, with an unambitious low house facing a somewhat uncared-for-looking forecourt, and an old-fashioned *chai*. Coutet is owned by M. Rolland-Guy and he has clearly lavished a good deal of money on it in recent years. As mentioned earlier, a former proprietor was a member of the ubiquitous Lur Saluces family, and the father of the last marquis; Coutet came to M. Rolland-Guy via his wife's father.

Climens for over a century has been in the hands of the Gounouilhou family, but the modest house is not occupied by the family. If Climens is less smart than Coutet I have continued to find the wine good. Unlike Yquem, both produced some '64 under their château labels, but Coutet had to de-class three-quarters of its production.

The area of Coutet is 33 hectares, made up of 80 per cent Sémillon, 15 per cent Sauvignon and 5 per cent Muscadelle. Average production is 330 *barriques*. Climens which has a more chalky soil also extends to 33 hectares of vines, but with a greater proportion of Sémillon: 95 per cent, with only 5 per cent of Sauvignon. It all depends on which grape suits best the particular soil. Climens usually bottles after three years, Coutet after two-and-a-half, but much depends on the vintage. Both wines are sold in cask as well as château-bottled. Some people, noting the great difference in price between Yquem and wines like these, like to ask whether the former is 'worth all that much more'. The question might be better put as 'are the first-growth Sauternes worth all that much less?' The answer is certainly no.

The next on the list of the classed growths and the top *deuxième* is a château whose wines are certainly little known in Britain nowadays: de Myrat. The mid-eighteenth century single-storey château, with an upper floor only in the middle – a '*chartreuse*' like Beychevelle and Langoa in the Médoc – is a charming building set in a pleasant park. It used to belong to the Martineau family but the owner is now the Comte de Pontac, of the family which once owned Haut-Brion. He has devoted a great deal of attention to restoring the house and furnishing it suitably. The vineyard is 22 hectares, and curiously enough contains no Sauvignon. The reason for this, I was told, was that the soil is very chalky and this does not suit the Sauvignon grape. So the *cépage* is 95 per cent Sémillon and 5 per cent Muscadelle. The production is 200 *barriques*. None is currently château-bottled, and I found this wine rather on the heavy side. The Count told me that sometimes the strength went as high as 19½ degrees. This is perhaps a doubtful recommendation.

Not far away are the two Doisys: Védrines and Daëne. (Dubroca, once a small vineyard of 4 hectares, producing 40 – 50 *barriques*, is now part of Climens.)

Doisy-Védrines is the larger of the pair, with a vineyard of 20 hectares, of which almost 80 per cent is Sémillon, 20 per cent Sauvignon and the balance a small quantity of Muscadelle. The average output is 200 *barriques*. It lies between Coutet and Climens, and is run by Mme Castéja on behalf of her husband, a brother of the proprietor of Lynch-Moussas and a Bordeaux wine merchant. As an example of the difficulties of selling even classed Barsacs these days, at Doisy-Védrines in the last few years they have been planting red wine grapes which can only be made into wine with the *appellation* Bordeaux Supérieur. I have drunk several very attractive sweet Doisy-Védrines, a rather full wine.

On the other hand Doisy-Daëne (pronounced Denne) has become known for its dry wine. Under the energetic proprietorship of M. Pierre Doubourdieu, who described his modest house to me as a 'cabine' and not a château, this dry wine has been developed and 120 *barriques* are made from a vineyard which is 60 per cent Sauvignon, 20 per cent Sémillon and – very unusual – 20 per cent Riesling. This dry white wine is bottled after six months and with a fresh nose and clean flavour, it is reckoned to be drunk young. The whole estate is 13 hectares, with about 80 per cent Sémillon and 20 per cent Sauvignon for the sweet wine, of which 120 *barriques* are made in good years. This is bottled after two years. Daëne is the more widely known of the two Doisy growths.

The remaining four classed Barsacs are not now well known widely whatever they were in the past. They follow each other in the 1855 list. Broustet is the first, consisting of 16 hectares, with 60 per cent Sémillon, 30 per cent Sauvignon and 10 per cent Muscadelle. Production averages 165 *barriques* in the small, low-ceilinged *chai*. The proprietress is Mme Veuve Pierre Fourneu. Nairac is a fine two-storeyed château facing the main road on the outskirts of the village of Barsac. The vineyard is immediately behind. Production is about 120 *barriques* and some red wine is made. Caillou, a lofty building lying further into the countryside is a larger property owned by the energetic M. Bravo. The area under white grapes is 22 hectares, planted in the proportion of 65 per cent Sémillon, 25 per cent Muscadelle and 10 per cent Sauvignon. Just over 400 *barriques* are normally made, including 30 *barriques* of dry wine called Domaine Sarraule. Some 3 hectares are planted in Cabernet-Sauvignon and Merlot to produce 25 *barriques* of red wine, sold as Clos du Clocher. There is even a little *rosé* produced, known as Rosé St-Vincent. To illustrate the difference in wine-making methods within a small area, M. Bravo begins his white wine fermentation in cask for two to three weeks, and then transfers the wine to cement vats for a month. After that it returns to casks early in the year following the vintage, and at the beginning is racked as often as once a fortnight, and later on every two months. In the third year before it is bottled it is racked twice more. I found the wine on the light side, as is to be expected. Most of it is sold privately. M. Bravo also owns or runs one or two other *bourgeois* Barsacs.

The last classed Barsac is Suau, situated between the main road from Barsac to the south and the railway from Bordeaux. The château is small, but rather like a small English country house, except that it has a round turret at one corner. It is owned by M. Biarnez, and production is only about 60 *barriques*. A little red wine is made here.

There are a considerable number of *crus bourgeois* in Barsac and some of them are well known. There are several Roumieux. The Goyaud family own 13 hectares, and the Bernardet family 8, while a third section is owned by the Lacoste family. In all, the three make about 240 *barriques* from 55 per cent Sémillon, 30 per cent Sauvignon and 15 per cent Muscadelle. I have seen this wine on one or two lists.

Piada was once in the hands of the Lur Saluces family, and at one point adjoins Coutet. I was told at the *chai* that the property dated back to the times of the English King Edward I. The present proprietor is M. J. Lalande, and he makes dry as well as sweet wine from his 13 hectares. Of this 150 *barriques* are sweet and 50 dry, sold allusively perhaps as Clos du Roy. I found it sweeter than the dry Doisy-Daëne. This dry wine comes from two-thirds Sauvignon and one-third Riesling. Before bottling the wine is heated sufficiently as to be slightly pasteurized; another variation in local production. Other fairly well-known Barsacs are Dudon, Liot and Menauta. The last of these has an enclosed walled courtyard in the style of Yquem.

A quick way to sample Barsacs is to visit the Office Viticole in the middle of the village, opposite the fine sixteenth-century Gothic church. It is possible to taste and buy wines, as well as obtain information about the local châteaux and their situation. The nearness of the Garonne is demonstrated by two high flood marks in the church: one mark is dated 7 April 1770 and the other 6 March 1930.

Adjoining Sauternes are four other small sweet white wine areas: Cérons, St-Pierre-du-Mons, Ste-Croix-du-Mont and Loupiac. At one time both Cérons and St-Pierre-du-Mons used to be part of Sauternes, and no doubt some of their wines contrive to be sold as Sauternes still. Cérons, situated on the left bank of the Garonne, downstream from Sauternes, is the largest and its *vignoble* is part of the Barsac plateau. The *appellation* is Cérons for wines with an alcoholic strength of 12·5 degrees (half a degree less than for Sauternes), and this extends to the communes of Podensac and Illats. In style the Cérons wines are between those of Graves and Barsac, but nearer the latter in their sweetness which owes something to the *pourriture noble*. However in order to meet the current taste for dryer wines a certain amount of dry Cérons is produced, although in my view it is the richer wines which represent the true Cérons. These are not widely known abroad, but in fact can be delicious, and are very modestly priced. Although the name-boards of châteaux greet passing motorists on the main road, and there is even a Château de Cérons, owned by Jean Perromat, yet château names are not all that important. The *cépage* is much the same as for Sauternes, but there tends to be a higher proportion of Muscadelle. For those who enjoy sweet wines but find the Sauternes either too luscious or too expensive, Cérons is an excellent alternative; discriminating wine merchants usually list one or two. St-Pierre-du-Mons produces wines similar in style.

Ste-Croix-du-Mont and Loupiac adjoin each other on the right bank of the river, opposite Sauternes and Barsac. Their wines are similar enough to treat them as one. Loupiac was delimited as recently as 1926. Each has its own *appellation*, with a minimum strength of 13 degrees like Sauternes, but with a much larger permitted crop of 40 hl. to the hectare, the same as Cérons. Physically these two small districts are part of the Entre-Deux-Mers, and vinously adjoin the Premières Côtes de Bordeaux. From the terrace by the nineteenth-century Romanesque church whose tower is a landmark from the Sauternes country opposite, there is a splendid view. Below is the river and the 'port' of Barsac, and beyond spread out the network of vineyards, with their châteaux, *chais* and clumps of woodland. Right behind, the horizon, dark with the trees of the Landes, forms a great arc. Ste-Croix-du-Mont and Loupiac together produce about 33,000 hl., rather less than Sauternes. However, both communes are subject to frost and in 1963 the former produced hardly any wine with its *appellation* and Loupiac only 25 per cent of normal. The wines are perhaps rather heavier, less distinguished and 'simpler' than those on the opposite bank, but they can be very agreeable for all that. Their chief markets used to be in Holland, Prussia and pre-Revolutionary Russia, but all these fell away after the First World War, and their growers have been in difficulties since the World Slump in the 1930s.

The best known Ste-Croix growth is probably de Tastes, owned by Pierre Ginestet, the proprietor of Ch. Margaux. Another is Lamarque owned by the Rolland family, who were associated with the old Parlement de Guyenne. Like many other properties here, red wine is also made. Loubens is also a well-known Ste-Croix.

Many of the sweet white wines of this area have suffered from the general lowering of demand and standards in the last 30 years or so, and all are ripe for a revival. Their two publicity organizations are the *Commanderie du Bontemps de Sauternes et Barsac* and the *Commanderie du Bontemps de Ste-Croix-du-Mont*.

The local main town on this side of the river is Cadillac, just to the north of Loupiac. It is an attractive old walled town, dominated by the Renaissance château of the Ducs d'Epernon, which is now state-owned. To the south of Ste-Croix is Verdelais, best known not for its wine but for the burial place of Toulouse-Lautrec. His grave lies up a flight of steps across the street from the village church, and is situated somewhat incongruously among the artificial flowers which are the normal cemetery furniture of French burial grounds.

16. The Entre-Deux-Mers, Côtes

The Entre-Deux-Mers, whose name dates back to the Middle Ages deriving from the Latin *Inter Duo Maria*, is an extensive, expanding tongue of land between the rivers Garonne and Dordogne. The distance, as the crow flies from the confluence opposite Bourg to the limits of the Gironde department is roughly the same as the length of the Médoc, about fifty miles, but the width of land broadens out as the valleys of the two rivers diverge. The country and the soil change, from the flat land round the confluence at Bec d'Ambès, rising to the district of Carbon-Blanc through which the Bordeaux-Libourne main road runs, and thereafter presenting a generally hilly appearance of great charm. The Entre-Deux-Mers and the Premières Côtes, physically one and only vinously separate, certainly form the most agreeable and varied country in the Bordeaux region. The 'frontier' towns which once prevented – and at other times connived at – the entry of wines from the 'Haut Pays' are Castillon and Ste-Foy on the Dordogne and St-Macaire and La Réole on the Garonne.

Vinously this triangular region is sub-divided and split up. Entre-Deux-Mers itself has three main areas: in the north-west and west the districts of Carbon-Blanc and Créon; in the north the communes near the Dordogne around Libourne (left bank only), Branne and Pujols; in the centre and south the districts of Targon, Sauveterre, Monségur and La Réole. The southern part of this is the Haut-Benauge region.

There are also enclaves with *appellations* of their own. In the north, across the Dordogne from Libourne, is the small area of the Graves de Vayres, whose white wines can carry that *appellation*, with a maximum output of 43 hl. per hectare. The gravelly soil earned them their name, but the wine is less good than Graves. The main market is Germany, where it is often sold as plain Graves and popular because cheap. Output is about 29,000 hl. A little red wine is also produced bearing a Bordeaux *appellation*. On the other end of that part of the Dordogne valley in the Gironde department is the rather larger Ste-Foy, with its *appellation* of Ste-Foy-Bordeaux. Then on the other side of the region and bordering on the Garonne is the thirty-mile long strip of the Premières Côtes de Bordeaux, which runs downstream to the north of Bordeaux and upstream to the slopes opposite Langon. The old archiepiscopal vineyards in Cenon and Lormont were in what is now the Premières Côtes. Set into this long strip is Loupiac and Ste-Croix-du-Mont, and beyond them the Côtes de Bordeaux-St-Macaire, which hinges on the riverside town of that name.

The best red wine in the area comes from the northern part of the Premières Côtes, for the southern section of that long strip, about 30 miles long but only three to four miles wide, is largely but not exclusively devoted to white wines. To secure the *appellation* the red wine must be at least 10·5 degrees and the white 12. Both may produce up to 40 hectolitres per hectare. The best red wine communes in the Premières Côtes are Camblanes, Quinsac and Cambes; and the best whites come from Monprimblanc and Gabarnac. Average production for the district is 24,000 hectolitres of red and 93,000 of white. For the Côtes de Bordeaux-St-Macaire only the white wines are entitled to that *appellation* and they are allowed to produce 42 hectolitres per hectare at a minimum strength of 11·5 degrees. They are fairly sweet wines. The reds are ordinary. Yet in Ste-Foy on the borders of the Dordogne department the large output per hectare of 45 hectolitres is permitted, and the strength of red and white wines is 10·5 and 12 degrees respectively. The white wines are the better, but somewhat heavy and more like those of the Dordogne. Production averages 28,000 hl, and a very little red. From the Haut-Benauge area on the Garonne side comes rather ordinary white wines.

In the northern wine-growing part of this tongue of land is the Graves de Vayres, so-called because the soil is gravelly rather than preponderantly clay, as further south in the Entre-Deux-Mers, the minimum strength is only 10·5 degrees for red and white, and the permitted quantity is 43 hl. for whites and 40 hl. for reds. The output of red and white wines averages 25,000 hectolitres. To complete this statistical picture the extensive vineyards of the Entre-Deux-Mers are only entitled to that *appellation* for their white wines; the red must be sold as Bordeaux or Bordeaux Supérieur. The somewhat low status of the Entre-Deux-Mers white wines is shown by the fact that up to 50 hectolitres with an 11·5 degree minimum may be produced, while a white Bordeaux Supérieur of the region has to be 11·5 degrees with a 40 hectolitres maximum and fetches a correspondingly higher price. The red Bordeaux can be as low as 10 degrees, and the red Bordeaux Supérieur 10·5 degrees.

It should be mentioned here that these proletarian wines of Bordeaux and Bordeaux Supérieur *AC* have their own guild – the *Compagnons de Bordeaux*.

It will be seen that these are very much the basic wines of Bordeaux, particularly the whites. It is a reasonably safe assumption that a wine labelled Bordeaux Blanc comes from these parts, and possibly a Bordeaux Rouge also, but either might originate in Bourg or Blaye, where rather low-grade white wine is also grown. Much of the wine grown in the geographical Entre-Deux-Mers region is used for blending. As the visitor can see, this is a region of mixed agriculture, with lines of grapes running beside other crops. The attractive countryside is dotted with fine old manoirs and farmhouses. A large proportion of the wine is made in the 15 co-operatives in the Entre-Deux-Mers. One I visited at Romagne, founded in 1936, each year makes 35,000 hectolitres of wine for its 180 members. The largest co-operative in this area makes as much as 120,000 hectolitres; these co-operatives have done much for the survival as well as the improvement of local viticulture. The trend here and in the Premières Côtes is towards red wine, which hitherto has accounted for only about 10 per cent of the output in the region. Soon it might be 20 per cent. The Entre-Deux-Mers white wines are dry, but the Premières Côtes are largely sweet. Most of the former wines are sold without vintage as they do not vary much. An average price of Entre-Deux-Mers in 1966 was 700 – 800 frs. a *tonneau*, compared with 1,000 – 1,200 frs. for the Premières Côtes. Both look a long way off from Lafite '66 at 27,000 frs. Much of the decline in the area of the Gironde *vignoble* in the past 20 years has taken place in the Entre-Deux-Mers.

One feature of this part of the world is the high-culture system of vine-growing. This originated in its present form in Austria, where it was developed by Lenz-Moser in vineyards on the Danube near the Wachau. There and in Germany whither it has spread, the system is called after Lenz-Moser. The lines of vines are much more widely spaced than normal and are allowed to grow to a height of four or five feet. The result is that the same quantity is produced from half the number of vines, a useful economy in itself. Also this permits tractors and ploughs to work among the rows. Nearly all planting in the Entre-Deux-Mers district is now being done by the high-culture system, and this may well spread to the other areas of mass-production. However it does call for fairly rich soil, and would not be suitable for the Médoc, or so I was told. Another limiting factor is that the sugar content is slightly reduced, as the moisture in the long grape stalks does not rise so easily. It is said that this high-culture system is in fact a reversion to ancient practice, for in Roman times when the vineyards were hand-worked the vines grew high; only when ploughing with oxen came in were the straight, narrowly spaced rows of low vines introduced.

Over the past generation there has been a decline in the standards of the less fine white Bordeaux. In pre-war days *chaptalisation* was chiefly used to raise the alcoholic strength of a wine that was too light. Each 1·8 kilograms of sugar per hectolitre will raise the strength by 1 degree, and it is permitted under certain conditions to add a maximum of 3 kgs. per hectolitre. There is a tax on sugar used for this purpose. After the war the taste for sweet wines spread beyond the borders of France, and as in the Sauternes district across the river such wines were sold by alcoholic strength, the temptation to pile in the sugar was seldom resisted. So white Bordeaux lost its character, became flabbily sweet and disagreeably heavy instead of being fresh.

The move to change this in the Sauternes district has already been mentioned, but

ENTRE-DEUX-MERS

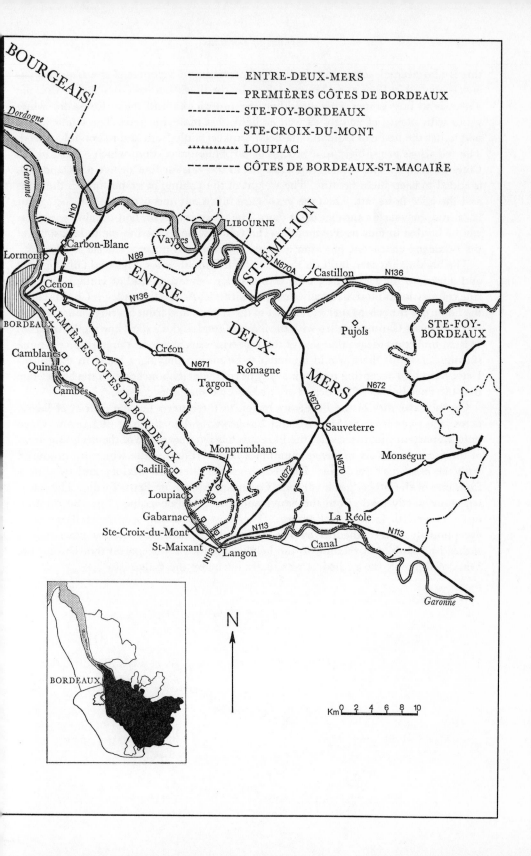

ENTRE-DEUX-MERS

PREMIÈRES CÔTES DE BORDEAUX

STE-FOY-BORDEAUX

STE-CROIX-DU-MONT

LOUPIAC

CÔTES DE BORDEAUX-ST-MACAIRE

BOURGEAIS

Dordogne

Garonne

N10

Carbon-Blanc

Vayres

LIBOURNE

Lormont

N89

ST-ÉMILION

N670A

Castillon

N136

Cenon

ENTRE-

N136

BORDEAUX

PREMIÈRES CÔTES DE BORDEAUX

Camblanes

Quinsac

Créon

DEUX-

Pujols

STE-FOY-BORDEAUX

Cambes

N671

Romagne

MERS

N672

Targon

N670

Sauveterre

Monprimblanc

N672

Monségur

Cadillac

N670

Loupiac

Gabarnac

La Réole

Ste-Croix-du-Mont

N113

St-Maixant

N113

Langon

Canal

N113

Garonne

N

BORDEAUX

Km 0 2 4 6 8 10

this is also needed across the river. One interesting development is a *Cave de Vinification* opened in 1966 at St-Maixant. Run by the Bordeaux firm of Sichel & Co., the object is to buy grapes from neighbouring proprietors and make fresh, dry white wines with plenty of acidity as well as light, fast maturing reds. The white wines, sold under the name of Domaine-de-Belair, are certainly fresh and reasonably priced. The red wines are subject to a process of carbonic maceration, which is used in the Côtes du Rhône. The whole grapes are put in the vats for four or five days, and CO_2 is added to keep them healthy. The weight of the volume of grapes breaks the skins and the juice flows out. Then the grapes are taken out and pressed before being put back into the vats for another eight days. The result is a fresh, non-tanniny wine that can be bottled in four or five months. The young wine seemed to me to lack some of the Bordeaux character, but after a year or so it should make a fair *vin de table*.

The St-Maixant *cave*, built on the side of a hill to allow for a natural fall of grapes and juice into the fermenting vats, is in a superb situation, and at vintage-time the ripe country looks more like Italy than the Gironde. Across the valley is Ch. Malagar, the home of François Mauriac, novelist of the region, and from his ridge one can look across the vast Garonne valley with the forest of the Landes a dark line on the horizon. It is an unfortunate fact that few of the best wines are made in the most picturesque surroundings, but there would be much to be said for having a house in the Entre-Deux-Mers and accepting the ordinary wines of the neighbourhood, in the knowledge that the finer bottles of Bordeaux are at hand for special occasions.

On the extremity of the Bordeaux region in these parts lies the district of Bazas, across the river from St-Macaire and La-Réole, and to the east of Langon. Once quite important quantitatively, the Bazadais has long been one of the declining areas of the Gironde. In six or seven communes both red and white wines are produced with the *appellation* Bordeaux. The red wines are one-third Malbec and two-thirds from one of the other 'noble' grapes, Cabernet, Merlot or Petit-Verdot. The white wines are partly made from the Sauvignon and Sémillon grapes, but also from an ordinary variety known as Enrageat. The most interesting feature of Bazas is its exceptionally long cathedral by French standards, with a nine-bay nave that is rather English-like in relation to the height. There is a fine portal too. During the Wars of Religion the cathedral was badly burnt by the Calvinists.

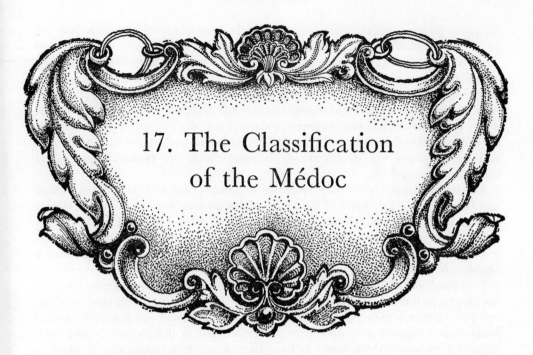

17. The Classification of the Médoc

Beginning his chapter with exactly the same heading as above, Wilhelm Franck, writing before the famous 1855 classification starts off with: 'Now we arrive at the most delicate section of our work'. This remains true today, for while there are many who say the classification is irrelevant, meaningless or outdated, it is a factor that has to be taken into consideration in any survey of Bordeaux. That the grading is still a subject of controversy is the best demonstration that it still counts for something: and the value of some kind of classification is shown by the fact that in recent years the leading Graves and the St-Emilions have been classified. I have heard no voices to suggest this should not have been done, although there are those who maintain that they should have been included in a comprehensive new classification embracing all the fine red wine areas.

For about the white wines there is little controversy. The urge for promotion and change is not apparent among the Sauternais who received recognition in 1855, and if the temporary omission of Haut-Brion-Blanc in the white Graves classification of 1959 caused a little stir, this has been rectified. So this chapter is almost exclusively concerned with the red wines. However, in spite of the title, it is impossible to discuss the Médocs in isolation from the wines of the other leading red wine districts of Bordeaux.

The origins of the Médoc classification are not clear, but it existed at least a century before 1855 and probably earlier, and the essential point was that class was based on price. It was not the reputation of estate or owner, the size or style of the château which counted, but the hard commercial facts as they existed on the Bordeaux market. I suspect that this classification began largely as a matter of convenience for the trade. By grouping the vineyards in classes – there were originally only four – it was easier to establish a price-structure for the roughly fifty to sixty best growths of the Médoc. Both the long standing of the classification and its basis are confirmed from letters written in 1823 by Lamothe, the *régisseur* of Latour to the proprietors and quoted by R. Pijassou in his chapter in *Bordeaux au XVIIIe Siècle* (1968). 'It is the trade itself which fixed the prices and formed the different classes of the wines of the Médoc a very long time ago'. He also referred to the fact that the relation of prices between the first and second growths had been established by the trade 'more than a hundred years ago'. Pijassou regards this as a slight exaggeration and dates its beginnings as between 1725 and 1735.

Also included was Haut-Brion, probably the senior of the first growths, for Graves had been the original centre of Bordeaux wine growing; but the other red Graves such as La Mission-Haut-Brion and Pape-Clément seem either to have been in a period of recession or were few enough not to have caused difficulty in pricing. There is a record of Haut-Brion being sold to the English in 1684 at 400 – 450 livres a *tonneau*, while other red wines (? of the Graves) only fetched 84 livres.

That some sort of classification existed by the mid-eighteenth century is shown by the fact there was a fixed scale of prices for all the growths in each class, with an equal step between each. No doubt the quality of wine produced by individual vine-yards caused periodic variations from the norm, but in the eighteenth and early nineteenth centuries there seems to have been much more uniformity of price in each class than exists today. Nor does there appear to have been any substantial movement from class to class. If not the good God, then the Bordeaux brokers made them high or lowly and ordered their estate. The classification probably grew up gradually, and without any preconceived idea that there should be so many different classes within it. The earliest reference I have found is a report dated 1730 and quoted by André Simon in *Bottlescrew Days* (1926). In this report are mentioned three principal classes of red wine. 'The first comprises the growths of Pontac, Lafitte and Château de Margo, which produce as a rule only about three hundred tuns a year; this is, however, the wine most highly esteemed of the province and it usually sells for 1,200 to 1,500 livres per tun. It is the English who buy the greater part of this wine.' After that came 'a very large number' of second-class growths, selling for 300 – 500 livres, and exported to England, Ireland, Scotland, Holland and Hamburg. Then there were the third class which went to northern France for 100 – 200 livres. Then were mentioned the 'unclassified' wines of the '*Palu*', the 'fine' costing 150 – 180 livres per tun, and the 'big' going for 90 – 100 livres. The first were bought in Holland, England, America and northern France; and the latter in America and Brittany.

Further, according to the Archives of the Gironde department, referred to by Pijassou, in the years 1735 – 1740 the four *premiers crus* achieved the highest prices on the Bordeaux market; rarely below 800 – 900 livres a *tonneau*, more commonly they sold for 1,200 – 1,800 livres, and even reached a peak of 2,000 livres. This is attributed to the fact that they were owned by the rich Parlement families, able to spend money on improving their profitable estates.

The first organized though not official classification arose from two reports addressed to the intendant by members of the Chamber of Commerce about 1750. It was called: *Tableau des paroisses d'où viennent les vins de Bordeaux et leurs différents prix*. Price, as will be seen, was an in-built feature; it is worth examining how this was worked out. The red Graves were included, and the leading growth of Pontac (Haut-Brion) was rated at 1,500 – 2,000 frs. per *tonneau*. It was, however, based much more on communes than particular growths, although that too was considered. For example the leading wines of Pauillac and Margaux fetched 1,500 – 1,800 frs. Yet the wine of M. de Ségur (Lafite), although fetching at least as much as 1,500 – 1,800 livres, could sell for 2,000. The wines of St-Julien, St-Mambert, Cantenac and St-Seurin de Cadourne made 800 – 1,200 livres, the same price as the wines of Pessac other than Haut-Brion. It is interesting to see the 'border' commune of Haut-Médoc, St-Seurin, included among the leaders, for even a hundred years later its wines were not highly regarded. St-Mambert, later called St-Lambert, is the small commune lying between St-Julien and Pauillac. Latour and Pichon-Lalande were at one time not Pauillacs but St-Lamberts; we may be thankful for the take-over, with one less commune name to grapple with.

The second-growth communes were Soussans and Labarde, whose wines were worth 600 livres a *tonneau*; Agassac (Ludon) (400 – 500 livres); Arsac, Arcins, Listrac and Moulis (400 livres). At the lowest level in the Médoc were St-Laurent, St-Estèphe, Le Pian, Macau and Ludon (300 – 400 livres); and the Gradignan and Cadaujac growths even less, at 200 – 300 livres. These low prices for the Graves demonstrate their comparative obscurity in the eighteenth century.

Malvezin reprints a list from the intendants' archives, giving a classification as in 1767. It is very similar to the slightly earlier one. The price is by commune, and there are three classes apiece for the red Graves and the Médoc, and two each for the '*vins de palus*', which include the Fronsadais and the white wines. In addition to the sweet wine communes, Blanquefort is included among the first white wine growths, but these only fetched 300 livres. A note records that 36 communes in what was then the '*sénéchaussée*' of Bordeaux made wine only for distillation into *eau-de-vie*. Also the St-Emilion wines were normally sold only on the home market.

That there was an accepted classification by the last quarter of the eighteenth century is shown by the notes that Thomas Jefferson, United States Commissioner and Minister in France, made after a tour of southern France in 1787. He visited Bordeaux in May of that year, and with his usual industry and attention to detail wrote the following report on the classed growths.

'There are 4 vineyards of first quality, viz. 1. Château Margau, belonging to the Marquis d'Agicourt, who makes about 150 *tonneaux* of 1000 bottles each. He has engaged to Jernon a merchant. 2. La Tour de Segur, en Saint Lambert, belonging to Monsieur Miromésnil, who makes 125 *tonneaux*. 3. Hautbrion, belonging 2/3 to M. le Comte de Femelle (Fumel), who has engaged to Barton a merchant, the other 1/3 to the Comte de Toulouse. The whole is 75 *tonneaux*. 4. Chateau de la Fite, belonging to the President Pichard at Bordeaux who makes 175 *tonneaux*. The wines of the three first are not in perfection till 4 years old. Those (of) de la Fite, being

249

somewhat lighter, are good at 3 years, that is the crop of 1786 is good in the spring of 1789. These growths of the year 1783 sell now at 2000 l. the *tonneaux*, those of 1784 on account of the superior quality of that vintage, sell at 2400 l., those of 1785 at 1800 l., those of 1786 at 1800 l., tho they sold at first for only 1500 l.'

He goes on to mention the '2nd quality wines', 'as Rozan, Dabbadie or Lionville, la Rose, Quirouen, Durfort; in all 800 *tonneaux* which sell at 1000 l. new.

'The 3d. class are Calons, Mouton, Gassie, Anboete, Pontette, de Terme, Candale; in all 2000 *tonneaux* at 8 or 900 l.

'After these they are reckoned common wines and sell from 500 l. down to 120 l. the tun. All red wines decline after a certain age, losing colour, flavour and body. Those of Bordeaux begin to decline at about 7 years old.'

While in Bordeaux Jefferson sent a relative in America six dozen 'of what is the very best Bordeaux wine. It is of the vineyard of Obrion, one of the four established as the very best, and it is of the vintage of 1784, the only very fine one since the year 1779'.

Jernon (Gernon), the merchant who took and sold the wine of Ch. Margaux, was one of the English traders of the time. From Jefferson's description of the state of readiness of the first growths it would appear that for the most part they must have been drunk very soon after bottling.

Jefferson's own purchases throw an interesting light on the predominance of the first growths even before the Revolution. He bought Ch. Margaux 1784 and wrote, 'it is the best vintage that has happened in nine years, and is one of the four vineyards which are admitted to possess exclusively the first reputation. I may safely assure you therefore that, according to the taste of this country and of England, there cannot be a bottle of better Bordeaux produced in France. It cost me at Bordeaux three livres a bottle, ready bottled and packed. This is very dear'.

In February 1788 he wrote to President Pichard asking to buy 250 bottles of La Fite 1784, asking him to put it in bottle and '*emballer chez vous*', as this would be a guarantee that the wine was natural and the racking, etc. had been well done. He also requested that while in France and after his return to America he might apply to him for his wines.

The letter was sent on to Pichard at Libourne, as the Parlement was then situated there, but in April the Président replied that he had no '*vin de Lafitte*' 1784 left, and though he would like to serve Jefferson in future he only had the 1786 which was not yet drinkable.

The American Consul in Bordeaux, J. Bondfield, in enclosing this negative reply, mentioned that the 'vins d'Hautbrion, belonging to Monsr. le Comte de Fumel' were esteemed as next in quality and a few hogsheads of the 1784 were still available. Thereupon Jefferson settled for 125 bottles of this wine. However, it turned out that the Comte only retained 4 hogsheads of the 1784, and refused an offer of 600 livres for 1 hogshead, so Jefferson was to have two cases [more than a dozen and probably 50 bottles apiece – E.P.-R.] of the first hogshead bottled.

Bondfield added, 'It is urging and too much to pay three livres in Bordeaux for a Bottle of Bordeaux Wine, but so great has been the demand for that Vintage that the holders obtain that exorbitant price'. Three livres was about the equivalent in English money then of 2s.6d.

Shortly before the Revolution, according to André Simon, the prices per *tonneau* of the Médocs were as follows:

1st growths –1,600–2,400 livres 3rd growths–900–1,400 livres
2nd growths–1,300–2,100 livres 4th growths–600–850 livres
Other Médocs–400–500 livres

The range of prices in each class reflected variations in the quality of the vintages.

André Simon gives the English prices per hogshead (*barrique*) of the classed growths at the end of the eighteenth century as being:

1st growths–£24 3rd growths–£18
2nd growths–£20 4th growths–£12

Then Wilhelm Franck, in the first edition of his *Traité sur les Vins du Médoc* (1824), in an appendix to a table of Bordeaux prices from 1782 to 1823, lists by communes the prices of the red wines of the 'good years of 1745, etc.' Some communes have four classes, others fewer. Margaux and Cantenac, bracketed together, are given first and Château Margaux is the single *premier cru* (1,500 – 1,800 livres a *tonneau*). Then follow eight seconds, including familiar names such as 'Rosan ainé' and Durfort, (1,000 – 1,300 livres), twelve thirds (600 – 1,000 livres) and nine fourths (400 – 600 livres). Growths are listed in seven other communes, including Labarde, Macau, St-Julien, St-Lambert, Pauillac, St-Estèphe and St-Seurin-de-Cadourne, in that order. They all have a *premier cru* but at very different prices. For example, the one in Macau is Villeneuve (Cantemerle), but its price is only 300 livres. Giscours the top wine of Labarde is in the 1,500 – 1,800 livres price-bracket, while Brane-Mouton, the only named second growth is, surprisingly, only priced at 400 – 600 livres, while Pichon-Longueville in St-Lambert is 400 – 500 livres.

Interesting too is a list of six red Graves communes, which include Pessac, Mérignac, Cauderan, Taillan and Blanquefort (these last two now the southern 'frontier' communes of the Médoc), Léognan and Gradignan. Haut-Brion is the only first growth of Pessac, in the 1,500 – 1,800 livres price range, followed by La Mission and Savignac as seconds, with the surprisingly high price of 1,200 – 1,300 livres. There are two thirds, one belonging to Mme Sabourin (800 – 1,200 livres) and Giac (500 – 800 livres). Three fourths follow, and even Mérignac, now largely lost to wine under the developers' excavators and the aircraft runways, has three classes, headed by Bouran (500 – 800 livres). Of the others only Cadauran has any growths mentioned and Léognan, esteemed today, sold for 300 – 400 livres only.

A further note by Franck shows that the price of Château Margaux in 1822 was the same as in 1722, 2,500 livres (frs.). Its output averaged 100 – 120 *tonneaux*. The stability of Bordeaux wine prices over very long periods is difficult to understand in these inflationary times. In 1824 Lafite commonly secured the top price, followed by Latour and Margaux in that order.

The prices given above are, of course, growers' prices, i.e. what they received for their wines when sold to the merchants in Bordeaux. The latter, with the expenses of stockholding and sale, have traditionally secured a good margin on their purchases. From the point of view of merchants' prices to their trade customers at home and abroad, as well as from that of the classification, a price list of Beyerman of this period is doubly interesting. The date is probably 1828, for the red wines of 1825 and 1826 are offered, and the whites of 1827. As the prices show, 1825 was a far better vintage than 1826, and the wines were, of course, a year older at the time of offer. The main listings are as follows:

Vins Rouges	1825	1826
1 *Crus*, Ch. Margaux, Latour, Lafitte, Ch. Haut-Brion	6,000 frs.	2,000 – 2,100 frs.
2 *Crus*, Rauzan, Léoville, Larose, Branne-Mouton	5,500 – 5,700	1,600 – 1,800
3 *Crus*, Kirwan, Pichon-de-Longueville, Ch. d'Issan, etc.	4,800 – 5,200	1,200 – 1,300
4 & 5 *Crus ou Bourgeois supérieurs* de Margaux, St-Julien, Pauillac, St-Estèphe	4,200 – 4,400	700 – 1,100
Bons Bourgeois de Médoc	3,500 – 3,800	500 – 600
Bourgeois Ordinaires de Médoc	1,900 – 2,800	360 – 400
Graves, Pessac, Talence, etc.	1,800 – 3,000	400 – 850
Graves, Pessac, Talence, *Ordinaires*	700 – 800	–
St-Emilion & Canon *1er qualité*	800 – 900	380 – 400
St-Emilion & Canon *2e & 3e qualité*	650 – 750	300 – 330
Bonnes Côtes & Bonnes Palus	400 – 450	–
Vins Blancs		
Haut-Preignac, Ht. Barsac, Bommes, Sauternes	900 – 1,200 – 2,600	500 – 800
Bas Preignac, Bas Barsac	600 – 700	400 – 425
Cérons, Ste-Croix, Dumont, Loupiac, et St-Pey, Langon, Fargues, Virelade, Landiras, etc.	450 – 700	280 – 425

The spelling of the names is as on the list. It is interesting in particular to note the relatively small difference in prices between the 1825 classed growths, and their relation to the other wines. Also the relatively low prices of the best Graves and the very modest position of the St-Emilions are shown. At this period Beyerman was part-proprietor of Haut-Brion.

It will be observed that the prices of the 1825s, although a distinguished vintage, were high in relation to the likely cost of the wines at source. Franck in 1824 was listing the average growers' prices for the three Médoc *premiers crus* as 2,300 – 2,400 frs. a *tonneau*, and 2,000 – 2,100 frs. for the same four *deuxièmes* as offered by Beyerman. For the eight *troisièmes*, which included Gorse, Pichon-de-Longueville, Cos, Calon, Lascombes and Bergeron (St-Julien), the growers' prices were 1,500–1,800 frs., while for the 18 *quatrièmes*, headed by Kirwan and ended by Boyd, were 1,200 – 1,400. There were no *cinquièmes* in Franck's list of 33 classed growths. Neither in his list nor in the merchant's did the first growths then greatly exceed the seconds.

Franck makes clear that at this period the first growths went to England. Of Latour he wrote that the English were the biggest buyers, and of Lafite 'nearly all is drunk in England'. 'The English also normally buy all the other *premiers crus* of this commune' (Pauillac).

The fifth class gradually evolved from the fourth, which at one time was divided into the first fourths and the second fourths. Franck in the first edition of his book (1824) in listing the prices of the classed and other growths from 1782 to 1823 gives the same prices for what were to be fourth and fifth growths, but in later editions shows them separately and at different average prices. A. L. Henderson in his *The History of Ancient and Modern Wines* (1824) lists five classes in tables of prices for the 1815, 1818 and 1822 vintages. Three firsts sold for 3,100 frs. and six seconds at 2,300 frs. Then follow six in the next rank, including Malescot, Castelnau, Brane-Cantenac, Gorse, Pichon-de-Longueville and Cabarrus (Lagrange) at 1,800 frs.; a fourth rank, including Giscours, Poujet and Laujac at 1,400 – 1,500 frs; and a fifth and final one, with Pontet-Canet and St-Guiron (Grand-Puy-Lacoste) at 1,200 frs. A long way below these comes St-Emilion at 500 – 600 frs. and Sauternes and Barsac at 650 – 800 frs. Some of the Médoc prices look very high.

It would be wearisome to follow all the price variations over the years up to 1855, and a selection taken from the more successful vintages will be found in Appendix A. The essential factor in each vintage was the basic price of the first growths; the others then fell into line. In general the norm in the 1820s and 1830s in a good year was 2,400 – 3,000 frs. a *tonneau* for the first growths, and then a descending scale of 300 frs. less per class; so the fifth growths sold at half the price of the first. However, there was so much variation in this that it was only a rough guide, and as the century advanced, the first growths tended to draw ahead of the others, as has happened much more dramatically in the past dozen years. Henderson mentions that the four first growths fetched 20 – 25 per cent more than any other wines of the region, and also says that Brane-Mouton sold for one-third less than Lafite. These differences, however, varied from vintage to vintage, and according to whether or not a vineyard made particularly good wine in a certain year. Although Lafite usually headed the list, in the excellent vintage of 1831 Latour's price was 2,600 frs. a *tonneau*, compared with 2,400 frs. for Lafite, 2,100 frs. for Mouton and 2,500 frs. for Rausan-Ségla. It was rare, nevertheless, for a second growth to challenge a first growth in price.

Perhaps before 1855 the classes were less rigid, because unofficial. For example, Cyrus Redding in 1833 says: 'The wines are classed by the brokers, who decide to which class the wine of each grower shall belong. The latter use all their efforts to place their wines in a higher class, and thus emulation is kindled, and they are justified in their efforts by the profits. The price of their wines, too, is less governed by particular merit, than by the number they occupy in the scale of classification. It often costs them sacrifices to reach that object. They will keep their wine many years to give it a superior title, instead of selling it the first year according to custom. By this means an individual will get his wine changed from the fourth to the third class, which he had perhaps occupied before for many successive years.' However, it is not clear that the proprietors were successful in their efforts but if the 1855 classification had been similarly flexible, who can doubt that Bordeaux would have been occupied with a non-stop game of snakes-and-ladders ever since?

That the pre-1855 classifications were not a closed corporation, as its successor turned out, is shown by the admission of Montrose and Palmer in the 1820s, when these vineyards were new and their wine young. Montrose, partly carved out of Calon's estate, was generally accepted as a second growth in 1825 and, based on Gascq, Palmer a third about the same time. However, allowing for changes of name and some variations in grading, the pre-1855 lists, as printed by Franck in his 1853 edition, are surprisingly similar to those set forth for the Paris Exhibition of 1855. Franck was careful to print his list of seconds to fifths in alphabetical order, to avoid controversy that was evidently as brisk then as later, but the only omissions from his list of second growths were Montrose and Ducru, both then placed as thirds. The third-growth list, with this pair added and Palmer subtracted, is little different from 1855, allowing for some changes of name, and one or two other relegations, including Calon and La Lagune, to the fourth class. Here and in the fifth growths the pattern is a little more confused, but the well-known estates such as Beychevelle, Talbot, St-Pierre and Duhart-Milon are there; and among the bottom rank the variations between the pre- and post-1855 listings are surprisingly small, although Château Popp may not immediately be recognized as Camensac. There are one or two outsiders in the list, notably La Mission 'près Haut-Brion', with the surprisingly small output of 30 – 40 *tonneaux*, compared with 80 – 90 today. Also Liversan and Monpelou are now no longer classed growths. It is interesting to see Cantemerle listed in 1853, for at that time it was not sold on the Bordeaux market but exported to Holland *en totalité*.

Too often the 1855 classification has by inference been presented either as the beginning of things, rather like the Creation; or, to use another Biblical simile, like the Tablets of the Law, handed down by the brokers of Bordeaux to the Médocain proprietors assembled on the Quai des Chartrons – with Haut-Brion's owner smuggled in on the old-boy network. As will have been seen already, the 1855 was no more produced suddenly out of thin air than Man was created in Seven Days. It was little more than a codification of previous practice and classification. Devised on the occasion of the Universal Exposition of Paris in 1855, and carried out by the Syndicate of Brokers, it was then endorsed by the Bordeaux Chamber of Commerce, which was careful to point out that 'this classification has been sanctioned by experience extending back more than a century'. It included 22 Sauternes and Barsacs in addition to the sixty-odd Médocs and the solitary Haut-Brion from the Graves.

What was fresh, however, was a new or at least newly formalized order of the growths in the classification. Whereas Franck in the appendix to his first edition had thought alphabetical order by commune was the better part of valour – so he put Ch. Margaux of Margaux at the head of the firsts, Haut-Brion as an outsider being tacked on at the end of this class – the brokers boldly placed the growths, red and white, in order if not of merit then certainly of price. So Lafite is at the top of the firsts and Mouton-Rothschild, however unwillingly later, leads the seconds.

This order of precedence continues throughout the list, demonstrating that they considered Rausan-Ségla superior to its neighbour Rauzan-Gassies, the Baron to the Comtesse of Pichon-Longueville and Grand-Puy-Lacoste to Grand-Puy-Ducasse. They may or may not have been right at the time, but that is how they saw it. The only errors on their showing at the time may have been the classification of Palmer as a third and the placing of Cantemerle at the bottom of the whole list; for the former was in the hands of receivers and the latter was sold on the Bordeaux market only the year before the classification, so therefore there was no list of prices to use as a guide. But even this is only speculation. In Appendix A will be found representative classed growth prices in some of the more important vintages.

It is a highly debatable point whether the 1855 classification has been of assistance to Bordeaux or to the consumer; but it has certainly helped the châteaux at the head of the list. The immediate result was a widening of the price differential between the first growths and the rest. D'Armailhacq in the third edition of his treatise *De La Culture des Vignes* (1867) comments that between 1855 and 1865 the first-growth prices rose from 2,800 to 5,600 frs. but the seconds only from 1,500 to 2,100 frs. and the fifths from 900 to 1,300 frs. It appears, that the new 'official' classification may have done no more than hasten and emphasize a trend already in existence.

It is probably true that the first growths have helped indirectly to raise above those of the non-classed properties the prices of the seconds and of all the classed growths, but whether this has been beneficial is again arguable. The *crus bourgeois* have probably secured less than their worth, and some at least of the *crus classés* have from time to time been 'carried' by their classmates. They still are. Moreover the rigidity of the 1855 classification over more than a century has removed even the theoretical incentive to betterment mentioned by Redding prior to 1855. So far as I am aware none of the Médoc classed growths below *premier cru* level advertise their rank in the classification on their labels, unlike the army of *premiers crus* in St-Emilion and Pomerol; and Lafite, 'first of the firsts', apparently scorns to do so. Indeed, so far as the consumers are concerned, there is little evidence of class-consciousness, except for the first growths.

However this has not prevented periodic skirmishes in the Médoc class war, particularly from the Rothschilds of Mouton. Even by 1867 Charles Lorbac, in his description of Mouton in *Les Richesses Gastronomiques de la France*, says the question of making Mouton a first growth had been raised, for it always sold for more than the other seconds. Docteur Aussel in *La Gironde A Vol D'Oiseau; ses Grands Vins et ses Châteaux* (1865) wrote of Mouton: 'this growth tends to achieve the first rank'.

Then Alfred Danflou in *Les Grands Crus Bordelais* (1867) writes somewhat rhetorically that he is convinced the classification is not definitive and the syndicate of brokers will be called to render justice to those growths which have risen to a rank they lacked at the time of classification. At one time, he continues, were not the wines of Bourg the leaders, and eighty years previously some growths, scarcely known today had a European reputation. He instances La Bégorce, Gorse, Prevôt de Lecroize in Margaux, Dubosc in St-Julien, Liversan in St-Sauveur and Angludet in Cantenac.

It may well be that Danflou had been listening to the complaints of Mouton, for he rather goes out of his way to depreciate the established *premiers crus*. According to him, Margaux was the only first with a reputation in the seventeenth century, Lafite was little known until the end of the reign of Louis XIV (d. 1715), while Latour and Haut-Brion's position dated in reality only from the end of the eighteenth century. This last point is certainly not true, as we have seen. He concludes by suggesting that Lafite and Latour might pay a public tribute to Mouton, state that the public considers it their equal and then admit it to parity. For good measure Danflou suggests that some unnamed other growths might also become firsts. (Seconds he particularly praises are Rausan, Léoville and Larose.)

According to Danflou, Mr Scott, described as one of the most important members of the Bordelais trade and presumably Scott the Consul, as well as M. Merman, the well-known broker, who were both members of the jury at the 1862 London Exhibition (when Cheval-Blanc secured its still label-publicized bronze medal), stated that Mouton above all equalled them (the first growths) in many years.

In the famous vintage of 1858 Mouton, Lafite and Haut-Brion all sold for the same price – 4,000 frs. – but Margaux, which had a special reputation *en primeur* fetched 5,000 frs. and Latour 4,800. Among the seconds Léoville-Poyferré made 3,500 frs.

In 1865 Mouton sold for 4,000 frs., compared with 2,750 for Palmer and 2,400 for Léoville Barton. But Lafite, bought by a syndicate of six Bordeaux merchants, fetched 5,600 frs. However, it is not easy to compare prices at this period, because it was not uncommon for a property to make a contract for five or ten years to buy the crop each year, irrespective of quality. Obviously such a speculation on the part of a Bordeaux merchant or group of merchants meant a lower price for the best years, so from 1863 – 72 Margaux was sold for 4,200 frs. to an English syndicate of three merchants: J. Alnutt, Trowers & Lawson, and Boord, Son & Beckwith. The terms of this contract, which had been negotiated by a Mr Clarke, were not disclosed, but in Bordeaux no deals remain secret for very long, and not only did the price emerge, but also the fact that in a crop averaging 130 *tonneaux* the first wine was sold for £42 per *barrique* and the second wine for £21.

At the height of the pre-phylloxera golden era, the 1868 edition of Cocks et Féret included a table (on the opposite page) showing the relative prices of the various classes of the excellent 1865 vintage, both *en primeur* and two years later. Mouton, as will be noted, is singled out from the second growths. Also the lower classes appreciated proportionately more in price than the first growths.

These prices do not always coincide with those given for Mouton and Palmer above, taken from Tastet et Lawton's records which, of course, reflect their own

	En primeur	Le 16 Novembre 1867
1ers Crus	5,600 frs.	7,000 – 8,000 frs.
2e Cru Mouton	3,500	5,500 – 6,000
2es Crus autres	2,500 – 2,600	5,000 – 5,500
3es Crus	1,900	3,600 – 4,000
4es Crus	1,500 – 1,600	3,000 – 3,400
5es Crus	1,200 – 1,400	2,500 – 2,800
Bourgeois supérieurs	1,000 – 1,200	1,800 – 2,000

dealings. Other prices given in this chapter and elsewhere are subject to normal market variations, but show the general trend. Cocks et Féret commented in 1868 that the first growths fetched about 25 per cent more than the seconds, the fifths always sold more or less at half the price of the seconds, while the thirds and fourths were roughly half-way between the seconds and the fifths. These rough approximations made business much easier.

Broadly speaking up to the phylloxera period Lafite generally secured the top price, which was sometimes equalled by the other first growths but not by Mouton. But the latter was, nevertheless, much more expensive than any of the other seconds, and usually by more than 1,000 frs. a *tonneau*. In 1874, for example, Mouton was sold immediately after the vintage for 4,200 frs. and its nearest rival among the seconds was Gruaud-Larose-Sarget at 3,000. Yet Lafite went for 5,500 frs. and Latour for 5,000.

After the phylloxera Lafite appears to have gone through a bad period, with one or other of the other first growths securing higher prices. For example, in 1890 Latour made 4,100 and Margaux 4,000 frs., compared with 3,000 for Lafite, and in the great year of 1899 Haut-Brion achieved the top price of 2,600 frs., followed by Margaux at 2,200, and Latour and Lafite at 2,000. But Mouton was also in a disappointing patch too, so far as opening prices were concerned. According to the Tastet et Lawton records, the 1890 Mouton was not sold until 1894 and then for a knock-down price of 2,000 frs., while the 1899 only went for 1,800. Later, however, the reckoning might have been different, as Mouton-Rothschild 1899 turned out one of the finest '99s.

During the first twenty years of the present century prices of the first growths in comparison with others are difficult to compare, because it was a period of extensive contract-making. In the golden vintage epoch from 1858 – 78 the contracting proprietors probably did less well than the merchants, but in the poor succession of vintages after 1900, the boot was on the other foot. For trade was not very good. Mouton was the monopoly of Calvet between 1907 and 1912, but the 1913 was so poor that Calvet refused it, and the contract ended. Lafite from 1907 – 16 was the monopoly of Rosenheim and Lebègue, and then of Rosenheim alone. Both the other Médoc first growths made contracts for the same decade, Margaux with Schröder & Schÿler and Eschenauer, and Latour with Mestrezat and others.

The contract price for Mouton paid by Calvet was identical with the first growths:

1,650 frs. a *tonneau*. Whatever was the assessment earlier, in this century and particularly since 1920 or thereabouts, Mouton-Rothschild as a wine has, I believe it fair to say generally received the same regard as the wines classed as *premiers crus* in 1855, and, often better, as the Twenties were not the best period for all the latter.

In 1917, a dismal war year, most of the leaders renewed their contracts for five years, for an increased price of 2,650 frs. Eschenauer and Calvet headed the Lafite group, Calvet the Margaux, while Ginestet had the monopoly of Latour for 1917 and 1918 only. As a result several of these first growths, committed to 2,650 frs., did not receive very satisfactory prices for the fine 1920s while third-growth Palmer secured 4,500 frs. After that the monopoly/contract system declined, although Rosenheim had a monopoly of Haut-Brion in 1929. While it lasted this contract system distorted the price structure, for the *premiers crus* which had tended to set the pace were largely out of the running. At the retail stage the first growths, with which Mouton must now be classed in common parlance, were not much more expensive than the runners-up.

In the 1920s the franc ran into difficulties and prices in terms of money rose sharply. The 1926s were the most expensive red Bordeaux ever sold up to that date, for the crop was small and the franc re-valued. All the leaders reached upwards of 40,000 frs., while Palmer went for 23,000. As a result this vintage was little bought in Britain and therefore seldom seen later. The '28s made up to 20,000 frs. for the leaders.

Sample prices of the famous '29s opened as follows:

First Growths	20,000 frs.	Cantemerle	9,000 frs.
Gruaud-Larose-Faure	12,000	Léoville-Barton	8,000
Léoville-Poyferré	11,000	Léoville-Las-Cases	8,000
Brane-Cantenac	10,000	Gruaud-Larose-Sarget	7,500
Beychevelle	10,000	Langoa	7,500
Pontet-Canet	9,000		

I quote a number of these opening prices as they demonstrate that position in the classification was now far less important than the estimated quality of the wine. Léoville-Poyferré, as indicated in the chapter on Bordeaux vintages, was exceptionally fine and superior to most of the *premiers crus* as well as to Gruaud-Larose-Faure. This was the year of the New York Stock Exchange crash which in October 1929 heralded the World Slump as the young wines were still in the fermenting vats. Within eighteen months the first-growth '29s could be re-bought for 10,000 frs., exactly half their opening prices. Not until after the Second World War were classed-growth prices to recover.

If time brought a re-adjustment of certain châteaux standing, the surprising thing was that the classification by and large had retained so much of its validity after three-quarters of a century; and this is still true today. The subsequent down-grading of some growths may well be owing more to bad husbandry than to anything else; and the reverse applies. Yet in the mysterious way that certain vineyards are esteemed all over the world, it is situation and soil which counts first.

Although I have devoted some attention to the question of Mouton because it is the most obvious anomaly, and the one most felt by a proprietor, this is not the only one; and after the last war voices began to be heard suggesting a re-organization of the 1855 classification or an entirely new one. Some merely proposed changes in the Médoc growths, with or without accessions from the leading *crus bourgeois*.

This category of *bourgeois* growth appears to be of indeterminate origin. Franck in 1853 lists seven *bons bourgeois*, following the fifth class, and fetching between 700 and 1,000 frs., according to quality. These were, as described by him:

Growth		Commune
Bel-Air	—	Soussans
Paveil	—	Soussans
Le Boscq	—	St-Estèphe
Cru-de-Morin	—	St-Corbian, St-Estèphe
Lanessan	—	Cussac
Pédesclaux	—	Pauillac
Tronquoy-Lalande	—	St-Estèphe

Of these the first is now Bel-Air-Marquis-d'Aligre, the second is Paveil de Luze. There is a Morin in St-Estèphe, but is not outstanding nowadays. The last on the list is now Bel-Orme-Tronquoy-de-Lalande and is in St-Seurin-de-Cadourne. Franck admits that his list of *bons bourgeois* is not comprehensive, and also mentions La-Tour-de-Mons of Soussans, and Pommiers and Morange of Ludon. The former of this Ludon pair appears not to exist now, but in 1853 it had a solid reputation in Holland, like the neighbouring Cantemerle. The second edition of Cocks et Féret's *Bordeaux et ses Vins* (1868) makes no such distinction among the better *crus bourgeois*.

Later on a category of *cru exceptional* was developed, but although no doubt similar in standing to the *bons bourgeois* was no more constant. In the 1929 Cocks et Féret it was limited to three—Bel-Air-Marquis-d'Aligre, Chasse Spleen and Villegeorge. In 1932 what might be called an unofficial market classification of these *exceptionals* was made by Bordeaux brokers at the request of owners of *crus bourgeois*, but was repudiated. The title itself was not well received, as one might consider an 'exceptional' growth superior to a mere 'first'. The selection too was controversial, but here it is:

Growth		Commune
Angludet	—	Cantenac
Villegeorge	—	Avensan
Bel-Air-Marquis-d'Aligre	—	Soussans
Chasse-Spleen	—	Moulis
Moulin-Riche	—	St-Julien
La Couronne	—	Pauillac

In the authoritative Larmat maps of Bordeaux issued in 1944, Villegeorge, then in partial eclipse, was not in the list.

Several other minor 'orders' came into being many years ago: *cru bourgeois supérieur du Haut-Médoc*; *cru bourgeois du Haut-Médoc*; and *cru bourgeois du Médoc*. This last applied to the Bas-Médoc. At the same time there were *crus paysans* and *crus artisans*. More recently, however, the peasantry was wiped out, though the artisans were spared. Now there are no *crus paysans* but the *crus artisans* persist, precariously one might think. To complete this *bourgeois* revolution, it only remained to ennoble some of the *haute bourgeoisie* or, in Bordeaux terms, the *bourgeoisie supérieur*.

During the last world war a significant official price grading, carried out, in 1943, at the Vichy Government's order, by the National Syndicate of the wine trade, gave some idea of how the classed growths then stood in relation to each other and to the rest of the Bordeaux estates. The purpose of this was to establish maximum prices at which these wines could be sold per *tonneau* of 900 litres. From a list running to 26 pages I take a few examples of interest.

		frs.
Médoc	Lafite (and other first growths)	100,000
,,	Mouton-Rothschild	100,000
Graves	Haut-Brion	100,000
St-Emilion	Ausone	100,000
,,	Cheval-Blanc	100,000
Graves	La Mission-Haut-Brion	88,000
Médoc	Other second growths	80,000
Pomerol	Pétrus	80,000
Graves	Haut-Bailly and Domaine de Chevalier	80,000
Médoc	Third growths (Giscours, La Lagune, and Palmer)	75,000
,,	Fourth growths (Beychevelle and Branaire-Ducru)	75,000
St-Emilion	Canon, La Gaffelière and Clos Fourtet, etc.	75,000
Pomerol	Vieux-Ch.-Certan, Certan, La Conseillante, etc.	75,000
Médoc	Other third growths	70,000
,,	Fourth growth (Talbot)	70,000
,,	Fifth growths (Cantemerle, Mouton d'Armailhacq and Pontet-Canet)	75,000
St-Emilion	Figeac, Belair, Trottevieille, etc.	70,000
Pomerol	Gazin, Lafleur	70,000
Graves	Fieuzal	70,000
Médoc	Other fourth growths	65,000
,,	Fifth growths (Batailley and Lynch-Bages)	65,000
Médoc	Other fifth growths	60,000
St-Emilion	La Dominique, Pavie, Bellevue, etc.	65,000
Pomerol	La Fleur-Pétrus, Le-Gay, Domaine de l'Eglise, etc.	65,000
Graves	Bouscaut, Olivier, Carbonnieux, Smith-Haut-Lafitte	60,000
St-Emilion	Cadet-Bon, Ripeau, Le Couvent, etc.	60,000
Pomerol	Beauregard, Croix-de-Gay, Nenin, etc.	60,000

The *bourgeois* Médocs of renown fetched between 40,000 and 50,000 frs., although

Chasse-Spleen was listed at 58,000 and Angludet at 52,000. The St-Emilion and Pomerol *crus bourgeois* fetched similar prices to the Médocs. The lowest listed prices for red Bordeaux were 28,000 to 30,000 francs.

It may be noted that among the Sauternes Yquem was clearly top of all Bordeaux at 130,000 frs., while the first growths were fixed at 90,000, and the seconds from 77,000 frs. down to 70,000 frs. The price average in this region was high, around 65,000 frs. Even some of the Ste-Croix-du-Monts were as high as 65,000, while the Cérons and Loupiacs averaged 55,000 frs. Perhaps they were in demand to satisfy a wartime shortage of sugar.

In passing it is of interest to mention that the prices fixed for Romanée-Conti and Montrachet were 32,500 and 28,000 frs. respectively per cask of 228 litres, while Chambertin and Musigny headed the other red Burgundies at 25,000 frs., and Bâtard-Montrachet and Corton-Charlemagne were only 16,000 frs. To compare these prices with Bordeaux they should be multiplied roughly four times.

Such was the state of play under wartime conditions a quarter of a century ago, and this shows a somewhat different appraisal of various growths than they would receive today.

After the war some reformers began thinking not only of re-classifying the classed growths but of embracing all the important red wines of Bordeaux. During the 1940s controversy simmered rather than raged, but the growing importance of the American market was an argument used by the re-classifiers. Across the Atlantic the existing system meant nothing, and was in fact highly misleading; and there was the nagging problem of the St-Emilions, not to mention wines labelled *premier cru* from elsewhere in France. Yet no evidence was produced that Americans, armed with classification cards as well as vintage charts, dismissed such wines as Grand-Puy-Lacoste with the curt comment, 'only a fifth growth with a rating of five'.

Meanwhile, the red Graves were classified in 1953 and the leading St-Emilions were officially classified by 1955, the latter being a provisional one designed only to last ten years, pending the hoped-for re-classification of the Médoc. Among the major districts only Pomerol now remains unclassified.

At one point in the 1950s the classed-growth owners of the Médoc conferred together and there was a majority for a new classification. In 1959 a committee was set up in Bordeaux to examine the matter. Proposals were made by a commission to omit no fewer than nineteen of the lesser classed growths from a new classification. True three or four of these no longer existed or had been amalgamated, but they made a clean sweep of St-Laurent's trio, as well as Lagrange, Dauzac, St-Pierre and other fourths and fifths. They also proposed to add a dozen *bourgeois* growths, including several of the *crus exceptionnels* and Gloria, Lanessan, Siran, Labégorce, etc., but left out others with fair claims to inclusion. Not surprisingly such proposals, although never made public officially, were badly received.

A suggestion was then made for an entirely new classification, based on a new 'competition' and an examination by an expert 'jury'. Who were to be the jurors? the critics asked suspiciously. In 1965 it looked as if this new classification scheme would go through, with the blessing of the French Government. However several distinguished classed growths let it be known they would boycott any such competition. It was also discovered nothing could stop growths classified in 1855 from continuing legally to announce the fact, even if compelled to add the information that it was of that classification.

Meanwhile Mr Alexis Lichine, associated with two classed growths and a member of the original examining committee, had in 1959 produced his own proposed classification. This took in the Graves, St-Emilion and Pomerol and added four of the *crus exceptionnels* and a dozen *crus bourgeois supérieurs*. The whole comprised nearly 150 growths, thanks to large contingents from St-Emilion and Pomerol. Numerical classification was avoided by the use of other terms in the five categories retained and within each class the wines were listed alphabetically. The top rank, occupied by the original four, plus Mouton-Rothschild, Cheval-Blanc, Ausone and Pétrus, was called *crus hors classe*. Then came *crus exceptionnels*, *grands crus*, *crus supérieurs* and *bons crus*. Who indeed could object to drinking just a *bon cru*?

Mr Lichine also pointed out that some of the existing classed growths no longer produced wines, others occupied somewhat different situations, while a third section no longer made good wine; some, however, were making much better wine. On this score he demoted Lagrange from third to fifth (*bon cru*) class and elevated Cantemerle to second (*cru exceptionnel*).

There was also a plan to classify 13 *crus exceptionnels* and divide the other *bourgeois* into *Crus Grands Bourgeois* and *Crus Bourgeois*.

Basically these proposals seem sensible, both in drawing in wines from other districts and in avoiding a numerical sequence. The inclusion of Mouton-Rothschild, Cheval-Blanc and Pétrus in the top class is surely correct, although I might be a little doubtful about placing Ausone there. I would have several other reservations and additions to suggest, but so would others; Alexis Lichine's proposals although slightly revised in 1966 are essentially already 10 years old, and the standing of vineyards can rise and fall in that period. I believe if and when there is a new classification it will be on these lines. Nevertheless to date nothing has been done; the forces of opposition and inertia have been too strong.

Meanwhile, it must be emphasized that one should not drink on class lines. The 1855 classification was criticized at the time on the grounds that it represented the views of the brokers buying these wines *en primeur*. That Lafite sold for twice the amount realized by Pichon-Longueville-Baron or Palmer did not mean in the end that a bottle of the former was necessarily better than or even as good as the latter pair. All that can be said is that all things being equal the top classed growths are more likely to make a finer wine than the lesser-classed vineyards; but things are often far from equal, as the comments on various châteaux and vintages in this book show.

Moreover in so far as the concentration on the first growths, nowadays principally sold in the U.S.A. (as they once were to Britain), has distorted the price structure of the leading clarets, the existing classification is to be deplored. The prices of Pétrus, Cheval-Blanc, Ausone and other growths only just behind the classified leaders have advanced in their wake while excellent wines of lower official status have often not secured their due return. This has all been affected by the rivalry that preceded the advent of the Rothschilds, but has certainly been accentuated by Baron Philippe's intense conviction that Mouton-Rothschild is as good as any first growth and for his money better than most. The only way this can be demonstrated is by asking a price as high as any other first growth and higher than most. Thanks to the devotion of Baron Philippe and his staff, to the quality of the wine and to its high reputation, especially in the United States hitherto, he has been able to do this successfully. But if the price trends of the mid-1960s are maintained, the top rank in a new classification may turn out for most claret lovers not merely to be *hors classe* but *hors cave* and *hors dégustation* as well.

18. The Bordeaux Vintages

This chapter is largely a personal assessment of clarets of various vintages that have come my way, along with general information I have been able to acquire; but even of the more recent years I cannot claim even to have sampled all the representative wines. There is also some appreciation of the Sauternes, though these do not appear on our tables with such regularity as the red Bordeaux. Lacking the longevity and experience of André Simon, revealed, for example, in his *Vintagewise* (1945) in which, *inter alia*, he surveyed the claret vintages from the 1840s onwards, I cannot properly discuss every vintage. Indeed I have never drunk a bottle of claret of the 1840 decade, although it is fair to add that in 1945 André Simon admitted to having drunk only one: Lafite 1846. So it would be for me an academic, somewhat arid account, and probably of little interest to readers today. Now and again a wine already mentioned in the various districts may be discussed again here, but in the context of its vintage equals or rivals.

Accordingly I take together all the pre-phylloxera vintages, then deal as a whole with the years to the close of the last century, and follow with those up to the end of the First World War and its immediate aftermath. Then a more regular, annual comment is possible up to the last vintage which is at this time assessable in bottle: 1964.

The Pre-Phylloxera Epoch

There was a succession of fine vintages in the 1770s, and 1784 was a celebrated year sought after by Thomas Jefferson. However what may be described as the first 'modern' fine vintage was the wonderful 1798. This can be called modern because it occurred not long after the development of the modern type of bottle which made it possible to lay down wine for maturing. Significantly perhaps, the *Vinothèque* at Lafite was established only a year before the remarkable 1798s, which had a very long life. At a Christie's wine sale in London in 1802 Château Margot (*sic*) 1798 'celebrated vintage, bottled in London in 1802' fetched the very high price of £9.2.6d. a dozen, and in the same sale 'Barnes's 1802 claret' (Barnes was a famous London merchant of the time and he had imported the Margaux 1798) bottled as late as 1807 fetched £8.2.6d. a case. This was of course at the height of the Napoleonic War scarcity, and after the 1798 the next famous vintage of the era was 1802. Other outstanding vintages in the first quarter of the nineteenth century were 1811, the famous 'Comet' year, 1815 a vintage long remembered, 1819 and 1825. Both 1822 and 1825 were exceptional white wine vintages. The 1825 wine was made after a very fine summer, prices were very high but as the wines took a long time to come round, considerable losses were incurred by merchants holding them. Fine were 1803, 1807, 1814 and 1822. I have already described the bottle of Lafite 1803 drunk at Bristol in 1967. The 1811 '*Vin de Comète*' Lafite was served at a celebrated lunch to several hundred guests at the château in 1926 and was proclaimed in excellent condition.

In the next quarter of this century the leading vintages were 1828, 1831, 1834, 1841, 1844, 1847 and 1848. The 1828s were very famous in their day, and were described by Tastet et Lawton as '*merveilleuse d'élégance, de grâce, de bouquet, goût délicieux*'. The first growths were particularly esteemed but the most celebrated of them all was the Mouton. There is a story, well known in Bordeaux, about a dinner party given probably about 1860 by the British Consul in Bordeaux, Mr T. G. D. Scott, who so far as I know had no connection with the Scotts of Lafite, and lived at what is now 29 Cours Xavier Arnozan. The story is told in Paul de Cassagnac's *French Wines* (1936) translated by Guy Knowles. One of the guests was M. Duffau-Dubergier, Mayor of Bordeaux and a very rich man. The crowning wine was the Mouton '28. It was greeted with great enthusiasm and the mayor at once asked, 'Have you much of it left?' 'Alas, only a dozen bottles.' The mayor replied, 'Well, my dear fellow, I'm going to make you a proposition. Twelve bottles, twelve thousand francs' (almost £500 and the equivalent today of at least £2,500).

'You are asking an impossibility of me, my friend' answered Scott, 'But to show you how much I desire to fall in with your wishes, I'll agree to share it with you, and we'll say six bottles, six thousand francs'.

'My dear Scott', remarked M. Duffau-Dubergier, 'if I buy wine at a thousand francs a bottle, it is on condition that I am the only man that can give it to his friends to drink'.

Scott thought it over a moment. 'Right; we'll say no more about it'. Then, turning to his butler, he said: 'Bernard, decant us two more bottles of the 1828 Mouton'. Another version of the story gives the wine as Lafite.

The winter of 1830 – 1 was exceptionally severe with ice-floes on the Garonne, with temperatures of minus 10 degrees Centigrade, followed by heavy hail in August.

The crop was small, but fine.* The white wines were particularly successful, as they were in 1834, when after spring frosts and summer hail storms the crop was again much reduced. The summer had been exceptionally hot and the vintage started on 9 September, the earliest year of the century until 1865, when picking began three days earlier. In 1834 there was bad weather later in September, and those who waited until October were rewarded for their patience. However conditions must have been not unlike the very hot year of 1921, and some of the wines were 'pricked', i.e., turned to vinegar in the vats; others had at first a taste of decay, but outgrew it to become a very distinguished vintage.

The next rank of vintages of the second quarter of the century included 1840 (for white wines) and 1846 (also for white wines). The 1840s were a period of exceptionally fine vintages. According to André Simon, 1846 was the first vintage of Lafite bottled at the château. This, however, as with many other details about Bordeaux in the past, is not certain. Christian Cruse has suggested that it was 1847, when his great-grandfather bought the whole crop and asked the château to bottle most of the wine, as he had no room in his Bordeaux cellars. In this period Lafite merely branded its château-bottled wine with 'C.L.' accompanied by the date. There was no label, and the wine merchants who purchased the wine were accustomed to use their own labels. When Cruse bought the whole crop of Lafite '47, he sold some of it in cask to Barton & Guestier, Clossmann and Johnston, who bottled their lots themselves. Cruse, who had no room in his cellars for the vast quantity of 1847s that he had bought, arranged for Lafite to bottle all the rest of its own wine. The 1847s were at first largely disregarded and very cheap, but later had a great success, particularly in northern Europe and the United States. The 1848s were even finer for reds, but not for the whites. The '47s and '48s form one of the famous 'pairs' of claret vintages.

If the 1840s were prolific in fine vintages, the 1850s were the reverse, owing to the oidium from 1853 – 7 (but first noticed in 1852). Gruaud Larose, which produced 160 *tonneaux* in 1848, made 20 in 1854 and 35 in 1855. Crops were decimated and when they recovered with the abundant and excellent 1858 prices were high. In 1858 began what is sometimes called the 'Golden Age' of claret, with a succession of vintages not only remarkable in themselves but in many cases with exceptional staying power. They provide most of the backing for the argument, impossible yet of resolution, that post-phylloxera clarets have never lasted so well. This period ended in 1878.

I have at least tasted one 1858 – the Lafite. This was from a remarkable collection of wines from the cellars at Dalmeny and Mentmore of the Earl of Rosebery, sold at Christie's in May 1967. These included no fewer than 19 magnums and 7 bottles of the 1858. Before the sale the auctioneers opened one bottle for two or three of us. It had a real aroma of fine claret, but on the palate there was some decay. Perhaps the magnums, which fetched up to £41 apiece were fuller, but if not this is scarcely surprising as 1858 was the vintage with which George Saintsbury started his cellar in

---

*From 1831 onwards prices of representative wines in fine or for other reasons interesting vintages may be found in Appendix A on page 305.

the late seventies, and he described them as then being 'a trifle old'. Yet André Simon in *Vintagewise* describes an 1858 as being perfect in Bordeaux in 1935.

It should be said right away there is little doubt that wines which have either never been moved from the château cellars or have lain a long age in Bordeaux are more likely to last well than those which have suffered a journey; especially difficult is movement when they are old. Therefore it would not be correct to assume that certain old wines that taste very well in the Bordeaux region will necessarily be good abroad; and, of course, one seldom knows how the latter wines have been kept in the meantime.

With the 1860s we enter the great pre-phylloxera period proper. Early in the decade some fine wine was made. In 1861 there was a very short crop owing to an exceptional frost in early May, and good wine was dear although moderate only. Christian Cruse has told me that in 1966 he and his son Edouard drank with great pleasure a bottle of Lafite 1862, which some years before he had re-corked. It was a fairly successful, prolific vintage. The classic vintage, however, was 1864, which was plentiful as well as of the highest quality, and the leading growth was certainly Lafite. A magnum of this was sold in the Rosebery sale for no less than £82.

By the kindness of Anthony Berry of Berry Bros. & Rudd I was able to taste this famous wine in February 1968. Having read that I had never drunk Lafite '64 and did not expect ever to do so, he invited me to lunch with him and his partners, and with Harry Waugh as the other guest. Preceded by two bottles of the Gruaud-Larose-Sarget '74 – good wines but in decline – we then had two bottles of the famous Lafite '64, served in separate glasses. Both were distinctly better than the two '74s. One was showing its age a little but the other was perfectly round, gentle and soft and with a 'sweet' nose. All its faculties were present, though only just. The other bottle too was also remarkably 'sweet'. Both wines had been decanted over an hour before we tasted them, and they showed no decline in the glass for at least half an hour; by that time we had despatched them.

Other '64s were also successful, and Yquem sold at 4,500 frs. a *tonneau*.

The 1865s were prolific and the quality good but they took some time to come round. Very large amounts of wine were made in this year, but the opening prices of the leading growths were even higher than for the '64s. Indeed, taking into account the changed value of money and allowing for the 1868s which did not keep their price, they were overall probably the highest for a normal vintage for about a hundred years, when the 1964 first-growth prices broke all bounds. Both Lafite, which produced 195 *tonneaux*, and Latour, where 103 *tonneaux* were made, sold for 5,600 frs. or £224 a *tonneau*. Allowing at least a fivefold decrease in the value of money since then, this was the equivalent of just on £1,100 a *tonneau*. In 1930 André Simon found the Lafite still excellent in London. Much more recently I had the privilege of drinking the Latour at the château. In October 1968 David Pollock, chairman of the company which now controls Latour, opened a bottle of this wine when my wife and I were dining there. Decanted just before drinking, it had a remarkably deep colour for a centenarian wine, with a powerful nose and a flavour so full and deep that there was almost a suggestion of port in its richness; perhaps it had been '*hermitagé*', although I doubt it. The wine began to fade about half an hour after first opening, but it was so big a wine that one would have thought it fifty years younger. Today 1859 is the oldest vintage in the private cellar at Mouton. The 1865 Mouton-Rothschild is also in the private cellar but the *maître de chai* has told me that it is now not so good as the 1870. The following two years were not of much account, but 1868 was better, and the first growths went ahead again in price, since the prosperity of the times gave the big 'names' an exceptional popularity, which was to be emulated in the 1960s. Some of the 1868 first growths fetched as much as 6,200 and 6,000 frs. However the wines were hard and unattractive, and the merchants who paid these prices made heavy losses, and one wonders whether history may not repeat itself over some of the exceptional prices paid at source for the 1964s and 1966s. However in 1965 I drank one superb example of the 1868s – and a fifth, not a first growth. This was Grand-Puy-Ducasse – the last bottle in the cellar at Pontet-Canet and opened for me by Christian Cruse. Although of course a little brown, yet full coloured for its age, it had that incomparable 'sealing wax' nose of really fine old claret; full of fruit and flavour with no sign of decay. Returning to the glass after an interval I found the wine remarkably sweet; class differences count for little at such an age if the wine is still in good heart, as this one was. It is interesting to read Tastet & Lawton's note that this vintage produced big wines, 'hard without charm', similar to André Simon's view of them.

However 1869 was another winner, well-balanced and again copious; the most plentiful of the decade, so prices fell. A bottle has not come my way. This was one of the famous years of Yquem, ranking alongside 1893 and 1921. As mentioned earlier, some ten years ago I was allowed a sample from a medicine bottle sent from Scotland to London by the owner of a bottle of this great wine who had decanted and posted off this sample. Although very dark it was still sound and luxuriously rich.

On the other hand I have been lucky enough to drink a number of 1870s. This was another fairly prolific vintage, which began early after a hot summer, the wine fetching similar prices to the '69s, although Mouton-Rothschild at 3,000 frs. a *tonneau* was higher and the equal of Latour. However the '70s chief repute for many years was that they were not ready for drinking; a classic slow-developing fine claret. Saintsbury talks about 'those unsatisfactory '70s', and regrets that for the money laid out on classed growths he did not buy three times the quantity of sound *bourgeois* wine. Incidentally he mentions that the seven dozen classed growths, including all four *premiers*, cost him 'at the high prices then ruling for claret' about £30. Presumably he bought these soon after he began his cellar when the wines were about ten years old; over 85s. a dozen was certainly not a very cheap price, particularly as the late Ian Campbell mentions in his *Wayward Tendrils of the Vine* (1947) that his firm bought a good part of the crop of Latour '71, bottled it in London, sold it to the trade at 26s. a dozen, and felt almost guilty of profiteering when later they raised the price to 36s.

Saintsbury described the '70s as 'dumb' at forty years of age, and older friends in Bordeaux tell me that they did not really unfold until about 1920. As a result later hard vintages, such as 1928, have often been queried as 'another 1870?'; but I doubt it.

The other side of this picture, so frustrating for our grandfathers, is that the wines lasted magnificently; and as they were rightly not considered ready to drink many were preserved. About 1960 my friend John Hadfield found himself the residuary legatee of nine or ten bottles of Léoville '70, which for many years had been lying in a Suffolk cellar near his home. I shared several of these bottles, and although those ullaged were not as good as the fuller bottles, none was undrinkable and the best were remarkable. One bottle was generously given me, and I drank it at home in June 1962 in the company of Ronald Avery, Harry Waugh and the late Douglas McClean. Surprisingly deep in colour, with a wonderfully full nose and flavour it had tremendous 'size', fruit and sweetness. This was a very distinguished wine on any count and it showed no sign of weakness, in spite of having been moved from one side of England to another in extreme old age. Even the next day the dregs in the bottle smelled sweet, and I count it among the finest bottles of claret I have drunk.

There were other remarkable '70s in my experience. The leading wine was said to be Lafite, and I drank that at Harveys, thanks to Harry Waugh who returned the compliment of my Léoville. Some Lafite and Langoa '70, all bottled by Harveys, had come up for auction at Restell's and the firm had bought them in the 1950s for what would now be considered the low price of £5 a bottle. I drank both wines and they had the same characteristics of deep colour and fruit noticed in the Léoville. The Lafite was somewhat ullaged and not so fine as the Langoa, which I drank in December 1965, while the Lafite was opened in August 1966. The quality of the Langoa may be gauged by the fact that when first tasted it was taken for a 1920.

Another celebrated '70 was the Mouton, and this I was able to taste on the spot – always a special pleasure and experience. I was able to drink this and other famous Moutons mentioned hereafter owing to the kindness of Baron Philippe de Rothschild, who in the course of several visits – for the sake of the cellar, fortunately mostly brief – more or less gave me the freedom of his incomparable cellar. I had the temerity to ask for the '70, and other wines on further occasions. The Mouton '70 had the same splendid nose and depth of flavour of the other '70s, but was perhaps rather more backward. The Latour '70 I sampled at a pre-auction tasting at Christie's early in 1969. English-bottled, it still had a good deal of vigour. It was later sold for just on £13 a bottle.

I am keeping these accounts of famous bottles to a minimum, for vicarious drinking is a limited pleasure to others, but such famous nineteenth-century wines are worth recording.

I have never drunk '71, '72 or '73, although the first of the three produced some notable, elegant wines and André Simon describes them as 'nearer the perfection of claret than any other, not excepting the wonderful '64s and '75s'. He particularly commends the Haut-Brion, Mouton and Lafite.

The '74s I have drunk several times, and some were past their best. It was a huge, expensive vintage, only surpassed in quantity by the record '75. The finest '74 that I have drunk was certainly Pontet-Canet (of which a tremendous crop of 275 *tonneaux* had been made), opened by Christian Cruse in Bordeaux in September 1967. In colour it was very brown, with almost a hint of orange, but the aroma and flavour were remarkable although not so big as the '70s. The nose had that concentrated, 'sealing wax' aroma of these great old clarets, and there was no lack of fruit. I was lucky enough to drink it again a year later at Christian Cruse's table. This bottle had more colour and was still quite a big fruity wine but was overshadowed by the Lafite '75 mentioned below. More recently, at a lunch given by Michael Broadbent, head of Christie's wine auction department, two magnums of Lafite 1874 formerly from the cellars of Viscount Boyne at Brancepeth Castle, Durham, were served. Both were slightly ullaged, one had been decanted the previous evening, the other immediately before lunch. Both had good noses but showed some decay on the taste, and the one decanted eighteen hours beforehand was the better. I suspect ullage was the trouble, as Latour '74 from the Rosebery cellar sampled in May 1967 had been a big rich wine for its age, with a real fine-claret nose.

I have referred to the declining Gruaud Larose '74 in connection with the Lafite '64, and in Bordeaux in October 1968 I drank a superb example of Lafite '75, the last wine in a remarkable assembly of nineteenth-century clarets which Christian Cruse opened for my wife and me. All find a place in these notes, but I imagined that the splendid Pontet-Canet '74 mentioned above completed the range. But then from the mantel-piece Cruse took an English claret jug, saying 'the gem of my cellar'. It was Lafite '75. The colour was light, almost like a deep Madeira, but the concentrated 'sealing wax' nose was that of really great old claret. The flavour was truly delicate and fine but with no hint of decay, and it had a distinctly fruity, sweet taste even two hours after decanting. For its delicate yet true flavour all the way, it was certainly one of the finest clarets I have drunk. As a souvenir Christian Cruse gave me the bottle, a hand-made one with a seal on the neck, inscribed '*Château Lafite – Grand Vin*'. The following day I showed this to M. André Portet, the *régisseur* of Lafite, and he told me that the bottle would have been supplied not by the château but by the merchant who then sent it to Lafite to be filled.

The 1875s from that record vintage were the reverse of the '74s. They were drink-able and delicate so early that in the Eighties and Nineties all the experts said they must be drunk up while they were so good. It was 'the wine of the evening' at a banquet given in 1895 by the Bordeaux Chamber of Commerce to representatives of the Corporation of the City of London. However, these wines in fact survived well into the Inter-War period. The only other example I have drunk was Ch. Margaux at Loudenne in October 1966. Alas both colour and nose had gone, although the wine was sweeter than one might have expected. Mouton was said to be one of the finest wines of the vintage.

The next year was not held in any esteem, though Christian Cruse and his son Edouard opened for me a bottle of Dauzac '76 at Pontet-Canet in October 1966. Edouard Cruse had never tasted a '76 before. It was pale, almost *rosé*, the nose was very fine and the fruit was attenuated but just there. A moderate wine which had not survived at all badly for 90 years.

The 1877s were irregular, as André Simon, whose birth year it was, assured me, but there was good report of a number of bottles presented to him on his ninetieth birthday. The only one I have tasted was Pichon-Longueville in Bordeaux. One bottle in 1966 was delicious, a second in 1967 was decayed; but there must always be uncertainty with old bottles.

The 'Golden Age' ended with the 1878s. The vintage was a fairly big one, but the wines were less expensive than the '74s or '75s. I have once or twice had thin, disappointing bottles in England, although at a lunch given by Rigby & Evens at Bristol in April 1967 one out of two magnums of Lafite was still fine claret, although near the end of its journey; the other had that 'mushroom' smell and taste of decay. At Mouton in October 1965 I had a superb bottle of its own wine. This had been decanted four or five hours before being drunk; nevertheless it was a splendidly complete, fruity wine, even better than the Mouton '70 which I drank a year later. Apart from periodic re-corking the '78 had not stirred from its original bin since 1881.

So ended the pre-phylloxera era. The American-imported louse had been active in Bordeaux for ten years, but it was not a widespread menace until after 1878. Whether or not the wines made from the ungrafted French vines were better or not must always remain a moot point, and most of us would settle cheerfully for wines of the quality of 1899 and 1900. It does seem more than likely, however, that these old wines did last longer than those made in the first 60 years of the post-phylloxera era. With one or two possible exceptions, it is almost certain they lasted better than will the clarets of the post-Second World War period.

The Phylloxera and After

Many people believe that the onset of the phylloxera, already discussed in Chapter One, led to an immediate deterioration in the quality of the wines. This is not so. What did suffer was the quantity, because the vines that were attacked wilted and died. It was the mildew which began in 1882 that affected the quality and produced miserable thin wines often with a taste of decay. Frequently too in the decade from 1879 the weather conditions were unfavourable, yet some good wines were made in the earlier years. André Simon has praised the Latour '79, and I have good reason to know that the Mouton '80, which also won his and Ian Campbell's commendation, was a very fine wine indeed. I drank this at the château in October 1966; the colour was deep, and the wine was extraordinarily full-flavoured and big. It could have been forty years younger. One could not wish for a better wine. In the same year I had Ausone '80 at Averys of Bristol. The colour was *rosé*, and neither the nose nor the palate suggested claret; yet it was not decayed. However Ronald Avery had already given me a bottle and this I opened, without much hope, in March 1967. It was surprisingly good. The colour, though pale, was much truer than the previous bottle, the nose was fruity, and the body had a fullness that actually did suggest a St-Emilion. Indeed the wine evoked a distinct suggestion of the aroma and flavour of very old vintage port. It had been château-bottled, and perhaps was *hermitagé*. I suspect the other bottle had been ullaged, whereas this one was up to the base of the neck. With an old wine the cork is the decisive factor, and that is why the leading châteaux re-cork their reserves of old wines roughly every twenty-five years.

The phylloxera-mildew years need not detain us. I have been told at Mouton that the '81 is still good. I once drank a surprisingly good Rausan-Ségla '85 when it was more than sixty years old, but '85 was not a good vintage, the quantity was the smallest of the decade, and only about a fifth of the output of '75. There was also a small crop in '87, but the wines were better but do not appear to have lasted well. The '88s were light but good, and the Ch. Margaux had a big reputation. Quantitatively this was the biggest vintage of the decade. The '89s were launched with hopeful noises by a trade desperately looking for good vintages to offer. Not that the wines of the Eighties were poured down the sink. They were sold and drunk. For example the Wine Society list of 1899 had Branon 1881 and 1884, both at 32s. a dozen, Léoville-Las-Cases 1883 at 43s. and Palmer-Margaux 1886 at 34s. (Branon-Licterie was listed as a leading Léognan in the 1868 edition of Cocks et Féret but is not included in recent issues.)

Recovery began properly in 1890 – a very expensive year although not considered a great vintage, for the wines were hard; yet I have drunk at least one fine bottle, a magnum of Pape-Clément, opened in 1948. It was full-bodied, deep coloured and with the nose of a fine old claret. Although vigorous, the wine had a slight after-taste which prevented it from being in the top class, but the flavour was good. Much older-tasting but with a fine 'sealing-wax' nose was the Gruaud-Larose from Sir Arthur Evans' cellar on Boar's Hill, Oxford, which was drunk in 1961; in flavour the wine was well on the way down.

The next two years, 1891 and 1892, had no reputation, but 1893 was different. After an exceptionally hot summer, the vintage began on 15 August, the earliest in 170 years of Bordeaux records. Ch. Margaux started picking on 17 August, and Lafite finished before the end of that month – for the first time ever in the history of Lafite. Owing to the immediate fame of this vintage the opening prices doubled within less than three years of the wine being made. The vintage was, like 1921, particularly successful for white wines, and Yquem '93 was one of the great wines of that château. The red wines lasted well, and David Peppercorn of the International Distillers & Vintners group and a serious-minded judge of claret, has written that in 1957 the Lafite '93 was still excellent, with a sweetness that reminded him of the '29s. I cannot recollect a claret myself, although the Yquem, also from Sir Arthur Evans' cellar, was remarkably fine in 1947 in spite of its dark golden colour.

The 1894s were poor, and another very hot summer in 1895 produced a lot of wines that were 'pricked', i.e. turned to vinegar, a fate the '93s had escaped. Christian Cruse has recounted to me an interesting story of that scorching late September vintage. Professor Ulysse Gayon (1845 – 1929), Director of the Bordeaux Station Agronomique et Oenologique from 1880 to 1920, pupil and friend of Pasteur, happened to be staying at Lafite. Observing that the temperature of the must in the vats was rising fast and likely to go over the top, to stop the fermentation and turn the wine to vinegar, he advised Baron de Rothschild to order a large quantity of ice to be sent immediately from Bordeaux, more than thirty miles away. The same advice was given to Mouton-Rothschild next door, blocks of ice were thrown into the vats and both wines were saved. The news spread to neighbouring châteaux and some of them, including Pontet-Canet, adopted this emergency measure; but elsewhere many wines went wrong. Cruse added that Mouton-Rothschild 1895 was one of the best clarets he had ever drunk. By good fortune I was enabled to drink this wine at Mouton in October 1968. I remembered Christian Cruse's story when going through the private cellar, and asked Raoul Blondin, one of the two *maître de chai* brothers, whether there was any '95 in the cellars, and if so what was it like. He replied that he did not think there was any and did not know the wine. However as the hovering candle light flickered over the bins I saw a label bearing the vintage in question behind a bin of other wines. There were indeed some bottles and two days later one was drunk with Philippe Cottin of La Bergerie, the firm that markets Mouton, and my wife. Cottin had not drunk the '95 Mouton either. In fact, it was a remarkable wine. The colour was deep, the nose was positively rich, and the flavour extraordinarily full and sweet. The wine was a complete claret, with no hint of decay. No doubt the residual sweetness was owing to the very hot year, as was the case with the '47 clarets. The following day I sought out Raoul Blondin, who had tasted the wine when decanting it. Beaming, he said: '*Monsieur, c'était un grand vin*'. It was.

The only other '95 I have tasted was during the same visit to Bordeaux and a consequence also of Christian Cruse's story. For he opened a bottle of the Montrose, apologizing for his lack of Mouton. This was brown in tint, but there was no hint of decay in the nose or taste. It had a slightly strong taste, and probably in youth it was a rather coarse, powerful wine as indeed Montrose can be. Now it was a fine big wine, but lacked the roundness of a great claret; it had probably not had the advantage of the ice treatment. Such a measure would be illegal nowadays, since the melted ice dilutes the must, so today it is lowered into the vats in bags; but I have heard of more recent cases of the ice being thrown in whole, notably in 1921 and 1947.

André Simon has also praised the Mouton '95 as well as the Lafite, and I have heard that the Carruades de Lafite lasted well for at least sixty years. There were other successes too, and David Peppercorn has mentioned the Pétrus as still being very fine in 1963.

The 1896s were light though agreeable (and Peppercorn has recorded an exceptional bottle of Lafite '96, drunk in 1954), but the following year was without reputation. The summer weather before the vintage was atrocious, the crop was small with many unripe grapes. The Gilbeys in the Loudenne diary refer to the 'complete failure of the 1897 vintage'. However, as recently as 1967 I drank a remarkable bottle of the Lafite, château-bottled. This was the prelude to the 1803, already referred to. The colour was deep and the flavour was strong, full and firm, as if it had once been a very hard wine. It had plenty of distinction and character now.

In 1898 the crop was small owing to disease and lack of rain after a dry summer. In fact some good wines were made, but they were over-shadowed by the extraordinary pair of years that immediately followed. In September 1967 I drank at the château the Mouton '98, which had an excellent colour for its age and a fruity nose, but the wine was showing its age; nevertheless a fine wine after just on seventy years for what was considered almost an off-vintage. A year later I drank with Christian Cruse a curiosity of the same vintage: Léoville Poyferré 1898 Vin de Goutte. As already mentioned in the Médoc chapter on Margaux, a *vin de goutte* in Bordeaux is a *vin rosé*, normally made for summer drinking for the proprietor's own use. This was the case with the Léoville Poyferré '98. The 70-year-old *vin de goutte* was the colour of a medium sherry rather than pink. It was still perfectly balanced, a light but still fruity and agreeable wine. The strength, I was told, was only 10·5 degrees, but it had survived. Indeed Cruse half-apologized to me for not serving the '78, but that was now finished.

The two final years of the nineteenth century did their best to make up for the unsatisfactory vintages of the previous twenty years. Both were prolific, 1899 making nearly 400,000 *tonneaux* (3,600,000 hectolitres), and 1900 well over 600,000 *tonneaux* (5,400,000 hectolitres), a figure not exceeded until the unhappy 1922s. The Bordeaux trade realized the exceptional quality of the '99s almost before they were made and the classed growths were snapped up as soon as they left the vats. On the other hand in 1900, after a fine summer, with a torrid August, the enormous crop brought prices down with a run; and not only for the new wine. The Gilbeys noted at Loudenne that Mouton-Rothschild '98, which had sold for £22 a hogshead in 1899, dropped to £7 in 1900. Suddenly there was too much good wine available – but for the last time for a score of years.

As early as 1903 the Loudenne diary records that the relative superiority of the 1899s or the 1900s was greatly discussed, comparisons being made with the '64s and '65s or the '74s and '75s. At that time it was thought that the '99s had more flavour and colour, while the 1900s had 'a remarkable softness and delicacy'. Such a comparison between two outstanding successive vintages was not to be possible again until 1928 and 1929. The prices of the 1900s were lower by one-third (they can be compared in the Appendix), and the Gilbeys bought large quantities. In 1904 their records showed stocks at Loudenne of 5,793 bottles of Latour and 5,830 bottles of Lafite; about 20 hogsheads worth apiece. In 1912 after a tasting of their wines the Gilbeys stated that 'Latour was by far the best of the 1900s'.

Between them these two years provided, in the drought of good vintages in the first two decades of the present century, the stand-by for *amateurs* of wines until well after the First World War. They were the wines to crown a wine dinner, as the finer '29s might today. They gave the lie to the pessimists who said that really fine claret on the pre-phylloxera pattern was a thing of the past. Further they provided a splendid arguing point as to which vintage was the superior. The '99s were perhaps more delicate wines than the '00s (the abbreviation is irresistible). André Simon twenty or or so years ago stated that the 1900s had stood the test of time better, and this is Ronald Barton's view, yet I have drunk some 1899s in first-class condition. I have not had the fortune to be able to compare them on the same occasion, and for some unknown reason, I have drunk more of the earlier year; with the 1900s so exceptionally prolific, one would have expected to have found a larger number of them surviving.

The first '99 I drank was the Branaire-Ducru, bought in 1941 from Avery's for 14s. a bottle, château-bottled, and opened in June 1942. Unused then to wine of such quality I and my guests were quite overcome; by its character, not by its alcohol. It was vigorous but smooth with an aroma that could truthfully be called a bouquet. It was certainly the finest wine I had drunk to date. In all I had five bottles of this wine – the last cost me as much as 21s! Although they varied, all were good, and the last, opened in October 1959 when exactly sixty years old, was superb, with the colour, nose, sugar and fruit that had impressed me over seventeen years earlier.

In 1942 I was invited to visit the then manager of the wine department of the Army & Navy Stores, A. M. Heath, a well-known claret-lover. Previous correspondence had shown him that I too was very interested in claret, and on his table was a splendid bottle of Mouton-Rothschild '99. We consumed it between us to the accompaniment only of wartime biscuits. He then sold me half a dozen bottles of another bottling. These were somewhat ullaged, and not as fine. It is fair to add he said they were uneven and charged me only 9s. a bottle.

I will not recite a list of the '99s I have drunk, but one particular occasion stands out in my memory. It was a dinner given in May 1950 by Ian Campbell and his wife at the Hind's Head Hotel, Bray, the scene of many chronicled wine dinners, where he then in his eightieth year was living. The other guests were his publisher, Jack McDougall and his wife, John Betjeman, Maurice Platnauer, then Vice-Principal and later Principal of Brasenose College, Oxford, Harry Waugh and myself. After some excellent La Mission-Haut-Brion 1934 and delicious Ch. Margaux 1929 we had the very last magnum of Latour 1899 in what had been the late Barry Neame's cellar. It was superbly full and rich; what one might hope for in an 1899 and a Latour. The next time I drank it was at a dinner given in London in January 1967 to Harry Waugh by his former associates and friends at Harveys. Two bottles of the '99 had been brought over three months earlier by Harry Waugh from the château, of which he was a director. They showed just a trace of tiredness, probably owing to the journey, but the wine had great colour, concentration of nose and a slightly 'roasted' taste.

In 1899 all the 'names' were good, and I had a couple of magnificent bottles of Haut-Brion. Also delicious was Haut-Brion 1900, though not as good as the '99, but the other top wines of 1900 had eluded me until 1967 at Mouton where my request to taste the 1900 was willingly acceded to. It was put to a hard test, for my suggestion for the previous wine had been Cheval-Blanc 1929, a tremendously sweet rich wine. Yet the Mouton 1900 had more body, prospect of life and distinction than the much younger St-Emilion. It had everything a really fine old claret in perfect condition should have. Château Margaux was another celebrated 1900, and said to be the finest Margaux of all, but I have never come across it.

The rather few other 1900s that I have drunk, among them Pape-Clément and Talbot, were all fairly delicate wines, and that the Mouton, drunk much later, certainly was not.

It might be thought that these wines, which in a way began as well as ended an era, would have been in great demand. Not, however, to judge from the lists of the I.E.C. Wine Society in the period before the First World War. True, this society, small then with only two or three thousand members, tended to concentrate on the less expensive wines. However in December 1902 was listed the Lafite '99, English-bottled as all this château's produce was at this period, and with a comment, unusual in those days, that it was 'one of the finest wines of this exceptionally fine vintage, suitable for laying down'. The price was 42s. a dozen, and it remained on the list at that price until 1910 when it was cautiously raised by 3s. a case, and a further 5s. in 1911. I have no idea of the quantity originally bought, but it is unlikely to have been large, yet the wine remained on the list for ten years and was only sold out in December 1912. It was of course not the cheapest '99 on a list no more heavily crowded by them than by the 1900s. In 1906 Pontet-Canet '99 came on at 25s. per dozen, Gruaud-Larose '99 at 28s. and Giscours '99 at the same price. In 1913 Gruaud-Larose '99, château-bottled, appeared at 58s. and Malescot 1900 at 43s. However, as George Saintsbury indicated in his *Notes on a Cellar Book*, this was a bad time for claret drinking; champagne had largely taken over. A few years earlier, in 1897, the Gilbeys had written, 'consumption in England has fallen off considerably for expensive after-dinner claret'.

1901–1919

This was not only a bad time for claret drinkers; it was a bad period for the growers and merchants too. It also provides a warning to those who believe nature has to some extent been tamed by chemistry and nowadays a good average of fair vintages is assured. True, the worst may not be quite as bad as they were, but both 1963 and 1965, to mention two recent disastrously poor vintages in Bordeaux, show us what nature can still effect. In the first nineteen years of the present century only one year can just be squeezed into the 'very fine' category: 1906.

Of the first three years, 1901 was not bad though variable; yet no one was much interested in such wines after their predecessors. The 1902s and 1903s were poor and after the failure of the latter vintage the Gilbeys were noting, 'no marketable wine has been made in the Médoc since 1900'. The 1904 offered more hopes but the wines appear to have lacked backbone and did not last, which is probably one reason why I have never drunk one.

The 1905s were rather better, for although light they were better balanced, and I have known bottles drinkable until the present time, including Léoville-Las-Cases and Figeac. However on the whole they did not make old bones. The 1906s were much sturdier. After a hot summer and a good vintage a rather small crop of exceptionally full-bodied wines was produced. Opinions have varied on the final outcome, and the only bottle I have ever cellared was a magnum of Lafite, château-bottled, which came from that treasure-house of old wines, Averys of Bristol, just after the war and was opened in 1949. It had not then the powerful quality associated with '06s, but was light, soft and delicate, good all the way but at the end of the journey. On the other hand Haut-Brion, which I have drunk, was outstanding and perhaps the best '06 in my experience.

However, once again in Bordeaux in the autumn of 1968 bottles were generously opened for me in the interests of my incomplete vinous education. At Cantemerle Henri Binaud wound up a lunch of his wines with the '06 Cantemerle. The colour was light, but the nose fine, followed by a concentrated fruity flavour, though the wine was beginning to show its age. I would have taken it for a '20 had I not known the vintage. Secondly, at Latour a bottle of '06 preceded the '65 mentioned earlier. Although a fine complete wine, it was rather lighter than expected for a Latour, and was to some extent overshadowed by its senior by 41 years; no mean compliment to the latter. A 1906 with a considerable reputation was La Lagune, but I have not drunk it.

The only 1907 I have ever had – two bottles of Ch. Margaux – also came from Averys. The vintage was exceptionally large, but apparently considerably affected by oidium, and the wine was light. The two bottles of Margaux, château-bottled, were drunk in 1943 and 1947 respectively. The first was very fine, with a remarkably fresh aroma, and a light but complete flavour; the second showed signs of fading, but it was ullaged. The bottle in good condition must have been well above the average in a vintage that did not generally last.

Of the 1908s, André Simon has stated that the only one he enjoyed was the Lafite; it was a hard, unattractive vintage. I have twice drunk the Haut-Brion with interest; the first a magnum in London in May 1965, which was past its best and had some decay; the second a far better bottle drunk at Mouton in October 1966. Very light in colour and with a fine old-claret nose, it was surprisingly big with a slightly strong burnt taste. Having, as is the custom at Mouton, been decanted several hours before dinner, it did decline in the glass, but was a distinguished wine while it lasted.

The 1909s aroused some expectations, but on the whole these were not realized. I once drank an Ausone '09 that was good, but I cannot recollect another wine of this year. The 1910s and 1911s have also passed me by. The former was notoriously one of the worst and smallest vintages of the century throughout France. ('It is necessary to go back a hundred years in the history of the Médoc to find a vintage as poor as this year', wrote the Gilbeys while staying at Loudenne during the vintage period.) The latter, much better after an exceptionally hot summer, was not a particularly successful Bordeaux vintage although a classic year in Burgundy. The intervention of the First World War resulted in many being bottled too late. The 1912s were affected by mildew, and the only two that have ever come my way were not very agreeable. The Cos d'Estournel in 1957 had quite gone and was in fact undrinkable. Eleven years later the Duhart-Milon was very brown and had a distinctly old nose, with a suggestion of decay. Yet it had some quality of fine claret and was at least drinkable. At this age, of course, there may be great variations between bottles, and one might expect better or even worse luck, particularly with an off-vintage. Generally the 1912s suffered from a great excess of acidity. Much the same applied to 1913. As it happened to be my birth year Tom Whelehan very kindly opened a bottle of Lafite '13 for me in Dublin in May 1966; it was very thin and rather acid, although drinkable. Another better '13 was Ausone, reasonably fruity for an off-year fifty-three years old. The 1914s had a rather better reputation, but did not last. Many of them were bottled too late. Yet an Haut-Brion '14 that I drank at Mouton in October 1966 was by no means disagreeable and had a distinction of flavour not lost under an end-taste of slight decline. It could fairly be called an interesting wine. This was a successful year for Sauternes, and Yquem made a fine wine, which I have enjoyed more than once in recent years.

Although 1915 was an outstanding Burgundy year, it was poor in Bordeaux and the best year of the First World War was certainly 1916. The wines were big and hard and in their youth were said to lack charm as hard claret can. I have once or twice drunk them in England and they were not good, but two excellent examples encountered at source were the Cantemerle and Mouton-Rothschild. The former I drank first at the château in 1964 and again in Bordeaux in the flat of the proprietor, Henri Binaud. It was a surprisingly full, *corsé* wine, vigorous but without the distinction and completeness of the Cantemerle '20 which preceded it on the second occasion. The Mouton '16 was from a magnum and in September '67 was in very good shape. Although there was some brownness in colour, for a wine of fifty years old its colour was deep. In flavour the wine was fairly delicate but had a fruity nose. It needed drinking and it was.

André Simon blames the war for the lack of success of the '17s, which were light and might have been better. The 1918s were of course exuberantly hailed at the end of the war, and were quite widely bought. The great Paris wine firm of Nicolas must have plunged heavily on them, since for many years they appeared in their famous special lists issued annually before Christmas. However the vintage was not very successful. It is surprising that the 1919s were not better, for again this was a fine year in Burgundy, although there the wines were tough and hard. Nevertheless I was surprised in September 1967 to drink Latour '19 at the château and find it so good. But then Latour is a celebrated surpriser. It was full coloured for its age, with that 'bigness' of flavour that is the mark of Latour. There was a slight descent in taste at the end, but I would certainly have taken it for '*un grand millésime*'. I cannot recollect many finer bottles of this sad claret period between 1901 and 1919, but we were now on the eve of one of Bordeaux's great periods.

Twenty-Five Vintages, 1920–1944

1920

I have always regarded 1920 as the finest claret year which I have had the luck to drink in relative plenty. They were about twenty years old when I first drank them and probably the vintage as a whole was at its peak in the next twenty years, up to about 1960. One has to admit that a good many of the wines are now in decline. However this is one of the factors to be taken into account with all wine. If longevity is the first consideration then judgments must be revised on many vintages, although for a leading year it is fair to demand a minimum period of, say, fifteen to twenty years. The '20s certainly passed the age test, but it was a great vintage also on quality. Many, perhaps most, people would put '29 ahead, for the later vintage was quite remarkably fruity and 'sweet'. But one cannot have everything, and if the '20s were a little drier they were also more refined and delicate, in my view more 'clarety'; whereas the '29s lacked this delicacy. It is a matter of choice. Ian Campbell, for example, found most '20s 'disappointingly dry'. Others found them not up to expectations too. Maurice Healy in his volume on *Claret* (1934) in the Constable Wine

Library described 1920 as 'that year, which has proved so disappointing to us all (except to Warner Allen, who always assured me that the 1920s would not last, and who may read here the record of his triumph over me).' He then called it 'that treacherous vintage', but had a good word for Latour. In 1936, as recorded in the *Wine & Food Quarterly*, at a dinner attended by André Simon, Maurice Healy, J. Murray Easton and James Laver, the last-named commented 'there is no other 1920 to compare with it (Latour), but we were lucky to drink it when we did, for it will probably never be better. Its sugar is all but gone and, like all the '20s, it does not appear to have any future'.

However in *Stay Me With Flagons* (1940) Maurice Healy revised his opinion of the '20s, stating, 'The 1920s seem all to have come back'. I attended a lunch with André Simon in Bristol in April 1967, and before the nineteenth-century Lafites we had some 'younger' wines, which included the Latour '20. It was at the top of its form, with a deep colour, wonderfully full nose and great distinction of flavour. Which goes to show. I have no doubt thirty years previously the '20s must have been passing through a bad phase, which certainly they had largely overcome by the 1940s.

It would be wearisome for the reader if I went through all the '20s I have had and enjoyed, but two in particular stand out: the Latour, already referred to above, and the Cheval-Blanc. The latter I will leave to discuss along with the '21, but the Latour '20 today is still one of the finest bottles of claret one could wish for, although I have had disappointing bottles, probably because they were not kept well over the years. But a bottle in good condition is still full, rich and yet not too 'bold', as some might think its rival, the Latour '29. The other leading growths I have tasted were distinguished too, the Lafite fine and delicate, the Haut-Brion fuller, and the Mouton too. The Margaux was probably too old when I drank it only a few years ago, for it was then disappointing, but the excellent Mouton is certainly also in decline now.

In their day the Palmer, Pape-Clément and Ausone were very fine wines. I do not think I have tasted a really first-class Ausone since. Nor a Rauzan-Gassies, whose '20 in magnum was still excellent in 1964. There was the minor La Closerie from Moulis which was fine for a lesser growth as late as the 1950s. Much later still, Cantemerle was in light but perfect condition in Bordeaux in 1966, and in the same year I drank with no little pleasure the La Mission-Haut-Brion '20 at the château; an old wine but still fruity. Lanessan, whose '29 is mentioned below, made an excellent '20, still full-coloured and only pardonably showing its age in 1968 when I drank it at Loudenne. All in all 1920 was a fine year for *amateurs* of fine but delicate claret.

1921

Every other wine made after this exceptionally hot summer was overshadowed by the Cheval-Blanc, one of the most extraordinary clarets I have ever drunk. Rather like the '47 from the same growth, it became a legend early in its life, and was expensive at a time when most fine clarets were very cheap. I remember it on Avery's list in 1938 for 300s. a dozen, at a time when Lafite '20 could be bought for 120s. The reason for its success lay in its quite extraordinary sweetness and sugar. This excess of sugar at the vintage which began on 15 September had been the ruin of a number of '21s, notably the Lafite which turned vinegary in the fermenting vats in the course of a single night. So far as I know there never was any '21 Lafite; it was sold as Pauillac or to Calvet as *vin rouge* for 1600 frs. a *tonneau*. The sun was so hot that the grapes were scorched, and I remember some Margaux '21, which seemed to me to have a slightly burnt taste; and the Gruaud-Larose as recently as April 1967 had a curiously strong flavour, though also fruity. On the whole the Médocs were not very successful, although those that survived to old age were agreeable enough. For example Palmer '21, opened by Christian Cruse in Bordeaux in September 1966, was very brown but still fruity, sweet and of fine claret flavour. In the Médoc the '21s were not unlike the '95s.

Certainly it was the St-Emilions that scored and not only the Cheval-Blanc. In St-Emilion itself in 1964 I drank Canon '21, with a fine nose that really came out of the glass. The flavour had a certain hardness that no doubt had preserved the wine, but it was a splendidly generous-flavoured wine, which had been decanted by Edouard Cruse in Bordeaux five hours before we drank it at the well-known La Plaisance restaurant in St-Emilion. There was also the fine Clos Fourtet '21, which I drank in 1964, on the last occasion I encountered the Cheval-Blanc, in Bristol with Ronald Avery, André Simon and two or three others. The Clos Fourtet was by no means an inferior wine, yet there was lacking the peculiar richness of the Cheval-Blanc, by then distinctly pale, pinkish rather than brown, but still with a remarkable concentration of nose and flavour that reminded one strangely enough of a great luscious German white wine.

The most interesting occasion on which I drank the '21 Cheval-Blanc was at my home in Wiltshire in July 1954; interesting because the company, which included Norman Alexander, Douglas McClean and Harry Waugh, was able to compare it with the '20. Contrary to my almost invariable practice, I served the '20 first, because I thought otherwise the older wine would be overwhelmed by the astonishing sweetness of the '21. The '20 had more colour, for the '21 already had the rosy hue much more pronounced ten years later. The nose of the '20 was distinctly better, and on the palate it was more complete and velvety. On the other hand the '21 though markedly sweet was not cloying and revealed gradations of flavour that made its rival seem almost lacking in distinction and interest. The '21 'finished' with a special quality – almost a flourish. However this was by no means a unanimous view and the table was, as it were, split down the middle, with Alexander and McClean supporting the '20, Waugh and I backing the '21. Probably the '20 was the more complete wine – and outstanding in its year – but the '21 was the more interesting; its fruitiness and flavour was enhanced not cloaked by the sweetness, and at the same time I wondered whether the sugar would stay as the body ebbed; I think it did, as shown by the bottle opened ten years later. I may add I drank the '20 a number of times subsequently, and it did begin to go downhill; the last bottle, tasted in August 1965 against the Pétrus (which showed finely but tired and less good than the Cheval-Blanc) was good all the way but not the wonderfully rich wine it had been earlier.

Throughout Europe 1921 was a very great year for white wines, and not least in the Sauternes. Elsewhere I have commented on the Yquem, which among white Bordeaux enjoyed a similar reputation to Cheval-Blanc in the reds. Too much of this great easy-to-drink wine was, I fear, drunk on luxurious picnics or at race meetings, where a fine bottle of Sauternes took second place to more topical affairs. The other Sauternes were excellent too, and I remember a very fine Coutet. For sheer lusciousness the vintage has probably never been equalled since, certainly not excelled.

1922

More wine was produced in the Gironde this year than ever before or since – 7,192,657 hectolitres or just on 800,000 *tonneaux*. Owing to the operation since 1937 of *appellation contrôlée* restricting output, it is unlikely that this figure will ever be attained again. Unfortunately quantity was not matched by quality, although the wines, if light and rather lacking in acidity, were not bad. There had been three prolific years, no one much wanted the '22s, and I have never come upon one, although no doubt some bottles lie in Bordeaux yet, still unwanted.

1923

This also was a prolific year; indeed more wine was produced in Bordeaux in the Twenties than in any other comparable period. It was a much better vintage than '22, but the wines were light and on the whole did not last. One of the celebrities was Domaine de Chevalier, but when I drank it ten years ago at home the wine was pale and in decline, although still fruity to the end. On the whole the vintage was past its best when I began to drink it shortly before the last war, and in any case this was not a widely-bought vintage in Britain; the merchants went more for the '24s. However, I did have a really splendid Duhart-Milon '23, which had come to me direct from France, and which drank beautifully from 1940 to 1950. In the last few years I have come upon others: Ch. Margaux at Angludet in 1965, La Lagune and Ausone in Bristol. The first two were very light, but the Ausone was still surprisingly fruity and agreeable; a fine wine. A most charming light but true wine was the Palmer '23 which drank beautifully well into the 1960s and may do so still. An outstanding St-Emilion was Clos Fourtet, which when forty-five years old was still very fruity. At the same age Cantemerle, though brown, had a delicious aroma and a sweetness on the palate that suggested a '29.

1924

This was really the vintage when, as it were, I came in, and so I have always had a special feeling for it. Not that it was my birth year, but it was the vintage of the first really mature clarets I drank when they were nearly fifteen years old. The wine was Grand-Puy-Lacoste, purchased from a wine merchant in Nantes, who was one at least of the suppliers of that omnivorous drinker Hilaire Belloc. It was part of a small consignment, and of the Grand-Puy-Lacoste there were but three bottles which cost me all of 4s. apiece. I opened the first bottle in July 1939 and the last, fearing the worst from bombs, on my birthday in March 1940. Here for the first time I smelled that wonderful bouquet of fine mature claret, an aroma which I then associated with that of blackcurrants. They were delicious bottles and I have never forgotten them.

There were of course many more notable '24s, although some of them were hard and did not develop evenly. The crop was again large (5,605,405 hl.), only surpassed since 1900 by 1922. Latour, Lafite, Mouton-Rothschild, Pichon-Longueville and Gruaud-Larose-Sarget were among wines I enjoyed from time to time, although I never owned more than three or four of each. They did vary and sometimes they seemed to be going through a 'dumb' patch. Latour, disappointing in 1942, was superb in 1955, but has declined. Some, like Ausone, were rather coarse. Ch. Margaux made the last really fine wine for its class for a long period, and a bottle drunk in 1967 was still surprisingly full and fruity. So too was Palmer in the same year, a wine that twenty-five years earlier had seemed fine but on the delicate side. Giscours made a notable '24 and, though old in flavour when drunk in 1968, it had more fruit than expected and was very enjoyable. All three Léovilles made excellent wines in 1924, and I do not think I have tasted a better Médoc of the vintage than the Poyferré, then in an exceptionally fine era. I drank that in 1949. Much more recently I have had the Las-Cases which had faded badly. However in 1967 when staying at Langoa I persuaded Ronald Barton, no great admirer of the '24s, to open a bottle of his Léoville. The colour was deep, the nose and flavour almost powerful; an exceptionally fine wine, which I would have taken for a '29, except it had more finesse.

So far as I was concerned, the St-Emilions and Graves were particularly successful in '24. The Cheval-Blanc was a splendid wine and so was Clos Fourtet, rich and full. Pape-Clément, much more delicate, was fine, but perhaps the Graves I remember best was the Domaine de Chevalier, of which between 1942 and 1946 Justerini & Brooks let me have more than a dozen bottles, beginning at 9s. each and rising over the wartime years to what then seemed the high price of 20s, but was of course very cheap for the quality of the wine. I drank them between 1942 and 1952 and I never had other than really fine bottles: true, delicate, refined claret. Towards the end the wine seemed so light that the next bottle must prove to have lost its body, but this was not so. Haut-Brion made a notable '24, but I do not recollect drinking it.

I am afraid by and large the '24s are in decline now. Some people, including Ian Campbell, never liked them, but on the whole I was fortunate. It was a fine year for Sauternes.

1925

A very prolific, undistinguished year in which the wines lacked maturity and tasted green. However as recently as May 1969 a bottle of Petit-Village, clearly an old wine, had a fine nose and a surprising amount of fruit and body for a Pomerol of this age and vintage.

1926

Until very recent years at least this was always spoken of as the 'most expensive claret vintage ever'. The high prices were caused not by the rapacity of growers and merchants after an exceptionally small vintage for the period (under 3 million hectolitres), but through a revaluation of the franc. The vintage began late in the first week of October, the wines were hard and on the dry side. As trade was not too good and English merchants at least were well supplied with the earlier vintages of this bountiful decade, very little expensive '26 was bought here. So not many have come my way until recent years. No doubt they are fine claret, but they tend to lack softness and charm. The most immediately attractive I have had is Cheval-Blanc, still in good form as far as I know, with plenty of sugar. So too was Gruaud-Larose-Sarget when I shared in a magnum in 1965. In the same year Mouton-Rothschild '26 at the château was a shade dry but distinguished and fruity all the way, while Haut-Brion – making indifferent wine generally in this period – tasted well when consumed at the château in September 1967: brownish in colour, a little dry but distinguished claret all the same. Latour is, as might be expected, bigger and fruitier to this day, albeit with the typical austerity of the vintage. A special favourite of mine has been La Lagune, light though true, but which has varied from bottle to bottle owing to poor small corks. Another better-than-average '26 has been Cantemerle. Lafite was distinguished but dry. Probably the best '26 I have drunk in recent years was Cos d'Estournel, a surprisingly big and fruity wine, with a splendid nose and more 'generosity' of flavour than most of its fellows. Another successful survivor in the later 1960s was Lagrange, that back-country St-Julien which has seldom appealed to me. The '26 when forty-plus had more fruit than I would have expected.

1927

Certainly the worst vintage of the Twenties, and so far as I know it has left no trace.

1928

The most controversial vintage of the decade and perhaps of the century so far. In those days 'vintages of the century' were not so prolific as now, but when the 1928s turned up they were hailed as the next best thing. Many wine merchants who had not bought '26 and so had nothing since '24 were only too ready to accept the '28s, which had been made in conditions of great heat, and were plentiful. We have André Simon's word for it that when bottled in 1931 they were 'as good as one can hope any young clarets to be'. They were bought widely. In fact they mostly turned out very hard wines, and although encouraging voices muttered 'another '70', there was not now the same inclination to wait for fifty years. When the fruity, easy-to-drink '29s came along the battle was joined between supporters of the two vintages, and it is not yet over; although there is no doubt that in popular estimation the '29s won. The protagonists of the '28s aver with some truth that they will outlive their juniors, and that may be correct. Some have already done so but it is not agreed that even these are all that attractive; for they tend to lack charm. In 1964 I was visiting Latour and asked the *maître de chai*, M. Metté, which vintage of the two he preferred for Latour. He replied 1928, but when later at luncheon we were able to compare the two, the unanimous view round the table was for 1929. However Latour '29 is an exceptional wine, and in some other cases, a château's '28 is now better than the '29, which is in decline. Mouton-Rothschild '28 and '29 are examples of this.

Two of the first growths made very disappointing wine in '28: Lafite and Haut-Brion. Owing to the extremely hot conditions at the vintage, the Lafite had to be pasteurized, and the same is said to have been done with Haut-Brion. The Bordeaux wine merchants who had bought Lafite *en primeur* were so disappointed with the wine that they brought a legal action against the château and returned the wine which had to be sold off later. I have drunk Lafite '28 in recent years, and it had a curiously dead flavour, with none of the distinction associated with this great growth.* Haut-Brion is distinctly odd too. Margaux has always been rather hard and disappointing when I have drunk it, and certainly Latour is the best of the first growths. Mouton '28, drunk at the château in 1966, was a fine big wine, still a little severe.

However, I believe the best Médoc of the year to be Léoville-Las-Cases, a superb wine, with plenty of body and fruit that reminds one of a '29 and yet also with the breed and delicacy of fine claret. It is one of the few '28s that has out-distanced a '29 at the same table; yet on the one occasion I compared it with its own '29, the younger wine won by being even fruitier.

Léoville-Poyferré was not far behind it but without quite so much body, and both the Léoville-Barton and the Langoa are fine too. Another excellent Médoc has been Brane-Cantenac, also Gruaud-Larose.

However the two '28s which stand out in my mind alongside the Las-Cases are Cheval-Blanc and Domaine de Chevalier. For years the former was a wonderful wine, with enough sugar to overcome the traditional '28 hardness. Then rather suddenly early in the 1960s it seemed to go brown in colour and lose its fruit. I cannot remember another really fine wine declining so quickly. Figeac made a fruity, firm wine, surprisingly deep-coloured after forty years. The Domaine de Chevalier was of course much more delicate, and I drank the wine years ago, when it was still wonderfully complete. However I did have a fellow Léognan, Haut-Bailly '28 much more recently, and although still a little firm it had an abundance of fruit, and was in the top rank of '28s I had drunk. The oddest '28 that has come my way was Vieux-Château-Certan drunk at Henri Binaud's table in Bordeaux in September 1967. The nose was very rich, the colour brown, but the taste was so strong it almost seemed as if a dollop of port had been added. There was a hint of burnt taste too, no doubt owing to the torrid vintage time.

Although some '28s probably have still to yield of their best, others seemed to have given up the unequal struggle with their tannin and have dried up. The Sauternes were very good, and Yquem was exceptional, better even than the '29.

---

* Such is the way things go that a couple of years ago I heard of this wine being sold in California for $75 a bottle.

1929

One may argue the comparative merits of this vintage, but there is no doubt so far it has proved the most satisfying vintage of the century. Nearly every château made a good and plentiful '29. Deep-coloured, fruity and undeniably sweet, they were drinkable from so early an age that many believed they could not last. Ian Campbell, whom I once asked what was the first thing he looked for in a claret replied 'sugar'; elsewhere he testified to a doubt about the '29s lasting, on account of their sweetness. True a large number are now in decline, but they stood up for a good thirty years.

To give a list even of the '29s I have drunk would be dull indeed, so I will mention only a few. Latour, there is little doubt today, is the finest of them, still so big and fruity a wine that one feels it must go on for many years still. However, one of the strange things about this almost universally successful year is that two and perhaps three of the first growths were by no means up to their class. Neither Lafite nor Haut-Brion were very attractive wines, and Margaux varied considerably, because, I have been told, one part of the wine was good and another part not. On the other hand Mouton-Rothschild the *premier cru* challenger, was for many years considered the finest '29, and excellent it was too, but this fellow-Pauillac has failed to stay the course so well as Latour. In any event, '29 is a good example of put-not-your-(entire)-trust-in *premiers crus*.

My favourite candidate for the top rank among the '29s is Léoville-Poyferré. Until May 1969 it had been some years since I had drunk a wine that had refinement and distinction as well as fruit, and a typical fine Médoc bouquet. It was a racehorse, whereas many of the '29s were chargers. Then Jack Rutherford opened a bottle in the company of Edouard Cruse and Christopher Tatham. It still maintained its elegance and fruit, and was not in decline. Cruse even preferred it to the succeeding Latour '20, but here he was in a minority. Las-Cases '29, has on more than one occasion seemed just about on a par with its neighbour. The Barton was more variable, as this was the first occasion when château-bottling was granted; the corks were not always up to standard. A bottle drunk at Langoa in 1966 was still very fruity, but showed some sign of decline; another in England in 1968 lacked finish. This was the last vintage for about thirty years in which the Poyferré and Las-Cases parts of the Léoville vineyard were really good, although the Poyferré '34 was above average for that disappointing year. Two other fine '29 St-Juliens I have enjoyed were Gruaud-Larose-Faure and Talbot.

Two Pauillacs that achieved splendid wines in this year were Pichon-Longueville-Baron and Pontet-Canet. The first, in the past at least, seemed to me to have more distinction of flavour than the overwhelming Latour. In 1964 it was still at the top of its form but a later bottle showed signs of decline. The Lalande, while good, never had the vinosity and fruit of its neighbour. I have already referred to the Pontet-Canet served at a dinner in London in 1962. I have drunk a bottle more recently at the château and this was just as fine. Being so 'sweet' it has more than once been taken by me for a Pomerol; an exceptional wine. As an example of the trade prices ruling when these wines were first offered, the Pontet-Canet '29 was £36 a *barrique*; the '28 had been £28.

Among the '29s of Margaux and its neighbours, the Rausan-Ségla was one of the great successes, with the delicacy to be expected as well as the fruit. There were the same qualities in Ch. Margaux '29 – obviously from the good *cuves* – which I drank in 1964 in the office of Corney & Barrow, the City wine merchants. It had lain in the City since 1932, unharmed by the blitz. In its day Cantenac-Brown '29 was an admirable wine, distinguished as well as fruity; alas the last fine wine from this château that has come my way. Giscours, another growth later producing indifferent wine for many years, also achieved a very fine '29, which I drank in Bordeaux as recently as 1966. The brown colour suggested a much older wine, but it was still fruity.

I have never leaned much towards the St-Estèphes but there were certainly some good '29s. The Cos d'Estournel twenty years ago was very fine, and the Montrose, a big wine with a powerful flavour even as late as 1967, was rounder than I usually find this growth.

It should not be imagined, some first growths apart, that all the classed Médocs made excellent wine. I can recall thin, disappointing Rauzan-Gassies and d'Issan, while the Mouton-d'Armailhacq was so sweet as to suggest sugaring. On the other hand there were some very fine wines from such *bourgeois* growths as Lanessan (Cissac) – still a big fruity wine today – and La Closerie (Moulis). La Tour-de-Mons made a '29 still very fruity when nearly forty years old.

I did not drink many of the '29 red Graves in their prime, but Haut-Bailly was excellent when at its best in the late 1940s and early 1950s. La Mission-Haut-Brion made a fine '29 although still a little hard – unusual for this vintage — when drunk at the château in 1966. It had a distinguished nose. Domaine de Chevalier followed its outstanding '28 with a fruity '29. A lesser Graves of fine quality was the Laburthe-Brivazac, a vineyard no longer in existence, as already mentioned.

As might be expected, the St-Emilions scored in 1929, and Cheval-Blanc I rate among the leaders of the vintage. It lasted better than the '28, for the last time I tasted the wine was at Mouton-Rothschild in 1967. It had a marvellously fruity nose. The colour was light but not brown. There was just a touch of age on the palate, and the fine wine was beaten by the Mouton-Rothschild 1900 that followed. I have drunk the Ausone several times but it has never seemed to me as outstanding as one might have hoped for. The Clos Fourtet, however, maintained its splendid tradition during the 1920s, a big 'warm' wine. An exceptionally fruity '29 St-Emilion, already referred to, was La Gaffelière-Naudes.

The Pomerols were not so popular in Britain before the war as they have since become, so they were not widely shipped. Accordingly my experience of '29 Pomerols has been limited; and as they do not last so well as Médocs those I have tasted have been on the old side. An excellent example in recent years I do remember, however, is l'Enclos. Early in the last war, I acquired from the Wine Society some Bel-Air-Lalande '29, C.B., and this was fruity, round and bountiful up to the time when I drank the last bottle in 1951.

On the whole the '29s are, alas, now on the way down, but fine bottles, well kept, from successful growths, are still among the most enjoyable clarets to be drunk. Nothing as good appeared for another sixteen years, until 1945.

This was also a very fine year for the Sauternes, and Yquem hit one of its high spots. This is now very dark in colour, but still tastes better than it looks.

1930, 1931, 1932

This was the worst trio of successive years in the Gironde since the phylloxera-mildew era of the 1880s; they are years not worth discussing separately. The 1930s produced light, thin wines little seen outside the region, though I have heard that the Cheval-Blanc was quite palatable. The 1931s were slightly better, and there were two successes, Cheval-Blanc and Domaine de Chevalier. As it rained heavily during the vintage and the wines generally were light and acid, it is fair to assume that these two wines were 'assisted'. One may suspect that a little sugar was added to save the wine, and why not? Thanks to Rigby & Evens of Liverpool, I had a bottle of the Cheval-Blanc in December 1968 and though brown and in decline it was still surprisingly fruity. Oddly enough Yquem '31 was much better than expected, and although light is still pale and fresh. In 1932 the beginning of the vintage was the latest on record this century, beginning on 14 or 15 October. Only once before in modern times had a vintage begun later; in 1816, which Tastet et Lawton described as '*détestable*', while to the 1932 they awarded the comment '*qualité exécrable*'.

No doubt in the conditions of the World Slump even the first vintages would have been difficult to dispose of, but these were hard years indeed for Bordeaux, and they stimulated the development of the co-operatives which spread throughout the Gironde and saved many of the small growers.

1933

After three bad years, and accompanied by a slight lifting of the economic cloud over the world by the time that these wines were offered, there were optimistic expectations of the '33s. I drank a good many of them during the war years, but on the whole they were very light and rather short of fruit; some were acid. The wines lacked 'guts', and among the Médocs the Pauillacs came out best. Even now Latour and Mouton-Rothschild are light but fairly complete wines, and as recently as 1968 a magnum of the Mouton in particular had the characteristically powerful nose of this growth, though the flavour was beginning to thin out. Berry Bros., of London, who made several very large purchases of the '33s, including Beychevelle, shared the whole crop of Mouton-Rothschild with the firm of Cruse. The wine was of course château-bottled and kept at the château. Unfortunately to distinguish their share, Berry's had their cases marked with their name and city. Most of this wine was still there in the Second World War when the Germans occupied Mouton. The 'enemy wine' was at once confiscated, and some fine wine went down unworthy, occupying throats.

In the mid-1940s the Ch. Margaux was still a pleasing soft wine, and as late as 1966 a bottle of Lascombes '33, drunk at Alexis Lichine's La Prieuré was surprisingly distinguished for its age. However over the years the most enjoyable '33 I drank was the Cheval-Blanc, a comparatively delicate foil to the more robust and round '34.

1934

This is generally reckoned to have been the best vintage of the Thirties, and after a series of small harvests since 1929, a very large crop was made this year; 6·8 million hectolitres, only beaten in the last hundred years by 1922. Naturally it was a much publicized vintage, with varying views as to the respective merits of '33 and '34. Unfortunately the wines contained an excess of tannin, particularly the Médocs and the Graves, and they have never outgrown this; the hardness was too much for the underlying fruit and most of the wines dried up. The best of the first growths was Latour, but even that remained dry. I am inclined to think the most agreeable Médocs came from St-Julien, for Léoville-Poyferré and Barton, as well as Langoa, were less uncompromising wines than the others. Perhaps the best thing about the '34 Médocs was their low price. The Wine Society of London bought Beychevelle '34 for £12. 5s. a hogshead; thirty years later the '64 cost them at least £150.

On the other hand the St-Emilions and Pomerols were remarkably good in '34, as they had less tannin and more fruit. Cheval-Blanc '34 was the best Bordeaux of the vintage, and from birth fetched a correspondingly high price. It was and is a very velvety, round wine in the best tradition of this château. Another excellent '34 which I bought before and during the last war was La Gaffelière-Naudes, a rich full-flavoured wine. It cost between 2s. 6d. and 3s. 4d. a bottle. I drank my last bottle, a Wine Society bottling, in 1958 and the wine was still full of colour, fruit and flavour. I dare say it still is. Clos Fourtet also produced a typically full wine this year.

The Pomerols were no less successful, but I have drunk fewer of them, and none better than La Pointe, bottled by Averys: a rich full wine to this day. I am told the Pétrus was good, but I have never drunk it. Among the Graves the same is true of Domaine de Chevalier, but I can vouch for La Mission-Haut-Brion as recently as 1966. It had a little of the '34 hardness, but well-above-average fruit for the year. The Sauternes were good in this year.

1935, 1936

Although '35 was a notable port year and a fine one for cognac, in Bordeaux this was an indifferent, rather late vintage and the grapes lacked maturity; much the same applied to the '36s, which were even worse. Neither year was generally shipped to Britain, although I once had some Pauillac '36 from Averys, which was said to be declassified Lafite. It was very light, had a curious aromatic, almost resinous nose and was quite agreeable. I cannot recollect drinking another '36 until the beginning of 1969, when two of very different rank presented themselves. The first was Latour, which was still surprisingly – if one continues to be surprised by off-vintage Latours – deep-coloured and fruity. I would have taken it for a much younger wine, but when it had been open half an hour its age began to show and the fruit to depart; however a fair innings. The other was Coufran, on the edge of the Haut-Médoc. In 1968 Michael Broadbent of Christie's gave me as a curiosity a bottle of Coufran '36 château-bottled. Although indubitably brown and in decline this lesser wine from the outskirts of the Haut-Médoc was still palatable after about a third of a century.

1937

This was the first vintage since the application in the autumn of 1936 of the new law of *appellation contrôlée*. Together with further decrees issued during the ensuing war, this restricted the permitted area, the types of grape allowed and the output per hectare in districts covered by the *AC* writ. The result was a big drop in output of wines of the higher *appellations*. The 1937 vintage was average only, and the Médocs were hard like the '34s, but even more so. This was the last vintage shipped before the Germans overran France in 1940. Indeed a good deal of wine belonging to British wine merchants was left in Bordeaux, and some of it miraculously survived to replenish their tiny stocks after the war. So the '37s were welcome enough to wine drinkers in the later 1940s and early 1950s, until the fine run of post-war vintages became drinkable. I have drunk all the first growths and none were very agreeable, on account of the excess of tannin. In recent years I have come across one or two more acceptable wines, notably Léoville-Poyferré in a magnum, which in 1965 was soft if a little old in taste; Léoville-Las-Cases, very fruity still in 1968, and Pichon-Longueville-Lalande which, though pale in colour, was so finely rounded that I took it for a light '29. This was opened at the château in October 1966. The following year at Langoa the Cos-d'Estournel surprised me. Although rather hard and strong-flavoured, there was more distinction than one would have expected. I see no future for the '37 Médocs, and believe they will dry up like the '34s.

The Graves, St-Emilions and Pomerols were, as in '34, much better. I would put Domaine de Chevalier '37, which I drank a number of times up to the early 1960s, as one of the outstanding wines of '37, only excelled by Cheval-Blanc, which once more turned out a most agreeably fruity wine. Another excellent Graves was Haut-Bailly, while Canon and Gaffelière-Naudes showed very well among the St-Emilions, whose extra fruit masked the tannin. The Sauternes were excellent, notably Climens and Yquem, in that order, while white Domaine de Chevalier was a very fine white Graves.

1938, 1939

Unattractive though the '37s generally were, this was the last relatively successful vintage of a disappointing decade. The '38s were light wines and under normal conditions might have been acceptable, for they were quite well balanced though without much body. They were all consumed during the war years, and this also happened to the much larger vintage of 1939, harvested at the beginning of the deceptive 'phoney war' period. A few years ago I tasted Latour '39 at the château, but even at that home of lost vintages, the wine was brown, old-tasting and rather tired.

1940, 1941, 1942

These years are not worth discussing separately. Crops were small and quality was good only in 1942. The only '40 of any distinction I have drunk is Latour, and oddly enough this is still a fine though light wine today. Some might find it too light, but the fruit is still there and the flavour goes all the way. The Latour '42 was a bigger wine and surprisingly full-flavoured a few years ago. In the mid-Fifties I drank the La Mission-Haut-Brion '42 and that too then was a distinguished wine. There may well be good bottles of these other wartime vintages still lying in Bordeaux, but very few were exported.

1943

This was certainly the best vintage of the war years, and the one most commonly shipped to Britain after the war and available until the early Fifties. The wines varied considerably, owing no doubt to the difficulties of wartime production, with labour short and the anti-disease chemicals even more deficient in supply. There was also a shortage of bottles, so one finds French-bottled wines often in light green bottles used for both red and white wines. Although I drank a fair number of them between 1947 and 1953 they have left little impression. Most of the wines were on the light side, including the first growths. Latour was a fair wine, Lafite less so, but the Médoc which I remember best was the Pichon-Longueville-Baron, a fine fruity wine for its year. In Bordeaux in 1967 I drank Beychevelle '43 and was surprised by its fruity quality; a little dry at the end, but what would one expect of a twenty-four year old wine originally light?

Other '43s have come my way in recent years, mostly in Bordeaux. At a lunch at Grand-Puy-Lacoste in October 1965, Sir Solly Zuckerman, a fellow-guest, asked Raymond Dupin, the proprietor, whether after his '53 and '47 wines we might conclude with the '43. A magnum was brought straight from the cellar and I expected disappointment. But in fact although the wine was obviously an old one, the colour was good and the wine was fruity, not dry. The following year a bottle of Rausan-Ségla in London had still a lovely nose and was surprisingly fruity, if a little 'short' at the end. But the most surprising pair of '43 Médocs I drank together in September 1967 with their proprietor, Henri Binaud, were La Tour-de-Mons and Cantemerle. The colour of the first was paler than the second and implied age, but on the palate was more complete than the rather bigger Cantemerle. Considering the style of this vintage they were remarkably good for those who like their claret to be delicate but fruity.

The St-Emilions were fuller, and for some years the Clos Fourtet '43 was very attractive, but fell away when eight or nine years old. Cheval-Blanc was made of sterner stuff. In 1965 I was given a bottle by a Swiss friend; it had lain in Switzerland for many years, probably since the initial shipment. I drank it in August 1966. The colour was surprisingly deep, the flavour unexpectedly full and complete; a fine wine by any standards.

I have drunk one or two Pomerols of this vintage, but the one I remember best was La Croix-de-Gay, the first of a series of delicious wines from this small growth. It lasted very well, and was fruity to the end, even when the colour, like most old Pomerols, had browned. Surprisingly, in a way, the Sauternes were good, and a Climens which I drank at Loudenne in October 1966 had everything one would expect of such a growth.

1944

A plentiful but light year. The wines lacked body but some were attractive of their type; I remember Haut-Brion as almost *rosé* in colour at ten years old, and Lafite of the same age, soft and delicate if a little attenuated. An unexpected success was Rausan-Ségla. Latour, predictably, was a bigger wine and a bottle consumed in the company of André Simon and his son in 1966 had still a sufficiency of colour, a full nose and a light but true taste. Later in the same year I drank Mouton-Rothschild at the château. It had the delicious nose of fine claret, but the wine fell away. This of course was made when Mouton was particularly discriminated against so far as disease-combating chemicals were concerned through being of Jewish ownership and Vichy-controlled.

Another surprisingly good '44 was Pontet-Canet. A bottle opened in London in 1967 was extraordinarily full and with so deep a flavour I took it for a Pomerol. No doubt it had been 'assisted'.

The Post-War Score: 1945 – 1964

1945

This vintage has had more *réclame* than any other in the post-war period, as therein it must narrowly be counted; the only, much younger rival in prestige has been 1961. Both vintages were similar in being exceptionally short. The '45s suffered from a disastrous spring frost on 2 May, and the crop was the second smallest of the century to date (only 1915 was smaller), and totalled 1·48 million hectolitres. Moreover conditions in the vineyards were understandably far from perfect. Ronald Barton has told me that when he first returned to Langoa in the summer of 1945, the normally trim vineyards were covered with weeds. Although an excellent vintage, which began early, around 10 September, not all chateaux were able to produce successful wines. For example, Margaux seems to lack fruit and to have been disappointing in its class, while a considerable proportion of Cheval-Blanc was 'pricked', or vinegary. Moreover the one fault of the wines was that they had an excess of tannin, and there have not been lacking long-memoried pessimists who have murmured, 'another '28'. This is unfair, but no doubt those who bought '45s when first offered between 1948 and 1950 have had to wait a long time before finding their wines ready. I am among these. Layers-down of vintage port may resign themselves to waiting a score of years before opening a bottle, but this is a long period for claret drinkers. Fortunately many more earlier-maturing vintages have intervened. At one time the '47s were more immediately attractive and had their champions as against the '45s, but the Médocs of '47 certainly did not hold up as expected. It is sometimes said that the '45s were the last clarets 'made in the old way', i.e., with a prolonged fermentation on the skins, resulting in slow development and fruity but tanniny wines; for the tannin comes from the skins and the pips.

With the possible exception of Margaux all the first growths and Mouton made very fine wine. There are those who place Lafite first, and it is indeed a wine of great breed and finesse, but Mouton-Rothschild is an extraordinarily full-bodied wine, quite different in style from its neighbour, but nonetheless remarkable. It is far from ready, although there have been periods when it seemed to be breaking through. Latour is still a great big fruity, but backward wine, with almost too powerful a flavour and a 'strong' nose, while Haut-Brion has long been the most advanced of them, with the typical earthy taste of Graves. La Mission-Haut-Brion, similar in style and a little more rounded when I drank it some years ago, was then also excellent.

Partly because of the fact that a good many '45s were drunk up too young in the period of post-war shortage, and partly because they have been held back owing to their backwardness, I have not drunk as many '45s as one might have expected to do; and I still tend to guard my own reserves. Very few, however, have been other than good, although some have been a little hard and green even after twenty years. Léoville-Barton is very fruity, and better than the other two Léovilles. Pontet-Canet is unusually full, with the same hint of Pomerol on the nose and palate that I have noted in the '29. Among the St-Estèphes the Cos d'Estournel has stood out.

Particularly attractive, because they mature fairly rapidly, are the Pomerols. Pétrus '45, drunk in 1966, lacked the graciousness and completeness of the '47, but if still a little hard, it had the typical 'concentrated' flavour. Gazin is another wine of the same character and such wines as L'Enclos and La Croix-de-Gay are highly agreeable.

I have had a number of disappointments with wines bottled in England, and can only think they were shipped and/or bottled too late, for they lack fruit. The best of the Médocs may well last into the next century as Baron Philippe de Rothschild certainly expects of his Mouton-Rothschild; and if ever there is a Latour that might emulate its pre-phylloxera predecessors in longevity it surely is the '45. On the other hand if the pessimists are proved correct, some of the wines with an excess of tannin might dry up and lose their fruit, as indeed a number of the '28s have done. The more elegant wines, of which Lafite is the best example known to me, might not have enough 'behind them' to last so long as the bigger types. But 'size' is not everything, and balance is at least equally important. So '45 remains a controversial vintage.

This was a great year for Sauternes, albeit a small crop. I doubt whether Yquem '45 has yet been surpassed in the post-war era.

1946

A distinctly off-year, but one in which I have come upon two surprisingly good wines: Latour and Mouton-Rothschild. At a tasting in 1964 at the château of off-vintage

Latours this unexpectedly turned up as my favourite in a selection stretching back from 1963 to 1939. Since then I have acquired a small stock and drunk it a number of times with enjoyment. The wine has plenty of fruit, flavour and expectation of life, but without quite the finish of a great year. The Mouton '46 was one of my 'discoveries' at the château in 1968. As Mouton-Rothschild, like Latour, often succeeds in off-years, and remembering the Latour, I enquired about the Mouton '46. Not surprisingly it is not one of the most frequently sought-after vintages in that famous cellar, and opinions on the wine were as vague as on the '95, referred to earlier, and in fact drunk on the same occasion as the '46, which immediately preceded it at table. Deep in colour, and with plenty of flavour, the wine had a little of the dryness at the end noticed in the Latour, but very well balanced for the year. Perhaps it was even better than the Latour. Certainly, I was heretical enough to have preferred the '46 as a glass of mature claret to the much more famous '45, of which a bottle had been decanted from the adjoining bin and drunk only the previous night. That does not imply, however, that the '45 has such prospects. When in May 1969 I drank Latour '46 alongside Mouton '46, the latter showed more fruit and flavour.

1947

After a very hot summer wines of great charm were made, although the excessive heat was the undoing of some. There was so much natural sugar present during the fermentation that not all was converted into alcohol, with the result there was volatile acidity in the wine. So quite a number of them, particularly the Médocs, soon showed a little sourness in their tail. These included Lafite, Latour, Lascombes, Léoville-Barton and many other classed growths. Two exceptions were part at least of Ch. Margaux and Mouton-Rothschild; both very fine wines. La Mission-Haut-Brion was good and Grand-Puy-Lacoste and Angludet above average. For their first ten years or so the '47 Médocs were very attractive, with a sweetness reminiscent of '29s, but they lacked that year's balance, and acidity began to obtrude.

However, it was the classic post-war vintage for Pomerol and a fine one for St-Emilion where, of course, Cheval-Blanc was and remains the star wine. In Dublin in May 1966 Tom Whelehan, whose generosity is not bounded by the capacity of his guests, produced among other wines Cheval-Blanc '47 and Pétrus '47. Both were remarkable: Pétrus rather sweeter and more overwhelming, Cheval-Blanc slightly more restrained yet distinguished. I was in a minority in preferring the latter for its greater depth of flavour, but both wines are among the most attractive post-war clarets of the richer, fuller type one could wish to drink. The Cheval-Blanc is as much *hors concours* as the '21, and for much the same reason: a very hot summer. This is still an enormous, port-type wine, untypical of claret and I would think it would last for years, although some suggest not. Owing to its great sweetness and easiness-to-drink Cheval-Blanc '47 has become much in demand for those with deep purses, and has already reached over £10 a bottle at Christie's wine auctions.

No other St-Emilion I have had approaches it, but a number of the Pomerols are more or less in the Pétrus class, including Vieux-Château-Certan, Certan, Petit-

Village, Nénin and the fruity La Croix-de-Gay, bottled by Harveys – my first introduction to '47 Pomerols and drunk with pleasure over the years.

White Graves do not figure much in these notes, not because they are unworthy of comment, but because they seldom remain in the memory. Moreover their standards of quality vary less from vintage to vintage than with the red wines, or with the Sauternes. However 1947 was a remarkably fine year for white Graves, and the most distinguished one I often came across was Domaine de Chevalier, a flowery honeyish wine with a dry finish; dry, that is by white Bordeaux standards. No doubt Haut-Brion-Blanc was good too, but I do not remember drinking it.

The Sauternes, produced after this hot summer, were also very fine, almost up to the '45s. The two I have found most attractive have been Climens and Yquem.

1948

A neglected year between two celebrated successes. I remember tasting the '47s and '48s in cask in the summer of 1949; the former were charming already, the latter very astringent. The only one of the '48s I liked then was the Brane-Cantenac, and indeed this has turned out one of the best Médocs of the year. The wines have always been on the firm side, and some have an excess of acidity which has become increasingly apparent with the years. Both Lafite and Palmer which used to be fine examples of the year are now too acid. The finest Médoc of the year is, however, Léoville-Barton, a fruity, big wine that to my knowledge has been excellent since 1957, when I was introduced to it by that great claret lover, Sir Guy Fison of Saccone & Speed. Unfortunately the two other '48 Léovilles are thin and disappointing. None of the first growths or Mouton equal the Barton, although both Latour and Mouton are well above average and could still develop, particularly the former. One of the most attractive is Malescot, and both Talbot and Cantemerle have been very agreeable. Among the Graves La Mission-Haut-Brion is outstanding with a very distinguished flavour. The future of any '48 depends on its acidity-sugar balance.

On the other side of the river Cheval-Blanc is rich and fruity though firm, and I still prefer it to the more celebrated '49. Since 1948s were hardly shipped to this country except by Averys of Bristol they have been hard to come by, so my range of St-Emilions and Pomerols tasted has been restricted, but La Dominique is good. Pétrus, on the other hand, rather lacked fruit on the only occasion I tasted it.

1949

This year was greatly acclaimed initially, but has not always fulfilled its promise, for many of the wines have an edge and hardness that have persisted. Others, such as Latour and Léoville-Barton, surely have yet to show their full qualities; both are fine, with plenty of body. It may be that another few years must pass before the status of this vintage is finally established. However, there is little doubt on present showing that the outstanding Médoc is Mouton-Rothschild. This is a wine of such enormous concentration of nose and flavour that it almost suggests a Burgundy, or at least a

Pomerol. In this wine particularly have I detected the 'cedar-wood' or 'lead pencil' nose associated with Mouton. Like the '45 it is typical Mouton, and utterly different from the rather delicate, distinguished but perhaps over-light Lafite '49. The Mouton embraces one, while the Lafite slips away from one's grasp. Ch. Margaux is fine too in its delicate way.

Other '49 Médocs I have liked, have been the very fruity Lynch-Bages, St-Pierre-Sevaistre and Cantemerle, but recently some '49 Médocs have seemed variable and may be in decline. But how good the '49 Pomerols have been: Pétrus, La Conseillante, Certan, La Croix-de-Gay – these and others have been of the same pattern as the '45s and '47s, although perhaps not quite so good as the latter. Cheval-Blanc, though an excellent wine has sometimes seemed a bit on the dull side; but it is now waking up at last. Gaffelière-Naudes was good when young but did not last a great time. I recollect Ausone as being better than I expected for this long-disappointing growth, but I do not remember ever tasting Figeac or Canon, both of which may have been very good. This was a not very successful period for many of the leading Graves. I have preferred the La Mission-Haut-Brion to Haut-Brion.

Another good white Graves and Sauternes year, with a wonderful Yquem, and splendid Coutet, Climens and Rieussec among others.

1950

Vast quantities of wine were made in Bordeaux this year. The output of 3·17 million hectolitres with *appellation contrôlée* was almost half as much again as in 1949, and the total was not matched until 1962. With three acclaimed vintages in the previous five years behind them, there was not much initial enthusiasm for the '50s, watered by a wet summer. However, they were very cheap and so were widely bought. A large number of them turned out better than expected and some are still good drinking today. For example in 1954 I bought Latour for 16s. 6d. a bottle; so they proved excellent bargains. The pattern of success was uneven and depended no doubt on the skill of the wine makers, plus perhaps a judicious proportion of added sugar, although not legalized until the following year. The Pomerols and St-Emilions, which sometimes do better than the Médocs in a poor year, were the most consistent wines, with Pétrus, Certan, Cheval-Blanc, Figeac and Ausone as wines still good when tasted in the last year or two. They tend to be a little short in flavour compared with, say 1949, but fruity and enjoyable all the same. Latour and Margaux were the best among the Médoc leaders, and when the latter in magnums was served as the final claret at the *Ban de Vendange* dinner in the magnificent white-pillared *chai* of Château Margaux in September 1967, it was as charming a light but true claret as one could have wished for. Latour, of course, was made of sterner stuff and still has a future. Both Mouton and Lafite were disappointing, but another Pauillac, Pichon-Longueville-Baron was a fruity wine, and Gruaud-Larose and Léoville-Barton, were notable successes in the adjoining St-Julien. Palmer was always light but hung on successfully for the better part of the twenty years. Although La Mission-Haut-Brion, and its junior partner La Tour-Haut-Brion, both made very attractive '50s I have never liked Haut-Brion, which has seemed too rich to be true. All in all a surprisingly successful off year.

Although I had drunk and enjoyed Haut-Brion-Blanc '49, I think it was the '50 that first attracted me to this often distinguished wine. In those days it was possible to ship the wine in cask, so that it was not over-expensive for its quality. I acquired a few bottles for not much more than 16s. 6d. a bottle, imported and bottled by Harveys. Along with Domaine de Chevalier of the same year, this was an unusually good recommendation for white Graves, with a honeyish nose which at first led one to expect a rather sweeter wine than showed on the palate. Sauternes came up exceptionally well in this year, and some Sauternes enthusiasts place 1950 as among the greatest post-war years. Yquem, Coutet and Climens were delicious; and they were decidedly inexpensive.

1951

This was the first year when *chaptalisation*, or adding sugar to the vats at the time of fermentation in order to increase the alcoholic content of the wine, was permanently legalized. Since then each year it has been an *ad hoc* decision made by the Minister of Agriculture through the *préfet* of the department shortly before the vintage. Originally intended only for bad years, there is little doubt that the practice has spread, and even in good years like 1964 and 1966 sugaring was permitted. Some maintain this was a 'sell-out' of the essential qualities of Bordeaux, and a sign that the Gironde was going the way of the Côte d'Or. It is already being suggested that yearly approval should be dispensed with and the growers be allowed to use their own judgment – and buy their sugar in good time. This may well come about, but my view is that while it is legitimate to save a bad or indifferent wine by sugaring, to add sugar in a good year detracts from the quality of a claret. A sugared wine tends to lack distinction and depth. It should be borne in mind that this decision in 1951 legalized but did not create the practice. There was one very fine '29 that in fact had been *chaptalisé*, and it seems likely that Pomerols were often 'assisted' in the past.

Certainly 1951 was a year for such 'assistance'. It was miserably wet and the crop was very small. The only wines drinkable must have been well sugared. Even today those wines which have survived are deceptive, for some suggest the sweetness of a '47 or even '29, and of course have an 'old' colour. Among these are Cheval-Blanc, an agreeable, but in appearance and flavour highly misleading, glass of wine; and neither Latour nor Mouton need to be apologized for on any table. Lafite, as might be expected, is more delicate and when I drank it last in 1967 it faded in the glass, no great condemnation sixteen years after a very bad vintage. I have also enjoyed recently Bel-Air, and earlier on I had some Gaffelière-Naudes which had cost me only 7s. a bottle from Harveys, and was a bargain at the price.

1952

The crop with *AC* was no larger than the previous year, but the wines were much better. I tasted many when first available in London in 1955, and at this early stage, they seemed most attractive; but in fact the Médocs contained an excess of tannin which obscured the fruit and has persisted to this day. Thus they lack the charm of the following '53s. Certainly in the last few years they have 'unbuttoned', and one or two wines I used to find almost disagreeable are now far less so, but I wonder whether they will ever lose their hard core. It is the old question of whether the fruit or the tannin will win, and usually but not always it is the latter. The next two or three years should show. Owing to their retarded quality I have tended to keep my '52s and drink my '53s; therefore I have not drunk anything like so many wines of the prior vintage. However Latour seems definitely better than Lafite and by 1968 was showing a fruity roundness that augured well, La Mission-Haut-Brion is more developed and round than Haut-Brion, which seems to lack acidity and tastes a little flat. Cantemerle has come on well from a hard beginning, and Talbot is another supple '52 Médoc; but Lascombes is too supple and sweet.

However, the story is quite different across the rivers, and although the Pomerols and St-Emilions show a hard streak, they have much more fruit and charm. At least until 1961 there was not another vintage to compare with them in quality. Although the '52s have not the elegance of the '49s some of them are in the tradition of the outstanding St-Emilions and Pomerols of the later 1940s. Perhaps the Pétrus of this year is even better than the Cheval-Blanc, but both are excellent and the latter should have a good future. Among the Pomerols I would pick out Vieux-Château-Certan, Lafleur-Pétrus, La Croix-de-Gay and Clos René, as excellent growth which I first met in this vintage. Some of the St-Emilions are more austere, but Figeac and Gaffelière-Naudes made firm wines, yet without the distinction of Cheval-Blanc. I have had several good '52 Sauternes, but it was probably a less good year than '50. But Yquem for the second year in succession produced no wine under the château label owing to frost or hail.

1953

This may not be the greatest post-war vintage but probably the most agreeable to date. Curiously enough it was a late vintage, starting only at the beginning of October, generally a bad omen, but following storms the weather combination just managed to turn out right; excellently balanced, soft wines were produced, which were already drinkable five years after they were made. The crop was reasonably large, 2·98 million hl. The wines are notable for lack of tannin and a natural sweetness which early made them most attractive. What is uncertain about them is how well they will last, because although their fine balance is in their favour, some at least are rather light in body. From the beginning Lafite was generally accepted as leading the field, and a very attractive wine it has been, with all the grace in aroma and flavour of a fine claret. But three or four years ago it was suggested Lafite '53 was not quite what it used to be, and many people now believe Margaux to be the better wine. Certainly the latter is a very elegant well-balanced claret. Partly owing to the fearsome frosts of February 1956, Lafite was bottling its '53 from December 1955 to June 1956, and it would be surprising if this did not entail some variation in the wine. I know this as I was at Lafite in June 1956, a week after they had finished. The better bottles are still very fine claret. Latour, which I visited next, had recently completed their smaller bottling programme in three months. So far, however, Latour has been rather a disappointing wine, somewhat strong, coarse and unbalanced. The other great success is Mouton-Rothschild, typically different from its nearest neighbour, and a big rich wine which drinks beautifully, with all the traditional concentration of Mouton, but not a wine for those who seek delicacy in claret.

There are so many fine '53 Médocs that a list would include a considerable slice of the classed growths including Léoville-Barton (but not the other two Léovilles, which are thin), Palmer, Grand-Puy-Lacoste, Cantemerle, Lynch-Bages, Talbot, Gruaud-Larose and Langoa. Ronald Barton declared his Langoa '53 to be the best he had ever made. Some of the Pauillacs, like the two Pichons and Pontet-Canet, are a bit on the 'hefty' side. However, three non-classed growths stand out in my memory, La Tour-de-Mons, Siran and Angludet. The first is a firm and powerful wine for a '53; in fact one of the best clarets of the year. Some of the Médocs already look a little brown, not a good sign.

Although Haut-Brion '53 is a very pleasant, soft wine, in my view it is over-shadowed once more by La Mission-Haut-Brion, which produced a wine with a special reputation from the start. Domaine de Chevalier, after so many disappointing post-war years so far as the red wine was concerned, somewhat returned to form with its '53.

The St-Emilions and Pomerols on the whole did not come up to the Médocs and Graves. They seem to lack the depth of flavour of the '52s, although perhaps better balanced. Cheval-Blanc '53 is a very agreeable wine, but misses the special character of the growth, and one might say the same of Pétrus and Vieux-Château-Certan too; indeed both were finer in '55. There were some particular successes in both communes, including Figeac in St-Emilion and Clos René, L'Enclos and Certan in Pomerol. Clos René, bottled by Harveys, and retailed at 9s. a bottle was one of my better buys. Until '61 neither district again produced such notable wines.

The '53 white Bordeaux were not so good as the '52s; nor so outstanding in their year as the reds, but nevertheless it was a fine vintage.

1954

This was the worst year since '46, but better than '56. As in '51, skill and sugar saved the crop for some châteaux, but others may have suffered worse micro-weather at the vintage late in October. Not altogether surprisingly Latour and Mouton-Rothschild made very drinkable wines; they still are. Another good Médoc was Léoville-Barton, a bit 'short' in flavour but surprisingly fruity. On the other hand Rausan-Ségla drunk in Bordeaux in October 1966 was so brown and old-smelling that one might have guessed a 1920 in decline. I remember being offered by Ronald Avery very cheaply, and slightly contemptuously rejecting Cheval-Blanc '54, when it was about three years old and not very attractive. In fact it turned out very pleasantly, while Pétrus still drunk surprisingly well in 1968, although by then distinctly pale in colour. Very few '54s came to Britain. One that did was Yquem '54, which may not have had the lusciousness of a great year, but was not a wine to despise.

1955

This was the first vintage when classed-growth prices began to rise markedly, a process accelerated by the two poor or short-crop succeeding years and continued in successful years ever since. The '55s, which were plentiful – up to then the largest successful vintage since the war, with 3·1 million hectolitres and not to be surpassed in quantity until 1962 – were also highly praised. They seemed rather expensive at the time, but not of course dear by later standards (25s. a bottle for Lafite '55 compared with 20s. for the '53). Many, including myself, bought the St-Emilions and Pomerols because they were 'the last good vintage' before the frost devastation early in 1956.

The '55s are certainly good wines, but their fault has been a certain lack of definition and a slight dull flatness arising from a shortage of acidity, or so they have seemed to me; but there are others who yet predict a bright future for them, and say they are 'passing through a phase'. On the whole those estates who make rather 'big' wines were most successful, including Latour, Mouton-Rothschild, Cos d'Estournel and Cantemerle; whereas the more delicate wines of Margaux have been thin and disappointing so far. I remember drinking a good Marquis-d'Alesme in 1966. Lafite has much of its traditional quality, and is elegant. Many people regarded Cantemerle as one of the most successful wines of the vintage.

Among the first growths, Haut-Brion '55 stands well, although at least equalled by La Mission which has seemed to have more acidity. The most attractive red Graves was surely Pape-Clément, which was a very elegant wine, and its only fault was that it had rather a short pontificate, for it has thinned off sadly.

The trans-riverine wines suffered from the same slight dullness. Among '55s Cheval-Blanc stands out for its fruitiness, but I would not call it an outstanding example of this growth. Two of its neighbours, La Dominique and Figeac did well but not brilliantly. The finest '55 Pomerol has always seemed to me to be Vieux-Château-Certan, one of the most attractive wines of the whole vintage, and better than Pétrus. Two successful Pomerols I know well are La Conseillante and La Grave-Trigant-de-Boisset. Trotanoy made good wine too. It will be interesting to see whether the '55 red Bordeaux have further development possibilities. I wish I were more confident, as there is a big gap until the next fine year – 1959.

The whites in this year were certainly good, and among the dry wines I remember an excellent Haut-Brion-Blanc and a very well-rounded Laville-Haut-Brion. Domaine de Chevalier was good but no more. The sweet wines were successful too without being outstanding. It was the last fine year for them until 1959.

1956

A really terrible year, with production down to about one-third of the previous vintage. The February frosts, particularly damaging, as they occurred after a spell of unusually mild weather causing the sap to rise in the vines, ensured a small crop; and the summer was bad too. Even Latour could not pull out anything very attractive, and Mouton made a sharp, thin wine, though no worse than others. I remember an acceptable Talbot, obtainable for a period on British railway restaurant cars; but otherwise the vintage is best forgotten. It was said at the time that St-Emilion and Pomerol would not recover their normal quality for at least ten years, owing to the number of vines killed. This proved exaggerated, as many vines put out shoots from the bottom, but above the graft. Nevertheless the next really good vintage for these districts was '61. The Médocs and Graves were less spectacularly damaged, but they suffered loss too. French wine-growers take their losses sadly, and it was commonly mourned as the worst disaster since the phylloxera. It was certainly a set-back to those classed-growth proprietors who had been making reasonable profits only for the last few years, and for the often hard-pressed lesser growths. Things turned out not to be as bad as advertised, but at the time the more far-seeing (or credulous) went out and bought even more '52s, '53s and '55s. I was among them.

1957

The amount of *AC* wine declared this year was scarcely greater than in '56. The later summer was poor and it was another October vintage. Not surprisingly the Bordelais put a brave face on the results which was well publicized, but the wines were hard indeed and lacking in charm. The only wines that have surprised me by their excellence are Haut-Brion – better balanced than most – and Haut-Bailly, while Lynch-Bages, strong and fruity, is good but not very Médocain in style. Talbot has given me some pleasant drinking too. The vintage has always had its adherents, and they promise great things by the 1970s. If so I shall be caught very short, as I scarcely bought a bottle.

1958

Another very small, mid-October vintage. The wines were all light, with some successes in the context of such a vintage. Cos d'Estournel made a very agreeable wine, and so did La Mission-Haut-Brion, although light. Latour and Mouton had none of the punch these two châteaux usually provide in their very different ways, but produced wines with more body and fruit than the average. Another good wine of the vintage is Cantemerle, which was particularly firm and fruity. No long life was to be expected for the '58s. The St-Emilions and Pomerols were still licking their wounds after '56, and although they produced rather more wine in '58, those I have tasted have had rather a 'made' taste.

1959

It was not surprising, after three unsatisfactory years for quantity as well as quality that 1959 was hailed somewhat extravagantly; a good vintage was on the order of the day. Moreover the summer was unexpectedly fine and hot even in Britain, and the not-so-initiated wine-drinking public equates a hot year with a fine vintage. In fact, as 1921 and 1947 showed, this brings considerable problems. Too much sun means too little fixed acidity, and the danger of volatile acidity. However, before the grapes were gathered, '59 had been declared the Vintage of the Century (we have had two others since then: '61 and '64). Journalists have been blamed for this headline, but it certainly was not those who write regularly about wine, for they are commendably cautious. The crop of red and white *AC* wines was not in fact very large – 1·85 million hectolitres and almost the same as the notoriously short '61; but the whites suffered more than the reds, and there seemed no initial lack of Médocs of quality.

It is now generally agreed that '59 is probably not such a fine year as originally thought, because there is a certain lack of acidity in many of the wines, so they are rather soft and lack stamina; some are a little flabby. On the other hand the best wines are very good and have the true style of fine claret. All three Pauillac leaders made good wine, typical of their varying styles, but I have found Margaux disappointing on the one or two occasions tasted. However the adjoining Palmer is good; and both Léoville-Las-Cases, now returned to form, and Léoville-Barton have plenty of flavour, so has Ducru-Beaucaillou. Gruaud-Larose is another fruity St-Julien; Cantemerle again scored a success. Haut-Brion was particularly attractive after some years of relative disappointment, and another red Graves that was very winning was Pape-Clément. The St-Emilions and Pomerols had now recovered some but certainly not all of their quality, and tended to show brown in colour when relatively young. Canon, l'Angélus, Pavie and Figeac have all been good in their way, but do not suggest long life. This also applies to Cheval-Blanc, which in my experience has varied prematurely from bottle to bottle. I must admit to having no final view at this time on a great many '59s, as I have tended to keep my own until the full quality of the better wines should be revealed. For fine claret I try to follow the ten-year rule of abstinence.

As might be expected in such a hot year, '59 was an excellent vintage for the Sauternes, and none of the well-known châteaux have made as good a wine since. Yquem is splendidly luscious, though perhaps a slightly weighty wine.

1960

This vintage was at first treated in rather the same way as 1950, for the weather had been similarly wet, although this year the vintage was not late; yet now there was a shortage of wine in Bordeaux. Also *chaptalisation* was permitted. The result was that some very drinkable wines were made in this fairly large vintage. Much depended, I suspect, on adroit use of sugar. Some put in too little, and the wines are thin, some too much and the wines are sweet enough to lose a good deal of their Bordeaux quality. Those however that had 'the mix' right did well. I would put Latour top of the list, Palmer second and Cantemerle third, but I do not claim to have drunk a great range. Grand-Puy-Lacoste is another attractive '60 and so certainly is Mouton-

Rothschild, which has an affinity with Latour. Haut-Brion has proved much too sweet for my taste, and Léoville-Las-Cases a bit mawkish. Ausone made a very charming light wine, although its very brown colour after only six or seven years did not suggest long life. Cheval-Blanc was bigger and rather more acceptable. Clos Fourtet, however, was a thin, acid, despairing sort of wine. A great virtue of the '60s was that they were inexpensive and, provided one found the right wine, they were very good buys for the not so exceptional occasion. They were also a warning not to be put off too much by cries of 'off-vintage'.

1961

This chapter is largely a summary of wines I have drunk rather than a vintage report. Although nowadays one cannot take as gospel the old Bordelais axiom that one should not drink fine claret until it is ten years old, the really distinguished wines have now become so expensive that there is a strong disincentive to open irreplaceable bottles before their time. My experiences of '61 have hitherto been at other people's expense and mostly at tastings. This vintage was abnormally short and as we thought at the time excessively dear. In fact, such has been the progress of inflation and the advance of first-growth prices (followed by others), that looking back the '61s now seem to have been not all that dear when first offered. Moreover on the whole the British wine trade, with plenty of '59s in its cellars in addition to older years, plus some '60s, shied off buying the more expensive wines. To offer Lafite '61 at 50s. or so a bottle at opening prices seemed an extravagant exercise. Later the '66 was to open at over 80s.

Soon there was no doubt of the quality of the '61s, which have plenty of fruit and, lacking the excessive tannin of the '45s, are well balanced, with plenty of body. Accordingly it is today generally accepted as being the best vintage since '45, and possibly since '29. The wines are also regrettably drinkable, whereas the '45s to some extent were protected from infanticide by their tannin covering. Haut-Brion, for example, is already agreeable and seems almost prematurely complete. Latour, and to a lesser extent Mouton, are usually slow developers in such years, but both while still unready, have a splendid balance making them palatable when relatively young. A wine which has appealed to me most in its own style is Ch. Margaux, which combines fruit with delicacy; it might be another '53, but fruitier.

I had an opportunity of drinking, as well as tasting, a number of leading wines at the Lebègue tasting in October 1967. This was one in the famous series of mammoth French wine tastings which Lebègue have organized in their vast cellars below London Bridge railway station since the late 1940s. Every professional and many amateur wine drinkers have been in their debt for this unparalleled opportunity to taste young and old clarets, Burgundies, etc. Fortunately the rate of expectoration is high, though its level happily low, so guests after sampling their choice from nearly two hundred wines, are still able to drink a special selection with the ensuing lavish lunch.

At the 1967 session, Guy Prince and his colleagues had arranged a tasting of the '66, '64, '62 and '61 vintages of Pétrus, Cheval-Blanc, Haut-Brion and Margaux. Certainly the '61s showed their quality, and it was the only one of the four vintages in which I liked all the wines. After the Margaux I placed the Pétrus unhesitatingly second; a wonderfully rich, deep-coloured wine; I put the Cheval-Blanc last, after the Haut-Brion, although to date the former is probably the best wine from this vineyard since the 1956 frosts, and is expected to turn out remarkably well.

Since nearly everyone seems to have made a good '61 it is pointless to particularize. Lafite certainly produced a wine of great distinction. One curious wine, however, is La Lagune, which perhaps had not yet achieved a properly balanced vineyard after re-planting in 1957. Twice I have taken La Lagune '61 for Burgundy. It showed age far too soon.

The '61 white wines were not so outstanding as might be expected, even Yquem was a trifle disappointing; the '62 was better.

This is certainly a vintage that should be well represented in the cellar of every claret lover. Soon, these are the only places it will be found, outside the wine auctions.

1962

This was the abundant vintage every Bordeaux grower and wine merchant had been praying for. Although it started well into October the grapes were generally sound, and the wines were well balanced though on the light side. The quantity of 3·74 million hectolitres *AC* wines was the biggest since the last war and up to and including 1967. There were no great wines made in '62, but most of them have turned out very pleasantly and with a good deal of the charm and lightness of true claret. The Médocs were certainly better than the St-Emilions and Pomerols, and probably better than the Graves too. Cheval-Blanc was disappointing, although Pétrus retained most of its typical fullness. Ausone had a certain distinction all too often absent in the last generation, but Figeac made a splendidly fruity Pomerol-reminiscent wine. A lighter but agreeable Pomerol is Vieux-Château-Certan. I have not drunk a great range of '62s to date, but have liked the Latour which has more character than most. Mouton-Rothschild, Margaux and Lafite have disappointed me. The Palmer is a charming wine; so is Léoville-Las-Cases. It is doubtful whether these '62s will have a very long life, but this does not mean they have to be drunk up too soon. The future of a claret vintage is notoriously hard to predict. This was the last passable year for Sauternes until 1966.

1963

This vintage was another abundant one, but abundance that caused no joy, for the wines were very poor indeed after a bad summer and a cheerless October vintage. It is an arguable point as to whether '63 or '65 is the worse vintage, although the '63 may have won the unwelcome palm. Even sugaring could not save them. It is true that in Bordeaux I sampled one or two not undrinkable very, very light wines. They were almost the colour of *vin rosé* when three or four years old. The only wine with any claim to quality I have come on is Latour, which did its best to maintain its off-vintage reputation and just succeeded; one can guess why it tastes sweet.

This was a terrible year for the sweet white wines, and although Yquem actually bottled some '63, its dark colour suggested a wine old before it was young, and for a leading growth this was no credit.

1964

Whoever was responsible for calling 1959 'the vintage of the century', there is no doubt that for '64 much of the responsibility can be firmly pinned on M. Edgard Pisani, the French Minister of Agriculture who in August 1964 proclaimed a wonderful vintage. It was another of those misleadingly hot summers. Nevertheless conditions were good, in spite of some deficiency of rain. The vintage started in the last week of September and those who picked at once generally made fine wine, but certain growths which often like to hang on to attain '*surmaturité*' delayed. Then on 8 October the heavens opened and it rained for a fortnight. The late-pickers included Lafite, Mouton-Rothschild and Lynch-Bages, and their wines were correspondingly disappointing and light. The early pickers included Latour, who probably made the best wine of the year. However, although there has been a tendency to divide the '64s into 'early' and 'late' pickers this is an over-simplification. Some that picked early did not produce a particularly successful wine, while others were caught by the bad weather half-way through their vintaging.

The St-Emilions and Pomerols overall were more fortunate than the Médocs, partly because their picking usually takes place a few days earlier. The red Graves also did well in '64, and La Mission-Haut-Brion has a particularly good reputation.

The prices attained by the first growths were extremely, many would say excessively, high; but the '66s were to be higher.

This was another disappointing year for Sauternes and I was told at Yquem that no '64 would be sold under the château label. Climens and Coutet did bottle some of their wine this year.

It is far too early to say how the '64s will turn out, but so far they have not been surpassed by later vintages; and about these it is pointless as yet to comment.

1965

As a footnote to the post-war score, the '65s appear to have little merit. Some growths by a process of ruthless selection made light clean wine: among these were La Mission-Haut-Brion and Cantemerle. Ch. Margaux, involved in its non-vintage blends, did not sell any wine with this vintage label. Both Latour and Mouton-Rothschild did, in my view mistakenly as there was a taste of rot in the wine.

Appendix A:

Opening Prices

Below are two tables giving the opening prices of clarets. The first shows a representative selection of classed-growth Médocs, with Haut-Brion included when the prices have been available, from 1831 to 1934, the last good vintage before the Second World War. The second concentrates on the *premiers crus* and Mouton from the officially fixed prices in that war up to 1967, the latest vintage of repute when this book went to press. The first list has been compiled from the incomparable records of Tastet et Lawton, the brokers; the omission of Haut-Brion, particularly in the early years, was because they did not deal in this red Graves, but I have been able to secure some figures from the château. To show a comparative *deuxième*, when possible I have included Léoville-Barton. With both lists it must be emphasized that while these were actual prices paid to the châteaux, such prices varied, not only according to the state of the market but also how long after the vintage the deal took place. This might mean a higher price than at first, or a lower one, as in the case of Mouton-Rothschild 1890, which, as noted below, passed through the brokers' hands in 1894 at a very low price compared with that given for the other leaders. Moreover there has long been established in Bordeaux the practice of a château selling its wines in two *tranches* (slices). The first is nearly always the larger, and where I have had figures for both I have given the earlier price. It is sometimes argued that opening prices are not always genuine, and either involved very small quantities to test the market or to try to establish a favourable price for the grower, or were on a returnable basis if the Bordeaux merchant could not sell all the wine. No doubt there is some substance in these objections, but by and large I have no doubt that the figures listed below did represent the opening prices of the various wines. It used to be the custom for a merchant or a group of merchants to make five- or ten-year contracts with the leading growths, guaranteeing to take all their crop over this period at a fixed price; who benefited most from this depended upon the run of the vintages. One celebrated vintage in which the first growths certainly lost was 1920. All the prices are given in francs per *tonneau*.

1831	Lafite	2400	Latour		2600
	Margaux (under contract)		Brane-Mouton		2100
	Rausan-Ségla	2500	Léoville-Barton		2000
	Dauzac	1250	Palmer		1480
1834	Lafite	2800–3200	Latour		2400
	Margaux	4000	Brane-Mouton		2100
	Léoville-Poyferré	2100	Beychevelle		1550
1841	Lafite	5500	Latour		1800
			(contract with Barton & Guestier)		
	Margaux	2500	Brane-Mouton		1400
	Palmer ('*en primeur*')	700	Dauzac		550–600
1847	Lafite (contract with Cruse)	1025	Latour (contract with Barton & Guestier, 1844–1853)		1750
	Margaux (under contract 1844–1852)	2100	Brane-Mouton		800
	Pichon-Longueville	525	Dauzac		400
1848	Lafite	2800	Latour		1750
			(contract with Barton & Guestier)		
	Margaux (under contract)	2100	Brane-Mouton		900–1400
	Léoville-Barton	850	Gruaud-Larose		1000
	Langoa	750			
1854	Lafite (December 1854)	5000	Latour		5000
	Margaux (December 1855)	5500	Mouton-Rothschild (December 1854)		5000
	Rausan-Ségla (under contract)	1200	Palmer		4000
1858	Lafite	4000	Latour		4800
	Margaux	5000	Haut-Brion		4000
	Léoville-Poyferré	3500	Mouton-Rothschild		4000
	Léoville-Las-Cases	3250	Léoville-Barton		3000

	Palmer	2400	Langoa	2400
	Pontet-Canet	1500	Lynch-Bages	1500–2000
	Dauzac	1500	Cantemerle	1500
1864	Lafite	5000	Latour	4500
	Margaux (under contract 1863–1872)	4200	Mouton-Rothschild	3100
	Pichon-Longueville	2400	Léoville-Poyferré	2000
	Palmer	2500–3000	Léoville-Barton	2000
	Dauzac	1350	Lynch-Bages	1200
	La Tertre	1350	Batailley	1200
1865	Lafite (exclusive to six merchants)	5600	Latour	5600
	Margaux (under contract)	4200	Mouton-Rothschild	3500–4000
	Palmer	2250	Léoville-Barton	2400
	Batailley	1500	Langoa	1900
	Grand-Puy-Ducasse	1200	Cantemerle	1400–1500
1870	Lafite	4500	Latour	3000
	Margaux (under contract)	4200	Mouton-Rothschild	3000
	Pichon-Longueville	2000	Léoville-Barton	1000
	Palmer	1000	Cantemerle	1000
	Beychevelle	1450		
1874	Lafite	5500	Latour	5000
	Margaux	3200	Mouton-Rothschild	4200
	Pichon-Longueville	2400	Léoville-Barton	2600
	Gruaud-Larose-Sarget	3000	Pontet-Canet	1400
	Gruaud-Larose-Faure	2400	Lynch-Bages	1000–1400
	Mouton d'Armailhacq	1000–1300	Cantemerle	1100
	Batailley	1200		
1875	Lafite	4000	Latour	5000
	Margaux	3500	Mouton-Rothschild	3000
	Rausan-Ségla	2300	Léoville-Barton	2000
	Pichon-Longueville	2500	Brane-Cantenac	2500
	Gruaud-Larose (both)	2500	Palmer	1600–1800
	Beychevelle	950	Lynch-Bages	1200–1300
	Batailley	1050	Lynch-Moussas	600
			Cantemerle	1100
1878	Lafite	4000	Latour	4000
	Margaux	4000	Mouton-Rothschild (November 1878)	2800
	Palmer	1700–2200	Léoville-Barton	2200
			Langoa	1600–1700
1880	Lafite	3600	Latour	3800
	Margaux	3800	Mouton-Rothschild	3600
	Haut-Brion	3200	Léoville-Barton	1800
	Pontet-Canet	1600		
1887	Lafite	3800	Latour	3250
	Margaux	3800	Haut-Brion	3200
	Léoville-Barton	3400	Mouton-Rothschild	2900
1890	Lafite	3000	Latour	4100
	Margaux	4000	Haut-Brion	2500
	Pichon-Longueville	1600	Mouton-Rothschild (1894)	2000
			Léoville-Barton	3100
1893	Lafite	2000	Latour	1750
	Margaux	1750	Mouton-Rothschild	1300
	Cos d'Estournel	1200	Léoville-Barton	1100
	Palmer	1050	Langoa	950

1899	Lafite	2000	Latour	1750
	Margaux	2200	Haut-Brion	2600
	Rausan-Ségla	1400	Mouton-Rothschild	1800
	Cos d'Estournel	1000	Léoville-Barton	1200
	Pichon (Baron)	850	Brane-Cantenac	1400
	Pontet-Canet	850	Cantemerle	900
	Mouton d'Armailhacq	600	Palmer	1200

(Owing to the immediate fame of the vintage many of these prices were paid in November 1899.)

1900	Lafite	1200	Latour	1150
	Margaux	1150	Haut-Brion 1.50 frs. per bottle	
	Rausan-Ségla	650	Mouton-Rothschild	950
	Brane-Cantenac	650	Léoville-Poyferré	600
	Pontet-Canet	600	Léoville-Barton	600
			Cantemerle	625

(These prices, much lower than for the preceding year, reflected both the existence of that vintage and the very large crop in 1900. Most of these prices were paid in the spring of 1901.)

1906	Lafite	2100	Latour	1650
	Margaux	2100	Mouton-Rothschild	
			(under contract to Calvet 1901–1913)	1650
	Rausan-Ségla	1400	Léoville-Barton	1200
	Gruaud-Larose (both)	1225	Brane-Cantenac	1500
	Palmer	1200		

1920	Lafite (under contract)	2650	Latour (under contract)	2650
	Margaux (under contract)	2650	Mouton-Rothschild (1923)	8 frs. per bottle
	Rausan-Ségla	4500	Léoville-Barton	4500
	Gruaud-Larose-Sarget	3000		

(The price of Mouton was equivalent to 7680 per *tonneau*, but as it will have included bottling charges this is not a strictly comparable price, although but for contracts the leading prices might well have been about 7000.)

1924	Lafite	9000–9500	Latour	8000
	Margaux	8000	Mouton-Rothschild	9000
	Rausan-Ségla	5000	Léoville-Poyferré	5000
	Pichon (Baron)	5000	Léoville-Barton	5000
	Cos d'Estournel	5000	Gruaud-Larose-Faure	5000
			Cantemerle	5000

1926	Lafite	40,000	Latour	40,000
	Margaux	40,000	Mouton-Rothschild	40,000
	Pichon (Baron)	15,000	Léoville-Poyferré	12,500
	Gruaud-Larose-Faure	22,000	Léoville-Barton	12,500
	Palmer	23,000	Cos d'Estournel	11,000
	La Lagune	15,000	Mouton-d'Armailhacq	5,600
	Pontet-Canet	18,000		

1928	Lafite	20,000	Latour	20,000
	Margaux	20,000	Mouton-Rothschild	20,000
	Brane-Cantenac	7,500	Léoville-Poyferré	9,000
	Palmer	9,000	Léoville-Barton	8,500
	Talbot	6,500	Léoville-Las-Cases	7,500
	d'Issan	10,000	Giscours	10,000
	Calon-Ségur	7,000	Pontet-Canet	7,000

1929	Lafite	20,000	Latour	20,000
	Margaux	20,000	Mouton-Rothschild	20,000
	Rausan-Ségla	8,000	Léoville-Poyferré	11,000

	Cos d'Estournel	8,500	Léoville-Las-Cases	11,000
	Pontet-Canet	9,000	Cantemerle	9,000
	Grand-Puy-Lacoste	5,400		
1934	Lafite	10,000	Latour	10,000
	Margaux	10,000	Mouton-Rothschild	10,000
	Ducru-Beaucaillou	3,200	Léoville-Barton	3,500

Opening Prices of First Growths and Mouton-Rothschild 1943–1967

The franc has been subject to several devaluations and changes since the last war. In 1957 it was devalued by 20 per cent, and at the end of 1958 by a further 17½ per cent. On 1 January 1960 the New Franc was introduced, by which one New Franc represented 100 old francs. At this point £1 was equal to 13.82 francs, and the $1 to 4,972 francs. In November 1967 sterling was devalued by 14⅔ per cent and the £1 has since been the equivalent of 11.83 francs. In the following table the old franc is used up to and including the 1958 vintage, but the following one was generally sold in terms of new francs.

1943	Lafite	100,000	Latour	100,000
	Margaux	100,000	Haut-Brion	100,000
			Mouton-Rothschild	100,000
1945	Lafite	225,000	Latour	225,000
	Margaux	225,000	Haut-Brion	225,000
			Mouton-Rothschild	225,000
1947	Lafite	200,000	Latour	130,000
	Margaux	130,000	Haut-Brion	200,000
			Mouton-Rothschild	200,000
1949	Lafite	360,000	Latour	285,000
	Margaux	250,000	Haut-Brion	250,000
			Mouton-Rothschild	350,000
1952	Lafite	350,000	Latour	350,000
	Margaux	300,000	Mouton-Rothschild	375,000
1953	Lafite	300,000	Latour	300,000
	Margaux	300,000	Haut-Brion	300,000
			Mouton-Rothschild	350,000
1954	Lafite	300,000	Latour	300,000
	Margaux	300,000	Haut-Brion	300,000
			Mouton-Rothschild	300,000
1955	Lafite	500,000	Latour	300,000–400,000
	Margaux	300,000–400,000	Haut-Brion	500,000
			Mouton-Rothschild	550,000
1956	Lafite	400,000–500,000	Latour	400,000–450,000
	Margaux	380,000–450,000	Haut-Brion	450,000
			Mouton-Rothschild	450,000
1957	Lafite	750,000	Latour	700,000
	Margaux	700,000	Haut-Brion	700,000
			Mouton-Rothschild	780,000
1958	Lafite	650,000	Latour	600,000
	Margaux	500,000–600,000	Haut-Brion	600,000
			Mouton-Rothschild	525,000
1959	Lafite	11,000	Latour	7,250
	Margaux	7,250	Haut-Brion	7,250
			Mouton-Rothschild	9,500
1960	Lafite	14,000	Latour	10,000
	Margaux	8,500–11,810	Haut-Brion	12,000
			Mouton-Rothschild	11,000
1961	Lafite	27,000	Latour	20,000

	Margaux	17,000	Haut-Brion	21,000
			Mouton-Rothschild	22,760
1962	Lafite	16,500	Latour	12,000–15,000
	Margaux	10,000–14,800	Haut-Brion (1964)	20 frs. per bottle
			Mouton-Rothschild	15,000

(For four years Haut-Brion took to selling by the bottle some time after the vintage. Allowing 960 bottles to the *tonneau* this would give the price of the 1962 as 19,800 frs., including bottle charges. Although first growths and Mouton-Rothschild are sold without keeping charges, the price of Haut-Brion in bottle in July 1964 would take into account interest charges, and the wine would not in fact be as expensive as the leaders.)

1963	Lafite	9,750	Latour	8,500
	Margaux	7,000	Haut-Brion	11 frs. per bottle
			Mouton-Rothschild	10,000
1964	Lafite	23,000	Latour	18,000
	Margaux	15,000	Haut-Brion	18 frs. per bottle
			Mouton-Rothschild	20,000
1965	Lafite	13,000	Latour	12,000
	Margaux—not sold with vintage date		Haut-Brion	11 frs. per bottle
			Mouton-Rothschild	13,000
1966	Lafite	27,000	Latour	24,000
	Margaux	19,000	Haut-Brion	20,000
			Mouton-Rothschild	27,000
1967	Lafite	27,000	Latour	19,000
	Margaux	15,300	Haut-Brion	17,000
			Mouton-Rothschild	27,000

Appendix B:

Rainfall in the Gironde 1952–1967

The crucial annual factors affecting the success of a vintage are the rainfall and the amount of sunshine and temperature levels. Of these the rainfall is the most important, and so the annual totals and monthly averages are given below. The sunniest month on average is July with 247 hours, compared with 230 hours for June and 227 hours for August. But August is the warmest month with a maximum average of 79°F. (26·3°C.). December is the least sunny month with an average of 64 hours, but January is the coldest with a maximum average of 48·5°F. (9·3°C.) and a minimum of 35°F. (1·8°C.). For all the statistics I am indebted to M. Pierre Leglise of the Station Climatologique, Pont de la Maye, Gironde.

Annual Rainfall in Millimetres				*Average Monthly Rainfall in Millimetres*			
1952	1145·4	1960	1194·7	January	95	July	57·9
1953	577	1961	716·6	February	73·6	August	62·2
1954	807·3	1962	695·3	March	63·5	September	80·4
1955	905·7	1963	812·5	April	55·2	October	99·6
1956	740·4	1964	836·1	May	63·9	November	101·9
1957	746·1	1965	1131·9	June	63·4	December	120·8
1958	1047·6	1966	1116·8				
1959	885	1967	711·3				

One cannot equate fine vintages with dry years, although some of the best have had small rainfall. Among earlier years, for example, there were only 612·7 mm. of rain in 1929, and 650·4 mm. in 1945, but in 1928 there was 876·2 mm. Moreover although the heaviest rainfall since 1924 was in 1960 when the total was 1,194·7 mm, backed by 1,149·7 mm. in the disastrous year of 1930, these records were closely followed by the above-average 1952 when 1,145·4 mm. fell.

In fact more important than the total annual rainfall is that in the two months before and during the better vintages: August and September, as shown below from 1952–1967.

Rainfall in August and September 1952–1967 in Millimetres

1952	151·5	1956	193·4	1960	259·2	1964	103·4
1953	86	1957	105·9	1961	36·1	1965	255·7
1954	168·7	1958	178·1	1962	56·1	1966	75
1955	70·8	1959	132·2	1963	167·4	1967	100

In these 16 years the wettest August was 1958 (126·3 mm.), although this was exceeded in 1968, outside these records, with 161·2 mm. The wettest September was 1965 (212·8 mm.) which goes far to explain the failure of the vintage. Also to be noted is that on average October has been the third wettest month in the 16 years listed, although over a longer period January can claim that place. Nevertheless in most years the vintage continues well into that hazardous month, particularly in Sauternes. The celebrated variation in the 1964 wines, depending on whether the growers finished picking before or after the rain which began on 7 October is demonstrated in rainfall figures. In that year 231·5 mm. fell in the month, only being exceeded in the period by half a millimetre in 1960 when 232 mm. were recorded; well over twice the average. The driest summer of the period was certainly 1961 when only 69·7 mm. fell between June and August. It was also the finest vintage. Since the prevailing wind in the Gironde is off the sea from the west and north-west the highest incidence of rainfall is near the coast and in the Médoc, with a mean annual average of about 950 mm. In the east, in the Garonne Valley, it sinks to about 750 mm.

Annual Rainfall Totals and Abstract from Mid-September to the End of February, 1924–1965

	Total mm	Totals from 15/9 to the end of February mm		Total mm	Totals from 15/9 to the end of February mm
1924	709·0	341·5	1945	650·4	285·2
1925	753·5	495·6	1946	692·5	540·9
1926	942·1	486·5	1947	843·4	483·1
1927	1,027·1	405·6	1948	590·6	187·7
1928	876·2	399·2	1949	700·9	463·4
1929	612·7	501·8	1950	847·7	665·4
1930	1,149·7	691·8	1951	1,089·3	513·1
1931	972·9	248·7	1952	1,145·4	689·3
1932	1,002·8	406·1	1953	577·0	352·4
1933	850·3	438·1	1954	807·3	504·7
1934	898·3	556·4	1955	905·7	380·0
1935	925·3	678·0	1956	740·4	332·6
1936	805·5	349·9	1957	746·1	358·9
1937	1,042·7	532·0	1958	1,047·6	341·1
1938	626·9	439·8	1959	885·0	657·1
1939	810·0	380·1	1960	1,194·7	830·2
1940	808·6	598·4	1961	716·6	496·4
1941	973·0	366·6	1962	695·3	383·8
1942	678·4	380·0? (war year)	1963	812·5	285·7
1943	752·9	348·9	1964	836·1	531·1
1944	738·0	538·2	1965	1,131·9	800·0

Appendix C:

Wine Organizations

Bordeaux is full of organizations associated with wine and the wine trade. There are professional organizations of growers, brokers and merchants; and a *Union des Crus Classés*. The Bordeaux Chamber of Commerce is naturally deeply concerned with the wine trade. However such bodies are not of great interest to the general reader, while the publicity bodies associated with each district are referred to in their proper place.

However the *Conseil Interprofessionel du Vin de Bordeaux* (*C.I.V.B.*) is worthy of brief mention, and its headquarters are in the Maison du Vin, 1 Cours du XXX Juillet, on the corner of the Allées de Tourny facing the Théâtre. It began, like similar bodies in other French wine-growing districts, in the last war, in 1943. It was somewhat differently named and organized then, and its present form dates from 1948, with a further re-organization in November 1966. The role of this officially organized body is to regulate the trade and to see that the regulations made by the *Institut National des Appellations d'Origine des Vins et Eaux-de-Vie* (*I.N.A.O.*) appertaining to Bordeaux are carried out. The *C.I.V.B.* is also responsible for economic and statistical surveys, for seeing that there is permanent contact between growers and merchants; and finally to promote the reputation of and demand for the *AC* wines of Bordeaux.

The composition of the *C.I.V.B.* is made up of 24 growers, 18 merchants, 2 brokers, 4 members nominated by the Ministry of Agriculture on the proposition of the Prefect of the Gironde department, including a consumers' representative, and 6 important local civil servants, among them the director of the Bordeaux Oenological Station. Also the regional delegates of the *I.N.A.O.* take part in the conseil's deliberations in an advisory capacity. The president of the *C.I.V.B.* now is M. Henri Martin, owner of Gloria, associated with the general direction of Latour, and prominent in both national and regional wine affairs. The Vice-President is M. Roger Dourthe, of the merchant firm. The director of the *C.I.V.B.* is M. J. M. Courteau.

What might be called a centralized propaganda organization is the *Académie du Vin de Bordeaux* presided over by Pierre Ginestet of Château Margaux and many other concerns. Like the great *Académie Francaise* of Paris it has 40 members, some of them local, others nationally known. Periodical dinners and other suitable celebrations are arranged.

Finally to be mentioned is the notable *Station Oenologique*, situated in the new university of Bordeaux buildings in Talence. It is associated with agronomy in the university, and the first director of the *Station Agronomique* was Professor A. Baudrimont (1806–1880). He was succeeded by the celebrated Professor Ulysse Gayon (1845–1929), assistant and friend of Pasteur, who advised him in 1880 to take the vacant post in Bordeaux. He arrived at an unpropitious time as the phylloxera was starting and the mildew, with which he was greatly concerned, only a few years away. Although offered other important posts, including the directorship in 1904 of the Pasteur Institute in Paris, he preferred to remain at Bordeaux until 1920. Today the director of the station is his son-in-law Professor Jean Ribereau-Gayon, and his other leading colleague is M. Peynaud. The work of the station consists of research and analysis. All wine exported is tested by chemical analysis to ensure that it is sound, and that there is adequate alcohol and acidity.

Appendix D:

Table of Minimum Strengths and Maximum Crop in Hectolitres Permitted under the Bordeaux *Appellations Contrôlées*

Appellations	*Degrees*		*Permitted Maximum crop per hectare in hectolitres*
Barsac	Blanc	13°	25
Blayais	Blanc ⎫ Rouge ⎬	10°	45 50
Bordeaux	Rouge	10°	50
	Blanc	10·5°	50
Bordeaux clairet ou rosé		11°	50
Bordeaux-Côtes-de-Castillon	Rouge	11°	40
Bordeaux-Haut-Benauge	Blanc	11·5°	50
Bordeaux-Mousseaux	Blanc	10°	50
Bordeaux-Supérieur	Blanc	11·5°	40
	Rouge	10·5°	40
Bordeaux Supérieur Côtes de Francs	Blanc	11·5°	40
	Rouge	10·5°	40

Appellations		*Degrees*	*Permitted Maximum crop per hectare in hectolitres*
Bourg, Bourgeais,	Blanc	11°	50
Côtes-de-Bourg	Rouge	10·5°	50
Cérons	Blanc	12·5°	40
Côtes-de-Blaye	Blanc	11°	42
Côtes-de-Bx-St-Macaire	Blanc	11·5°	42
Côtes-Canon-Fronsac	Rouge	11°	42
Côtes-de-Fronsac	Rouge	11°	42
Entre-Deux-Mers Haut-Benauge	Blanc	11·5°	50
Entre-Deux-Mers	Blanc	11·5°	50
Graves	Blanc	11°	40
	Rouge	10°	40
Graves-Supérieures	Blanc	12°	40
Graves de Vayres	Blanc }	10·5°	43
	Rouge }		40
Haut-Médoc	Rouge	10°	43
Lalande-de-Pomerol	Rouge	10·5°	40
Listrac	Rouge	10·5°	40
Loupiac	Blanc	13°	40
Lussac-St-Emilion	Rouge	11°	42
Margaux	Rouge	10·5°	40
Médoc	Rouge	10°	45
Montagne-St-Emilion	Rouge	11°	42
Moulis	Rouge	10·5°	40
Néac (merged with Lalande)	Rouge	10·5°	40
Pauillac	Rouge	10·5°	40
Parsac-St-Emilion	Rouge	11°	42
Pomerol	Rouge	10·5°	40
1e Côtes de Blaye	Rouge	10·5°	50
	Blanc	11°	42
1e Côtes de Bordeaux	Rouge	10·5°	40
	Blanc	12°	40
1e Côtes de Bordeaux followed by a commune name	Rouge	11·5°	40
	Blanc	13°	40
1e Côtes de Bordeaux-Cadillac	Blanc	12°	40
1e Côtes de Bordeaux-Gabarnac	Blanc	12°	40
Puisseguin-St-Emilion	Rouge	11°	42
Sables-St-Emilion	Rouge	10·5°	42
St-Emilion	Rouge	11°	42
St-Emilion grand cru	Rouge	11·5°	42
St-Emilion grand cru classé	Rouge	11·5°	42
St-Emilion 1e grand cru classé	Rouge	11·5°	42
St-Estèphe	Rouge	10·5°	40
St-Georges-St-Emilion	Rouge	11°	42
Ste-Croix-du-Mont	Blanc	13°	40
Ste-Foy-Bordeaux	Blanc	12°	45
	Rouge	10·5°	45
St-Julien	Rouge	10·5°	40
Sauternes	Blanc	13°	25

Bibliography

This is a list of the books and articles consulted in the course of writing this book, rather than an extensive bibliography on a vast subject. I hope it may prove helpful to others.

Allen, H. Warner. *The Wines of France* 1924. *Natural Red Wines*, 1951. *A History of Wine*, 1961.

Barennes, J. *Viticulture et Vinification en Bordelais au Moyen Age*, 1912.

Bertall. *La Vigne—Voyages Autour des Vins de France*, 1878.

Boutruche, R. *La Crise d'une Société: Seigneurs et Paysans du Bordelais pendant la Guerre des Cent Ans*, 1947.

Bowley, A. L. *Wages and Incomes in the United Kingdom*, 1935.

Campbell, Ian M. *The Wayward Tendrils of the Vine*, 1947.

Carus-Wilson, E. M. *The Effects of the Acquisition and of the Loss of Gascony on the English Wine Trade*. Bulletin of the Institute of Historical Research, 1947.

Cassagnac, Paul de. *French Wines*. Tr. Guy Knowles, 1930.

Cocks, Charles & Féret, Edouard. *Bordeaux et Ses Vins*, various editions, 1868–1949.

Danflou, Alfred. *Les Grands Crus Bordelais*, 1867.

D'Armailhacq, A. *De la Culture des Vignes dans le Médoc*, 1850, and subsequent editions to 1867.

Dion, Roger. *Histoire de la Vigne et du Vin en France dès Origines au XIXième Siècle*, 1959.

Dunham, A. L. *The Anglo-French Treaty of Commerce of 1860 and the Progress of the Industrial Revolution in France*, 1930.

Féret, E. *St-Emilion et Ses Vins*, 1893.

Forster, Robert. *The Noble Wine Producers of the Bordelais in the Eighteenth Century*. Economic History Review, 1961.

Franck, Wilhelm. *Traité sur les Vins du Médoc et les Autres Vins Rouges et Blancs du Département de la Gironde*, 1824 and subsequent editions to 1868.

Guillon, E. *Les Châteaux Historiques et Vignobles de la Gironde*, 1866.

Healy, Maurice. *Claret and the White Wines of Bordeaux*, 1934. *Stay Me With Flagons*, 1940.

Henderson, A. L. *The History of Ancient and Modern Wines*, 1824.

Higounet, Charles. Ed. *Histoire de Bordeaux*. Seven volumes (Vols. 1–5 only issued), 1962–68.
    1. *Bordeaux Antique*, par R. Etienne, etc., 1962.
    2. *Bordeaux Pendant le Haut Moyen Age*, par Ch. Higounet, etc., 1964.
    3. *Bordeaux sous les Rois d'Angleterre*, sous la direction de Y. Renouard, 1965.
    4. *Bordeaux 1453 à 1715*, sous la direction de R. Boutruche, 1966.
    5. *Bordeaux au XVIIIe Siècle*, sous la direction de François-Georges Pariset, 1968.

Hyams, Edward. *Dionysus: a Social History of the Vine*, 1965.

Jacob, E. F. *The Fifteenth Century (Oxford History of England*, Vol. 6), 1961.

James, Marjory K. *The Fluctuations of the Anglo-Gascon Wine Trade during the Fourteenth Century*. Economic History Review, 1951.

Jefferson, Thomas. *The Papers of Thomas Jefferson*. Edited J. L. Boyd. Vols. 9–15, 1956–58.

Jullian, Camille. *Histoire de Bordeaux depuis les Origines jusqu'en 1895*, 1895.

Jullien, A. *Manuel du Sommelier*, 1826.

Kirby, J. L. *The Siege of Bourg*, 1406. History Today, 1968.

Kressman, Jean. *Le Défi d'Edouard*, 1959.

Lafforgue, Germain. *Le Vignoble Girondin*, 1947.

Lichine, Alexis. *The Wines of France*. Revised edition, 1969.
    Encyclopaedia of Wines and Spirits, 1967.

Lodge, Eleanor C. *The Estates of the Archbishop and Chapters of St André of Bordeaux under English Rule*. Oxford Studies in Social and Legal History, Vol. 3, 1912.
    Gascony under English Rule, 1926.

Lorbac, Charles. *Les Richesses Gastronomiques de la France: Les Vins de Bordeaux*, 1867.

Malvezin, Frantz. *Histoire de la Vigne et du Vin en Aquitaine*, 1919.

Malvezin, T. *Histoire du Commerce de Bordeaux*, 1892.

Malvezin, T. and Féret, E. *Le Médoc et Ses Vins*, 1876.

Michel, Francisque. *Histoire du Commerce et de la Navigation à Bordeaux*, 1867.

Perraux, F. *Prise de Vues sur la Croissance d'Economie Française 1780–1950*, 1950.

Perroud, Régine. *Eleanor of Aquitaine*. Tr. P. Wiles, 1967.

Pijassou, P. *Un Château du Médoc: Palmer*, 1964.

Plumb, J. H. *Men and Places*, 1963.

Powicke, Sir F. M. *King Henry III and the Lord Edward*, 1947.

Ray, Cyril. *Lafite: The Story of Château Lafite-Rothschild*, 1968.

Redding, Cyrus. *A History and Description of Modern Wines*, 1833.

Renouard, Yves. *Bordeaux sous les Rois d'Angleterre*. Economic History Review, 1951.

Ribadieu, Henri. *L'Histoire des Châteaux de la Gironde*, 1856.

   Histoire de la Conquête de la Guyenne par les Français, 1866.

Riol, J. L. *Le Vignoble de Gaillac*, 1913.

Roger, J.-R. *Les Vins de Bordeaux*, 1955 (translated into English 1960)

Saintsbury, George. *Notes on a Cellar-Book*, 1920.

Salavert, Jan. *La Commerce des Vins de Bordeaux*, 1912.

Sée, Henri. *Histoire Economique de la France: Les Temps Modernes 1789–1914*, 1942.

Shand, P. Morton. *A Book of French Wines*, 1928. (Revised edition, edited Cyril Ray, 1960. Paperback edition, 1964).

Shaw, Thomas George. *Wine, the Vine and the Cellar*, 1863.

Sichel, Allan. *The Penguin Book of Wines*, 1965.

Simon, André L. *History of the Wine Trade in England*, 1906–09.

   Bottlescrew Days, 1926.

   Vintagewise, 1945.

Viallate, A. *L'Activité Economique en France de la fin du XVIIIe Siècle à Nos Jours*, 1937.

Younger, William. *Gods, Men and Wine*, 1966.

General Index

L'Activité Economique en France de la Fin du XVIIIe Siècle à Nos Jours, 79
d'Adhémar, Count, 65, 148
Agen, 35; wines from, 48
d'Alesmes family, 60
Algeria, 23, 143, 161; wine from, 80
altise (vine pest), 19
America, United States of,
  economic difficulties with, 81, 82;
  estates owned by Americans, *see* Bouscaut, Haut-Brion, Le Prieuré;
  trade with, 32, 74, 76, 79–83, 87, 88, 94, 101, 102, 261;
  vine-stocks from, 17, 19, 21, 184;
  see also Jefferson, T.
America, South, trade with, 78, 100
Analyse Chimique des Grands Vins de la Gironde, 117
Anglo-French Treaty of Commerce (1860), *see* trade
Angoulême, Isabella of, 39
Anjou (district), wines of, 47
anthracnose (vine disease), 19
appellation contrôlée, 15, 20, 24, 32, 61, 81, 164, 281;
  legislation on, 85, 86, 106, 289;
  appellation d'origine, 81, 84, 86;
  appellation simple, 86;
  see also Institut National des Appellations d'Origine (I.N.A.O.) *and* Appendix
Aquitaine, Eleanor of, 29, 36, 38, 51;
  Prince of, 43;
  Principality of, 42, 64
Arcins (commune), *167 and* 148, 249
armagnac, 38, 169
d'Armailhacq, A., 119, 129, 254
Arsac (commune), *160, 161 and* 69, 147, 155, 249
L'Art de faire, de gouverner et de perfectionner le Vin, 23, 24
assemblage, *see égalisage*
d'Aulède, Marquis, 62
Aussel, Dr., 255
Avensan (commune), *167 and* 33, 46
Averys of Bristol, 143, 157, 195, 207, 271, 276, 279, 294
Avery, Ronald, 86, 105, 113, 194, 269, 298

Bacalan, Quai de, 32, 100
Baltic countries, exports to, 55, 73, 99
Ban de Vendange, 29, 166, 295
Barbanne (river), 212
barrique bordelaise, 25, 30, 33, 65
Barsac (commune), *237–240 and* 33, 56, 226
Barton family, 68, 90–92, 137, 142, 249
Barton, Ronald, 14, 92, 105, 119, 120, 138–142, 152, 181, 198, 274, 282, 291, 298
Barton & Guestier (firm), 68, 89–92, 95, 97, 124, 126, 137, 196, 266
Bas-Médoc, *see* Médoc
Bass-Charrington (firm), 102
Bastiat, Frédéric, 76
bastide towns, 41
Bayonne, 39, 42, 43
Bazas (commune), 40, 85, 246
de la Beaumelle family, 96
Beaumont family, 66, 116
Bec d'Ambès, II, 34, 220, 242
Bégadan (commune), 97, 170
Benedictine Order, vineyards owned by, 63, 66, 183
Bergerac, 34; wines from, 48, 55, 73, 74
La Bergerie (firm), 101, 129
Berland, Pey, Archbishop of Bordeaux, 43–45, 52
Berry Bros. & Rudd (firm), 215, 267, 287
Beychac, 32
Beyerman family and firm, 55, 68, 89, 90, 95, 164, 175, 252, 253
Beylot (firm), 95, 201
La Bidure grape, 13

Binaud, Henri, 89, 95, 119, 162, 164, 276, 278, 290
Black Death, the, 50
Black Prince, the, 42, 43, 200
Blanquefort (commune), 33, 46, 54, 165, 249, 251;
  Sch. of Agriculture at, 165;
  Jalle de Blanquefort, 33, 106, 109, 172
Blaye, *221, 222 and* 12, 16, 27, 29, 32–35;
  its ferry, 171;
  fighting over, 40–43, 45, 49, 119;
  price of wines (1647), 56
blending of wines, 31, 34, 35, 57, 82, 92, 224;
  by Dutch merchants, 55;
  with Algerian wine, 80;
  edict against, 90, 91;
  non-vintage blend, 133, 143, 150;
  'travail de l'Anglaise', 93
  see also égalisage
Blondin, Pierre and Raoul, 123, 273
de la Boétie, Etienne, 36
Bommes (commune), 56, 226, 233
Bontemps du Médoc et des Graves, 29, 110
A Book of French Wines, 63
Bordeaux, Archbishops of, as vineyard owners, 32, 46, 59, 243
Bordeaux Chamber of Commerce, 17, 77, 249, 254, 270
Bordeaux, Compagnons de, 243
Bordeaux, countryside surrounding, 11, 12, 167;
  vineyards ousting other crops, 48, 61;
  draining of marshes, 56, 60;
  great extension of vineyards, 60, 61;
  contraction, 88
Bordeaux de 1453 à 1715, 52
Bordeaux au XVIIIe Siècle, 61, 66, 74, 248
Bordeaux, early history of, 28–36; connections with England, 37–51;
'Bordeaux mixture' (*bouillie bordelaise*), 18, 161
Bordeaux University, 18, 43
Bordeaux et ses Vins, 145 (*see* Cocks et Féret)
Borie family, 126, 131, 141;
Borie-Manoux (firm), 126
bottles, for wine, 26, 27, 31, 48, 63;
  early use of, 64, 265;
  manufacture of, 95;
  glass-stoppered, 118;
  extra-large, 122, 123
bottling of wine, time of, 121; chateau-bottling, 114, 126
Bottlescrew Days, 60, 248
Bouchet grape, 13, 14, 187
Bourg, *218–220 and* 12, 27, 32–35;
  fighting over, 41–43, 45; re-fortified, 63;
  wines from, 56, 256
Bouteiller, M., 124, 127
Boutruche, Robert, 52
Brane (Branne), Baron Hector de, 119
Branne, 242
Bretigny, Treaty of (1360), 42
Bristol, 31, 46, 47, 51;
  emigration of Bordelais to, 52;
  Earl of, 60, 63, 64
brokers, wine, *courtiers*, 102, 103, 248, 253;
  Syndicate of, 254
Bureau, Jean, 44, 227
Burgundy (area), 24, 30, 38, 59;
  Dukes of, 38;
  wine from, 46, 50, compared with claret, 104, 105, 204, 294, 302;
  vintages, 277, 278

Cabernet-Franc grape, 13, 14
Cabernet-Sauvignon grape, 13–17;
  introduced to the Médoc, 119
Cadaujac (commune), *185 and* 32, 249
Cadillac, 32, 44, 45, 240
Cahors, 35; wines from, 48, 95
calendar, Gregorian, 59; Julian, 30
Calvet (firm), 99, 100, 163, 235, 257, 258

Campbell, Ian, 268, 271, 275, 278, 282, 284
Cambes (commune), 243
Camblanes (commune), 243
Canada, wine sales to, 95
Cantenac (commune), *156–163 and* 33, 61, 63, 147, 155
Capus, Jean, 86; 'le Loi Capus', 86
Carbon-Blanc, 29, 32, 242
Carruades plateau, 18, 115, 125
Carmenère grape, 14
casks, for wine, 25, 30; Haut-Pays type, 34;
  of Baltic oak, 66;
  price of, 121; extra large, 134;
  wine drunk from the cask, 31, 64
Cassagnac, Paul de, 265
Castéja, Jean, 124, 128, 237
Castelnau, 33, 85
Castille, Eleanor of, 40
Castillon, 35, 44, 45, 49, 242;
  Battle of, *202 and* 44, 64, 116, 144
Castillon-de-Médoc, 36, 41
Cauderan (commune), 251
Cayrou, M., 69
Cenon, 29, 32; liqueurs made at, 35
Cérons (commune), *173 and* 11, 32, 33, 223, 240, 261
Chaplin, W. H. (firm), 153
Chaptal, Jean André, Comte de Chanteloup 23, 24, 93
chaptalisation, 23, 24, 244, 301;
  economic effects of, 84;
  legislation on, 296
Charente, 15, 35, 38; rise of spirit trade, 73
Chartrons, Quai des, 11, 32, 34, 44, 54, 55;
  merchants in, 71, 78, 89–99;
  Pavé des Ch., 11, 89, 99
châteaux, see index on 318
de Chavanas, M., 64, 116
cheese (English) and claret, 51
Chiapella, J., 132, 179
Christie's (Christie, Manson & Wood), 60, 65, 79, 148, 176, 265, 266; wine catalogues, 112–116, 119, 123, 228, 229
Christophers' (firm), 79, 132, 210
Church, the, as vineyard proprietor, 59, 62, 63, 66, 181
Cissac (commune), 166, 168
clairet, 30
claret, early use of word, 54; in 18th century, 65; in 19th century, 93;
  compared with Burgundy, 104, 105, 204, 294, 302
classification of wines, *247–263 and* (Médoc), 108, 109, 121;
  (St. Emilion), 190–192, 261; (Pomerol), 206; (Sauternes), 228, 237;
  (red Graves), 261; crus bourgois, 259, 262
  re-classification, proposals for, 261, 262
Clausel family, 64, 116, 162
Clément V, Pope, 32
Clossman (firm), 99
Cobden, Richard, 72, 76, 80
cochylis (vine pest), 19
Cocks et Féret, 15, 18, 145, 190–193, 204, 212, 256, 259
Cognac (area), 35, 134; cognac, 35, 72, 288
Coloms, the, 40
Colbert, Jean-Baptiste, 55, 57, 64
Colombar grape, 15
'Comet Year' (1811), 75, 112, 113, 265
Le Commerce des Vins de Bordeaux, 82
Commonwealth, 56
Conynck, M., 95
co-operatives, growers', 84, 287; in the Médoc, 107, 131, 135, 166–170; in St. Emilion, 197, 201; in Bourg and Blaye, 221; in the Entre-deux-Mers, 243
coopers, *tonneliers*, 30
Cordial Médoc, 35
Cordier, Jean, 134, 141, 142, 144, 155
  Cordier (firm), 101, 233
Cordouan, Rapids of, 91

315

corks, early use of, 63, 64; importance of, 271
Cottin, Philippe, 101, 129, 273
coulure (vine disease), 14, 19, 21
Coutras (commune), 216
Cowdray family, 66, 116
Crébat, 36
Cripps, Sir Stafford, 77
Crouzet, F., 74
Cruse family, 69, 94–97, 134, 151, 158, 161, 165, 170, 204, 221;
Christian, 97, 125, 127, 167, 231, 266–272, 280
Cruse et Fils Frères, 97, 124–126, 130, 210, 227, 287
Cubzadais (area), 218
De la Culture des Vignes dans le Médoc, 129, 254
Cunliffe, Dobson (firm), 95
Cussac (commune), *167, 168 and* 148

Danflou, Alfred, 255, 256
Danglade family and firm, 102, 188, 215, 216
Dax, 39, 43
Delor family and firm, 99, 152
Delsoters, the, 40
Dillon, Clarence, 176
diseases of the vine, *see* altise, anthracnose, cochylis, *coulure*, mildew, *millerandage*, oidium, peranospora, phylloxera, *pourriture grise*, red spider;
remedies against, 17–19, 29
'distillateurs liquoristes', 35
distillation of wine, 35, 249; legislation on, 35
see also eau-de-vie, marc
Domitian, Emperor, 28, 61
Dordogne, the (river), 11, 12, 16, 29, 32–38, 41, 49, 242
Dourthe (firm) 94, 130, 162, 166, 233
Dubos family and firm, 95, 160, 162, 163
Dupin, Raymond, 119, 127, 290
Dutch Republic and Bordeaux wine, 55, 57; merchants, 71, 89, 95
see also Netherlands
duty on Fr. wines entering England, 57, 71, 73, 76;
ad valorem, 76;
'bottle surcharge', 77
entering Ireland and Scotland, 74

eau-de-vie, 35, 72, 73, 249
égalisage or *assemblage*, 26, 27, 209, 229
égrappage, 22, 27, 66, 93
Encyclopaedia of Wines and Spirits, 204
England, connections with Bordeaux, *37–51* and 28, 29, 32–34; trade with, 36, 39, 44–50, 56–58, 130, 253;
viticulture in, 40;
Engl.-owned estates, *see* Angludet, Courant, Latour, Langoa, Léoville-Barton, Lynestre, Rausan-Ségla
Engl. taste in wine, 54
England, Kings of: Henry II, 29, 36–38; Richard I, 'Coeur-de-Lion', 38, 39; John, 37, 39, 46–48; Henry III, 31, 39, 40, 47; Edward I, 39–41, 50, 51; Edward II, 42, 49; Edward III, 33, 36, 42; Richard II, 'of Bordeaux', 43; Henry IV, 43, 48; Henry V, 43; Henry VI, 43; Henry VII, 43; Elizabeth I, 54; Charles I, 54, 56, Charles II, 57, 71; William III, 57, 71; Victoria, 76, 120
as purchasers of wine, 47, 49, 50;
influence of royal taste, 47
Enrageat grape, 246
Entre-deux-Mers (district), *242–246 and* 11, 12, 16, 29, 32, 215, 220, 240;
price of wines from, 56; export of, 73, 91
Eschenauer, family and firm, 90, 98, 181, 183, 184, 257, 258
Evelyn, John, 60
Exhibitions, International: (Paris, 1855), 76, 193, 254; (Paris, 1867), 193; (London, 1862), 77, 99, 193, 256 *and see also* Int. Exh. Co-operative Wine Society

Fargues (commune), 226, 235
Faringdon, Sir William, 41
Faure, M., 117
fermentation, process of, 23–26, 30, 229; in 18th century, 66, 67; *'fermentation froide'*, 23, 179; malolactic, 25, 178; ferm. vats, steel, 117, 118, 178; use of ice, 272, 273
Filhot, M. de, 63
fining, *collage*, 26, 30, 233
'first growths', *see* classification of wines
Flanders, trade with, 36
flowering (of the vine), *floraison*, 21
The Fluctuations of the Anglo-Gascon Wine Trade during the Fourteenth Century (Economic History Review), 49
Folle-Blanche grape, 15
Forster, Robert, 60
Fould family, 68, 145, 148
fouloir-égrappoir, 22, 25
France, Kings of: Louis VII, 38; Louis VIII 40; Louis IX, 40; Philip the Fair, 41, 42; John, 42; Charles VII, 43, 44; Charles VIII, 53; Louis XIV, 45, 192; Louis XV, 109, 175; Louis XVI, 175; Napoleon, 46, 47, 67, 75; Louis XVIII, 67; Louis-Philippe, 68, 75, 97; Napoleon III, 120
Franck, Wilhelm, 76, 118, 137, 164, 176, 192, 204, 218, 247, 251–254, 259
French colonies, trade with, 71, 73, 74
French Wines, 265
Fronsac, *214, 215 and* 12, 15, 17, 33, 41, 213; fighting over, 43, 44;
Côtes de, 12, 214
frost damage to vines, 21, 59, 61, 187, 188, 198, 230, 299
Fumel family, 175; Joseph, Marquis de, 62, 66, 148, 249, 250

Gabarnac (commune), 243
Gaillac, 28, 34; wines from, 40, 48
Garonne, the (river), 11, 13, 16, 28–32, 43, 49, 242
Gascony, *passim*, and see especially 28–51;
also:
extent of region, 38;
Merchant Wine Tonners of, 42
Gascony under English Rule, 41
de Gascq, Président, 61, 63
Gasqueton family, 96, 133, 161, 185
Gaunt, John of, 43
Gayon, Ulysse, 96, 272
Germany, trade with, 73, 83, 85, 94, 98, 157, 166, 243;
German colony in B., 73; G. occupation, 87, 216, 287;
G. wines, 36, 47, 50, 54, 243
Gers, the, 38
Gilbey family and firm, 17, 18, 188, 273–277; buy Loudenne, 69, 169
Ginestet family and firm, 99–101, 132–135, 149–154, 197, 200, 211, 240, 258
Gironde (Department), *passim* and see especially: extent of *vignoble* in 18th and 19th centuries, 61, 75, 78; in 20th century, 81, 83–85, 88, 243
Gironde, the (river), 11, 29, 34, 116, 171 islands in, 170; ships of war on, 43, 44; Engl. wine fleet in, 48, 49, 53, 54
La Gironde A Vol d'Oiseau; ses Grand Vins et ses Châteaux, 255
Girondins, the, 11, 75
Gladstone, W. E., 57, 72, 77; 'Gladstone's claret', 77, 78
Gods, Men and Wine, 59
Gradignan (commune), 32, 249, 251
de Grailly, Jean, Seneschal of Gascony (1268), 41
Les Grands Crus Bordelais, 255
grape varieties, *13–15*; their influence on flavour, 13; proportions planted (Médoc), 107; (Graves), 173, 185; (St-Emilion), 187; (Pomerol), 206; (Bourg and Blaye), 220; (Sauternes), 223; *and see also* individual estates *passim; see also* names of varieties: La Bidure, Bouchet, Cabernet-Franc, Cabernet-Sauvignon;

Carmenère, Colombar, Enrageat, Folle Blanche, Malbec, Merlot, Muscadelle, Pressac, Riesling, Sauvignon, Sémillon, Ugniblanc, Verdot, *vitis riparia, vitis rupestris, vitis vinifera*
Graves (district), *172–186 and* 11–13, 16, 18, 21, 32, 33;
early history of, wines from, 54–56; classification (1953), 261
Graves-St-Emilion, *197 and* 192, 193
Graves de Vayres, 12, 186, 242, 243
du Guesclin, Bertrand, 43
Guestier family, 91, 92, 145, 157; *see also* Barton & Guestier
Guîtres (commune), 216
Guyenne, 21, 38, 63; relations with England 45; *Parlement de*, 111, *Conétablie de*, 222

Hadfield, John, 269
hail damage to vines, 230
Hanseatic cities, trade with, 53, 55, 73, 166
Harveys of Bristol, 99, 116, 118, 207, 210
Haut-Benauge, 242, 243
Haut-Médoc, *see* Médoc
Haut-Pays, rivalry with B., 34, 48, 49; wines from, 28, 31, 35, 45, 57, 74; tax or restrictions on, 53; distillation of, 72
Healy, Maurice, 60, 104, 105, 221, 278, 279
Henderson, A. L., 253
Henry VI (Shakespeare), 44
Hermitage (wine), 92, 93; 'hermitaging' (blending), 92, 93, 100, 267, 271
Hervey, John Earl of Bristol, 60, 63, 64
Histoire du Commerce de Bordeaux, 56, 175
Histoire du Commerce et de la Navigation à Bordeaux, 119
Histoire Militaire de Bordeaux, 115
Histoire du Vigne et du Vin en Aquitaine, 64, 73
Histoire de la Vigne et du Vin en France dès origines au XIXe Siècle, 28, 29
Historique description du sauvage et solitaire pays du Médoc, 36
History of Ancient and Modern Wines, 253
History of Wine, 92
History of the Wine Trade in England, 48, 53
Holt, John (firm), 98, 151, 184
Huguenots, the, 57, 72, 192

Ile de France wines, 39, 73
Illats (commune), 173, 240
Institut National des Appelations d'Origine (I.N.A.O.), 24, 106, 190;
see also appellation contrôlée
International Exhibition Co-operative Wine Society, 83, 86, 141, 164, 195, 207, 275
Ireland, trade with, 46, 72–74; blending of wine in, 90, 91;
Irish in B., 60, 90
Italy, wine from, 28, 80, 81

Jefferson, Thomas, 91, 172, 228, 249, 250, 264
Joan of Arc, 43
Johnston, Nathaniel, 18, 69, 91–94, 141, 161;
Johnston, W. & N. (firm), 93–94, 266
Jullien, A., 93
Justerini & Brooks (firm), 182, 282

Koenigswater, M., 69, 160
Kressman (firm), 100; Jean, 184

Labarde (commune), *161 and* 147, 155, 249, 251
labels, for wine bottles, 121, 122, 144, 178
Lafforgue, Germain, 15
Lafite, 63, 111
Lalande, Armand, 69, 99, 158; (firm), 99
Lalande-de-Pomerol (district), 206, 212, 213
Lamarque (commune), 12, 62, 167
Lamothe, M., 91, 248
Lancaster, Henry of, Earl of Derby, 42, 49
Landes, the, 11, 13, 240, 246
Langon, 42, 56, 186, 243
Langoiran, 32
Languedoc, 34
Lawton family and firm, 91, 94, 96, 99
see also Tastet et Lawton

Lebègue (firm), 114, 257, 302
Lenz-Moser system, 243
Léognan (commune), *181–184 and* 32, 33, 46, 251
Lesparre, 12, 33, 44, 85, 146, 170
Libourne, 12, 16, 33, 35, 51, 192;
 origin of name, 41; fighting over, 42–45, 49;
 as wine port, 48, 49, 74, 188; merchants in, 95, 102, 188, 201;
 wines from, 213
Lichine, Alexis, 148, 153, 160, 183, 204, 262, 287; (firm), 90, 102
Liqueurs, distillation of wine for, 35, 96
Listrac (commune) *165–168 and* 12, 33, 46, 249
livre tournois (currency), value of, 31n.
London, wine-drinking in, 31, 40, 48; wine auctions in, 65, 79 (*and see* Christies');
 Vintners' Company of, 42
Lorbac, Charles, 192, 193, 255
Loubat, Mme., 207, 211
Louis, Victor (architect), 11, 67, 218, 221, 229, 235
Loupiac (commune), 32, 223, 240, 243, 261
Ludon (commune), *164, 165 and* 99, 173, 249
Lur Saluces family, 63, 227–229, 232, 236, 237, 239
Lussac (commune) 201
de Luze family and firm, 98, 99, 158, 163
Lynch, Count, 67, 128, 161; (firm), 90

maceration, carbonic, 236, 246
Macau (commune), *163, 164 and* 33, 41, 45, 173, 249, 251
maderisation, 186, 231
Mahler-Besse (firm), 100, 159, 197
Malbec grape, 14, 15, *and see* grape varieties
Malvezin, Franz, 64; Théophile, 17, 56, 73, 175, 249
Manuel du Sommelier, 93
marc, 30, 75
Margaux (district), *147–155 and passim*
Marie Brizard et Roger (firm), 35
Marne, the (river), 37, 46
Martillac (commune), 184, 185
Martin, Henri, 145
Médoc (district), *104–171* and also:
 height above sea-level, 12; draining of marshes, 56, 60, 64; grape varieties grown in, 13–16; cultivation of vines in, 20–23, 33, 36; expansion of estates, 68, 69; prizes in Int. Exhibitions, 193; classification of wines, *247–263* and 108, 109, 121
Médoc, Bas-, *169–171 and* 12, 17, 19, 33, 106
Médoc, Haut-, *109–168 and* 12, 17, 33, 106
Médoc, Fort du, 64, 171
Men and Places, 64
Merchant Wine Tonners of Gascony, 42
Merignac (commune), 32, 46, 251
Merlot grape, 13–15; Merlot-Blanc, 15; *and see* grape varieties
Merman (firm), 91, 99, 130, 256
Mestrezat family and firm, 96, 181, 257
Mestrezat-Preller (firm), 96
Methuen Treaty, 71
Miailhe, Jean, 167, 168; William-Alain, 124, 159, 162
Midi, the, 16; vineyards in, 80, wine from, 93
mildew (vine disease), 18, 21, 69, 187, 271
millerandage (vine disease), 19, 21
Moissac, Abbey, 48; wines from, 40, 48
Monbazillac, wines from, 74
Monprimblanc (commune), 243
Monségur, 7
Montagne-St-Emilion (commune), 12, 197, 201, 212
Montesquieu, Charles Louis de Secondat, Baron de la Brède, 185, 186
de Montfort, Simon, 40
Moueix family and firm, 102, 188, 196, 200, 208, 211;
 their Ch. Videlot, 201

Moulis (commune), 165, 166 *and* 12, 33, 46, 62, 249
Moytié, M., 60
Muscadelle grape, 15, 223, *and see also* grape varieties
Musée du Vin (Beaune), 30; (Mouton), 122, 123; (St-Estephe), 135

Nantes, Revocation of the Edict of, 56, 72, 192
Néac (district), 212 *and* 206
Nérac, 34
Netherlands, trade with, *71–88 and* 46, 47, 53–56, 95, 163, 254;
 in spirits, 72
Nicolas (firm), 103, 115, 200, 207, 278
Normandy, wine from, 36, 46
Notes from a Cellar Book, 204, 276

oidium, *oidium tuckeri*, (vine disease), 15, 16, 21, 69, 76, 120, 266
l'Ombrière, Château de, 34, 39, 43
Orleans, Duke of, 43; Orleanais wines, 39
ouillage, see ullage
Oxford, wine price in, 54

palus (marsh), 12, 14, 16, 20, 32, 94, 167, 248, 249;
 soil from, 198; wines from, 54, 73, 248, 249;
 vineyards abandoned, 81
Palmer, General, 61, 68, 159
Parempuyre (commune), 165
Parlement, of Bordeaux, 52, 55, 61, 62, 250
Parsac (commune), 201
Pauillac (commune), *104–131* and 13–15, 46, 251;
 Co-operative de, 131; *Société Vinicole de*, 101
Peppercorn, David, 169, 272, 273
Pepys, Samuel, 54, 60, 172
peranospora (vine disease), 19
Pereire family, 68, 148, 159, 160
Pessac (commune), *174–181 and* 15, 29, 32, 33, 46, 54, 251;
 archiepiscopal vineyards in, 59; estates in 60
Peyrelongue family, 96, 133
phylloxera, *phylloxera vastatrix*, (vine disease), 15–19, 35, 169; effect on wine trade, 69, 79, 170, 271;
 pre- and post-phylloxera vintages, 264–276
Le Pian-Médoc (commune), 165, 249
Pichard, Président, 62, 111, 233, 249, 250
Pichon, Jacques, Baron de Longueville, 62, 123
Picquigny, Treaty of, 53
Pijassou, R., 61, 66, 248
Plassac, 29
Ploughs, ploughing of vineyards, 20–22; with oxen, 29, 33, 244
Plumb, J. H., 63
Podensac (commune), 33, 173, 240
Pointe de Grave, 12, 146
Poitiers, 38; Battle of, 42
Poitou, Count of, 38, 42, 46
Pollock, David, 119, 267
Pomerol (district), 203–213
Pont de Pierre, 39, 98
Pontac, 54, 60, 62, 63, 172; Arnaud de, 60, 172; family, 175, 185, 234, 237
Portet, André, 107, 115, 270
Portugal, wine from, 50, 53, 61; duty on, 57, 58, 71, 72
pourriture grise, 19, 187, 226;
pourriture noble, botrytis cinerea, 15, 33, 173, 226, 240
Preignac (commune), 226, 235
Premières Côtes (district), *242–246 and* 11, 12, 29, 32, 240
Pressac grape, 14, 187, *and see also* grape varieties
pressing, *foulage*, 30
prices of wine, *71–88 and*
 in 14th century, 50; in 15th and 16th, 53, 54; in 17th, 56, 57; in 18th century, 64, 65, 249–252; in 19th, 75, 76, 78, 97, 112, 176, 227, 252–254; in 20th cen-

tury, 82, 87, 114, 115, 207, 230, 258 (of the '29s) 258; during World War II, 260; compared with Burgundies, 261
Promis, Marc, 68, 161
Puisseguin (commune), 201
Pujols, 33, 242

Quercy, 34
Queyries, 32, 91
Quinconces, Place des, 11

racking (*soutirage*), 26, 67
Ray, Cyril, 63, 111n.
Redding, Cyrus, 177, 253, 255
La Réole, 43, 242
Revolution, the French (1789), 21, 29, 32, 35; effect on wine trade, 66, 67, 75, 111; (1848), 97
Rhine (river), wines from, 31, 47, 50, 54; compared with Sauternes, 227, 234
Rhone (river), 16; wines from, 92, 93, 100, 246; Rh. Valley, 28
Ribadieu, Henri, 115
Richelieu, Louis Francois Armand du Plessis, Duc de, 109
Les Richesses Gastronomiques de la France, 192, 255
Riesling grape, 13, 15, 237, 239
La Rivière (commune), 215
La Rochelle, 35, 46, 38, 47
rosé wine, *see vin rosé*
Rosebery, Earl of (sale of his wines), 114, 118, 266, 270
Rosenheim (firm), 114, 176, 257, 258
Rothschild family, 111, 112, 255; Baroness de, 22, 123; Barons Nathaniel, 68, 69, 120, 122; James, 68, 69, 119, 120; Henri, 119; Guy, 112; Elie, 112; Philippe 101, 119–123, 129, 159, 164, 263, 269
Rouen, 43, 50
Roullet, Georges, 96
Royan, 40; 'Custom of Royan', 49
Russia, exports to, 73, 88, 227, 240; wines from, 84
Rutherford, Osborn & Perkin (firm), 210, Jack R., 285

St-Aignan, 215
St-André, Cathedral of, 33, 42, 46
St-André de Cubzac, 32, 218
St-André, feast of (30th Nov.), 34
St-Christoly-de-Médoc (commune), 36, 170
St-Christophe-des-Bardes (commune), 201
St-Emilion (district), *187–202 and* 20; vintage in, 22, 29; history of wine-growing in, 33; fighting over, 43, 45, 49; classification of wines (1955), 261
St-Emilion (town), 188; *Jurade de*, 201
St-Estèphe (commune), *131–135 and* 12, 33, 62, 249, 251;
 Marquis de (co-operative), 135
St-Etienne-de-Lisse (commune), 201
St-Georges (commune), 201
St-Germain d'Esteuil (commune), 170
St-Germain-la-Rivière, 215
St-Gervais, 164
St-Hippolyte (commune), 201
St-Julien (commune), *136–145 and* 147, 251
St-Lambert (St-Mambert), (commune), 110, 117, 249, 251
St-Laurent (commune) 146, 147 *and* 12, 62, 249
St-Laurent-des-Combes (commune), 201
St-Macaire, 32, 34, 40, 43, 49, 242, 243
St-Maixant, 246
St-Martin, feast of (11 Nov.), 31, 34, 48, 216
St-Michel-de-Fronsac (commune), 215
St-Pey d'Armens (commune), 201
St-Pierre-du-Mons (commune), 240
St-Sauveur (commune), 168
St-Seurin-de-Cadourne (commune), 168, 169, 249, 251
St-Sulpice-de-Faleyrens (commune), 201
St-Sulpice d'Izon, 32
St-Symphorien (commune), 85

St-Vivien, 12
St-Yzans (commune), 169
Ste-Croix, Abbey of, 63, 183
Ste-Croix-du-Mont (commune), 223, 240, 243, 261
Ste-Foy-la-Grande, 30, 55, 56, 73, 242, 243
Saintes, 40, 42
Saintsbury, George, 204, 266, 268, 276; Saintsbury Club, 207
Salavert, Jean, 82–84
Saluces family, *see* Lur Saluces, 20
Sauternes (district), *223–241, and* 20, 22, 27; wines from (historical), 55, 56, 66, 76; vintage in 22; estates in 62, 63
Sauternes (commune and village), 226, 232
Sauveterre, 242
Sauvignon, Petit-Sauvignon, grape, 15; *and see also* grape varieties
Scandinavia, *see* Baltic countries
Schröder & Schÿler (firm), 90, 94, 157, 257
Schÿler, Alfred (firm), 94; Guy, 94
Scotland, trade with, 36, 58, 73, 74, 133
Scott, Sir Samuel, 111, 132
Scott, T. G. D. (Consul), 256, 265
de Ségur, Marquis, 62, 66, 109, 111, 116, 133, 249; family, 64
Sémillon grape, 15; *and see also* grape varieties
Shand, P. Morton, 63, 203
share-cropping system, 59, 62
shipping, of wine, 34, 36, 48–51, 54; development of Engl., 51, 53; Navigation Act (1651), 56, 57
Sichel, Allan, 100, 159; family and firm, 100, 159, 160, 231, 246
Simon, André, 54, 56, 58, 113, 118, 251, 266–273, 283, 291;
History of the Wine Trade in England, 48, 53
Bottlescrew Days, 60, 248
Vintagewise, 79, 182, 207, 264, 267
soil, soils, for wine-growing, 106, 167, 173, 223
Solesse, 33
Soulac (commune), *170 and* 33, 53
Soussans (commune), 162, 163 *and* 33, 147, 155, 249
soutirage, see racking
Spain, 35; Spanish labour, 22; wine, 36, 50, 53, 61, 71, 224
duty on, 57, 58; used for blending (Benicarlo), 90, 92
sparkling wine, from the Médoc, 141, 162
spider, red (vine pest), 19, 20
Station Agronomique et Oenologique, 96, 272
Stay Me with Flagons, 104, 279

Strabo, 28
sugar, addition of to wine (*chaptalisation*), 23, 24, 30, 84, 244, 296; tax on, sulphur, 16, 19, 173, 184, 185
Le Taillan (commune), *165 and* 33, 46, 251
Talbot, John, Earl of Shrewsbury, 44, 52, 116, 144, 202
Talence, (commune), 32, 172
Talleyrand-Périgord, Charles Maurice de, 175
Targon, 242
Tarn, the (river), 28, 38
Tastet et Lawton (firm), 22, 94, 256, 257, 265, 268, 287
tax, taxes, on wine in France, 31, 34, 39–44, 50, 52, 67, 75, 81–83; Grande Coutume 31, 39, 47, 49; Petite Coutume, 31; Custom of Royan, 49; on wine in England, 50, 56
Tesseron, Guy, 134
Tokay, 226, 227
tonneau, size of, 25, 30
Tourny, Allées de, 11, 32, 51; Marquis de, 61
trade in wine, *37–51, 71–88*, Anglo-Fr. Commercial Treaty (1860), 77–80, 120; treaties with other countries, 77–80
Traité sur les Vins du Médoc, 76, 118, 251
de la Tresne, Jean-Baptiste, 60
Trompette, Château, 34, 52
Ugniblanc grape, 15, 223
ullage, *ouillage*, 26, 134
Van den Bussche fils (firm), 143
Vaucluse, 17
Vayres, 32
Verdot grape, 14, *and see also* grape varieties
Vieille Cure liqueur, 35
Vertheuil (commune), 168
Viallate, A., 79
Le Vignoble Girondin, 15
Villenave-d'Ornon (commune), *185 and* 33, 46, 62
Villeneuve family, 62
Villeneuve-les-Avignon, 16
vin de l'année, 48; '*vin de Comète*', 111, 113; *vin de consommation*, 55; *vin de goutte*, 27, 152, 229, 273; *vin gris*, 30; *vin de lie*, 26; *vin lymphaté*, 30; *vin de presse*, 25, 30, 206; *vin de queue*, 25; *vin rosé*, 27, 30, 152, 185, 239, 273

Vinification, Cave de, 246
vineyards, composition of, 15; cultivation of (ploughing, pruning etc.) 19–22, 33); replanting of, 17, 18, restrictions on, 86; history of v. planting, 28–36, 59–70; rents for (*agrières*), 59; ancient vines in, 184; Lenz-Moser system, 244
Vins de Bordeaux, see Cocks et Féret
vintage, *vendange*, 21–24, 29, 30; effect of vine diseases on, 18; starting dates of, 21, 30, 59, 187, 226, 266, 272, 283, 287, 297 (*and see* individual estates)
vintages, *millésimes*, 264–304, *and* 113, 129, 276, 277, 283, 287
Vintagewise, 79, 182, 207, 264, 266
Vintners Company of London, 42, 56
Visigoths, the, 29
Viticole, Office, (Barsac), 239
Viticulture, College of, 233
vitis riparia, rupestris, vinifera, 19
Walpole, Robert 63
War, First World, 19; effect on wine trade, 85; vintages, 277
War, Franco-Prussian, 16
War, the Hundred Years, 42–45, 59, 202
War, Second World, effect on wine trade, 87; prices during, 260; vintages, 290
Wars, Napoleonic, 65, 72, 75, 94, 113, 265
Wars of the Roses, 43
Warner Allen, H., 92
watering of wine, *mouillage*, 84
Waugh, Harry, 210, 231, 267, 269, 275, 280
Wayward Tendrils of the Vine, 268
wine-growing, history of, 27–36
wine-making process, *20–27*, 66, 67; maturing first practised, 64–67
wine merchants, in Bordeaux, *89–103 and* 56, 57, 68, 78, 84; modern rôle of, 102, 103
wine names, misuse of, 81, 84
wine, price of, *see* prices
Wine Society, *see* International Exhib. co-operative Wine Society
Wines of France, 204
woad, *pastel*, 35
Woltner, family and firm, 101; Henri, 23, 101, 119, 179, 180
Xavier, Arnozan, Cours, 11, 89, 95, 99
Younger, William, 59
Zuckerman, Sir Solly, 127, 290

Index of Châteaux

L'Abbé-Gorsse de Gorsse, 162
L'Angélus, 197, 301
Angludet, *160 and* 100, 159, 162; classification, 256, 259, 261; vintages, 293, 298
d'Arche, 62, 232
Arche Vimeney, 233
Ausone, *194 and* 67, 102, 128, 188, 192, 193; classification, 256, 262; vintages, 271, 277, 279, 281, 286, 295, 302, 303

Bahans-Haut-Brion, 176
de Barbe, 220
Barbé, 221
Baret, 185
Bastor-Lamontagne, 237
Batailley, 69, 126, 260
Beaumont, 168
Beauregard, 260
Beau Rivage, 164
Beauséjour, *196 and* 192, 193,
Beauséjour (Médoc), 135
Bégadanais (co-operative), 170

Bel-Air, *195 and* 190, 192, 193, 260, vintages, 296
Bel-Air-Lalande, 212, 286
Bel-Air-Marquis d'Aligre, 162, 259
Belgrave, 147
Belles-Graves, 212
Bellevue, 260
Bel-Orme, 168
Bel-Orme-Tronquoy-de-Lalande, 259
Bergeron, 253
Beychevelle, *144, 145 and* 62, 64, 68, 86; classification, 254, 258, 260; vintages, 287, 288, 290
Beychevelle (Cubzadais), 218
Blissa, 221
Bodet, 215
Le Boscq, 90, 135, 259
Bougneuf, 212
du Bouilh, 67, 218
Bouran, 251
Bouscaut, 185, 260
Le Bourdieu, 168
Bouscaut, 185, 260
du Bousquet, 220

Boyd-Cantenac, 154, 253
Branaire, 23
Branaire-Ducru, *143, and* 105, 260; vintages, 274
Brane-Cantenac, *157, 157 and* 119, 152; classification, 253, 258, 284; vintages, 294
Branne-Mouton, 65, 66, 68, 92, 119, 120; classification, 251, 253
Branon-Licterie, 272
La Brède, 186
Broustet, 238
Brown-Cantenac *see* Cantenac-Brown

Cabarrus, 253
Cadet-Bon, 260
Caillou, 239
Caillou-Blanc, 144
Calon-Ségur, *133. and* 64, 96, 111; classification, 253, 254
Camensac, 147, 254
Cameron, 235
Camponac, 98, 181
Canet, 66

Canon, *195 and* 65, 190, 192, 193; classification, 260; vintages, 280, 289, 301
Canon (Frousac), 214, 215
Canon-La-Gaffetière, 196
Canteloup, 135
Cantemerle, *163, 164 and* 22, 33, 70, 95, 251; classification, 254, 255, 258, 260, 262; vintages, 276, 278, 279, 281, 283, 290, 294, 295, 296, 297, 298, 299, 300, 301, 304
Cantemerle, Cru, 164
Cantenac, 124
Cantenac-Brown, *158, and* 68, 69, 99; vintages, 286
Capbern, 135
Carbonnieux, *183 and* 62, 63, 66, 69, 260
Cardaillan, 237
Carruades de Lafite, 111, 115, 273
Castelnau, 253
Castelot, 201
du Castéra, 170
Cérons, 240
Certan, 260; vintages, 293, 295, 298
Certan-Demay, 209
Certan-Giraud, 209
Certan-Marzelle, 209
Chasse-Spleen, 166, 259, 261
La Chatelerie, 168
Chauvin, 200
Cheval-Blanc, *197–199 and* 13, 87, 102, 104, 105, 176, 190, 193; prices, 207–260; classification, 256, 260, 262; vintages, 275, 279–302
Cheval-Noir, 197
Chevalier d'Ars, 167
Cissac, 168
Citran-Clauzel, 167
Clarke, 166
Clerc-Milon-Mondon, 130
Climens, 231, 237, 238; vintages, 289, 291, 294, 295, 296
Clinet, 212
Clos du Clocher, 239
Clos Fourtet, *196 and* 101, 102, 190, 192; classification, 260; vintages, 280, 281, 282, 286, 288, 290, 302
Clos Haut-Peyraguey, 233
Clos des Jacobins, 197
Clos Labère, 235
Clos du Marquis, 138
Clos René, 210; vintages, 297, 298
Clos du Roy, 239
La Closerie, 166, 279; vintages, 286
La Clotte, 102, 196, 197
Colombier-Monpelon, 131
La Commanderie, 212, 213
La Conseillante, 209, 260; vintages, 299
Corbin d'Espagne, 200
Corbin-Michotte, 200
Cos d'Estournel *132, and* 97, 101, 124; classification, 253; vintages, 277, 283, 286, 289, 292, 299, 300
Cos Labory, 132, 134
Coufran, 168, 169, vintages, 289
Couhins, 185
Courant, 167
La Couronne, 99, 131, 259
Coutet, *237, 238 and* 227, 229, 231; vintages, 281, 295, 296
Le Courent, 197, 260
Le Crock, 99
La Croix, 215
La Croix-de-Gay, *210 and* 204, 260; vintages, 291–295, 297
La Croix-Millorit, 221
Croizet-Bages, 131
Croque Michotte, 200
Cronte, Charlus, 221
Cru Canternerle (Cubzadais), 218
Cru Patache, d'Aux, 170
Cru St-Marc, 233

La Dame Blanche, 165
La Dauphine, 215
Dauzac, *161, 162 and* 18, 67, 69, 94, 124; vintages, 286
Desmirail, 153, 154, 159
Dillon, 165
Doisy-Daëne, 230, 237

Doisy-Védrines, 237
Domaine-du-Balardin, 154
Domaine de Belair, 246
Domaine de Chevalier, *182 and* 260; white, 289, 294, 296, 299; vintages, 281–298
Domaine Clarence Dillon, 165
Domaine de l'Eglise, 212, 260
Domaine, de l'Ermitage Lamourous, 99
Domaine de Lamothe, (Ch. des Ramparts) 237
Domaine du Mayne, 237
Domaine Sarraule, 239
Domaine de Toumalin, 215
La Dominique, *200 and* 190, 193, 260; vintages, 294, 299
Dubignon-Talbot, 154, 155
Dubosc, 256
Dubroca, 237
Ducru-Beaucaillou, *141, and* 18, 69, 94, 126; classification, 254; vintages, 301
Dudon, 239
Duhart-Milon, 124, 125, 254; vintages, 277, 281
Duplessis, 166
Durfort-Vivens, *152 and* 68, 69, 70, 97, 99, 251
Dutruch-Grand-Poujeaux, 166

L'Enclos, 210; vintages, 286, 292, 298
L'Enclos-du-Presbytère, 212
L'Evangile 197, 209
Eyquem, 221

Farques, 63
de Ferrand, 193, 201
Ferrière, 154
Fieuzal, 183, 260
Figeac, *199 and* 67, 190, 193; classification, 260; vintages, 276, 284, 295, 297, 299, 301, 303
Filhot, 227, 230, 232
La Fleur-Pourret, 197
Fonbadet, 131
Fonbedeau, 64, 140
Fonroque, 102
Fourcas-Dupré, 166
Fourcas-Hostein, 166
La France, 215
Franc-Petit-Figeac, 200

Gaby, 215
La Gaffelière, *195, 196 and* 190, 193; classification, 260; vintages, 286, 288, 289, 295–297
La Garde, 98, 185
Le Gay, 211, 260
Gazin, 211, 260; vintages, 292
Giac, 251
Giscours, *164 and* 66, 68, 69, 97; classification, 251, 253, 260; vintages, 276, 282, 286
de Glana, 146
Gloria, 145, 261
Gorse, 251, 253, 256
Grâce-Dieu, 197
Grand-Barrail-Lamarzelle-Figeac, 200
Grand Corbin, 200
Grand Listrac, 166
Grand-Pontet, 196
Grand-Puy-Ducasse, 105, 125–127; classification, 255; vintages, 268
Grand-Puy-Lacoste, 65, 126, 127, 253; classification, 255, 261; vintages, 281, 290, 293, 298, 301
Grand St-Julien, 146
Les Grandes Murailles, 193, 196
La Grave Figeac, 200
La Grave-Trigart-de-Boisset, 210, 299
Gressier-Grand-Poujeaux, 166
Gruand-Larose, *140, 141 and* 64, 101, 125, 144; classification, 257, 258; vintages, 266, 267, 270, 272, 276, 280, 282–285, 295, 298, 301
Guiraud (and Pavillon Sec de Ch. Guiraud) 232
La Gurgue, 162

Haut-Bages, 125

Haut-Bages-Averous, 131
Haut-Bages-Libéral, 130
Haut-Bailly, *181 and* 96, 260; vintages, 284 286, 289, 300
Haut-Batailley, 126
Haut-Bommes, 234
Haut-Brion, *175–179 and* 14, 24, 54, 60–68, 74, 105, 172; classification, 248–251, 254–258, 260; vintages, 269, 275–277, 282–285, 291, 292
Haut-Brion Blanc, 179, 247; vintages, 294, 295, 299
Haut-Sarpe, 201

Issan, *157, 158 and* 64, 97, vintages, 286

Junayme, 95, 215

Kirwan, 157, 252, 253

Labégorce, 162, 256, 261 *see also* L'Abbé-Gorsse-de-Gorsse
Labégorce-Zédé, 162
Laburthe-Brivazac, 181, 286
Lacabanne, 211
Lafaurie-Peyraguey, 233
Lafite, *110–115 and* 13, 18, 21, 23, 59–66, 74, 97, 264; prices in 18th century, 249–251; in 19th century, 79, 100; the 1803, 105, 113; purchase by Rothschild, 68; sales to England, 253; classification, 255–258, vintages, 265–304
Lafleur-du-Gazin, 211, 260
Lafleur-Pétrus, 102, 211, 260; vintages, 297
Lafon, 233
Lafon-Rochet, 133, 134
Lagrange, 102, 142, 262, vintages, 283
La Lagune, *164, 165 and* 15, 70; classification, 254, 260; vintages, 277, 281, 283, 303
Lagrange (Pomerol), 212
Lamarque, 157
Lamarque (Ste-Croix), 240
Lamothe, 64, 148, 232, 233; (Cissac), 168
Lamothe-de-Bergeron, 168
Lamothe-Bergey, 233
Lanessan, *167, 168 and* 124, 259, 261; vintages, 279, 286
Langoa, *142 and* 14, 92, 105, 124, 138, 140 152; classification, 258; vintages, 269, 284, 288, 298
L'Archeveque, 215
Larcis-Ducasse, 201
Laroque, 193
Larose, 92, 256
Larose Trentaudon, 146
Larrivet-Haut-Brion, 184
Lascombes, *153, and* 20, 102, 148, 152; classification, 253; vintages, 287, 293, 297
Lassègue, 201
Latour, *115–119, and* 13, 14, 62–65, 105, 249; archives of, 66, 67, 91, 109; price in 19th century, 79; in 1930s, 86; classification, 253, 256–258, vintages, 267–304
Latour-Pomerol, 102, 211
Latour-Rauzan, 142
Laujac, 97, 170, 253
Laville-Haut-Brion, 101, 180, 299
Léoville, *137, 138 and* 60, 66, 73, 120, 256; vintages, 269
Léoville-Barton, *137–140 and* 14, 92, 97, 105, 142; classification, 256, 258; vintages, 282, 284, 285, 288, 292–295, 298, 301
Léoville-Las-Cases, *137, 138 and* 97, 105, classification, 258; vintages, 272, 276, 282, 284, 285, 289–303
Léoville-Poyferré, *137, 138 and* 69, 99, 105, 152, 204; classification, 258; vintages, 273, 282, 284, 285, 288, 289
Lescadre, 221
Liôt, 239
Liversan, 168, 254, 256
Livran, 170
Loubens, 240
Loudenne, *169, 170 and* 17, 18, 69, 168
La Louvière, 184
Lynch-Bages, *127, 128 and* 69, 260; vintages, 295, 298, 300, 304

Lynch-Moussas, 128
Lyonnat, 201

Magdelaine, *196 and* 102, 190, 192, 193
Malartic-Lagravière, 183
Malescot St-Expuéry, *153, 154 and* 64, 253, 276, 294
de Malle, 236
La Maqueline, 94, 161
Marbuzet, 99, 135
Margaux, *148–150 and* 62–69, 97, 101, 105 classification, 249–251, 255–258; vintages, 265, 270, 272, 275, 276, 279–304
Marquis d'Alesme Becker, 153, 154, 299
Marquis de Terme, 154
Martinens, 160
Martinet, 201
Maucaillou, 166
Maurian, 165
Mauvezin, 166
Médoc (Ch.), 146
de Menandat, 221
Menauta, 239
Mendoce, 221
Meyney, 134
Mille-Secousses, 221
La Mission-Haut-Brion, *179, 180 and* 23, 24, 63, 66, 92, 101, 105, 172; classification, 248, 251, 254, 260; vintages, 275, 279, 286, 288–295, 297–300, 304
Monbadon, 201, 216
Monbousquet, 201
Moncets, 212
Monconseil, 221
Monpelou, 131, 254
Mont-Moytié, 60, 64, 137
Montrose, 68, 132, 133; classification, 254; vintages, 273, 286
Morange, 259
Morin, 259
Moulin des Carruades, 115
Moulin d'Issan, 158
Moulin-Riche, 259
Moulin-â-Vent, 212
Moulinet, 95, 212
Mouton-Baron-Philippe (previously Mouton d'Armailhac) 64, 101, 129; classification, 260; vintages, 286
Mouton-Cadet, 101, 103, 129, 130
Mouton-Rothschild, *119–123 and* 13, 14, 22, 23, 62–68; meaning of name, 119; prices (1871), 100; post-war, 87; classification, 255–271; vintages, 265–304
Myrat, 175, 237

Nairac, 238
Nénin, 206, 211, 260; vintages, 294
Nexon-Lemoyne, 165

Olivier, 98, 183, 260
Ormes-de-Pez, 135

Palmer (Palmer-Margaux), *158–160 and* 13, 20, 22, 26, 100; origin of name, 68; classification, 254–256, 258, 260, 262; vintages, 272, 279–281, 294, 295, 298–303
Pape-Clément, *181 and* 32, 59, 248; vintages, 272, 275, 279, 282, 299, 301
Parempuyre, 165
Paveil-de-Luze, 98, 163, 259
Pavie, *196 and* 102, 190, 192, 260; vintages, 301

Pavillon-Blanc de Ch. Margaux, 149
Pavillon Rouge, 232
Pédesclaux, 130, 259
Peixotto, 234
Perganson, 146
Perron, 213
Petit-Figeac, 200
Petit-Village, 211, 282, 294
Petit-Arnauds, 221
Pétrus, *206–208 and* 87, 102, 104, 204; classification, 260, 262; vintages, 273, 280, 288, 292–298, 303
Peyrabon, 168
de Pez, 62, 134
Phélan-Ségur, 135
Piada, 239
Le Pian, 99
Pibran, 131
Pichon-Longueville, 123, 124; classification, 251–254; vintages, 270, 282
Pichon-Longueville-Baron, *123, 124 and* 65, 97, 105; classification, 255, 262; vintages, 285, 290, 295, 298
Pichon-Longueville Comtesse de Lalande, *123, 124 and* 65, 97; classification, 255; vintages, 289, 298
Pierre Bibian, 166
Plaisance, 201
Plantier Rose, 135
Plince, 212
La Pointe, 209, 288
Pomys, 132, 135, 166
Pontac, 65, 248; 'Pontack', 65, 175
Pontac-Lynch, 160
Pontac-Monplaisir, 185
Pontet-Canet, *125–126, 130 and* 18, 23, 105, 124; bought by Cruse family, 69, 97; classification, 253, 258, 260; vintages, 269, 270, 276, 285, 291, 292, 298
Poujèaux-Castaing, 166
Poujèaux Marly, 166
Poujèaux-Theil, 166
Poujet, 154, 160, 253
Preignac, 63
Prevôt de Lecroize, 256
Le Prieuré, *160 and* 64, 102, 153
Puy-Blanquet, 193, 201

Rabaud, 234
Rabaud-Promis, 161, 234
Rausan, *151, 152 and* 64, 69, 74, 97, 124; classification, 251, 256
Rausan-Ségla, *151, 152 and* classification, 253, 255; vintages, 272, 286, 290, 291, 298
Rauzan-Gassies, *151, 152, and* classification, 255; vintages, 279, 286
Raymond, 186
Raymond-Lafon, 232
Rayne-Vigneau, 234
Renouil-Franquet, 166
Rieussec, 235; vintages, 295
Ripeau, 190, 200, 260
Rochemorin, 186
Romer, 235
La Rose, 124
La Rose Paulliac, 131
Rosemont, 163
Rouet, 215, 216
Rouget, 212

Roumieu, 239
Rousset, 221

St.-Emilion-Royal, 197
St.-Julien, 142
St.-Pierre (Bontemps and Sevaistre), *143 and* 65, 254, 295
St.-Sauveur, 168
de Sales, 212
Sarpe, 193
Savignac, 251
Sénilhac, 99, 168
Siaurac, 212
Sigalas-Rabaud, 234
Siran, *162 and* 124, 261; vintages, 298
Smith-Haut-Lafite, *184 and* 98, 260
Sociando, 168, 221
Suau, 239
Suduiraut, 97, 235, 236, 237

Le Taillan, 97, 165
Talbot, *144 and* 101, 141; origin of the name, 44; classification, 254, 260; vintages, 275, 285, 294, 279–300
de Tastes, 240
Tauzia, 100
Tayac, 221
Terrefort, 218
du Tertre, 69, 158, 160, 161
Tertre-Dangay, 197
Thau, 221
La Tour Blanche, 233
La Tour-de-By, 170
La Tour-Carnet, 146, 147
La Tour-Figeac, 200
La Tour-Haut-Brion, 101, 180, 295
La Tour-de-Marbuzet, 135
La Tour-Martillac, 100, 184
La Tour-Milon, 131
La Tour-du-Mirail, 168
La Tour-de-Mous, 162, 163, 164; classification, 259; vintages, 286, 290, 298
La Tour-Pibran, 131
La Tour-du-Pin-Figeac, 200
La Tour-du-Roc, 167
La Tour-Séguy, 221
Tournefeuille, 212
des Tours (Montagre St-Emilion), 17
Les Trois-Moulins, 193
Tronquoy Lalande, 135
Troplong-Mondot, 192, 197
Trotanoy, 204, 211, 299
Trottevieille, 193, 196, 260

Valrose, 171
Vieux-Château-Certan, *208, 209 and* 104, 105, 204, 206, 260; vintages, 284, 293, 297–299, 303
Verdignan, 168
Vignonet, 201
Villegeorge, 167, 259
Villemarine, 197
Le Virou, 221
Vrai-Canon-Bodet-La-Tour, 215

Ygrec, 230
Yquem, *226–231 and* 15, 16, 23, 27, 44, 63; prices (1849) 97; (1867/8), 76, 79; (1943), 261; (1960s), 87; vintages, 267, 268, 272, 277, 281, 284, 286, 289, 292–296, 299, 301
Yon-Figeac, 200